ANNALS OF
ENGLISH LITERATURE
1475–1950

ANNALS OF
ENGLISH LITERATURE
1475–1950

*THE PRINCIPAL PUBLICATIONS OF
EACH YEAR TOGETHER WITH AN
ALPHABETICAL INDEX OF AUTHORS
WITH THEIR WORKS*

SECOND EDITION

OXFORD
AT THE CLARENDON PRESS
1961

Oxford University Press, Amen House, London E.C.4

GLASGOW   NEW YORK   TORONTO   MELBOURNE   WELLINGTON
BOMBAY   CALCUTTA   MADRAS   KARACHI   KUALA LUMPUR
CAPE TOWN   IBADAN   NAIROBI   ACCRA

© *Oxford University Press 1961*

First edition 1935
Reprinted with corrections 1936
Second edition 1961

PRINTED IN GREAT BRITAIN

PREFACE TO THE SECOND EDITION

In this revised edition numerous corrections have been made in that part of the text which ends at 1900, the section 1900 to 1925 has been completely reset, and a new section covering the years 1925 to 1950 has been added. This has made it possible to widen the scope of inclusion for the twentieth century and give a more extensive representation to works and authors from the Commonwealth and the United States. The opportunity has also been taken to improve the treatment in marginal entries of French and German literature especially. The Index has been revised and reset and the provenance of authors from outside the United Kingdom is indicated by the following abbreviations: Au (Australia); C (Canada); Ind (India); NZ (New Zealand); SA (South Africa); and US (United States of America).

The main work of revision was done by the late Dr. R. W. Chapman. Unfortunately, it is impossible for the publishers to make separate acknowledgement to the many scholars and friends on whom he drew for help. To all of them the publishers are much indebted. They would like to acknowledge the work done by Mrs. W. K. Davin in co-ordinating the results of Dr. Chapman's labours when illness made it impossible for him to continue. They would also like to thank Professor E. L. Stahl and Mr. Robert Baldick for help given with the German and French entries, and Miss M. A. Hennings for preparing the Index and seeing it through the press.

PREFACE TO THE FIRST EDITION

THIS little book has its origin in an aspiration of Sir Walter Raleigh, who used to dream of *Annals of English Literature*. How many volumes such a work would comprise, if it listed every publication under its year, was never calculated; guesses might now be based on the bulk of the *Short-Title Catalogue, 1475–1640*.

The more modest purpose of the present compilation is to give the student, at a glance, the main literary output of any year or series of years; to show what books people were likely to be reading at any time, and with what rivals a candidate for literary fame had to reckon. Though the main object is to discover any book in its chronological setting, and so to serve the ends of a work of reference, it has been found in practice that these brief annals can be read continuously with profit, and even with pleasure.

The Index of Authors gives at once a conspectus of any literary career, and the means of studying it, by reference to the text, in its proper environment.

It has necessarily been assumed that the date of publication is that at which any work became public property and passed into the stream of national consciousness. This inference must, of course, be drawn with reserve in the earlier period. Before the invention of printing there was no datable publication; and after the invention of printing there are many famous examples of books which had profoundly influenced their age before they came to be printed.

The dates assumed are in general those on the title-page. It is well known that books published near the end of a year were often dated the year following; and there are other sources of confusion. But the error is not serious for the purposes of an elementary manual.

The principle of choice has been the inclusion of all the books (but not all the occasional writings, contributions to periodicals, and the like) of the major authors, and a selection of the more influential publications of the minors. It is not expected that the choice will meet with uniform approval; but the attempt has been made to keep the work in focus.

To economize space, and to avoid tedious iteration, Christian names have not as a rule been given in the main text, except to obscure or ambiguously named writers. The space so saved is used for the birth-date (if known). Thus the author's age when he published a book is immediately apparent, and the reader is reminded that Pope was twenty-seven when he began to publish the *Iliad*, Dickens twenty-four when he began to publish *Pickwick*, and Hardy sixty-eight when he completed *The Dynasts*. If the Christian name is wanted, it will generally be found under the birth-year in the side column, and always in the Index. For posthumous works not the birth-date but the death-date is given, and the fact that publication was belated, and probably unauthorized, is at once apparent.

In the side-column are recorded the births and deaths of authors, the publication of newspapers, periodicals, translations, editions, and other compilations not to be classed as original literature; together with a selection of foreign events which had a bearing on the course of English literature.

The compilation of the Annals is the work of Mr. J. C. Ghosh, D.Phil.; the Annals 1901–25, and the Index, are the work of Miss E. G. Withycombe, B.A. The Index ends, in general, at 1925, but the opportunity has occasionally been taken to complete a literary career which has since been terminated by death, or to mention a recent edition of a classic. The publisher and compilers are indebted to a very large number of scholars who have read the work or parts of it in manuscript or in proof and have made valuable additions or removed serious errors.

Abbreviations:

P = Prose   T = Tragedy
V = Verse   C = Comedy
                D = Drama

Note on the Second Impression.

The rapid exhaustion of the first edition has made it necessary to reprint early. The opportunity has been taken to correct some errors and omissions; it is hoped that scholars will continue to report their discoveries.

1475

Gesta Romanorum, *c.* 1475.

Alexander Barclay b.?
Gavin Douglas b.?
Michelangelo b.
Caxton prints his first book
'Recuyell of the His-
tories of Troy' (trs.
Raoul Le Fèvre) c. 1475
at Bruges.

1476

Sir John Fortescue d.?
Caxton prints 'Game and
Playe of the Chess' (trs.
Jacobus de Cessolis) c.
1476 at Bruges.
Caxton sets up press at
Westminster.

1477

Caxton (1422?): History of Jason [n.d.]. P
Lydgate (d. 1450?): Temple of Glass [n.d.; prtd. Caxton; later edd. 1500 (?), 1530 (?)]. V
Horse, Goose and Sheep [n.d.; prtd. Caxton; another ed. 1500(?)]. P
Churl and the Bird [n.d.; prtd. Caxton; other edd. 1493 (?), 1520 (?)]. V
Wydeville, A., Earl Rivers: Trs. Dictes and Sayings of Philosophers [first book printed by Caxton in England]. P

1478

Chaucer (d. 1400): Canterbury Tales [n.d.; prtd. Caxton; also 1484 (?); prtd. Pynson 1492 (?), 1526; prtd. Wynkyn de Worde 1498; ed. Tyrwhitt 1775–8; Wright 1848–51; Furnivall 1868 ff.; Skeat 1894–7]. V
Trs. Consolation of Philosophy of Boethius [n.d.; prtd. Caxton]. P
Parliament of Fowls [incl. Gentilesse, Truth, Fortune, Envoy to Scogan, Anelida and Arcite, Compleynte to his Purse; n.d.; prtd. Caxton]. V
Wydeville, A., Earl Rivers (1442?): Trs. Moral Proverbs of Christyne de Pise [prtd. Caxton]. P

Sir Thomas More b.
First book printed at Ox-
ford c. 1478.

1479

Caxton (1422?): Book of Courtesy [n.d.]. P
Cordyale, or the Four Last Things [trs. attributed to A. Wydeville, Earl Rivers]. P
Lydgate (d. 1450?): Stans puer ad Mensam [n.d.]. V

Caxton (1422?): Chronicles of England [called Caxton's Chronicle; really The Chronicle of Brute]. P
Lydgate (d. 1450?): Court of Sapience [n.d.]. V

1481

Caxton (1422?): Reynard the Fox [trs. Dutch]. P
Mirror of the World [trs. Vincent de Beauvais]. P

Tully of Old Age [trs., through Fr., of Cicero]. P
Godfrey of Boulogne [trs. Fr.]. P

Pulci, 'Morgante Maggiore'.

1482

Chaucer (d. 1400): Troylus and Creseyde [n.d.; prtd. Caxton; prtd. Wynkyn de Worde 1517, Pynson 1526]. V
Trevisa, John (d. 1402): Trs. Ranulph Higden's Polychronicon [another ed. 1495]. P

1483

Caxton (1422?): Golden Legend [n.d.; trs. Legenda Aurea of Jacobus de Voragine; other edd. 1487 (?), 1493, 1498, 1512, 1527]. P
Gower, John (d. 1408): Confessio Amantis [other edd. 1493, 1532, 1534]. V
Lydgate (d. 1450?): Pilgrimage of the Soul [trs. Guillaume de Deguileville]. P

King Edward V.
King Richard III 1483–5.
Luther b.
Francesco Guicciardini b.

1484

Caxton (1422?): Trs. Æsop's Fables [Pynson's trs. 1497 (?), 1500 (?); Middleton's 1550(?)]. P
Order of Chivalry.
Book of the Knight of the Tower [trs. Fr.].
Lydgate (d. 1450?): Life of our Lady [n.d.; also 1531]. V

Ulrich Zwingli b.
Julius Caesar Scaliger b.
Pulci d.

1485

Caxton (1422?): Life of Charles the Great. P
Malory, Sir Thomas (d. 1471): Morte d'Arthur [trs. Fr.; prtd. Caxton; prtd. Wynkyn de Worde 1498, 1529; other edd. 1557, 1585 (?), 1626: see also 1947]. P

Henry VII 1485–1509.

Berners, Dame Juliana (1388?): The Boke of St Albans [2nd ed. 1496]. P

Chaucer (d. 1400): House of Fame [n.d.; another ed. with other works 1526 (?)]. V

Medwall, Henry: Interlude of Nature [acted between 1486 and 1500; prtd. *c.* 1525].

Bartolomeo Diaz circumnavigates the Cape.

Paston Letters (of the family of Sir John Paston: written 1440–86) concluded (two vols. of Selections first pub. 1787; two more 1789; and a fifth 1825; the Letters ed. J. Gairdner 1901).

1487

Caxton (1422?): Book of Good Manners.

1488

Miles Coverdale b.
Duke Humphrey's Library opened at Oxford.

1489

Caxton (1422?): Doctrinal of Sapience [trs. Fr.]. P
Governal of Health [trs. Lat.]. P
Blanchardin and Eglantine [trs. Fr.]. P

Thomas Cranmer b.
Villon, 'Le Grand Testament', 'Le Petit Testament'.

1490

Caxton (1422 ?): Eneydos [n.d. ; trs. Fr.].

Sir Thomas Elyot b.?
Sir David Lindsay b.

1491

Caxton (1422?): Art and Craft to know how well to die [trs. F.]. P

William Caxton d.

1492

Aretino b.
Columbus discovers the West Indies.

1493

1494

Hylton, Walter (d. 1396): Scala Perfectionis [also called Ladder of Perfection]. P
Devout Book to a Temporal Man. P
Lydgate (d. 1450?): Falls of Princes [trs. Boccaccio; also 1527–54–55(?)]. V

Boiardo d.
Angelo Poliziano d.
Sebastian Brandt, ' Narrenschiff'.
' Natura Brevium' in French (see 1532).

1495

Trevisa, John (d. 1412): Trs. De Proprietatibus
Rerum of Bartholomew Anglicus [rev. by
Stephen Batman as Batman upon Bartho-
lomew 1582]. P

John Bale b.
Rabelais probably b.
(1483 also suggested).
Clément Marot b.
Boiardo, 'Orlando Inna-
morato'.

1496

'Mandeville, Sir John' (Jean d'Outremeuse?):
Travels [n.d.; later edd. 1499, 1501–3–68–
83(?)–1618–25–40–68 (ed. T. Este); all these
from a defective MS.: the Cotton MS. first
prtd. 1725, the Egerton MS. 1889]. P
Rolle, Richard, of Hampole (d. 1349?): Abbaye of
the Holy Ghost [n.d.]. P
Skelton (1460?): Epitaffe of Jasper Duke of Bed-
deford [n.d.; doubtful if by S.]. V

1497

Trs. Æsop's Fables [prtd. Pynson; n.d.; another
ed. 1500 (?): see 1484]. P

John Heywood b.?
Cabot discovers American
Mainland.

1498

Lydgate (d. 1450?): Assembly of the Gods [n.d.;
also 1500 (?)]. V

Savonarola burned.
Vasco da Gama discovers
sea-route to India.
Erasmus visits Oxford.

1499

1500

Chaucer (d. 1400): Mars and Venus [n.d.]. V
Lydgate (d. 1450?): Story of Thebes [n.d.]. V

Robert Henryson d.?
Erasmus, 'Adagia' (Eng.
trs. 1539).

1501

Fernando de Roja, 'Celes-
tina'.

1502

Arnold, Richard: Chronicle.

1503

Atkinson, William: Trs. De Imitatione Christi of
Thomas à Kempis [first Eng. trs.].

Sir Thomas Wyatt b.?
Erasmus, 'Enchiridion'
(Eng. trs. 1533).

Matthew Parker b.
Colet Dean of St. Paul's.
Sanazzaro, 'Arcadia'.

1505

Barclay (1475?): Castell of Laboure [n.d.; earliest ed. b. d. 1506; earlier Paris ed. *c.* 1503; trs. Gringoire]. V
Hawes (1474?): Temple of Glass [n.d.]. V

Nicholas Udall b.
John Knox b.

1506

Rolle, Richard, of Hampole (d. 1349?): Contemplations of the dread and love of God. P

John Leland b.?
Columbus d.

1507

1508

Anon.: Maying or Disport of Chaucer [attr. Chaucer]. V
Dunbar, William (1460?): Poems prtd. by Chapman and Myllar [n.d.; incl. Ballade of Lord Barnard Stewart, Flyting of Dunbar and Kennedy, Goldyn Targe, Twa Marrit Women and the Widow, Lament for Makaris, Dance of the Seven Deadly Sins, Thrissil and the Rois. D.'s Poems ed. David Laing 1834].
Fisher (1459): Treatise concerning the Fruitful Sayings of David.
Henry the Minstrel ('Blind Harry'): Wallace [n.d.; a fragment; trs. Lat. of J. Blair; ed. J. Moir 1884–9].
Rolle, Richard, of Hampole (d. 1349?): Remedy against the Troubles of Temptation. P

1509

Barclay (1475?): Ship of Fools [trs. Brandt's Narrenschiff]. V
Hawes (1474?): Pastime of Pleasure [also 1517, 1554–5]. V
Conversion of Swearers [also 1530 (?)]. V
Coronation of Henry VIII [n.d.]. V

Henry VIII 1509–47.
Calvin b.
Erasmus, 'Moriae Encomium'.

1510

Anon.: Everyman: A Moral Play [n.d.; between 1510–30].
Hyckescorner: an Interlude [n.d.].
Cock Lorrell's Bote [n.d.]. V
Hawes (1474?): Example of Virtue [n.d.; also 1530]. V
Lydgate (d. 1450?): Treatise of a Gallant [n.d.; attrib. L.]. V
More (1478): Life of John Picus Earl of Mirandula [n.d.; trs. Giovanni Pico della Mirandola]. P

Colet founds St. Paul's School.

1511

Lydgate (d. 1450?): Governaunce of Kings and Princes.

Erasmus Greek Reader at Cambridge 1511–14.

1512

1513

Anon.: Flowers of Ovid [first Eng. trs. of Ars Amatoria].
Lydgate (d. 1450?): Troy Book [also 1553, 1555; trs. Guido delle Colonne]. V
Skelton (1460?): Ballade of the Scottish King [n.d.]. V

Battle of Flodden.
Machiavelli composes 'Il Principe'.

1514

Wolsey Archbishop of York.

1515

Barclay (1475?): Eclogues [i–iii only; n.d.; another ed. 1548 (?); Eclogues iv–v 1521 (?)]. V
Lydgate (d. 1450?): Testament of John Lydgate [n.d.]. V

Roger Ascham b.
Probable date of the John Asloan MS. of Scottish literature.

1516

Fabyan, Robert: Chronicles.
More (1478): A Merry Jest how a Sergeant would learn to be a Friar [n.d.]. V
Utopia [in original Lat. and prtd. at Louvain; first Eng. trs. by R. Robinson 1551; trs. Gilbert Burnet 1684; trs. Arthur Cayley 1808].

John Foxe b.
Erasmus, 'Novum Instrumentum'.
Ariosto, 'Orlando Furioso' (in final form 1532).

1517

Henry Howard, Earl of Surrey b.
Luther's 'Theses' at Wittenberg.

Lydgate (d. 1450?): Lamentation of Our Lady [attr. L.; n.d.; before 1519].

1519

Medwall, Henry: Interlude of Fulgens, Cenatoure of Rome [n.d.; before 1520].

John Colet d.
Cortes in Mexico.
First Journey round the World (Magellan 1519–20).

1520

Scots New Testament [of Murdoch Nisbet] *c.* 1520.
Anon.: Interlude of Youth [n.d.; fragment only; other edd. *c.* 1557, 1562].
   Trs. Terence's Andria [n.d.; earliest trs.]
   Trs. Four Cardinal Virtues of Mancinus [n.d.; earliest trs.].
Barclay (1475?): Chronicle of the War which the Romans had against Jugurtha [trs. Sallust; n.d.]. P
   Life of St. Thomas. P
Lydgate (d. 1450?): Damage and Destruction in Realms [n.d.; called Serpent of Division 1559]. P

Thomas Churchyard b.?
William Dunbar d.?

1521

Barclay (1475?): Introductory to write and pronounce French. P
   Eclogues iv–v [n.d.; see 1515]. V
Fisher (1459): Sermon against the Doctrine of Luther [n.d.].
Henry VIII (1491): Defense of the Seven Sacraments.

John Siberch prints books at Cambridge 1521–2.
Papal ban on Luther at the Diet of Worms.

1522

Anon.: Interlude of the World and the Child.

Gavin Douglas d.
William Lily d.
Luther's Bible 1522–34.

1523

Barclay (1475?): Mirror of Good Manners [n.d.; trs. Mancinus]. P
Bourchier, John, Lord Berners: Trs. Froissart's Chronicles, pt. i [ii 1525]. P
Fitzherbert, John: Book of Surveying [10th ed. 1587 (?)].
   Book of Husbandry [11th ed. 1598: these two books have been wrongly attr. to Sir Anthony Fitzherbert].
Skelton (1460?): Goodly Garland or Chapelet of Laurell. V

Stephen Hawes d.?

Anon.: Trs. Gesta Romanorum [prtd. by Wynkyn de Worde; n.d.; other translations of Gesta 1557, 1595].

Cox, Leonard: Arte or Crafte of Rhethoryke [n.d.]. P

Thomas Tusser b.?
Camoens d.
Ronsard b.
Luther, 'Geistliche Lieder'.

1525

Medwall, Henry: Interlude of Nature [n.d.].

Rastell, John: Interlude of Gentylness and No-bylitie [n.d.; sometimes attr. John Heywood].
   Interlude of the Four Elements [n.d.].
   Interlude wherein is described as well the beauty and good property of Women as their vices [n.d.; commonly known as Calisto and Melibea; adaptation of Celestina of Fernando de Rojas].

Tyndale, William: Trs. New Testament [pub. abroad: see 1530, 1531].

Walton, John: Book of Comfort [trs. De Consolatione Philosophiae of Boethius].

John Stow b.?
Sir Thomas Lyttleton, 'Tenures' in English (n.d.).

1526

Anon.: A Hundred Merry Tales [n.d.].

Boece, Hector: Scotorum Historiae [pub. abroad; for Eng. trs. see 1535].

1527

Colet (1467?): Æditio [incl. William Lily's Grammatices Rudimenta; developed with Erasmus's revisions into Eton Latin Grammar; see 1549].

Machiavelli d.
Castiglione, 'Il Cortegiano'.

1528

Copland, William: Jest of a Man called Howle-glass [n.d.; trs. Tyl Eulenspiegel].

Fisher (1459): Sermon had at Paul's [on 11 Feb. 1525] concernynge certaine heretickes [n.d.].

Roy, William: Rede me and be nott wrothe [n.d.; pub. abroad; first Eng. ed. 1546]. V

Tyndale, William: Obedience of a Christian Man [pub. abroad]. P
   Parable of Wicked Mammon [pub. abroad]. P

Execution of Patrick Hamilton and beginning of Reformation in Scotland.

1529

Fish, Simon: Supplication of Beggars [anon.; n.d.]. P

More (1478): Supplication of Souls [against the Supplication of Beggars above; n.d.]. P
   Dialogue of Diverse Matters. P

John Skelton d.
Fall of Wolsey.

Anon.: Everyman: a moral play [n.d.; between 1510–30].

Colet (d. 1519): Sermon made to the Convocation at Paulis [n.d.].

Poyntz, Sir Francis (d. 1528): Trs. Tables of Cebes the Philosopher. P

Tyndale, William: Trs. Pentateuch [pub. abroad; n.d.: see 1525, 1531].

Practice of Prelates [pub. abroad]. P

Cardinal Wolsey d.

1531

Golden Litany in English.

Elyot (1490?): The Boke named the Governour. P

Tyndale, William: Trs. Book of Jonah [pub. abroad: see 1525, 1530].

Answer to Sir Thomas More's Dialogue [pub. abroad; n.d.: see More 1529].

Ulrich Zwingli d.

1532

Chaucer (d. 1400): Works ed. William Thynne [all genuine works hitherto pub. or unpub., and the following that are spurious: Testament of Cresseid (by Henryson); Flower of Courtesie and Complaint of the Black Knight (Lydgate); Testament of Love (Thomas Usk); Letter of Cupid (Occleve); Cuckoo and Nightingale (Sir Thomas Clanvowe?); La Belle Dame sans Mercie (Sir Richard Ross); Assembly of Ladies (unknown); Lamentation of Mary Magdalen (unknown), and others.

Later edd. of Works with spurious poems added: ed. Thynne (Plowman's Tale) 1542, 1545 (?); ed. Stow (Court of Love and some short poems) 1561; ed. Speght (Flower and the Leaf, Jack Upland, Chaucer's A.B.C., and a new Chaucer's Dream) 1598, 1602, 1687; ed. Urry (Tale of Gamelyn, Pardoner and the Tapster, and Second Merchants Tale) 1721.

Modern edd. of Works: ed. Singer 1822, Morris 1866, Skeat 1894–7, Pollard 1897].

Elyot (1490?): Pasquil the Plaine. P

Henryson: (d. 1500): Testament of Cresseid [in Works of Chaucer above]. V

Hervet, Gentian: Trs. Xenophon's Treatise of Household. P

Lydgate (d. 1450): Flower of Courtesie, Complaint of the Black Knight [in Works of Chaucer above]. V

More (1478): Confutation of Tyndale's Answer [Second Part of Confutation 1533]. P

Henry VIII divorces Katherine of Aragon.
'Natura Brevium' in English.
Rabelais, 'Pantagruel', bk. i (bk. ii called Gargantua 1534, bk. iii 1545, bk. iv 1548–52, bk. v (of doubtful authenticity) 1562–4).
Ariosto, 'Orlando Furioso' (in final form: see 1516).
Machiavelli, 'Il Principe'.
Erasmus, 'Apophthegmata'.

Anon.: Trs. Erasmus's Enchiridion [prtd. Wynkyn de Worde].

Elyot (1490?): Of the Knowledge which maketh a wise man. P

Grimald, Nicholas: Trs. Three Books of Duties of Cicero. P

Heywood (1497?): Johan the husband, Tyb the wife and Sir Johan the Priest. D interlude.

The Pardoner, the Frere, the Curate and Neighbour Pratte. D interlude.

Play of the Wether. D interlude.

Lydgate (d. 1450?): Life of Albon and Amphabel. V

More (1478): Apology of Sir Thomas More. P

Skelton (d. 1529): Magnificence: a goodly Interlude [n.d.]. D

Tyndale, William: Treatise of the Sacraments. P

Supper of the Lord. P

Udall, Nicholas: Floures of Latin speaking, gathered out of Terence, and translated into English.

Montaigne b.
Ariosto d.

1534

Bourchier, John, Lord Berners: Trs. Huon of Bordeaux [3rd ed. 1601].

Colet (d. 1519): A Right Fruitful Admonition. P

Elyot (1490?): Sermon of Holy Saint Ciprian. Rules of a Christian Life [trs. Mirandola]. P

Doctrine of Princes [trs. Isocrates]. P

Castel of Health [see 1539]. P

Heywood (1497?): A Play of Love. D interlude.

Lydgate (d. 1450?): Life of St. Alban. V

Whytington, R.: Three Books of Tullyes Offices [trs. Cicero]. P

John Leland's antiquarian tour through England 1534–43 ('Itinerary' first pub. 1710; 'Collectanea' 1715. See 1549).
Rabelais, 'Pantagruel', bk. ii (see 1532).

1535

Bellenden, John: Chronicles of Scotland [trs. Hector Boece: see 1526]. P

Bourchier, John, Lord Berners: Golden Book of Marcus Aurelius [trs. Antonio de Guevara]. P

Coverdale (1488): Trs. Bible [pub. abroad: see 1537].

Fisher (1459): Spiritual Consolation to his Sister [n.d.]. P

Sir Thomas North b.?
Sir Thomas More executed.
John Fisher executed.
Act of Supremacy.
Suppression of religious houses 1535–9.
Calvin, 'Institution of Christian Religion' (last corrected ed. 1559; Eng. trs. 1561).

1536

Anon.: Remedy for Sedition [sometimes attrib. Sir John Cheke]. P

Copland, Robert: Hye Way to the Spyttel House [n.d.]. V

William Tyndale burnt.
Erasmus d.

Coverdale (1488): Trs. Bible [modified version of the trs. of 1535; first Bible prtd. in England].
Cranmer (1489) and others: Institution of a Christian Man. P
Fortescue (d. 1476?): De Laudibus Legum Angliae [in Latin]. P
Rogers, John: Matthews' Bible [so called because trs. under pseudonym of Thomas Matthews].

1538

Elyot (1490?): Dictionary [Latin-English; another ed. 1545; rev. by T. Cooper as Bibliotheca Eliotae 1548–52–59].
Lindsay (1490): Complaint of a Popinjay [earliest extant ed.]. V
Ockham, William of (d. 1349?): Dialogue betwene a knight & a clerke [Trs. from Latin: possibly not by Ockham].

1539

The Great Bible [also called Cranmer's Bible].
Elyot (1490?): Banquet of Sapience. P
  Castel of Health [earliest extant, i.e. 2nd ed.; originally in 1534]. P
Taverner, Richard: Trs. Bible.
  Garden of Wisdom. P
  Proverbs & Adagies [trs. Adagia of Erasmus]. P

1540

Anon.: Jack Upland [n.d.; sometimes attrib. Chaucer]. V
  Schoolhouse of Women [n.d.]. V
Bourchier, John, Lord Berners: Castell of Love [trs. D. de San Pedro; n.d.]. P
Elyot (1490?): Image of Governance [trs. Eucolpius]. P
Lindsay (1490): Satyr of Three Estates [acted: prtd. 1602]. D

Barnabe Googe b.
George Turberville b.?
Barnabe Rich b.?
Guicciardini d.

1541

Paracelsus d.

1542

Anon.: Plowman's Tale [attrib. Chaucer in ed. below: separately 1545 (?)]. V

Boorde, Andrew (1490?): Dietary of Health [n.d.].

Chaucer (d. 1400): Works, 2nd ed. by William Thynne [see 1532].

Halle, Edward: Union of the Families of Lancastre and Yorke [commonly known as 'Halle's Chronicle'; first ed. undated and a fragment; 2nd ed. 1548; 3rd the most complete 1550].

Lily, William (d. 1522): Introduction to the Eight Parts of Speech [final and approved form of L.'s Grammar].

Recorde, Robert: Ground of Arts, teaching Arithmetic.

Udall, Nicholas: Trs. Apophthegms of Erasmus. P

George Gascoigne b.
Sir Thomas Wyatt d.
Montemayor, 'Diana'.

1543

Hardyng, John (d. 1465?): Chronicle of England [with the Continuation by Richard Grafton].

More (d. 1535): History of Richard the Third [first pub. in Hardyng's Chronicle above; later in Halle's Chronicle 1548, and in M.'s English Works 1557; attribution to M. not certain]. P

Thomas Deloney b.?
Copernicus (d. 1543), 'De Revolutionibus'.
English Litany separately printed.

1544

Bale (1495): Chronicle concerning Sir John Oldcastle [pub. abroad]. P

Leland (1506?): Assertio Inclytissimi Arturii Regis Britanniae [in original Latin; trs. R. Robinson as Assertion of the Life of Prince Arthur 1582]. P

George Whetstone b.?
Tasso b.
Clément Marot d.

1545

The King's Primer.

Ascham (1515): Toxophilus. P

Elyot (1490?): Defence of Good Women. P
Preservative against Death. P

Heywood (1497?): The Four P.P. [n.d.]. D interlude.

Rhodes, Hugh: Book of Nurture for Men, Servants and Children [n.d.]. P

Skelton (d. 1529): Book of Phillip Sparrow [n.d.]. V

Colin Clout [n.d.]. V

Why come ye not to Court [n.d.]. V

Certain Books compiled by Master Skelton [n.d.; incl. Speak Parrot, Death of Edward IV, Treatise of the Scots, Tunning of Elinour Rumming, and other poems, enlarged 1565 (?)].

Sir Thomas Bodley b.
Nicholas Breton b.?
Council of Trent meets.
Rabelais,'Pantagruel', bk. iii (see 1532).

Bale (1495): Acts of English Votaries. P

Heywood (1497?): Proverbs [enlarged 1555, 1560, 1562]. V

Wiclif (d. 1384): Wyclif's Wicket [attrib. Wiclif]. P

Sir Thomas Elyot d.
Luther d.

1547

Book of Homilies [promoted by Cranmer].

Baldwin, William: Treatise of Moral Philosophy [trs. Diogenes Laertius, and others; enlarg. 1555(?) ed. Paulfreyman with additions 1557, 1564, 1567, 1584, 1620 (?)]. P

Bale (1495): Interlude manifesting Chief Promises of God [n.d.; pub. abroad; first Eng. ed. 1577]. D

Interlude concerning Temptation of our Lord [n.d.; pub. abroad; first Eng. ed. 1870]. D

Boorde, Andrew (1490?): Breviary of Health [also 1552].

First Book of the Introduction of Knowledge [n.d.]. P

Ingelend, Thomas: Interlude of Disobedient Child [performed *c.* 1547; prtd. *c.* 1570].

Sternhold, Thomas, and Hopkins, John: Psalms [first instalment: see 1549, 1562].

Wilkinson, John: Ethiques of Aristotle [first Eng. trs.]. P

Edward VI 1547–53.
Henry Howard, Earl of
Surrey, executed.
Cervantes b.

1548

Order of the Communion.

Bale (1495): Interlude concerning Three Laws of Nature [n.d.; prtd. abroad; first Eng. ed. 1562].

Kynge Johan [acted *c.* 1548; prtd. 1838]. D interlude.

Illustrium Majoris Britanniae Scriptorum Summarium [commonly called Catalogus; greatly enlarg. 1557–9].

Brinkelow, Henry: Complaynt of Roderyck Mors [n.d.]. P

Latimer (1485): A Notable Sermon preached at Paul's Church [Plough Sermon]. P

Lindsay (1490): Tragical Death of David Beaton [n.d.]. V

Udall, Nicholas: Trs. Erasmus's Paraphrase of the New Testament [vol. ii, 1549, but not by U.]. P

Rabelais, 'Pantagruel',
bk. iv 1548–52 (see
1532).

Book of Common Prayer [mainly the work of Cranmer; called the First Prayer Book of Edward VI; Second Prayer Book of Edward VI 1552; rev. as Elizabethan Prayer Book 1559; Prayer Book in final form 1662].

Anon.: Complaynt of Scotland [n.d.; prtd. at Paris?]. P

Baldwin, William: Canticles of Solomon in Englyshe Metres.

Cheke, Sir John: Hurt of Sedition. P

Cooper, Thomas: Chronicle [completed from unfinished work of Thomas Lanquet; other edd. 1560, 1565].

Latimer (1485?): Seven Sermons preached before the King in 1549.

Leland (1506?): Journey and Search for England's Antiquities given as a New Year's Gift to King Henry VIII. P

Sternhold, Thomas, and Hopkins, John: Psalms [2nd instalment: see 1547, 1562]. V

Wyatt (d. 1542): Certaine Psalmes drawne into English meter.

Giles Fletcher, senr. b.?
William Lily and John Colet, 'Short Introduction of Grammar'.
La Pléiade (Ronsard, Jodelle, Belleau, Baïf, Daurat, Joachim du Bellay, and Pontus de Tyard).
Du Bellay, 'Défense de la langue française'.

1550

Bansley, Charles: Tract showing the Pride and Abuse of Women [n.d.]. V

Cranmer (1489): Defence of the Catholike Doctrine of the Sacrement. P

Crowley, Robert: One and Thirty Epigrams. V

Halle, Edward: Chronicle [see 1542]. P

Harington, John: Book of Friendship [trs. Cicero].

Hunnis, William: Certain Psalmes in English Metre. V

Langland (d. 1400?): Vision of Pierce the Plowman [what is known as the B-text; another ed. with Crede of Pierce the Plowman added 1561; ed. Wright 1842, 1856, 1895; ed. Skeat 1869, 1896; A-text ed. Skeat 1867; C-text ed. Whitaker 1813, Skeat 1873; the three texts ed. Skeat 1886]. V

Nicolls, Thomas: Trs. History of Thucydides [earliest trs.].

Wiclif (d. 1384): Prologue written in an old English Bible.

Ronsard, 'Odes' and 'Amours de Cassandre' between 1550 and 1554.
Vasari, 'Lives of Painters' (concl. 1578).

1551

Robynson, Raphe: Trs. More's Utopia [also 1556, 1597; corrected 1624; another ed. 1639: see 1516]. P

Turner, William: A New Herball [pt. ii 1562, pts. i and ii rev. and pt. iii added 1568]. P

Wilson, Thomas (1525?): Rule of Reason. P

William Camden b.

Second Prayer Book of Edward VI [mainly the work of Cranmer: see 1549].

Forty-two Articles [promulgated by Cranmer: see 1560].

Churchyard (1520?): A Mirror for Man [n.d.]. V

Edmund Spenser b.?
Walter Raleigh b.?
Richard Hakluyt b.?
John Speed b.?
John Leland d.
Alexander Barclay d.
Autobiography and Diary of Dr. Simon Forman from 1552 to 1602 (pub. J. O. Halliwell-Phillips 1849).
Jodelle, 'Cléopâtre'.

1553

Anon.: Interlude of Jacke Jugeler [performed between 1553 and 1558; prtd. between 1562 and 1569].

Douglas (d. 1522): Trs. Æneid. V
Palace of Honour [n.d.; also 1579]. V

More (d. 1535): Dialogue of Comfort [corrected 1573]. P

Wilson, Thomas (1525?): Arte of Rhetorique. P

Queen Mary 1553–8.
Anthony Munday b.
Rabelais d.
Sir Hugh Willoughby sails for Cathay.
Mendoza (?) 'Lazarillo de Tormes'.

1554

Lindsay (1490): Dialogue betwixt Experience and Ane Courtier [n.d.; later edd., mostly with other works added, 1558, 1566, 1575]. V

Lydgate (d. 1450): Dance of Death [in ed. of Falls of Princes: see 1494]. V

Sir Philip Sidney b.
John Lyly b. ?
Fulke Greville b.
Richard Hooker b.?
Meeting of John Knox and Calvin at Geneva.
Stationers' Registers 1554–1640 (ed. E. Arber 1875–94).
Bandello, 'Novelle', vol. i–iii (iv 1573).
Ronsard, 'Amours de Marie' and 'Hymnes' between 1554 and 1560.

1555

Anon.: Institution of a Gentleman. P

Baldwin, William (ed.): Memorial of such Princes as have been unfortunate in the realm of England [suppressed first ed. of Mirror for Magistrates; n.d.: see 1559]. V

Bourchier, John, Lord Berners: History of Arthur of Little Britain [trs. Fr.; n.d.; another ed. c. 1582]. P

Eden, Richard: Decades of the New World or West India [trs. Peter Martyr]. P

Heywood (1497?): Two Hundred Epigrams [see 1546, 1560, 1562]. V

Lancelot Andrewes b.
Malherbe b.
Latimer and Ridley burnt.
Sir David Lindsay d.

The Genevan Psalter [pub. abroad: chiefly work of William Whittingham].
Colville, George: Book called Comfort of Philosophy [trs. Boethius].
Heywood (1497?): Spider and the Fly. V
Recorde, Robert: Castle of Knowledge. P

Thomas Cranmer burnt.
Nicholas Udall d.
Pietro Aretino d.

1557

Anon.: Interlude of Youth [n.d.].
More (d. 1535): Works written in English [ed. William Rastell].
North (1535?): Diall of Princes. Famous Book of Marcus Aurelius [trs. Antonio de Guevara; rev. and enlarg. 1568]. P
Recorde, Robert: Whetstone of Wit [first book of Algebra].
Surrey (d. 1547): Trs. Certaine Books of Virgil's Æneis [bks. ii and iv]. V
Tottel, Richard, and Grimald, Nicholas (compilers): Songs and Sonnets [called Tottel's Miscellany; contributors: Surrey, Wyatt, Lord Vaux, John Heywood, Edward Somerset, and others. Later edd. 1559, 1565, 1567, 1574, 1585, 1587; ed. J. Nott 1812; R. Bell 1854; E. Arber 1870, 1903; H. Rollins 1928–9].
Tusser (1524?): Hundreth Good Pointes of Husbandrie [see 1573]. V

Thomas Kyd b.?
Stationers' Company incorporated.

1558

Anon.: Interlude of Wealth and Health [n.d.]. D
Bullein, William: Government of Health [n.d.].
Knox (1505): First Blast of the Trumpet against the Monstrous Regiment of Women. P
Morwyng, P.: History of the Jewes Commune Weale [trs. Joseph ben Gorion]. P
Phaer, Thomas: Trs. Æneid, bks. i–vii [i–ix 1562; completed in 13 bks. by Thomas Twyne 1584]. V

Queen Elizabeth 1558–1603.
Thomas Lodge b.?
George Peele b.?
William Warner b.?
Julius Caesar Scaliger d.
Marguerite de Navarre, 'Heptameron' (concl. 1559).

Elizabethan Prayer Book [see 1549].
Aylmer, John: Harbour against the late blown
blast concerning Government of Women
[reply to Knox: see 1558]. P
Baldwin, William (ed.): Mirror for Magistrates
[later edd. with alterations and additions
1563, 1571, 1574 (ed. John Higgins), 1578
(ed. Thomas Blenerhasset), 1587 (ed. John
Higgins), 1610 (ed. Richard Nicols); 1815 (ed.
J. Haslewood); notable contributions: In-
duction and Complaint of Buckingham by
Thomas Sackville, Shore's Wife by Thomas
Churchyard, and Edward the Fourth by
John Skelton: see 1555]. V
Heywood, Jasper: Trs. Troas of Seneca [see 1581].
T

Act of Uniformity.
George Chapman b.?
Isaac Casaubon b.
*Jacques Amyot, trs. Plu-
tarch.*

1560

Geneva Bible [also called Breeches Bible; mainly
the work of William Whittingham; pub. at
Geneva].
Thirty-nine Articles.
Anon.: Interlude called the Nice Wanton [n.d.]. D
Interlude called Impatient Poverty [n.d.]. D
Interlude called Thersytes [n.d.; by Nicholas
Udall?]. D
Proud Wives Paternoster. V
Barker, W.: Trs. Bookes of Xenophon containing
Discipline and Education of Cyrus [n.d.]. P
T. C.,: Pleasant History of Galesus [trs. Boccaccio;
n.d.].
Fisher (d. 1535): Treatise declaring Benefits of
Prayer. P
Googe (1540): Zodiake of Life, bks. i–iii [bks. i–vi
1561; complete in 12 bks. 1565; trs. Marcellus
Palingenius]. V
Heywood, Jasper: Trs. Thyestes of Seneca [see
1581]. T
Heywood (1497?): A Fourth Hundred of Epigrams
[see 1546, 1555, 1562]. V
Howell, Thomas: Fable of Narcissus [trs. Ovid].
Knox (1505): Treatise on Predestination. P
Whitehorne, Peter: Trs. Machiavelli's Art of War
[concl. 1562]. P

Robert Greene b.?
*The anon. comedies 'Miso-
gonus' and 'The Bug-
bears' performed about
this date.*
*Ronsard, 'Discours des
Misères de ce temps'
and Epic 'Franciade'
between 1560 and 1574.*

Anon.: Pierce the Ploughman's Creed [see Langland 1550. Ed. Skeat 1867, 1906]. V
Godly Queen Hester. D moral interlude.
Beware the Cat [n.d.]. P
Chaucer (d. 1400): Works, ed. Stow [see 1532].
Eden, Richard: Art of Navigation [trs. Cortes].
Gilby, Goddard: Trs. Cicero's Epistle to Quintus.
Heywood, Jasper: Trs. Hercules Furens of Seneca [see 1581]. T
Hoby (1530): The Courtyer [trs. Castiglione]. P
Norton, Thomas: Trs. Calvin's Institution of Christian Religion. P

Francis Bacon b.
Robert Southwell b.?
Sir John Harington b.
'Gorboduc' acted at Inner Temple (see 1565).
Scaliger, 'Poetics'.

1562

Bale (1495): Interlude concerning Three Laws of Nature [see 1548]. D
Broke, Arthur: History of Romeus and Juliet. V
Bullein, William: Bulwark against all Sickness.
Grafton, Richard: Abridgement of the Chronicles of England [1563–64–70–72].
Heywood (1497?): Works [i.e. Proverbs and Epigrams: see 1546, 1555, 1560].
Ballad against Slander and Detraction. V
Jewel, John: Apology for the Church of England [both Latin original, and Eng. trs. by Ann, Lady Bacon: see 1567]. P
Latimer (d. 1555): XXVII Sermons [see 1571].
Sternhold, Thomas, Hopkins, John, and others: Whole Book of Psalms [first complete ed., and known as the Old Version; sectionally 1547–49–61. For New Version see 1696]. V

Samuel Daniel b.
Lope de Vega b.
Sir John Hawkins's Voyages 1562–8.
Rabelais, 'Pantagruel', bk. v 1562–4 (see 1532).

1563

Foxe (1516): Actes and Monuments [commonly called Book of Martyrs; edd. during F.'s lifetime 1570–76–83; other edd. 1596, 1610–32–41–84; ed. Cattley 1837–41, Stoughton 1877].
Golding, Arthur: Trs. Histories of Justin. P
Googe (1540): Eclogs, Epitaphs and Sonnets. V
Nevyle, Alexander: Oedipus [trs. Seneca: see 1581]. T
Rainolde, Richard: Foundacion of Rhetorike. P

Plague in London.
Michael Drayton b.
Joshua Sylvester b.
John Bale d.
Index Librorum Prohibitorum.

1564

Scots Psalter.
Bullein, William: Dialogue against the Fever Pestilence.

William Shakespeare b.
Christopher Marlowe b.
Henry Chettle b.
Galileo b.
Calvin d.
Michelangelo d.
Queen Elizabeth visits Cambridge.

Anon.: Interlude of Kyng Darius. D
  Contention between Liberalitie and Prodigalitie [acted: prtd. 1602]. D interlude.
Awdeley, John: Fraternity of Vagabonds. Twenty-five Orders of Knaves. P
Golding, Arthur: Trs. Ovid's Metamorphoses, bks. i–iv [complete: bks. i–xv 1567].
  Trs. Caesar's Exploits in Gallia. P
Grafton, Richard: Manual of the Chronicles of England [n.d.]. P
Norton, Thomas, and Sackville, Thomas: Tragedy of Gorboduc [called Ferrex and Porrex 1570].
Peend, T.: Fable of Hermaphroditus and Salmacis [trs. Ovid].
Stow (1525?): Summarie of English Chronicles [later edd., with additions up to date: 1566–67–70–73–74–75–87–90–98–1604; continued by Howes 1607–10; by Allde (?) 1618].
Underdowne, Thomas: Hermaphroditus and Salmacis [trs. Ovid].
Weaver, R.: Interlude called Lusty Juventus [n.d.]. D

John Davies of Hereford b.?
Thomas Cooper, 'Thesaurus Linguae Romanae et Britannicae'.
Cinthio, 'Hecatommithi.'

1566

Anon.: Albion Knight [n.d.]. D moral interlude.
Adlington, William: Trs. Golden Ass of Apuleius. P
Drant, Thomas: A Medicinable Moral, that is, two Books of Horace his Satyres.
Gascoigne (1542): Supposes [acted: see 1573; adapted from Ariosto]. C
  Jocasta [acted; see 1573; adapted from Euripides]. T
Grantham, H.: A Pleasant Disport entitled Philocopo [n.d.; trs. Boccaccio]. P
Lindsay (d. 1555): Deploration of Death of Queen Magdalen [in ed. of Dialogue between Experience and ane Courtier: see 1554]. V
Painter, William: Palace of Pleasure [vol. ii 1567; corrected and enlarg. 1575; trs. tales chiefly from Boccaccio and Bandello]. P
Studley, John: Trs. Agamemnon of Seneca [see 1581]. T
  Trs. Medea of Seneca [see 1581]. T
Udall (d. 1556): Ralph Roister Doister [n.d.]. C
Wager, Lewis: Life and Repentance of Mary Magdalene. D moral interlude.

Gowrie Conspiracy.
Queen Elizabeth visits Oxford.
Diary of James Melville, minister of Kilrenny 1566–1601 (pub. Bannatyne Club 1829).
Martin Luther, 'Tischreden'.

Anon.: Interlude called Trial of Treasure. D

Drant, Thomas: Arte of Poetrie, Pistles and Satyrs [trs. Horace]. V

Fenton, Sir Geoffrey: Certaine Tragicall Discourses [trs. Bandello]. P

Hake, E.: Trs. De Imitatione Christi.

Harman, Thomas: Caveat or Warening for Common Cursetors Vulgarely called Vagabones [earliest extant, i.e. 2nd, ed.]. P

Jewel, John: Defence of the Apologie of the Church of Englande [see 1562]. P

Mulcaster, Richard: A Learned Commendation of the Laws of England [trs. De Laudibus Legum Angliae of Sir John Fortescue]. P

Paynell, Thomas: Trs. Amadis of France. P

Pickering, John: History of Horestes, a new Interlude. D

Rastell, John: Expositions of the Termes of the Lawes. P

Sandford, James: Trs. Manual of Epictetus.

Turbervile (1540?): Epitaphs, Epigrams, Songs, and Sonnets.

Trs. Heroical Epistles of Ovid. V

Trs. Eclogues of Mantuan. V

Revolt of the Netherlands.
Sir William Alexander, Earl of Stirling b.?
Thomas Nash b.
Thomas Campion b.

1568

The Bishops' Bible [chiefly the work of Matthew Parker].

Anon.: History of Jacob and Esau. D interlude.

Baker, Humphrey: Well-Spring of Sciences [Book of Arithmetic].

Fulwell, Ulpian: Interlude entitled Like Will to Like.

Grafton, Richard: Chronicle at Large [2nd ed. 1569]. P

Howell, Thomas: Arbor of Amitie. V

New Sonnets and Pretty Pamphlets [n.d.]. V

Lindsay (d. 1555): Works [incl. all works except Satire of Three Estates (pub. 1602), and History of Squire Meldrum pub. in 1582 ed. of Works. Works ed. Laing 1879].

Skelton (d. 1529): Pithy, Pleasant and Profitable Works, now Collected [works ed. A. Dyce 1843].

Tilney, Edmund: Discourse of Duties in Marriage. P

Turbervile (1540?): Plain Path to Perfect Virtue [trs. Mancinus]. V

Mary Queen of Scots in England.
Sir Henry Wotton b.
Gervase Markham b.?
Miles Coverdale d.
Roger Ascham d.
Probable date of compilation of George Bannatyne MS. of Scottish literature (prtd. in entirety by Hunterian Club 1873–1902).
William Lambarde's 'Archaionomia'.

Hawkins, Sir John: True Declaration of his Voyage in 1567 and 1568 [his third voyage]. P

Newton, Thomas: Trs. Cicero's Paradoxa Stoicorum. P

Worthy Book of Old Age [trs. Cicero].

Sandford, J.: Trs. Cornelius Agrippa's Of the Vanitie of Artes and Sciences.

T., C.: Notable History of Nastagio [trs. Boccaccio].

Underdowne, Thomas: Trs. Æthiopian History of Heliodorus [n.d.]. P

Trs. Ovid his Invective against Ibis. V

Sir John Davies b.
Sir James Melville's 'Memorials of Transactions in Scotland' 1569–73 (first pub. 1683; prtd. Bannatyne Club 1827).

1570

Anon.: Marriage of Wit and Science [n.d.]. D interlude.

Ascham (d. 1568): The Schoolmaster. P

Barbour (d. 1395): Bruce [n.d.; also 1616, 1620]. V

Fenton, Sir Geoffrey: Discourse of Civil Wars of France [n.d.; trs. Fr.].

Foxe, John: Sermon of Christ Crucified. P

Googe (1540): The Popish Kingdom [trs. Thomas Kirchmayer].

Henryson (d. 1500?): Moral Fables of Æsop [also 1621] V

Ingelend, Thomas: Interlude called Disobedient Child [n.d.: see 1547].

North (1535?): Moral Philosophy of Doni [trs. Fables of Bidpai]. P

Phillips, John: Patient and Meek Grissil [n.d.]. D interlude.

Preston,Thomas: Cambises, King of Persia [n.d.]. D

Wilson, Thomas (1525?): Trs. Three Orations of Demosthenes.

Thomas Dekker b.?
Thomas Middleton b.?

1571

Edwards, Richard: Damon and Pithias. C

Grafton, Richard: Treatise containing many proper tables and rules [enlarg. 1611]. P

Latimer (d. 1555): Fruitful Sermons, pt. i [pts. ii and iii 1575; later collective edd. of Sermons 1578–84–94–1607–35].

Act for incorporation of the Universities of Oxford and Cambridge.
Kepler b.

Cartwright, Thomas: Second Admonition to Parliament. P

Churchyard (1520?): Trs. First three books of Ovid's Tristia [n.d.]. V

Fenton, Sir Geoffrey: Monophylo, or a philosophical discourse of love. V

Field, John, and Wilcox, Thomas: Admonition to Parliament. P

Parker, Matthew: De Antiquitate Britanniae Ecclesiae [supposed first privately printed book in England].

'R. H.': Trs. Ludwig Lavater's Of Ghosts and Spirits walking by Night.

Wilson, Thomas (1525?): Discourse upon Usury.

Massacre of St. Bartholomew.
Unattached companies of actors declared rogues and vagabonds.
Society of Antiquarians founded by Matthew Parker.
John Donne b.
John Knox d.
Camoens, ' Os Lusiados'.

1573

Anon.: New Custom. D moral interlude.

Gascoigne (1542): A Hundreth Sundry Flowers [n.d.; anon and unauthorized; cont. Supposes, Jocasta (b. d. 1566), Master Ferdinando Ieronimo, Devices of Sundry Gentlemen, Dan Bartholomew of Bath: see 1575].

Tusser (1524?): Five Hundreth Pointes of Good Husbandrie [enlarged 1580: see 1557]. V

Tyndale (d. 1536): Whole Works of Tyndale, John Frith and Doctor Barnes [cont. Lives of the authors extracted from Foxe's Martyrs.].

Ben Jonson b.?
William Laud b.
Bandello, 'Novelle', vol. iv (see 1554).
Tasso, ' Aminta'.

1574

Hellowes, Edward: Trs. Familiar Letters of Antonio de Guevara.

Higgins, John: Ed. Mirror for Magistrates [see 1559].

Parker, Matthew: Lives of the Seventy Archbishops of Canterbury. P

Rich, Barnabe (1540?): Dialogue between Mercury and an English Souldier [n.d.].

Scot, Reginald: Perfit Platform of a hop garden. P

Earl of Leicester's theatrical company formed.
Joseph Hall b.
Richard Barnfield b.

1575

Anon.: Gammer Gurtons Needle [William Stevenson now supposed author; formerly John Still]. C

B., R.: Appius and Virginia. D tragi-comedy.

Breton (1545?): Small handful of fragrant flowers. V

Churchyard (1520?): First Part of Churchyards Chippes. V

John Marston b.?
Cyril Tourneur b.?
Samuel Purchas b.?
Thomas Heywood b.?
Jacob Boehme b.
Matthew Parker d.

Fenton, Sir Geoffrey: Trs. Golden Epistles [trs. Spanish of Guevara; corrected 1577, 1582].

Gascoigne (1542): A Glasse of Government. D
Posies of George Gascoigne [cont. enlarged version of works 1573; adds Notes of Instruction concerning Making of Verse: see 1587].

Rolland, John: Treatise callit the Court of Venus. V

Turberville (1540?): Book of Falconrie [rev. and enlarg. 1611]. P
Noble Art of Venerie [n.d.].

1576

Edwards, Richard; Heywood, Jasper; Lord Vaux, and others: Paradise of Dainty Devices [later edd. 1578–80–85–96–98 (?)–1600–6]. V

Fleming, Abraham: Panoplie of Epistles [trs. Cicero, Pliny the Younger, and others].

Gascoigne (1542): Steele Glas. Complainte of Phylomene. V
Droomme of Doomesday [trs. Lat. of Conti]. P
Delicate Diet for Daintie mouthde Droonkardes. P
Princelye Pleasures at Courte of Kenelwoorth [with G. Ferrers, H. Goldingham, and W. Hunnis]. D masque or entertainment.

Gilbert, Sir Humphrey: Discourse of a New Passage to Cataia. P

Lambarde, William: Perambulation of Kent. P

Pettie, George: Petite Pallace of Pettie his Pleasure [n.d.]. P

Whetstone (1544?): Rocke of Regard. V and P

Sack of Antwerp.
Martin Frobisher's Voyages, 1576–7.
Erection of The Theater (first theatre in London).

1577

Bale (d. 1563): Chief Promises of God [see 1547]. D interlude.

Breton (1545?): Works of a Young Wit. V
Floorish upon Fancie. V

Eden, Richard (d. 1576): History of Travel in East and West Indies [completed by R. Willes]. P

Gascoigne (d. 1577): Spoyle of Antwerpe [n.d.]. P

Golding, Arthur: Tragedy of Abrahams Sacrifice [trs. Fr. of Theodore Beza]. D

Googe (1540): Four Books of Husbandry [trs. Conrad Heresbach]. V

Hellowes, Edward: Lives of Ten Emperors of Rome [trs. Spanish of Guevara]. P

Holinshed, Raphael: Chronicles [incl. Harrison's Description of England; enl. 1587]. P

Kendall, Timothy: Flowres of Epigrams. V

Peacham, Henry, senr.: Garden of Eloquence. P

Drake's voyage round the world, 1577–80.
The Curtain Theatre opened c. 1577.
Robert Burton b.
Thomas Coryate b.?
George Gascoigne d.
David Moysie's Memoirs of Affairs of Scotland, 1577–1603 (first pub. Bannatyne Club 1830).

Best, George: Discourse of the Voyages of Martin Frobisher. P

Churchyard (1520): Woful Wars in Flaunders. V
Discourse of the Queenes Entertainment in Suffolk and Norfolk. V

Day, Richard: Book of Christian Prayers.

Hellowes, Edward: Invention of the Art of Navigation [trs. Spanish of Guevara]. P

Lupton, Thomas: All for Money. D moral interlude.

Lyly (1554?): Euphues, the Anatomy of Wit [n.d.; corrected and augmented 1579; pt. ii Euphues and his England 1580; pts. i–ii combined 1617]. P

Proctor, Thomas: Gorgeous Gallery of Gallant Inventions [Verse collection].

Rich, Barnabe (1540?): Alarm to England. P

Whetstone (1544?): Promos and Cassandra. C
Remembrance of the Life of George Gascoigne [n.d.]. V

George Sandys b.
William Harvey b.
Thomas Blenerhasset ed.
' Mirror for Magistrates' (see 1559).
Du Bartas, 'La Semaine' ('La Seconde Semaine' 1584).

1579

Churchyard (1520?): General Rehearsal of Wars [n.d.]. V

Miserie of Flaunders. V

Day, Richard: Christ Jesus Triumphant. D

Fenton, Sir Geoffrey: History of the Wars of Italy [trs. Guicciardini]. P

Frampton, John: Trs. Travels of Marco Polo. P

Gosson, Stephen: School of Abuse. P
Ephemerides of Phialo [cont. Apologie for School of Abuse]. P

Lodge (1558?): Defence of Stage Plays [reply to Gosson; known copies want title and date; about 1579–80]. P

Munday (1553): Mirror of Mutabilitie. V

North (1535?): Trs. Plutarch's Lives [Lives of Epaminondas and Philip of Macedon added 1602; trs. through Fr. of Amyot]. P

Spenser (1552?): Shepheards Calender. V

Puritan Attack on the Stage: Gosson's *School of Abuse* (1579) and *Apologie for School of Abuse* (1579); Lodge's Reply to Gosson (1579); Gosson's *Plays Confuted* (1582) and Lodge's rejoinder in Preface to *Alarum against Usurers* (1584); Stubbes's *Anatomie of Abuses* (1583) and Nash's attack on Stubbes in *Anatomie of Absurditie* (1589).

John Fletcher b.

Bullokar, William: Book for the amendment of English Orthographie. P

Churchyard (1520?): Churchyardes Charge. V

Gifford, Humfrey: Posie of Gilloflowers. V

Lyly (1554?): Euphues and his England [see 1578]. P

Munday (1553): Zelauto, the Fountain of Fame. P
Pain of Pleasure. P

Roger, J.: Trs. De Imitatione Christi. P

Spenser and Harvey, Gabriel (1552?): Three Letters and two other Letters passed between two university men. P

Stow (1525?): Chronicles of England [n.d.; see 1592]. P

John Webster b.?
Raphael Holinshed d.?
John Heywood d.?
Thomas Tusser d.
Probable date of the MS. of the Collection of ancient Scottish Literature made by Sir Richard Maitland (1496–1586).
Camoens d.
Quevedo b.
Montaigne, 'Essais', bks. i, ii (bk. iii 1588; 'Essais' in final form 1595).
Belleforest, 'Histoires Tragiques' (concl. 1582).

1581

Hall, Arthur: Ten Books of Homer's Iliades. V

Heywood, Newton, Studley, Nevyle, and Nuce: Seneca his Ten Tragedies [collected; separately 1559–60–61–63–66]. P

Howell, Thomas: Howell his Devises. V

Lambarde, William: Eirenarchia. P

Mulcaster, Richard: Positions. P

Pettie, George: Trs. Civil Conversations of Stefano Guazzo, bks. i–iii [completed in 4 bks. by Bartholomew Young 1586]. P

Rich, Barnabe (1540?): Rich his Farewell to the Military Profession [enlarg. 1606]. P

Adventures of Don Simonides [vol. ii 1584]. P

Woodes, Nathaniel: Conflict of Conscience. D

James Ussher b.
Sir Thomas Overbury b.
Tasso, 'Gerusalemme Liberata'.

1582

The Rheims and Douay Bible [N.T. pub. at Rheims 1582; O.T. pub. at Douay 1609–10].

Gosson, Stephen: Plays Confuted in five actions [n.d.]. P

Hakluyt (1552?): Diverse Voyages touching Discovery of America. P

Lindsay (d. 1555): History of Squire Meldrum [see 1568]. V

Mulcaster, Richard: Elementarie. P

Munday (1553): Discovery of Edward Campion. P
English Roman Life. P

Parsons, Robert: Book of Christian Exercise [later called Christian Directory]. P

Stanyhurst, Richard: Trs. Æneid [bks. i–iv only]. V

Watson, Thomas: Ecatompathia, or a Passionate Century of Love [n.d.]. V

Whetstone, George (1544?): Heptameron of Civil Discourses [trs. Cinthio; as Aurelia 1593]. P

Plague in London, 1582–3.
Edinburgh University founded.
Phineas Fletcher b.
Shakespeare's marriage to Anne Hathaway.
George Buchanan, 'Rerum Scoticarum Historiae'.
R. Robinson Trs. Leland's 'Life of Prince Arthur' (see 1544).

Greene (1560?): Mamillia, pt. i [ii 1593]. P
Melbancke, Brian: Philotimus. P
Smith, Sir Thomas (d. 1577): De Republica Anglorum: the manner of Government of England. P
Stubbes, Philip: Anatomy of Abuses [enlarg. 1584–5, 1595]. P

Queen's Company of Players formed.
Edward Herbert, Lord Herbert of Cherbury b.
Philip Massinger b.
Grotius b.

1584

Greene (1560?): Myrror of Modestie. P
  Gwydonius. P
  Arbasto. P
  Morando. P
James VI of Scotland, I of England: Essays of a Prentice in the Art of Poesie.
Lodge (1558?): Alarum against Usurers. P
Lyly (1554?): Campaspe. C
  Sapho and Phao. C
Munday (1553): Watchword to England. P
Norden, John: Pensive Man's Practice. P
Peele (1558?): Arraignment of Paris. D pastoral.
Phaer, Thomas: Trs. Æneid [completed by Thomas Twyne: see 1558]. V
R., B.: Trs. History of Herodotus [translator sometimes supposed to be Barnabe Rich]. P
Robinson, Clement, and others: Handful of Pleasant Delites [earliest extant ed.; originally *c.* 1566]. V
Scot, Reginald: Discoverie of Witchcraft. P
Warner (1558?): Pan his Syrinx [n.d.; corrected 1597]. P
Whetstone (1544?): Mirrour for Magistrates of Cities. P
Wilson, Robert: Three Ladies of London. D moral Interlude.

William of Orange assassinated.
Raleigh's Charter of Colonization.
John Selden b.
John Hales b.
Francis Beaumont b.

1585

Bullokar, William: Trs. Æsop's Fables.
Munday (1553): Fedele and Fortunio [trs. Italian of Luigi Pasqualigo]. C
Watson, Thomas: Amynta [in Latin: based on Tasso's Aminta].

Leicester's Expedition to the Netherlands.
William Drummond of Hawthornden b.
William Rowley b.?
Shakespeare leaves Stratford.
Ronsard d.

Bowes, T.: Trs. Pierre de la Primaudaye's French Academy.

Camden (1551): Britannia [in Latin: other edd., corrected, 1587–90–94, 1600, 1610; Abridgement 1626; Eng. trs. by Philemon Holland 1610, 1637; ed. by Edmund Gibson 1695, 1722; by Richard Gough 1789].

Day, Angell: English Secretorie. P

Rowland, David: Trs. Lazarillo de Tormes [earliest extant, i.e. 2nd, ed.; originally *c.* 1576]. P

Warner (1558?): Albions England, bks. i–iv [rev. and enlarg. into 6 bks., 1589; into 9 bks., 1592; into 12 bks., 1596; into 13 bks., 1602; into 16 bks., 1606]. V

Webbe, William: Discourse of English Poetrie [reprinted 1815; Arber 1870]. P

Whetstone (1544?): English Mirror. P

John Ford b.
Sir Philip Sidney d.
With the object of checking the flow of Puritan pamphlets the decree is passed (under instigation of John Whitgift, Archbishop of Canterbury) by the Star Chamber forbidding all publications unless previously approved of by ecclesiastical authorities. This intensifies the episcopal controversy and leads on to the Martin Marprelate Tracts, 1588.

1587

Churchyard (1520?): Worthiness of Wales. V

Day, Angell: Daphnis and Chloe [trs. Amyot's version of Longus]. P

Fraunce, Abraham: Lamentations of Amyntas [trs. Thomas Watson's Latin version of Tasso: see 1585]. V

Gascoigne (d. 1577): Whole Works of George Gascoigne [see 1575; Works ed. W. C. Hazlitt 1868–9; ed. J. W. Cunliffe 1907–8].

Gifford, George: Discourse of Subtill Practices of Devils. P

Greene (1560?): Penelope's Web. P
Euphues his Censure to Philautus. P

Grove, Matthew: History of Pelops and Hippodamia. Epigrams, Songs, and Sonnets. V

Hakluyt (1552?): Voyages made into Florida. P

Hughes, Thomas: Misfortunes of Arthur [in Certain Devices and Shows presented to her Majesty]. D

Knox (d. 1572): History of the Reformation in Scotland. P

Mascall, Leonard: Book of Cattle. P

Penry, John: Treatise containing the Aequity of an Humble Supplication. P

Rankins, William: Mirrour of Monsters [anti-stage pamphlet]. P

Turberville (1540?): Tragical Tales [chiefly from Boccaccio]. V

Whetstone (d. 1587?): Sir Philip Sidney, his Honourable Life [n.d.]. V

Young, Bartholomew: Amorous Fiametta [trs. Boccaccio]. P

Execution of Mary Queen of Scots.
Nathaniel Field b.
George Whetstone d.?

Anon.: Trs. Six Idillia of Theocritus. V

Bigges, Walter: A summarie and true discourse of Sir Francis Drake's West Indian Voyage P

Byrd (1538?): Psalmes, sonets, and songs. V

Fraunce, Abraham: Arcadian Rhetorick. P

Greene (1560?): Perimides the Blacke Smith. P
Pandosto [called Dorastus and Fawnia 1636]. P

Munday (1553): Banquet of Dainty Conceits. V
Trs. Palmerin de Oliva [pt. ii 1597]. P
Palladins of England [trs. Fr.]. P

Udall, John: State of Church of England [commonly called Diotrephes]. P

Martin Marprelate Tracts 1588–9: (1) *The Epistle*; (2) *The Epitome*; (3) *The Minerall Schoolpoints*; (4) *Hay any work for Cooper*; (5) *Theses Martinianae or Martin Junior*; (6) *Just Censure and Reproof or Martin Senior*; and (7) *The Protestation*. Suspected authors: John Udall, John Penry, and Job Throckmorton.

Some Anti-Martin tracts: *Pappe with a Hatchet* by John Lyly; *Whip for an Ape* by John Lyly (?); *Pasquil's Apology* (anon.); *Return of Pasquil* (anon.); *Almond for a Parrat* by Thomas Nash (?); *Plaine Percivall* (anon.; Richard Harvey?); *Lamb of God* by Richard Harvey; *Martin's Months Mind* (anon.); *Admonition to People of England* by Thomas Cooper.

Defeat of Spanish Armada
Thomas Hobbes b.
George Wither b.
Martin Marprelate Controversy, 1588–90.
Thomas Kyd trs. 'Householder's Philosophy' of Tasso.
Maurice Kyffin trs. 'Andria' of Terence.
Montaigne, 'Essais', bk. iii (see 1580).

1589

Anon.: Rare Triumphs of Love and Fortune. D
A Copie of a Letter sent from sea by a Gentleman. P

Byrd (1538?): Songs of sundrie natures. V

Cooper, Thomas: Admonition to People of England. P

Devereux, Robert, 2nd Earl of Essex (1566): A True Coppie of a Discourse. P

Greene (1560?): Spanish Masquerado. P
Ciceronis Amor, Tullies Love. P
Menaphon [called Greene's Arcadia, or Menaphon 1599]. P

Hakluyt (1552?): Principall Navigations, Voyages and Discoveries [see 1598]. P

Lodge (1558?): Scillaes Metamorphosis [called Glaucus and Scilla 1610]. V

Nashe (1567): Anatomy of Absurditie. P

Peele (1558?): Farewell to Sir John Norris. A
Tale of Troy. V

Puttenham, George: Art of English Poesy [Lord Lumley also supposed to be author]. P

Davies (1569): Epigrammes [n.d.; cont. Marlowe's trs. of Elegies from Ovid]. V

Greene (1560?): Royal Exchange. P
  Greene's Mourning Garment. P
  Greene's Never Too Late. P

Holland, Henry: Treatise against Witchcraft. P

Lodge (1558?): Rosalynde. P

Marlowe (1564): Tamburlaine the Great, pts. i, ii. T
  Trs. Ovid's Elegies [see Davies above]. V

Munday (1553): Amadis de Gaul, pt. i [trs. Fr.; n.d.; pt. ii 1595; iii, iv 1618]. P

Nashe (1567): First Part of Pasquil's Apology. P

Sidney (d. 1586): Countess of Pembroke's Arcadia [augmented 1593, 1598]. P

Spenser (1552?): Faerie Queene, bks. i–iii [see 1596]. V
  Muiopotmos or Fate of the Butterfly. V

Sylvester, Joshua (1563): Canticle of the Victory of Henry the Fourth [trs. Du Bartas]. V

Vallans, William: Tale of Two Swans. V

Watson, Thomas: Eglogue upon the Death of Sir Francis Walsingham. V

Webbe, Edward: Rare and Most Wonderful Things E. W. has seen. P

Wilson, Robert: Three Lords and Three Ladies of London. D morality.

1591

Anon.: Troublesome Raigne of John King of England [first pub. anon. 1591; attrib. Shakespeare 1611 and 1622 edd.]. D

Robert Herrick b.
William Browne b.

Breton (1545?): Briton's Bower of Delights. V

Drayton (1563): Harmonie of the Church. V

Fletcher (1549?): Of the Russe Commonwealth. P

Fraunce, Abraham: Countess of Pembroke's Yvychurch, pts. i, ii [iii 1593]. V
  Countess of Pembroke's Emanuel. V

Greene (1560?): Greene's Farewell to Folly. P
  Notable Discovery of Coosenage [i.e. pt. i of Conny Catching]. P
  Second Part of Conny Catching. P

Harington (1561): Orlando Furioso in English heroical verse [rev. 1607, 1634]. V

Lodge (1558?): Robert Duke of Normandy. P
  Catharos. P

Lyly (1554?): Endymion, the Man in the Moon. C

Raleigh (1552?): The Fight about the Azores. P

Savile, Sir Henry: Trs. Histories of Tacitus. P

Sidney (d. 1586): Astrophel and Stella [first authorized ed. in 1598 ed. of Arcadia]. V

Southwell (1561?): Mary Magdalens Funeral Tears. P

Spenser (1552?): Complaints. V
  Daphnaida. V

Wilmot, Robert: Tancred and Gismund. T

Anon.: Arden of Feversham [pseudo-Shake-speare]. T

Hypneromachia, The Strife of Love in a Dream. V

Breton (1545?): Pilgrimage to Paradise. Countess of Pembroke's Love. V

Churchyard (1520?): Handful of Gladsome Verses given to the Queen's Majesty.

Constable, Henry: Diana [enlarg. 1594]. V

Daniel (1562): Delia [27 sonnets were published unauthorized in 1591 ed. of Sidney's Astrophel]. V

Complaint of Rosamond [in 2nd ed. of Delia; Delia and Rosamond augmented 1594, 1595, 1598]. V

Greene (d. 1592): Third Part of Conny Catching [see 1591]. P

Disputation between a hee Conny Catcher and a shee Conny Catcher. P

Black Bookes Messenger. P

Philomela. P

Quip for an Upstart Courtier. P

Groatsworth of Wit. P

Greene's Vision. P

Repentance of Greene.

Harvey, Gabriel: Four Letters and Certain Sonnets especially touching Robert Greene.

Kyd (1557?): Spanish Tragedy [n.d.]. T

Lodge (1558?): Euphues Shadow. P

Lyly (1554?): Gallathea. C

Midas. C

Nashe (1567): Pierce Penniless his Supplication to the Devil. P

Strange News of the Intercepting Certain Letters [called Apology of Pierce Penniless 1593]. P

Rich, Barnabe: Adventures of Brusanus. P

Sidney, Mary (Countess of Pembroke): A Discourse of Death; Antonius [both trs. Fr.]. D

Smith, Henry (d. 1591): Sermons [ed. Thomas Fuller 1657].

Stow (1525?): Annals of England [begun *c.* 1580 as Chronicles of England; re-issued by S. under present name and with additions up to date 1592, 1600, 1601, 1605; continued by Edward Howes 1615, 1618, 1631–2]. P

Sylvester, Joshua (1563): Trs. La Semaine of Du Bartas [completed in four instalments 1592–3–8–9; for collective ed. see 1605]. V

Plague revives in London.
Rose Theatre opened c. 1592.
Francis Quarles b.
Robert Greene d.
Philip Henslowe's Diary begins (see 1603).
Beginning of the quarrel between Greene, Nashe, and Gabriel Harvey (concl. 1597).
Montaigne d.

Greene-Nashe-Harvey Quarrel: Greene's *Quip for an Upstart Courtier* (1592) attacks Gabriel Harvey and his brother Richard; Nashe's *Pierce Penniless* (1592) attacks the Harveys; G. Harvey's *Four Letters Intercepted* (1592) attacks Greene; Nashe replies in *Strange News of the Intercepting Certain Letters* (1592; called *Apology of Pierce Penniless* in 1593); Nashe's *Christ's Tears over Jerusalem* with conciliatory preface (about Sept. 1593); G. Harvey's *Pierce's Supererogation* and *New Letter of Notable Contents* (written before he had seen *Christ's Tears*) issued in autumn of 1593; Nashe re-issues *Christ's Tears* with new Preface renewing attack in 1594; further attack by Nashe in *Have with you to Saffron Walden* (1596).

1593

Anon.: Phoenix Nest [verse collection].
   Life and Death of Jack Straw [attrib. Peele]. T
Barnes, Barnabe (1569?): Parthenophil and Parthenophe. V
Chettle, Henry: Kind Heart's Dream [n.d.]. P
Churchyard (1520?): Churchyard's Challenge. V
Drayton (1563): Idea, the Shepherds Garland [rev. as Eglogs in Poems 1606(?); as Pastorals in Poems 1619]. V
Fletcher (1549?): Licia, or Poems of Love [n.d.]. V
Gifford, George: Dialogue concerning Witches and Witchcraft. P
Harvey, Gabriel: Pierce's Supererogation. P
   New Letter of Notable Contents. P
Henryson (d. 1500?): Testament of Cressid [first separate ed.; originally in Chaucer's Works 1532]. V
Lodge (1558?): Phillis. V
   Life of William Longbeard. P
Markham (1568?): Discourse of Horsemanship. P
Marlowe (d. 1593): Trs. bk. i of Lucan's Pharsalia. V
Morley, Thomas (1557): Canzonets. V
Nashe (1567): Christ's Tears over Jerusalem. P
Norden, John: Speculum Britanniae [pt. i Description of Middlesex; pt. ii Description of Hertfordshire 1598].
Peele (1558?): Chronicle of Edward the First. D
   Honour of the Garter [n.d.]. V
Shakespeare (1564): Venus and Adonis. V
Watson, Thomas (d. 1592): Tears of Fancie. V
Whetstone, George (d. 1587?): Aurelia [see 1582]. P

Sir Richard Hawkins's Voyage.
Izaak Walton b.
George Herbert b.
Christopher Marlowe d.
Theatres closed in London between February and end of the year on account of the Plague.

Anon.: First Part of the Contention betwixt the
　　Houses of York and Lancaster [see 1595;
　　now regarded as a bad Quarto of Shake-
　　speare's 2 Henry VI]. D

　Tragical Raigne of Selimus [attrib. Greene]. D

　True Tragedy of Richard the Third. D

　Wars of Cyrus King of Persia. D

　Taming of a Shrew. C

　Knacke to Know a Knave. C

　Zepheria. V

Bacon, Richard: Solon his Follie. P

Barnfield (1574): Affectionate Shepherd. V

Carew, Richard (1555): Godfrey of Bulloigne [trs.
　　Cantos I–V of Tasso's Jerusalem Delivered]. V

Chapman (1559?): Shadow of Night. V

Daniel (1562): Cleopatra [in augmented ed. of
　　Delia and Rosamond: see 1592]. T

Davys, John: Seaman's Secrets. P

Drayton (1563): Piers Gaveston [n.d.]. V
　Matilda. V
　Ideas Mirror [sonnets, rev. and enlarg. 1599,
　　1602, 1605; final ed. 1619]. V

Greene (d. 1592): Historie of Orlando Furioso. D
　Looking Glass for London and England [with
　　Lodge]. D
　Friar Bacon and Friar Bongay. C

Hooker (1554?): Of the Laws of Ecclesiastical
　　Polity, bks. i–iv [n.d.; v 1597; vi and viii
　　1648 (also 1651); vii in Gauden's ed. of H.'s
　　Works 1662. Authenticity of bks. vi–viii
　　doubtful]. P

Kyd (1557?): Cornelia [trs. Fr. of Robert Garnier]. T.

Lodge (1558?): Wounds of Civil War. T
　Looking Glass for London and England [with
　　Greene]. D

Lyly (1554?): Mother Bombie. C

Marlowe (d. 1593): Edward the Second. T
　Tragedie of Dido [with Nashe]. T

Morley, Thomas (1567): Madrigalls to Four Voices.
　　V

Munday (1553): John a Kent and John a Cumber
　　[acted *c.* 1594; prtd. J. P. Collier 1851].

Nashe (1567): Terrors of the Night. P
　Unfortunate Traveller or Life of Jack Wilton. P

Peele (1558?): Battle of Alcazar. T

Percy, William: Sonnets to Fairest Celia. V

Shakespeare (1564): Lucrece [called Rape of
　　Lucrece 1616]. V
　Titus Andronicus. T

Sylvester (1563): Monodia [n.d.]. V

Willoby, Henry: Willobie his Avisa [corrected and
　　enlarg. 1605, 1611]. V

James Howell b.?
Barnabe Googe d.
*Erection of the Swan
Theatre between 1594
and 1600.*

Anon.: Alcilia. Philoparthens Loving Folly. V
 Tragedy of Locrine [attrib. Shakespeare on
 title-page]. D
 True Tragedy of Richard Duke of York [now
 regarded as a bad Quarto of Shakespeare's
 3 Henry VI; combined with First Part of
 Contention betwixt Houses of York and
 Lancaster (see 1594) as Whole Contention
 between Houses of York and Lancaster,
 1619]. D

Barnes, Barnabe: Divine Century of Spiritual
 Sonnets.

Barnfield (1574): Cynthia, with Certain Sonnets,
 and Legend of Cassandra. V

Beddingfield, Thomas: Trs. Florentine History of
 Macchiavelli [first Eng. trs.]. P

Breton (1545?): Marie Magdalen's Love. V

Chapman (1559?): Ovid's Banquet of Sence. A
 Coronet for Mistress Philosophy and other
 poems. V

Chettle, Henry: Piers Plainnes Seven Years Pren-
 ticeship. P

Churchyard (1520?): A Praise of Poetrie. V
 Consort of Heavenly Harmonie called Churchyard's Charitie. V

Copley, Anthony: Wits, Fittes and Fancies. Love's
 Owle. V and P

Daniel (1562): Civil Wars between Houses of
 Lancaster and York, bks. i–iv [bk. v added
 in 2nd ed. same year; bk. vi 1601, complete
 in bks. i–viii 1609]. V

Davys, John: World's Hydrographical Description. P

Drayton (1563): Endimion and Phoebe [n.d.]. V

Edwards, Thomas: Cephalus and Procris. V

Forde, Emanuel: Ornatus and Artesia [n.d.]. P

Lodge (1558?): Fig for Momus. V

Markham (1568?): Tragedy of Sir Richard Grenville. D

Morley, Thomas (1559): First Book of Ballets. V

Peele (1558?): Old Wives' Tale. C

Sidney (d. 1586): Apologie for Poetrie [another
 ed. same year called Defence of Poesy]. P

Southwell (d. 1595): Saint Peter's Complaint. V
 Maeoniae, or Certain Poems.
 Triumphs over Death. P

Spenser (1552?): Amoretti. Epithalamion. V
 Colin Clouts come home again [cont. Astrophel,
 and Mourning Muse, two poems on death of
 Sir Philip Sidney]. V

W. W.: Trs. of Plautus' Menaechmi. C

*Sir Walter Raleigh's Voy-
 age to Guiana.*
Thomas Carew b.?
Thomas May b.
Robert Southwell executed.
Thomas Kyd d.?
*Andrew Maunsell, 'Cata-
 logue of English Books'.*
Tasso d.
*Montaigne, 'Essais' (in
 final form: see 1580).*

Anon.: Delightful History of Celestina the Fair [trs. by W. Barley?]. P

Raigne of King Edward the Third [pseudo-Shakespeare]. D

Knacke to Know an Honest Man. C

The Goode Housewife's Jewell (cookery book).

Copley, Anthony: A Fig for a Fortune. V

Dannett, Thomas: Trs. History of Philip de Commines [another trs. by ' R. B. ' 1639]. P

Davies (1569): Orchestra. V

Dickenson, John: Shepherd's Complaint [n.d.]. V

Drayton (1563): Tragical Legend of Robert, Duke of Normandy. V

Mortemeriados [rev. as Barons' Wars 1603]. V

Griffin, Bartholomew: Fidessa more Chaste than Kind. V

Harington (1561): Metamorphosis of Ajax. P

Anatomy of the metamorphosed Ajax. P

Ulysses upon Ajax. P

An Apology or rather a Recantation [n.d.]. P

Lodge (1558?): Margarite of America. P

Wits Miserie. P

Devil Conjured. P

Prosopopeia [doubtful if by L.].

Lynche, Richard: Diella, certain sonnets. V

Markham (1568?): Poem of Poems, or Sion's Muse [n.d.]. V

Middleton (1580): Wisdom of Solomon Paraphrased. V

Munday (1553): Trs. Palmerin of England. P

Nashe (1567): Have with you to Saffron Walden. P

Raleigh (1552?): Discovery of the Empire of Guiana. P

Smith, William: Chloris or Complaint of Passionate Shepherd. V

Spenser (1552?): Faerie Queene [bks. i–iii revised, with addition of bks. iv–vi; also 1609, 1611: see 1590]. V

Prothalamion. V

Fowre Hymns. V

Blackfriars Theatre opened.

James Shirley b.

Shakespeare's son Hamnet dies.

Descartes b.

Bacon (1561): Essays. Meditationes Sacrae. Colours of Good and Evil [Ten Essays only; Essays enlarged 1612, 1625]. P

Beard, Thomas: Theatre of God's Judgements. P

Breton (1545?): Arbour of Amorous Devices [with others]. V

Auspicante Jehoua, Maries Exercise. V

Wits Trenchmour. P

Will of Wit or Wit's Will or Will's Wit [corrected 1606]. P

Dowland, John (1563?): First Book of Songs. V

Drayton (1563): England's Heroical Epistles. V

Gerard, John: Herball. P

Hall (1574): Virgidemiae, bks. i–iii [see 1598]. V

Hooker (1554?): Laws of Ecclesiastical Polity, bk. v [see 1594]. P

James VI, King of Scotland: Demonologie. P

Ling, Nicholas (ed.): Politeuphuia or Wits Commonwealth [John Bodenham also supposed to be editor; 12th ed. 1630 (?)].

Lok, Henry: Ecclesiasticus, with Sundrie Sonnets.

Lyly (1554?): Woman in the Moon. C

Montgomery, Alexander: The Cherrie and the Slae. V

Rowley (1585?): Birth of Merlin [acted between 1597–1607; prtd. 1662; alleged collaboration of Shakespeare]. D

S., E.: Discovery of the Knights of the Post [Edward Sharpham author?]. P

Shakespeare (1564): King Richard the Second. T

Romeo and Juliet. Q 1 [Q 2 1599]. T

Richard the Third. T

Tofte, Robert: Laura. V

George Peele d.?

Shakespeare buys New Place in Stratford.

Nashe's play 'Isle of Dogs' suppressed and author imprisoned.

Isaac Casaubon's diary 'Ephemerides' begins (ends with his death 1614; pub. 1850).

1598

Anon.: Comedy of Mucedorus [enlarg. 1610; pseudo-Shakespeare]. D

Famous Victories of Henry V. D

Pilgrimage to Parnassus. Return from Parnassus, pts. i, ii [acted *c.* 1598, *c.* 1601, *c.* 1602 at St. John's, Cambridge; pt. ii of Return prtd. 1606; the trilogy prtd. W. D. Macray 1886]. C

Sir Thomas More [written before this date; prtd. A. Dyce 1844; partly by Shakespeare?]. D

Barnfield (1574): Encomion of Lady Pecunia. Complaint of Poetry for Death of Liberality. Combat between Conscience and Covetousness. Poems in Divers Humours. V

Bastard, Thomas: Chrestoleros: seven books of Epigrams. V

Bernard, Richard: Terence in English [trs. Adelphi, Andria, Eunuchus, Heautontimoroumenos, Hecyra, Phormio]. D

Breton (1545?): Solemn Passion of the Soul's Love. V

Chapman (1559?): Blind Beggar of Alexandria. C

Seven Bookes of the Illiades [1st instalment of trs. Iliad]. V

Achilles Shield: other seven books of Homer [2nd instalment of trs. Iliad: see 1610,1611]. V

Chaucer (d. 1400): Works, ed. Thomas Speght [see 1532].

Forde, Emanuel: Parismus [pt. ii Parismenos 1599]. P

Greene (d. 1592): Scottish History of James the Fourth. D tragi-comedy.

Guilpin, Edward: Skialethia, or a Shadow of Truth in Certain Epigrams and Satires. V

Hakluyt (1552?): Principall Navigations, Voyages and Discoveries [concl. 1600; enlarg. from work of 1589]. P

Hall (1574): Virgidemiae, bks. iv–vi [see 1597]. V

Marlowe (d. 1593): Hero and Leander [completed by Chapman]. V

Marston (1575?): Metamorphosis of Pigmalion's Image, and Certain Satires. V

Scourge of Villainie [enlarg. 1599]. V

Meres, Francis: Palladis Tamia. P

Rankins, William: Seven Satires applied to the Week. V

Rowlands, Samuel: Betraying of Christ, with other Poems.

Shakespeare (1564): Henry IV, pt. i. D

Love's Labour's Lost. C

Southwell (d. 1595): A Short Rule of Good Life [n.d.]. P

Edict of Nantes.
Death of Burghley.
First quarrel between Ben Jonson and Marston (see 1601).
Giovanni Florio, 'World of Wordes' (Italian and English Dictionary; rev. 1611).
First Eng. trs. of Aristotle's 'Politics' by J. D. Voiture b.

36

Stow (1525?): Survay of London [another ed.
1603; contd. and enlarg., by Anthony
Munday 1618; Munday and Dyson 1633; ed.
J. Strype 1720, W. J. Thoms 1876, C. L.
Kingsford 1908].
Tofte, Robert: Trs. Orlando Inamorato of Boiardo
[bks. i–iii only]. V
Young, Bartholomew: Trs. Diana of George Mon-
temayor. P and V

1599

Anon.: Passionate Pilgrim [cont. two sonnets by
Shakespeare and poems by Barnfield and
others].

Warning for Fair Women. T

Sir Clyomon and Sir Clamydes [sometimes
attrib. Peele]. D

Tragedy of Solimon and Perseda [attrib. Kyd]. D

Comedy of George a Greene [attrib. Greene]. D

Allott, Robert (ed.): Wit's Theatre of the Little
World [verse miscellany].

Chapman (1559?): An Humorous Days Mirth. C

Cutwode, Thomas: Caltha Poetarum, or the
Bumble Bee. V

Daniel (1562): Musophilus. Letter from Octavia
to Marcus Antonius. V

Poetical Essays [collection of previously pub.
poems: see 1601].

Davies (1569): Nosce Teipsum [corrected 1602]. V
Hymnes of Astraea. V

Greene (d. 1592): Alphonsus King of Arragon. C
Orpharion. V

Hakluyt (1522?): Principall Navigations, Voyages
and Discoveries [completed: see 1598]. P

Hayward, Sir John: Life and Raigne of King
Henry IV. P

Heywood (1575?): King Edward the Fourth, pts.
i, ii. D chronicle.

James VI, King of Scotland: Basilikon Doron. P

M.,T.: Micro-cynicon, six snarling satires
[Thomas Middleton or Thomas Moffat?].

Nashe (1567): Nashes Lenten Stuffe. P

Peele (d. 1597?): Love of King David and Fair
Bethsabe. D

Porter, Henry: Two Angry Women of Abington.
D

Shakespeare (1564): Julius Cæsar [acted *c.* 1599;
printed 1623]. T

Weever, John: Epigrams in the Oldest Cut. V

*Edmund Spenser d.
Globe Theatre opened.*

37

1600

Anon.: Book of Merry Riddles [earliest known ed.].

Wisdom of Dr. Dodypoll. D

Weakest goeth to the Wall. D

Look about you. C

Maid's Metamorphosis [attrib. Lyly]. D

First Part of the Life of Sir John Oldcastle [now attrib. Munday, Drayton, and others. Another issue, dated 1600 but really prtd. 1619, attributes the play to Shakespeare]. D

True and Credible Report of a great and very dangerous fight at Sea. P

Allott, Robert (ed.): England's Parnassus [collection of verse by various hands].

Bodenham, John (ed.): England's Helicon [collection of verse by various hands; another ed. 1614].

Belvedere [collection of verse by various hands; another ed. 1610].

Breton (1545?): Pasquil's Fooles Cap. V

Pasquil's Mistresse. V

Pasquil's passe and passeth not. V

Melancholike Humours. V

Pasquil's Mad-Cap and Mad-Cappe's Message. V

Second Part of Pasquil's Mad Cap, entitled Fooles Cap. V

Strange Fortune of two Excellent Princes. P

Cornwallis, Sir William: Essayes [enlarg. 1610; Essays or Encomions 1616; Essays of Paradoxes 1616; Essays Corrected 1632].

Dekker (1570?): Shoemaker's Holiday. C

Comedy of Old Fortunatus. D

Dowland, John (1563?): Second Book of Songs. V

Fairfax, Edward: Godfrey of Bulloigne [trs. Jerusalem Delivered of Tasso]. V

Haughton, William: Grim the Collier of Croyden [acted *c.* 1600; prtd. 1662].

Heywood (1575?): Ovid's Art of Love [trs. by H., appropriated by H. Austin; n.d.; 1600–10(?)]. V

Holland, Philemon: Trs. Livy's Roman History. P

Jonson (1573?): Everyman out of His Humour. C

Kemp, William: Kemp's Nine Daies Wonder. P

Markham (1568?): Tears of the Beloved. V

Marlowe (d. 1593): Massacre at Paris [n.d.]. T

Trs. bk. i of Lucan's Pharsalia. V

Nashe (1567): Summers Last Will and Testament. C

Rowlands, Samuel: Letting of Humours Blood in the Head Vaine. V

East India Company founded.

Fortune Theatre opened.

Peter Heylyn b.

William Prynne b.

Richard Hooker d.

Thomas Deloney d. ?

William Gilbert, 'De Magnete'.

Sir Edward Coke's 'Reports' (of law suits) in French 1600–15 (in English 1658).

Calderon b.

Shakespeare (1564): Henry IV, pt. ii. D
  Henry V. D
  Merchant of Venice. D
  Midsummer-Night's Dream. C
  Much Ado about Nothing. C
  As You Like It [acted *c.* 1600; prtd. 1623]. C
Thynne, Francis: Emblems and Epigrams. V
Tourneur (1575?): Transformed Metamorphosis. V
Vaughan, William (1577): Golden Grove [enlarg.
    1608]. P
  Natural and Artificial Directions for Health. P

1601

Anon.: Jack Drum's Entertainment. C
Breton (1545?): A Divine Poem in two parts. V
  Upon the Longing of a Blessed Heart. V
Chester, Robert (ed.): Love's Martyr [cont. poems
    by Jonson, Chapman, Marston, and others,
    and The Phoenix and Turtle attrib. Shake-
    speare]. V
Cornwallis, Sir William: Discourses on Seneca. P
Daniel (1562): Works, newly augmented [cont.,
    among unpub. works, bk. vi of Civil Wars
    (see 1595) and Pastoral to the Delia Sonnets.
    Later edd. of Works, mostly rev. and enlarg.
    1605-7-11-23; ed. Grosart 1885].
Holland, Philemon: Trs. Pliny's Natural History. P
Jones, Robert (fl. 1616): First Booke of Songs &
    Aires. V
  Second Booke of Songs & Aires. V
Jonson (1573?): Everyman in his Humour. C
  Cynthia's Revels. C
Lyly (1554?): Love's Metamorphosis. C
Markham (1568?): Marie Magdalen's Lamenta-
    tions. V
Morley, Thomas (1557): The Triumphs of Oriana. V
Munday (1553): Death of Robert Earl of Hunting-
    ton [with Henry Chettle]. T
  Downfall of Robert Earl of Huntington [pt. ii
    of above]. T
Shakespeare (1564): Twelfth Night [acted *c.* 1601;
    prtd. 1623]. C

*Queen Elizabeth's Poor
  Law.
Execution of Essex.
John Earle b.
Thomas Nashe d.
Sir Thomas North d.?
Ben Jonson's quarrel with
  Dekker and Marston.*

Anon.: Liberalitie and Prodigalitie. D
  Chronicle History of Thomas Lord Cromwell
    [attrib. Shakespeare on title-page]. D
  A Larum for London. D
  How a Man may chuse a Good Wife from a Bad. D
Basse, William: Sword and Buckler. V
  Three pastoral Elegies. V
Beaumont (1584): Salmacis and Hermaphroditus
    [trs. Ovid: see 1640]. V
Beaumont, Sir John: Metamorphosis of Tobacco. V
Breton (1545?) Soule's Harmony. V
  Old Madcap's New Gallimawfry. V
  Mother's Blessing. V
  True Description of Unthankfulness. V
  Wonders worth the Hearing. P
  Poste with a mad Packet of Letters [enlarg.
    1603; pt. ii 1606; many edd. to 1637]. P
Campion (1567): Art of English Poesie. P
Carew, Richard (1555): Survey of Cornwall. P
Davies (1565?): Mirum in Modum. V
Davison, Francis: Poetical Rapsody [by various
    hands: enlarg. 1608, 1611, 1621]. V
Dekker (1570?): Satiro-mastix. C
Jonson (1573?): Poetaster, or the Arraignment. C
Lindsay (d. 1555): Satyr of the Three Estates
    [see 1540, 1568]. D
Lodge (1558?): Paradoxes.
  Trs. Works of Flavius Josephus.
Mansell, Sir Robert (1573): A True Report of the
    Service done upon certaine Gallies. P
Patricke, Simon: Means of Well Governing against
    Niccolo Macchiavel [trs. Gentillet]. P
Marston (1575?): Antonio and Mellida. T
  Antonio's Revenge [pt. ii of above]. T
Middleton (1580)?: Blurt Master-Constable. C
Rowlands, Samuel: Greenes Ghost haunting
    Conie Catchers. P
  Tis Merry when Gossips meet. V
Shakespeare (1564): Merry Wives of Windsor. C

William Chillingworth b.
Bodleian Library opens.
First Eng. trs. of Guarini's 'Il Pastor Fido' by Edward Dymock.
The anon. play 'Narcissus' acted at St. John's, Oxford, c. 1602-3 (prtd. 1893).

1603

Anon.: Bachelor's Banquet [trs. Quinze Joyes de
    Marriage]. P
Bacon (1561): Union of England and Scotland. P
Breton (1545?): Dialogue full of Pith and Pleasure
    between Three Philosophers. P
  A Mad World my Masters [also 1635]. P
Chettle, Henry: England's Mourning Garment. V
Daniel (1562): Panegyricke Congratulatorie to
    the King's Majestie. V Poetical Epistles. V
  Defence of Rhyme. P

Death of Queen Elizabeth. Accession of James I. Plague in London. Sir Kenelm Digby b. Shakerley Marmion b. Philip Henslowe's 'Diary' ends (began 1592; pub. 1845). John Barclay 'Euphormionis Satyricon' (concl. 1607).

Davies (1565?): Microcosmos. V
Dekker (1570?): The Wonderful Year 1603. P
  Patient Grissel [with Chettle & Haughton]. C
Dowland, John (1563 ?): Third Book of Songs. V
Drayton (1563): Barrons Wars [see 1596]. V
Florio, John: Trs. Montaigne's Essays. P
Fowldes, W.: Trs. Batrachomyomachia. V
Hall (1574): The King's Prophecie. V
Holland, Philemon: Trs. Plutarch's Morals. P
James I: True Law of Free Monarchies. P
Knolles, Richard (1550?): History of the Turks
  [enlarg. 1610–21–31–38]. P
Lodge (1558?): Treatise on the Plague. P
Norden, John: A Pensive Soul's Delight. P
Shakespeare (1564): Hamlet Q 1. T
  Troilus and Cressida [acted *c.* 1603; prtd. 1609].

1604

Anon.: Palladis Palatium [anthology].
Alexander (1567?): Aurora. V
  A Paraenesis to the Prince. V
  Monarchick Tragedies [Croesus, Darius: see
    1607]. T
Bacon (1561): His Apology. P
  Considerations touching better Pacification of
    the Church of England. P
Breton (1545?): Passionate Shepherd. V
  Grimello's Fortune. P
Churchyard (d. 1604): Churchyard's Goodwill. V
Daniel (1563): Vision of the Twelve Goddesses. D
Dekker (1570?): Honest Whore [pt. i; with
  Middleton? See 1630]. D
  Entertainment given to King James. D
Drayton (1563): The Owle. V
  Moyses in a Map of his Miracles. V
  Paean Triumphall for the Societie of Goldsmiths
    of London. V
Hayward, Sir John: Sanctuarie of a troubled
  Soul [pt. ii 1607; two pts. together 1616]. P
James I: Counterblast to Tobacco. P
Marlowe (d. 1593): Tragical History of Dr. Faus-
  tus. T
Marston (1575?): The Malcontent [another ed.
  same year enlarg. by Webster]. D
Middleton (1580): Father Hubbard's Tales. P
  The Blacke Booke. P
Rowlands: Look to it, for I will stab ye. V
Rich, Barnabe (1540?): A Souldier's Wish to
  Briton's Welfare. P
  Fruits of Long Experience [pt. ii of above]. P
Shakespeare (1564): Hamlet Q 2 [see 1603].
  Measure for Measure [acted *c.* 1604; prtd. 1623].
  Othello [acted; prtd. 1622].

Fall of Ostend.
Hampton Court Confer-
  ence.
Abolition of private pat-
  ronage of players.
English players at Fon-
  tainebleau.
Jasper Mayne b.
Thomas Churchyard d.

Anon.: London Prodigall [attrib. Shakespeare on
  title-page]. C
  First Part of Ieronimo [doubtfully attrib. Kyd]. T
  Chronicle History of King Leir. D
  Life and Death of Captain Thomas Stukeley. T
  Trial of Chivalry. D
  Fair Maid of Bristow. D
  History of the Triall of Chevalry, with Life of
  Cavaliero Dicke Bowyer. D
  School of Slovenrie [trs. Grobianus of Dede-
  kind].

Bacon (1561): Advancement of Learning. P

Breton (1545?): Soul's Immortal Crown. V
  Honour of Valour. V

Camden (1551): Remains of a Greater Work concerning Britain [see 1586]. P

Carew, Richard (1555): Excellency of the English
  Tongue [in Camden's Remains above]. P

Chapman (1559?): All Fooles, a comedy.
  Eastward Ho [with Ben Jonson and Marston]. C

Daniel (1562): Certaine Small Poems [Ulysses and
  the Siren and others]. Philotas. T

Davies, John (1565?): Humours Heaven on Earth
  [Civil Wars of Death and Fortune. Triumph
  of Death]. V
  Wits Pilgrimage [n.d.]. V

Drayton (1563): Poems [earliest collection; later
  collections mostly rev. and enlarg. 1606(?)
  8–10–13–19–20–30–7; Poems ed. J. P. Collier
  1856; ed. R. Hooper 1876; W. Hebel 1931].

Hall (1574): Meditations and Vows (enlarg. 1609,
  1621). P

Heywood (1575?): If you know not me, you know
  Nobody [see 1606]. D

Jonson (1573?): Sejanus his Fall. T
  The Masque of Blackness. D

Marston (1575?): Dutch Courtezan. C

Montgomerie, Alexander: Mind's Melody. V

Rowlands, Samuel: Hell's broke loose. V

Rowley, Samuel: When you see me you know me
  or Chronicle History of King Henry VIII. D

Shakespeare (1564): Macbeth [acted *c.* 1605; prtd.
  1623]. T

Sylvester, Joshua (1563): Du Bartas his Divine
  Weekes and Works [collective ed. of trs. of
  La Semaine and other works of Du Bartas;
  concl. 1606; later edd. 1608–11–13; with other
  works of Sylvester 1633–41: see 1592]. V

Wodehouse, Peter: Democritus his Dream; or the
  Contention betweene the Elephant and the
  Flea. V

Gunpowder Plot.
James I visits Oxford.
Sir Thomas Browne b.
Bulstrode Whitelocke b.
Thomas Randolph b.
Sir William Dugdale b.
William Habington b.
John Stow d.
*Imprisonment of the au-
  thors of 'Eastward Ho'
  for references to the
  Scotch.*
*'Don Quixote', pt. i (com-
  plete 1615).*

42

Anon.: Return from Parnassus, pt. ii [see 1598]. C
Wily Beguiled. C
Sir Gyles Goosecap. C
Burton, William: Seven Dialogues [trs. Colloquia of Erasmus].
Chapman (1559?): Monsieur D'Olive. C
Gentleman Usher. C
Daniel (1562): The Queen's Arcadia, a Pastoral tragi-comedy.
Day, John: Ile of Guls. C
Dekker (1570?): Seven Deadly Sins of London. P
News from Hell [enlarg. as A Knight's Conjuring 1607]. P
The Double P.P. V
Drayton (1563): Poems Lyrick and Pastoral [n.d.; among new poems: Ballad of Agincourt, Man in the Moon, To His Coy Love, To Cupid, The Virginian Voyage].
Hall (1574): Art of Divine Meditation. P
Heaven upon Earth. P
Heywood (1575?): If you know not me you know Nobody, pt. ii [see 1605]. D
Holland, Philemon: Trs. History of Twelve Caesars by Suetonius. P
Jonson (1573?): Hymenaei. D masque.
Marston (1575?): Parasitaster or the Fawne. C
Wonder of Women, or Tragedy of Sophonisba. T
Peacham, Henry, jnr.: Art of Drawing [called Graphice 1612]. P
Rich, Barnabe (1540?): Faults, Faults, and Nothing Else but Faults [called My Ladies Looking Glass 1616]. P
Rowlands, Samuel: Terrible Battle between the Consumers of the World. P and V
Southwell (d. 1595): Fourefold Meditation of Foure Last Things [? by Philip, Earl of Arundel]. V
Warner (1558?): Albions England [see 1586]. V
West, Richard: News from Bartholomew Fair. V

Sir William D'Avenant b.
Edmund Waller b.
Pierre Corneille b.
John Lyly d.

Anon.: Tragedy of Caesar and Pompey. T
Tragedy of Claudius Tiberius Nero [not to be confused with Tragedy of Nero 1624]. T
The Puritaine or Widow of Watling Street [pseudo-Shakespeare]. D
Alexander (1567?): Monarchick Tragedies [adds Alexandraean and Julius Caesar to those of 1604]. T
Barnes, Barnabe: The Devil's Charter. D
Beaumont (1584) **and Fletcher** (1579): The Woman Hater. D
Campion (1567): Masque presented in Honour of Lord Hayes.
Chapman (1559?): Bussy D'Ambois: a Tragedie.
Davies, John (1565?): Summa Totalis. V
Day, John: Travailes of Three English Brothers [with Rowley and George Wilkins]. D
Dekker (1570?): Whore of Babylon. D allegory.
History of Sir Thomas Wyatt [with Webster]. T
Westward Ho [with Webster]. C
Northward Ho [with Webster]. C
Jests to Make you Merry [with George Wilkins]. P
Knights Conjuring. P
Drayton (1563): Legend of Great Cromwell [altered as History of Life and Death of Lord Cromwell 1609]. V
Grimestone, Edward: Admirable and Memorable Histories. P
Hall (1574): Holy Observations. P
Heywood (1575?): A Woman kilde with Kindness. T
Fair Maid of the Exchange. C
Fortune by Land and Sea [acted; prtd. 1655; with Rowley]. D
Jones, Robert (fl. 1616): First set of Madrigals. V
Jonson (1573?): Volpone or the Fox. C
Markham (1568?): Cavelarice or the English Horseman. P
English Arcadia [pt. ii 1613]. P
Marston (1575?): What you will. C
Middleton (1580): Michaelmas Term. C
The Phoenix. C
Niccols, Richard: The Cuckow. V
Norden, John: The Surveyor's Dialogue. P
Rowlands, Samuel: Diogenes Lanthorne. V & P
Democritus, or Dr. Merriman his Medicines. V
Shakespeare (1564): Timon of Athens [acted; prtd. 1623].
Sharpham, Edward: Cupid's Whirligig. C
The Fleire. C
Tomkis, Thomas: Lingua, or Combat of the Tongue and the Five Senses. C

John Owen, '*Epigrams*' (*Eng. trs. 1619*).
*Final ed. of Camden's '*Britannia*' (see 1586).*
Scudéry b.
D'Urfé, '*Astrée*', *1607-27.*
Malherbe, '*Odes*' *between 1607 and 1628.*

Topsell, Edward: History of Fourefooted Beasts [trs. Conrad Gesner]. P
Tourneur (1575?) (?): Revenger's Tragedy. T
Walkington, Thomas: Optick Glass of Humours. P
West, Richard: Court of Conscience or Dick Whippers Sessions. V
Wilkins, George: Miseries of Inforst Marriage. D

1608

Anon.: Merry Devil of Edmonton. C
A Yorkshire Tragedy [attrib. Shakespeare on title-page]. T
Armin, Robert: A Nest of Ninnies. D
Breton (1545): Divine Considerations of the Soul. P
Chapman (1559?): Conspiracy of Charles Duke of Byron [two parts]. T
Day, John: Humour out of Breath. C
Law Tricks, or Who would have thought it. C
Dekker (1570?): Belman of London. P
Lanthorne and Candlelight [pt. ii of above; rev. in 1609; (O per se O); 1616 (Villanies Discovered); 1632 (English Villanies)]. P
The Dead Term or Westminster's Complaint. P
Grimestone, Edward: General History of the Netherlands. P
Hall (1574): Characters of Virtues and Vices. P
Six Decades of Epistles. P
Heywood (1575?): Rape of Lucrece. T
Two Most Worthy Histories [trs. Catiline Conspiracy and Jugurthan War of Sallust]. P
Jones, Robert (fl. 1616): Ultimum Vale. V
Jonson (1573?): Two Royall Masques [Of Blackness, Of Beauty].
Markham (1568?): Dumb Knight [with Lewis Machin]. C
Middleton (1580): Family of Love. C
A Mad World, my Masters. C
A Trick to Catch the Old One. C
Your Five Gallants [n.d.]. C
Perkins, William: Discourse of the Art of Witchcraft. P
Rowlands, Samuel: Humours Looking Glass [attrib. R.]. V
Shakespeare (1564): King Lear. T
Coriolanus [acted *c.* 1608; prtd. 1623]. T
West, Richard: Century of Epigrams.
Wiclif (d. 1384): Two Treatises against the Order of Begging Friars. P

John Milton b.
Thomas Fuller b.
Opening of the salon of the Hôtel de Rambouillet by Catherine de Vivonne, Marquise de Rambouillet.

45

Anon.: Every Woman in her Humour. C
Armin, Robert: Two Maids of More-clacke. D
  Italian Taylor and his Boy. D
Burton, Charles: Feminine Monarchie [3rd edition
  in phonetic spelling 1634].
Daniel (1562): Civil Wars between Houses of
  Lancaster and York [completed: see 1595]. V
Davies (1565?): Holy Roode. V
Dekker (1570?): Guls Hornbooke. P
  Ravens Almanack. P
  Four Birds of Noahs Ark. P
  Work for Armourers. P
Drayton (1563): Life and Death of Lord Cromwell
  [see 1607]. V
Greville (1554): Tragedy of Mustapha [improved
  version 1633]. D
Hall (1574): Discovery of a New World [Mundus
  alter et idem trs. by John Healy; n.d.]. P
  Solomon's Divine Arts. P
Heywood (1575?): Troia Britannica. V
Holland, Philemon (1552): Trs. Ammianus.
Jewel, John (d. 1571): Works ed. Fuller. P
Jones, Robert (fl. 1616): A Musicall Dream. V
Jonson (1573?): Case is Alter'd. C
  Masque of Queens.
  Epicoene. C.
'M., W.': Man in the Moon telling strange For-
  tunes. P
Rich, Barnabe (1540?): Roome for a Gentleman
  [pt. ii of Faults, Faults, 1606]. P
Rowlands, Samuel: Knave of Clubs [originally
  Tis Merry when Knaves Meet *c*. 1600]. V
  Whole Crew of Kind Gossips. V
Rowley (1585?): A Search for Money. C
Shakespeare (1564): Sonnets.
  Troilus and Cressida. D
  Pericles [with George Wilkins and William
  Rowley?]. D
Spenser (d. 1599): Two Cantos of Mutabilitie in
  new ed. of Faerie Queene [see 1590]. V

*Edward Hyde (Earl of
  Clarendon) b.*
Benjamin Whichcote b.
Sir John Suckling b.
Sir Matthew Hale b.
William Warner d.
*Bacon, 'De Sapientia
  Veterum Liber' (for
  Eng. trs. see 1619).*

1610

Anon.: Histriomastix [partly by Marston?]. C
Campion (1567): Two Books of Airs [n.d.: see
  1612]. V
Chapman (1559?): Homer Prince of Poets [3rd
  instalment of Iliad; n.d.: see 1598, 1611]. V
Daniel (1562): Tethys Festival. D masque.
Dent, Arthur (d. 1607): The Plain Man's Pathway
  to Heaven. P

George Turberville d.?
*Richard Niccols ed. 'Mir-
  ror for Magistrates'(final
  ed.; see 1559).*
Scarron b.
Hardy, 'Mariamne'.

Donne (1572): Pseudo-Martyr. P
Fletcher, Giles, jnr. (1588?): Christ's Victory and
Triumph, 2 pts. V
Fletcher (1579): Faithful Shepherdess [n.d.; 2nd
ed. corrected 1629; 3rd ed. enlarg. 1634]. D
Heath, John: Two Centuries of Epigrams. V
Holland, Philemon (1552): Trs. Camden's Britan-
nia [another ed. 1637: see 1586]. P
Jones, Robert (fl. 1616): The Muses' Garden of
Delights. V
Markham (1568?): Markham's Masterpiece. P
Rich (1540?): New Description of Ireland [called
New Irish Prognostication 1624]. P
Rich, Richard: News from Virginia. V
Scot, Thomas: Philomythie or Philomythologie
[enlarg. 1616, 1622; pt. ii 1625]. V
Selden (1584): England's Epinomis. P
Duello, or Single Combat. P
Shakespeare (1564): The Tempest, Cymbeline,
A Winter's Tale; acted between 1610 and
1612 [printed 1623].
Sharpe, Roger: More Fools Yet [epigrams]. V

1611

Authorized Version of the Bible.
Byrd (1538?): Psalmes, Songs, & Sonnets. V
Chapman (1559?): May Day, a comedy.
Trs. Iliad [complete: see 1598, 1610]. V
Coryate (1577?): Coryats Crudities. P
Coryats Crambe. P
Odcombian Banquet. P
Davies (1565?): Scourge of Folly [n.d.]. V
Donne (1572): Anatomy of the World [The First
Anniversary and A Funeral Elegy; 2nd ed.
with The Second Anniversary added 1612]. V
Ignatius his Conclave. P
Fenton, Roger: Treatise of Usury. P
Heywood (1575?): The Golden Age. D
Jonson (1597?): Catiline his Conspiracy. T
Middleton (1580): The Roaring Girl or Moll Cut-
purse [with Dekker]. C
Speed (1552?): History of Great Britain [rev.
1623, 1627; enlarg. 1632; originally com-
menced as Theatre of the Empire of Great
Britain 1611]. P
Genealogies recorded in Sacred Scriptures. P
Tourneur (1575?): Atheist's Tragedy. T

James Harrington b.
Sir Thomas Urquhart b.
Robert Leighton b.
Giles Fletcher senr. d.
*Shakespeare's retirement
to Stratford about this
date.*
*Randle Cotgrave, 'Dic-
tionary of French and
English Tongues' (ed.
with Eng.-Fr. Diction-
ary by R. Sherwood
1632; ed. J. Howell
1650–60–73).*

47

Alexander (1567?): Elegy on Death of Prince Henry. V

Breton (1545?): Wit's Private Wealth. P
Cornucopiae. Pasquil's Night Cap. V

Campion (1567): Third and Fourth Book of Airs [n.d.: see 1610]. V

Chapman (1559?): Widow's Tears, a comedy.
Trs. Petrarch's Penitential Psalms. V
An Epicede, or Funeral Song on Death of Prince Henry. V

Daniel (1562): History of England, pt. i [to end of Stephen; pt. ii, continued to Edward III, 1618]. P

Davies (1569): Discovery of Causes why Ireland was never subdued. P

Davies (1565?): Muse's Sacrifice, or Divine Meditations. V

Dekker (1570?): If it be not good, the Devil is in it. C
Troia Nova Triumphans.

Deloney (d. 1607?): Thomas of Reading [earliest extant ed.; first pub. probably 1602]. P

Dowland, John (1563?): A Pilgrim's Solace. V

Drayton (1563): Polyolbion pt. i [n.d.: see 1622]. V

Field, Nathaniel: A Woman is a Weathercock. C

Hall (1574): Contemplations, vol. i [ii 1614, iii 1615, iv 1618, v 1620, vi 1622, vii 1623, viii 1626]. P

Heywood (1575?): Apology for Actors [altered by William Cartwright as Actor's Vindication 1658]. P

Hooker (d. 1600): Learned Discourse of Justification. P
Sermon of the Nature of Pride. P
Answer to the Supplication of Mr. Travers. P
Remedy against Sorrow and Fear. P
Sermon of the Certainty and Perpetuity of Faith. P

Jonson (1597?): The Alchemist. C

Purchas (1575?): Purchas his Pilgrimage, or Relation of the World. P

Rowlands, Samuel: Knave of Hearts. V

Sylvester (1563): Lachrimae Lachrimarum [enlarg. 1613]. V

Webster (1580?): The White Devil. T

Wither (1588): Prince Henry's Obsequies. V
Epithalamia, or Nuptial Poems. V

Death of Henry, Prince of Wales.
Samuel Butler b.
Thomas Killigrew senr. b.
Sir John Harington d.
First Eng. trs. of 'Don Quixote', pt. i by Thomas Shelton (see 1620).

Bayly, Lewis, Bishop of Bangor: Practice of Piety [earliest extant, i.e. 3rd, ed.; first pub. earlier in the century]. P

Beaumont (1584): Masque of the Inner Temple [n.d.].

Knight of the Burning Pestle [with Fletcher]. D burlesque.

Browne (1591): Britannia's Pastorals, pt. i [n.d.; pt. ii 1616; iii prtd. T. C. Croker 1852]. V

Campion (1567): Songs bewailing the Death of Prince Henry. V

Entertainment given by Lord Knowles. D masque.

Chapman (1559?): Revenge of Bussy D'Ambois. T Masque of Middle Temple [n.d.].

Dekker (1570?): Strange Horse Race. P

Drummond (1585): Tears on Death of Meliades. V Mausoleum [elegies by D., Chapman, Wither, Rowley, and others]. V

Hayward, Sir John: Lives of the Three Norman Kings of England. P

Heywood (1575?): The Brazen Age. D The Silver Age. D

Markham (1568?): The English Husbandman [bk. ii 1614; rev. 1635]. P

Marston (1575?): Insatiate Countess. T

Rich (1540?): Opinion Defied. P Excellency of Good Women. P

Rowlands, Samuel: More Knaves Yet. V

Scoggin, John: Scoggin his Jests [earliest extant collection; originally *c.* 1565; Jests gathered by Andrew Boord 1626].

Shakespeare (1564): Henry VIII [acted; prtd 1623]. D

Wither (1588): Abuses stript and whipt [includes The Scourge and Epigrams]. V

Globe Theatre burnt.
Jeremy Taylor b.
Richard Crashaw b.?
John Cleveland b.
La Rochefoucauld b.
Sir Thomas Overbury d.
Sir Thomas Bodley d.

Alexander (1567?): Doomesday. V
Bacon (1561): Charge touching Duels. P
Brathwaite, Richard: The Scholar's Medley.
Browne (1591): Shepherd's Pipe [with poems by Wither, Christopher Brooke, and John Davies of Hereford]. V
Campion (1567): A Masque presented at Marriage of Earl of Somerset.
Chapman (1559?): Trs. Odyssey, bks. i–xii [n.d.: see 1615]. V
Cooke, John: Greene's Tu Quoque, or the City Gallant. C
Fletcher (1579): Bonduca [acted *c.* 1614; prtd. 1647]. T
Gentleman, Tobias: England's Way to win Wealth. P
Gorges, Sir Arthur: Trs. Lucan's Pharsalia. V
Heywood (1575?): Life and Death of Hector [modernization of Lydgate's Troy Book]. V
Jonson (1597?): Sad Shepherd [acted; prtd. 1641]. D
Bartholomew Fair [acted; prtd. 1631]. C
Lodge (1558?): Trs. Works of Seneca both Moral and Natural [enlarg. 1620]. P
Overbury (d. 1613): Characters [with A Wife now the Widow of Sir Thomas Overbury; enlarg. 1614, 1615, 1616, &c.; 16th ed. 1638]. P
Raleigh (1552?): History of the World [ed. with Life by William Oldys 1736]. P
Rich (1540?): Honesty of this Age. P
Selden (1584): Titles of Honour. P
Sylvester (1563): Parliament of Virtues Royal [n.d.; Second Session of the Parliament *c.* 1615; trs. Jean Bertaut; cont. other pieces by S.]. V
Tailor, Robert: The Hogge hath lost his Pearl. C

Henry More b.
John Barclay, 'Icon Animarum' (trs. Thomas May 1631).
John Napier's 'Mirifici Logarithmorum Canonis Descriptio'.
Isaac Casaubon d.
La Calprenède b.

1615

Anon.: Valiant Welshman. D
Andrews, John: Anatomie of Baseness. V
Beaumont (1584) **and Fletcher** (1579): Cupid's Revenge. D
Brathwaite, Richard: Strappado for the Devil. V
Breton (1545?): Characters upon Essays Moral and Divine. P
Chapman (1559?): Trs. Odyssey [complete in 24 bks.; n.d.: see 1614]. V
Daniel (1562): Hymen's Triumph. D masque.
Harington (d. 1612): Epigrams [enlarg. 1618]. V
Heywood (1575?): Four Prentices of London. D
Jonson (1573): Mercurie Vindicated. D masque.
Rowlands, Samuel: Melancholy Knight. V

King James visits Cambridge.
The Cockpit Theatre erected c. 1615.
Richard Baxter b.
Sir John Denham b.
William Camden, 'Annales', pt. i (pt. ii 1627; Eng. trs. of pt. i by Abraham Darcie 1627; of pt. ii by Thomas Browne 1629; of whole by Richard Norton 1630).
'Don Quixote' (completed, see 1605).

Sandys (1578): Relation of a Journey begun in 1610. P
Stephens, John: Satyrical Essays, characters. P
Tomkis, Thomas: Albumazar, a comedy.
Wither (1588): Shepherds Hunting. V
 Fidelia [corrected and enlarg. 1619]. V

1616

Beaumont (d. 1616) and Fletcher (1579): Scornful Lady. C
Breton (1545?): Crossing of Proverbs. P
Browne (1591): Britannia's Pastorals, pt. ii [see 1613]. V
Bullokar, John: English Expositor, teaching interpretation of hardest Words. P
Chapman (1559?): Whole Works of Homer [collective ed. of Iliad and Odyssey; n.d.: see 1611, 1615, 1624]. V
Coryate (1577?): Greeting from the Court of the Great Mogul. P
Cotta, John: Trial of Witchcraft. P
Davies (1565?): A Select Husband for Sir Thomas Overburie's Wife. V
Drummond (1585): Poems [see 1656].
Haughton, William: Englishmen for my Money, or A Woman will have her Will. C
James I, King of England: Works. P
Jonson (1597?): Works of Benjamin Jonson [1st vol. of the First Folio; cont. all plays pub. (1600–12) except Case is Altered, and adding Epicoene, Epigrams, The Forest, and eighteen masques and entertainments: see 1631, 1640, 1692].
Markham (1568?): Markham's Method or Epitome. P
Niccols, Richard: Sir Thomas Overburie's Vision. V

Joseph Beaumont b.
Roger L'Estrange b.
William Shakespeare d.
Francis Beaumont d.
Richard Hakluyt d.
William Harvey expounds theory of circulation of the blood to College of Surgeons (see 1628, 1651).
John Selden, ed. of Sir John Fortescue's 'De Laudibus Legum Angliae'.
Cervantes d.
D'Aubigné, 'Les Tragiques', 'Histoire Universelle' (concl. 1620).

1617

Davies (1565?): Wit's Bedlam. V
Drummond (1585): Forth Feasting. V
Greene (d. 1592): Alcida. P
Hall (1574): Quo Vadis? A just Censure of Travel. P
Lyly (d. 1606): Euphues [complete: see 1578]. P
Middleton (1580): A Faire Quarrell [with Rowley]. D
Moryson, Fynes (1566): Itinerary. P
Rich (d. 1617): The Irish Hubub, or the English Hue and Cry. P
Sylvester (1563): Tobacco Battered and the Pipes Shattered. V

Ralph Cudworth b.
Elias Ashmole b.
Barnabe Rich d.
Thomas Coryate d.
John Selden, 'De Diis Syris Syntagmata'.
D'Aubigné, 'Faeneste' (concl. 1630).
Théophile, 'Pyrame et Thisbé', c. 1617

Breton (1545?): The Court and the Country. P
Chapman (1559?): Trs. Georgics of Hesiod. V
Coryate (1577?): To his Friends in England: from Agra. P
Field, Nathaniel: Amends for Ladies. C
Harington (d. 1612): Epigrams [complete in 4 bks.: see 1615]. V
Holyday, Barten: Technogamia, or Marriage of the Arts. C
Mynshul, Geoffray: Essays and Characters of a Prison and Prisoners. P
Selden (1584): History of Tithes. P
Stow (d. 1605): Summary of English Chronicles [final ed., embodying all additions and continuations by S. and others: see 1565]. P

Synod of Dort.
Thirty Years War 1618–48.
Richard Lovelace b.
Abraham Cowley b.
Sir Walter Raleigh executed.
John Davies of Hereford d.
Joshua Sylvester d.
Meeting of Ben Jonson and Drummond of Hawthornden (see 1711, 1827).
J. Brinsley trs. Ovid's 'Metamorphoses'

1619

Anon.: Whole Contention between Houses of York and Lancaster [see 1594, 1595]. D
Beaumont (d. 1616) **and Fletcher** (1579): Maid's Tragedy. T
  A King and No King. T
Deloney (d. 1607?): History of John Winchcomb [earliest extant, i.e. 8th, ed.; first pub. probably before 1600]. P
Fletcher (1579): Humorous Lieutenant [acted; prtd. 1647]. C
  Little French Lawyer [acted *c.* 1619; prtd. 1647; written with Massinger]. C
Hutton, Henry: Folly's Anatomy. V
Middleton (1580): Inner Temple Masque.
  Triumphs of Love and Antiquity. D pageant.
Purchas (1575?): Purchas his Pilgrim. Microcosmus. P
Shakespeare (d. 1616): Quartos of Henry VI, Pericles, A Yorkshire Tragedy (ascribed to S.), Merry Wives of Windsor, Merchant of Venice, Lear, Henry V, Sir John Oldcastle (ascribed to S.), Midsummer-Night's Dream, printed by W. Jaggard, some with false dates.
Wither (1588): Preparation to the Psalter.

William Chamberlayne b.
Samuel Daniel d.
Webster's 'Appius and Virginia' acted before 1619 (prtd. 1654).
Sir A. Gorges, 'Wisdom of the Ancients' (trs. of Bacon; see 1609).
John Vicars trs. John Owen's 'Epigrams' (see 1607).

Anon.: Horae Subsecivae [Essays: attrib. Grey Brydges, Lord Chandos; or Gilbert Cavendish]. P

Trs. Boccaccio's Decameron [first complete trs., prtd. Isaac Jaggard]. P

Bloody Banquet, a tragedy.

Swetnam, the Woman Hater. C

Two Merry Milkmaids. C

Beaumont (d. 1616) **and Fletcher** (1579): Philaster. T

Brathwaite, Richard: Essays upon the Five Senses. P

Dekker (1570?): Dekker his Dreame. V

Middleton (1580): World Tost at Tennis [with Rowley]. D masque.

Peacham, Henry, jnr.: Thalia's Banquet. V

Quarles (1592): Feast for Worms [also Hymne to God, Eleven Meditations, Pentelogia]. V

Rowlands, Samuel: The Night Raven. V

Sylvester (d. 1618): Sacred Works, gathered into one volume. V

Woodman's Bear. V

Pilgrim Fathers emigrate to America.
John Evelyn b.
Thomas Campion d.
Bacon, 'Instauratio Magna'.
'Don Quixote', pt. ii translated (see 1612).
Sir Thomas Overbury trs. Ovid's 'Remedy of Love'.
J. Webbe trs. 'Familiar Epistles of Cicero' (anon.; n.d.).

1621

Burton (1577): Anatomy of Melancholy [later edd. 1624–8–32–8–51–2–60–76]. P

Culpeper, Sir Thomas: Tract against Usury. P

Fletcher (1579): Wild Goose Chase [acted: prtd. 1652]. C

The Pilgrim [acted: prtd. 1647]. D

Thierry and Theodoret. T

Hall (1574): Works [later collections, with additions, during H.'s life-time 1625–28–34: see 1660, 1662].

Heylyn (1600): Microcosmus [see 1652]. P

Mason, William: Handful of Essays. P

Middleton (1580): Sun in Aries. D pageant.

Entertainments Composed for the City. D

Mun, Thomas: Discourse of Trade unto the East Indies. P

Quarles (1592): Hadassa. V

Rowley (1585?) **with Middleton and Dekker**: Witch of Edmonton [acted *c.* 1621; prtd. 1658]. D tragi-comedy.

Wither (1588): Wither's Motto. V

Songs of Old Testament. V

Wroth, Lady Mary: Countess of Montgomerie's Urania. P

Trial and Condemnation of Bacon.
Andrew Marvell b.
Roger Boyle, Earl of Orrery, b.
John Barclay, 'Argenis' (trs. K. Long 1625).
La Fontaine b.

Bacon (1561): History of the Reign of Henry VII. P
    Historia Naturalis et Experimentalis [Latin]. P
Breton (1545?): Strange News out of Diverse
    Countries. P
Drayton (1563): Second Part of Polyolbion [see
    1612]. V
Hannay, Patrick: The Nightingale. V
Hawkins, Sir Richard: Observations in his Voyage
    into the South Sea. P
Mabbe (1572): The Rogue. P
Markham (1568?): Herod and Antipater [with
    William Sampson]. T
Massinger (1583): Virgin Martyr [with Dekker]. T
May (1595): The Heir. C
Peacham, Henry, jnr.: Compleat Gentleman. P
Shakespeare (d. 1616): Othello. T
Wither (1588): Fair Virtue. V
    Juvenilia. V

Henry Vaughan b.
Thomas Vaughan b.
The Weekly News-pam-
    phlets, 'The Corantos',
    begin (concl. 1641; in-
    terrupted 1632–8).
Molière b.

1623

Daniel (d. 1619): Whole Works. V
Drummond (1585): Flowers of Sion. V
    Cypress Grove. P
Feltham, Owen: Resolves [n.d.: see 1628]. P
Fletcher (d. 1623): Reward of the Faithful. P
Jonson (1573?): Pan's Anniversarie (masque).
    Neptune's Triumph (masque).
Massinger (1583): Duke of Milan. T
Shakespeare (d. 1616): First Folio, ed. J. Hem-
    inge and H. Condell [cont. 36 plays of which
    the following had not appeared before: Tem-
    pest, Two Gentlemen of Verona, Measure for
    Measure, Comedy of Errors, As You Like It,
    Taming of the Shrew, All's Well that Ends
    Well, Twelfth Night, Winter's Tale, King
    John, 1 Henry VI, 2 Henry VI, 3 Henry VI,
    Henry VIII, Coriolanus, Timon of Athens,
    Julius Caesar, Antony and Cleopatra, Mac-
    beth, Cymbeline. Pericles (see 1609) is
    omitted. See 1632, 1663, 1685].
Webster (1580?): Duchess of Malfi. T
    Devil's Law Case. C
Wither (1588): Hymns and Songs of the Church.

Massacre at Amboyna.
Sir William Petty b.
William Camden d.
Giles Fletcher jnr. d.
Bacon, 'De Augmentis'.
'The Spanish Gipsy' and
    'The Changeling' by
    Middleton and Rowley
    acted about this date
    (prtd. 1653).
J. Bingham trs. 'History'
    of Xenophon.
Pascal b.
Charles Sorel, 'Francion'.

Anon.: Tragedy of Nero. D
    Love's Garland [verse miscellany].
Chapman (1559?): Trs. Batrachomyomachia or
    Homer's Battle of Frogs and Mice [n.d.: see
    1616]. V
Donne (1572): Devotions upon Emergent Occa-
    sions. P
Massinger: The Bondman. D
    Parliament of Love [acted; prtd. 1805]. C
Quarles (1592): Job Militant. V
    Sion's Elegies. V
Smith, Captain John: General Historie of Virginia.
    P
Wotton (1568): Elements of Architecture. P

*War declared against
    Spain.
George Fox b.
Margaret Cavendish
    (Duchess of Newcastle)
    b.?
Thomas Heywood's 'Cap-
    tives' written before this
    date (first prtd. 1885).
Lord Herbert of Cherbury's
    'De Veritate' in Paris
    (first Eng. ed. 1645):
    his Autobiography ends
    (pub. 1764).
Jacob Boehme d.
Opitz, 'Von der deutschen
    Poeterey'.*

1625

Bacon (1561): Essays [in final form: see 1597]. P
    Apophthegms New and Old. P
    Trs. Certain Psalmes. V
Dekker (1570?): Rod for Runaways. P
Markham (1568?): The Souldier's Accidence. P
Middleton (1580): Game at Chess [n.d.]. C
Purchas, Samuel: Hakluytes Posthumus, or Pur-
    chas his Pilgrims. P
Quarles (1592): Sion's Sonnets sung by Solomon. V
    Alphabet of Elegies. V
Wither (1588): Scholar's Purgatory [n.d.]. P

*Accession of Charles I.
Plague in London.
Thomas Lodge d.
John Fletcher d.
John Webster d.?
Abraham Darcie trs.
    Camden's 'Annales',
    pt. i (see 1615).
K. Long trs. John Bar-
    clay's 'Argenis'.
Grotius, 'De Jure belli et
    pacis'.
Racan, 'Les Bergeries'.*

1626

Breton (d. 1626?): Pasquils Mad-Cappe. V
    Fantasticks. P
Donne (1572): Five Sermons [collected: separ-
    ately 1622–3–5–6].
Drake, Sir Francis, jnr.: Sir Francis Drake re-
    vived [relation of D.'s voyage to West Indies].
    P
Hall (1574): Contemplations [completed: see
    1612]. P
Parrot, Henry: VIII Cures for the Itch: Characters,
    Epigrams, Epitaphs. V
Roper, William (d. 1578): Life of Sir Thomas
    More. P
Sandys (1578): Trs. Ovid's Metamorphoses. V
Smith, Captain John: Accidence for Young Sea-
    men [amplified into Seaman's Grammar
    1653].
Vaughan, William (1577): Golden Fleece. P and V

*Francis Bacon d.
Sir John Davies d.
Cyril Tourneur d.
Samuel Purchas d.
Nicholas Breton d.?
William Rowley d.
Sir Henry Spelman, 'Glos-
    sariumArchaiologicum'.
Abridgement of Camden's
    'Britannia'.
Mme de Sévigné b.*

Bacon (d. 1626): Sylva Sylvarum [cont. New Atlantis]. P
Bernard, Richard (1568): The Isle of Man. P
Drayton (1563): Battaile of Agincourt, Miseries of Queen Margarite, Nimphidia, Quest of Cynthia, Shepherd's Sirene, The Moon Calfe. V
Fletcher, Phineas (1582): Locustæ [The Locusts; in 2 pts.; Eng. and Latin]. V
May (1595): Trs. Lucan's Pharsalia [concl. 1630]. V
Niccols, Richard: The Beggers Ape. V

Robert Boyle b.
John Hall b.
Dorothy Osborne b.
Richard Barnfield d.
Thomas Middleton d.
Camden, 'Annales' pt. ii (see 1615).
Bossuet b.
Honoré D'Urfé, 'Astrée' (final ed.: earliest prt. 1610).

1628

Anon.: Britain's Idea [Phineas Fletcher now supposed to be author; sometimes wrongly attrib. Spenser]. V
Anon.: Robin Good Fellow [earliest extant ed.].
Clavell, John: Recantation of an ill-spent Life.
Coke, Sir Edward: Institutes of the Laws of England [pt. ii 1642; iii and iv 1644].
Earle (1601): Microcosmographie [enlarg. 1629 –30–3–8]. P
Feltham, Owen: Resolves [complete; first instalment *c.* 1623]. P
Fletcher, Francis: The World Encompassed by Sir Francis Drake. P
Gomersall, Robert: Tragedy of Lodovick Sforza. D
Raleigh (d. 1618): Prerogative of Parliaments. P
Reynolds, Henry: Tasso's Aminta Englisht. D pastoral.
Wither (1588): Britain's Remembrancer. P

George Villiers, Duke of Buckingham, b.
John Bunyan b.
Fulke Greville d.
Sir William Temple b.
William Harvey's system of blood circulation set forth in 'Exercitatio Anatomica de Motu Cordis et Sanguinis in Animalibus' (see 1616, 1651).
Perrault b.
Malherbe d.
Charles Sorel, 'Le Berger Extravagant'.

1629

Adams, Thomas: Works, being the Summe of his Sermons.
Andrewes, Lancelot (d. 1626): XCVI Sermons [also 1631, 1635].
Bacon (d. 1626): Certain Miscellany Works, ed. Rawley. P
Advertisement touching a Holy War. P
Beaumont, Sir John (d. 1627): Bosworth Field. V
Carlell, Lodowick: The Deserving Favourite. D
Chapman (1559?): Justification of a Strange Action of Nero. Trs. Fifth Satire of Juvenal. V

Whitefriars Playhouse.
John Speed d.?
Thomas Browne trs. Camden's 'Annals', pt. ii (see 1615).
W. Cross trs. Works of Sallust.
Pierre Corneille, 'Mélite'.

D'Avenant (1606): Tragedy of Albovine. D
Ford (1586): Lover's Melancholy. C
Hobbes (1588): Trs. Peloponnesian War of Thucy-
    dides. P
Lightfoot, John: Erubhim, or Miscellanies Chris-
    tian and Judaicall. P
Markham (1568?): Markham's Faithful Farrier. P
Massinger (1583): Roman Actor. T
Parkinson, John: Paradisi in sole, Paradisus Ter-
    restris. P
Quarles (1592): Argalus and Parthenia. V
Shirley (1596): The Wedding. D

1630

Anon.: Pathomachia, or Battle of Affections. D
'B., A.': Merry Tales of the Mad Men of Gotham
    [sometimes attrib. Andrew Boorde].
Bacon (d. 1626). Maxims of the Law. P
Brathwaite, Richard: The English Gentleman. P
D'Avenant (1606): The Cruel Brother. T
    The Just Italian. D
Dekker (1570?): Second Part of the Honest
    Whore [pt. i 1604]. D
Drayton (1563): Muses Elizium [Noah's Flood;
    Moses his Birth and Miracles (see 1604);
    David and Goliah]. V
Hall (1574): Occasional Meditations. P
Hayward, Sir John (d. 1627): Life and Reign of
    King Edward VI. P
Higgeson, Francis (d. 1630). New England's
    Plantation. P
Massinger (1583): The Picture. D tragi-comedy.
    The Renegado. D tragi-comedy.
Middleton (d. 1627): A Chaste Mayd in Cheap-
    side. C
Randolph (1605): Aristippus. The Conceited Ped-
    ler. C
Shirley (1596): Grateful Servant. C
Taylor, John (1580): All the Works of John
    Taylor the Water Poet [reprtd. Spenser
    Society 1868-9; other works not in this col-
    lection reprtd. same Society 1870-8].

Isaac Barrow b.
John Tillotson b.
Charles Cotton b.
Edward Phillips b.
Gabriel Harvey d.
Richard Norton trs.
    'Annals' of Camden
    (both parts: see 1615).
Kepler d.
Balzac, 'Dissertations',
    1630-40.
Pierre Corneille, 'Clit-
    andre'.

Anon.: Comedie of Fair Em. D

Brathwaite, Richard: The English Gentlewoman. P
Whimzies, or a new cast of characters. P

Chapman (1559?): Wars of Pompey and Caesar [also called Caesar and Pompey]. T

Chettle, Henry: Tragedy of Hoffman, or Revenge for a Father [acted 1602]. D

Dekker (1570?): Match me in London, a tragi-comedy.
Penny wise pound foolish. P

Fletcher (1582): Sicelides, a Piscatory. D pastoral.

Fuller (1608): David's Heinous Sinne. V

Heywood (1575?): Fair Maid of the West, pts. i, ii. C
England's Elizabeth, her Life and Troubles. P

Jonson (1597?): Bartholomew Fair. Devil is an Ass. Staple of News [see 1640]. C
New Inne, or The Light Heart [see 1692]. C
Love's Triumph (masque).
Chloridia (masque).

Lenton, Francis (fl. 1630–40): Characterismi. P

Lloyd, David: Legend of Captain Jones [enlarg. 1648; another ed. 1656]. V

Mabbe, James ('Don Diego Puede-Ser'): Spanish Bawd, represented in Celestina; or the tragick comedy of Calisto and Melibea [trs. Fernando de Rojas].

Markham (1568?): Way to get Wealth. P

Massinger (1583): Believe as You List [acted; prtd. 1849]. C

May (1595): Tragedy of Antigone. D
Mirror of Minds [trs. John Barclay's Icon Animarum, 1614].

Powell, Thomas: Tom of all Trades. P

Quarles (1592): Historie of Samson. V

Shirley (1596): School of Compliment [called Love Tricks 1667].

Stow (d. 1605): Annals of England [final ed. embodying all additions by S. and continuations by E. Howes; Appendix, &c. 1632: see 1592]. P

Charles I visits Cambridge.
John Dryden b.
John Phillips b.
Catherine Philips ('Matchless Orinda') b.
John Donne d.
Michael Drayton d.
John Selden, 'De Successionibus'.

1632

Brome, Richard: Northern Lass. C

Donne (d. 1631): Death's Duell [his last sermon]. P

Heywood (1575?): The Iron Age, pts. i, ii. D

Holland, Philemon: Trs. Cyropaedia of Xenophon. P

Lupton, Donald: London and the Countrey carbonadoed and quartred (characters). P

Marmion (1603): Holland's Leaguer. C

John Locke b.
Anthony à Wood b.
Thomas Dekker d.
Spinoza b.

Massinger (1583): Emperor of the East. D tragi-comedy.
  Fatal Dowry [with Nathaniel Field]. T
  Maid of Honour. D
  City Madam [acted; prtd. 1658]. C
Quarles (1592): Divine Fancies. V
Raleigh (d. 1618): Instructions to his Son. P
Randolph (1605): Jealous Lovers. C
Reynolds, Henry: Mythomystes, wherein a Short
  Survey is taken of true poesy [n.d.]. P
Rowley (d. 1626): A New Wonder, A Woman
  never Vext. C
Shakespeare (d. 1616): Second Folio [contents
  same as First Folio: see 1623].
Shirley (1596): Changes, or Love in a Maze. C
Wither (1588): Psalms of David translated. V

1633

Anon.: The Costlie Whore. C
Cowley (1618): Poetical Blossoms [enlarg. 1636,
  1637]. V
Donne (d. 1631): Poems [later edd., mostly with
  additions, 1635-9-49-50-4-69; ed. Grosart
  1872, Chambers 1896, Grierson 1912].
  Juvenilia, or Paradoxes and Problems. P
Fletcher (1582): Purple Island [with Piscatory
  Eclogues and other poetical miscellanies]. V
Ford (1586): The Broken Heart. T
  Love's Sacrifice. T   Tis Pity She's a Whore. T
Forde, Emanuel: Famous History of Montelyon. P
Greville (d. 1628): Certain Learned and Elegant
  Works [Humane Learning, Fame and
  Honour, Treatise of Wars, Cœlica, Tragedy
  of Alaham, Tragedy of Mustapha (see 1609)].
Herbert (d. 1633): The Temple. V
Heywood (1575?): The English Traveller. D
Marlowe (d. 1593): Jew of Malta. T
Marmion (1603): A Fine Companion. D
Massinger (1583): New Way to pay old Debts. C
  The Guardian [acted; prtd. 1655].
May (1595): Reigne of King Henry the Second. V
Prynne (1600): Histrio-mastix. P
Quarles (1552): Divine Poems [collection of all
  biblical paraphrases pub. hitherto, and
  Alphabet of Elegies, 1625].
Rowley (d. 1626): All's Lost by Lust. T
  A Match at Midnight. C
Shirley (1596): Bird in a Cage. C
  Witty Fair One. C
  Contention for Honour and Riches. D masque.
  Triumph of Peace, a masque.
Spenser (d. 1599): View of the Present State of
  Ireland [i.e. in 1596; pub. in Sir James Ware's
  Two Histories of Ireland]. P

*George Savile (Marquis of
  Halifax) b.
Samuel Pepys b.
Wentworth Dillon (Earl of
  Roscommon) b.?
George Herbert d.
Anthony Munday d.
Prynne pilloried for ' His-triomastix'.
W. Saltonstall trs. Ovid's
  ' Tristia'.*

Charles I] **1634**

Carew (1595?): Coelum Britannicum, a masque.
D'Avenant (1606): Temple of Love, a masque.
Fletcher (d. 1625): Two Noble Kinsmen [with Shakespeare]. T
Ford (1586): Chronicle History of Perkin Warbeck. D
Habington (1605): Castara [enlarg. 1635, 1640]. V
Heywood (1575?): Late Lancashire Witches [with Richard Brome]. C
  A Maidenhead Well Lost. C
Rowley (d. 1626): The Noble Soldier. T

Robert South b.
Mme de La Fayette b.
John Marston d.
George Chapman d.
Sir John Reresby d.
Meric Casaubon trs. 'Meditations of Marcus Aurelius'.
Pierre Corneille, 'La Veuve', 'La Suivante'.

1635

D'Avenant (1606): Triumphs of Prince d'Amour. D masque.
Heywood (1575?): Hierarchie of Blessed Angels. V
  Philocothonista, or the Drunkard. V
May (1595): Victorious Reigne of Edward the Third. V
Quarles (1592): Emblems. V
Rutter, Joseph: The Shepherd's Holiday. D pastoral.
Shirley (1596): The Traitor. T
Swan, John: Speculum Mundi. P
Wither (1588): Collection of Emblems. V

Sir George Etherege b.?
Edward Stillingfleet b.
Thomas Sprat b.
Thomas Randolph d.
John Selden, 'Mare Clausum' (Eng. trs. by M. N. 1652).
Académie Française founded.
Pierre Corneille, 'Medée'
Lope de Vega d.

1636

D'Avenant (1606): The Wits, a comedy.
  The Platonick Lovers. D tragi-comedy.
Davies (d. 1618): Writing Schoolmaster [16th ed.; no earlier copy extant]. P,
Dekker (d. 1632): Wonder of a Kingdom. D tragi-comedy.
Heylyn (1600): History of the Sabbath. P
Heywood (1575?): Love's Mistress, or the Queen's Masque.
  Challenge for Beauty. D
  Discourse of two Upstart Prophets. V
Massinger (1583): Great Duke of Florence. C
  Bashful Lover [acted; prtd. 1655]. C
Sandys (1578): Paraphrase upon Psalms of David [called Paraphrase upon Divine Poems 1638]. V
Wither (1588): Nature of Man [trs. Nemesius]. P

Charles I visits Oxford.
Joseph Glanvill b.
J. Carpenter trs. Ovid's 'Remedy of Love'.
W. Saltonstall trs. Ovid's 'Epistles'.
William Prynne, 'News from Ipswich' (attack on Bishop of Norwich).
Annalia Dubrensia (on Dover's Cotswold Games).
Boileau b.
Pierre Corneille, 'Le Cid'.

60

Alexander (1567?): Recreations with the Muses. V
Deloney (d. 1607?): The Gentle Craft [earliest extant ed.; first pub. probably 1597]. P
Fletcher (d. 1625): The Elder Brother. C
Heywood (1575?): Royal King and the Loyal Subject. D
Pleasant Dialogues and Dramas [trs. Lucian]. P
Hobbes (1588): Art of Rhetorique [trs. Aristotle; n.d.]. P
Jordan (1612?): Poeticall Varieties. V
Marmion (1603): Cupid and Psyche. V
Milton (1608): A Masque presented at Ludlow Castle [Comus: acted 1634].
Nabbes, Thomas: Hannibal and Scipio. T
Microcosmus, a moral masque.
Shirley (1596): The Example. D
The Gamester. D
Hide Park. C
Lady of Pleasure. C
Young Admiral. D

Thomas Traherne b.?
Ben Jonson d.
Gervase Markham d.
Joseph Rutter trs. 'Le Cid' of Corneille (pt. ii 1640).
Descartes, 'Discours de la Méthode'.
Gomberville, 'Polexandre.'
Desmarets, 'Les Visionaires'.
Brian Duppa, ed. 'Jonsonus Virbius'.

1638

Brathwaite, Richard: Barnabae Itinerarium. V
Chillingworth (1602): Religion of Protestants a safe way to Salvation. P
Cowley (1618): Love's Riddle, a pastoral comedy.
D'Avenant (1606): Madagascar and other Poems.
Ford (1586): Fancies, Chaste and Noble. C
Heywood (1575?): Wise Woman of Hogsdon. C
Killigrew, Henry: The Conspiracy [called Pallantus and Eudora 1653]. T
Milton (1608): Lycidas [in Obsequies to the memorie of Mr. Edward King]. V
Nabbes, Thomas: Covent Garden. C
Tottenham Court. C
Quarles (1592): Hieroglyphikes of Life of Man. V
Randolph (d. 1635): Poems. Muses Looking Glass. D
Amyntas. D
Rowley (d. 1626): A Shoemaker a Gentleman. C
Shirley, Henry: The Martyr'd Souldier. T
Shirley (1596): The Royal Master. D
The Duke's Mistress. D
Suckling (1609): Aglaura. D tragi-comedy.

Thomas Shelton, 'Tachygraphy'.
Henry Peacham, jnr., 'Truth of our Times'.

Beaumont (d. 1616) **and** Fletcher (d. 1625): Bloody
    Brother [Rollo, Duke of Normandy 1640]. T
    Wit without Money. C

Carlell, Lodowick: Arviragus and Philicia, pts. i,
    ii. D

Cartwright, William: The Royal Slave. D

Chapman (d. 1634) **and** Shirley (1596): The Ball. C
    Chabot, Admiral of France. T

D'Avenant (1606): Salmacida Spolia, a masque.

Davenport, Robert: New Trick to Cheat the Devil. C
    A Crowne for a Conqueror. V

Fletcher (d. 1625): Monsieur Thomas. C

Ford (1586): The Ladies Trial. D

Fuller (1608): History of the Holy War. P

Glapthorne, Henry: Argalus and Parthenia. D
    Tragedy of Albertus Wallenstein. D

Massinger (1583): The Unnatural Combat. T

May (1595): Tragedy of Cleopatra. D
    Tragedy of Julia Agrippina. D

Mayne (1604): The City Match, a comedy.

Shirley (1596): The Maid's Revenge. T

Sir Charles Sedley b.?
Sir Henry Wotton d.
Thomas Carew d.?
Shakerley Marmion d.
W. Page trs. 'De Imi-
tatione Christi'.
J. Sherburne trs. Ovid's
'Heroical Epistles'.
Sir Henry Spelman, 'Con-
cilia Decreta Leges Con-
stitutiones' (concl. 1664).
Z. Catlin trs. Ovid's
'Tristia'.
Racine b.
Pierre Corneille, 'Horace',
'Cinna'.

1640

Beaumont (d. 1616): Poems [see 1602].

Brome, Richard: The Antipodes, a comedy.
    Sparagus Garden, a comedy.

Carew (d. 1639?): Poems [Collected; also 1642,
    51–71–2; ed. Maitland 1824, W. C. Hazlitt
    1870, Ebsworth 1893, Vincent 1899].

Donne (d. 1631): LXXX Sermons, with Life by
    Izaak Walton [i.e. vol. i of collective ed. of
    Sermons pub. by D.'s son; vol. ii L Sermons
    1649; vol. iii XXVI Sermons 1660].

Fletcher (d. 1625): The Nightwalker. C
    Rule a Wife and Have a Wife. C

Fuller (1608): Joseph's Party-Coloured Coat. P

Glapthorne, Henry: The Hollander, a comedy.
    The Ladies Privilege, a comedy.
    Wit in a Constable, a comedy.

Greville, Robert, Baron Brooke: Nature of Truth. P

Habington (1605): Queen of Arragon. D
    History of Edward the Fourth of England. P

Hall (1574): Episcopacy by Divine Right. P
    Christian Moderation. P

Harvey, Christopher: The Synagogue, or Shadow
    of the Temple. V

Herbert (d. 1633): Wit's Recreations with a thou-
    sand outlandish Proverbs [anthology of
    verse by various hands].

Heywood (1575?): Exemplary Lives and Memor-
    able Acts of Nine Most Worthy Women.

Howell (1594): Dendrologie, Dodona's Grove. P

Long Parliament.
John Crowne b.
William Wycherley b.?
Aphra Behn b.
Philip Massinger d.
Sir William Alexander,
Earl of Stirling, d.
John Ford d.?
Robert Burton d.
John Selden, 'De Jure
Naturali'.
First Eng. trs. of Mac-
chiavelli's 'Prince' by
Edward Dacres.
J. Gower, 'Ovid's Festi-
vals' (trs. 'Fasti').
John Parkinson, 'Thea-
trum Botanicum'.
Bay Psalm Book.
Mme de Maintenon's first
series of letters about
this time.
Pierre Corneille, 'Poly-
eucte'.

Jonson (d. 1637): Works of Benjamin Johnson [2nd vol. of First Folio (see 1616); cont. Bartholomew Fair, Devil is an Ass, Staple of News (all dated 1631); Magnetic Lady, Tale of a Tub, Sad Shepherd (dated 1641), Mortimer his Fall, Underwoods, Horace his Art of Poetry, English Grammar, Timber, or Discoveries (dated 1641), Masques: see 1616, '92].

Mabbe (1572): trs. Cervantes' Exemplary Novels. P

Milton (1608): Of Reformation touching Church Discipline. P

Nabbes, Thomas: Unfortunate Mother. T
The Bride, a comedy.

Quarles (1592): Enchyridion. P

Rawlins, Thomas: The Rebellion. T

Richards: Messalina the Roman Empress. T

Sandys (1578): Christ's Passion. V

Selden (1584): Discourse concerning the Power of Peers and Commons of Parliament. P

Shirley (1596): A Pastoral called the Arcadia. D
Constant Maid. C
Humorous Courtier. C; Love's Cruelty. T
The Opportunity. C; St. Patrick for Ireland. D
The Coronation [prtd. as by Fletcher]. C

Suckling (1609): Discontented Colonel [n.d.]. T

Walton (1593): Life of Donne [see Donne above; rev. and separate ed. 1658]. P

1641

Cavendish, George: Negotiations of Thomas Woolsey [2nd rev. ed. 1667]. P

Day, John: Parliament of Bees. D masque.

Habington (1605): Observations upon Historie. P

Hartlib, Samuel: Description of Macaria. P

Jonson (d. 1637): Sad Shepherd [see 1640]. C
Timber, or Discoveries [see 1640]. P

Killigrew (1612): The Prisoners. Claracilla [see 1664]. D tragi-comedy.

Marmion (d. 1639): The Antiquary, a comedy.

Sandys (1578): Paraphrase upon the Song of Solomon. V

Sylvester (d. 1618): Collected Works. V

Whiting, Nathaniel: Albino and Bellama. V

Wither (1588): Hallelujah [hymns].

The Episcopacy Controversy: Joseph Hall, *An Humble Remonstrance in Favour of Episcopacy* (1641); 'Smectymnuus' (Stephen Marshall, Edmund Calamy, Thomas Young, Matthew Newcomen, and William Spurstow) *Answer to An Humble Remonstrance* (1641); Hall's *Defence of the Remonstrance* (1641) and *Vindication of the Answer* (1641) by 'Smectymnuus'; Milton's *Reformation touching Church Discipline, Of Prelatical Episcopacy* and *Animadversions upon the Remonstrant's Defence* in 1641, and *Reason of Church Government urged against Prelaty* and *Apology for Smectymnuus* in 1642; James Ussher's *Original of Bishops and Metropolitans* (1641).

Execution of Strafford.
Irish Rebellion.
Thomas Rymer b.
Thomas Heywood d.
The Episcopacy Controversy.
Evelyn's Diary begins (ends 1706; pub. 1818).
George Thomason Collection of Tracts, 1641–62 (catalogued Fortescue 1908).
Pierre Corneille, 'La Mort de Pompée'.
Scudéry, 'Ibrahim'.

Bacon (d. 1626): Reading on the Statute of Uses. P
Baron, Robert: Mirza. D
Denham (1615): The Sophy. T
    Cooper's Hill [final version 1655]. V
Fuller (1608): Holy State and Profane State. P
Hartlib, Samuel: Reformation of Schools [trs. Comenius]. P
Howell (1594?): Instructions for Foreign Travel [enlarg. 1650]. P
Kynaston, Sir Francis: Leoline and Sydanis. V
Milton (1608): Reason of Church Government urged against Prelaty. P
    Apology for Smectymnuus. P
More (1614): Psychodia Platonica, a Platonical Song of the Soul [see 1647]. V
Raleigh (d.1618): The Prince, or Maxims of State. P
Selden (1584): Privileges of Baronage. P
Taylor (1613): Sacred Order and Offices of Episcopacy. P.

Civil War.
Theatres closed.
Isaac Newton b.
Thomas Shadwell b.?
Sir John Suckling d.
Milton's first marriage (with Mary Powell).
Hobbes, 'De Cive' (see 1651).
Jeremiah Rich and William Cartwright, 'Semigraphy'.
Henry Peacham, jnr., 'Art of Living in London'.
Galileo d.
Pierre Corneille, 'Le Menteur'.
La Calprenède, 'Cassandre' (concl. 1645).

1643

Baker, Sir Richard: Chronicle of the Kings of England [contd. to 1660 by Edward Phillips 1660; 9th ed. with successive continuations 1696; contd. to end of George I's reign 1730]. P
Browne (1605): Religio Medici [first authorized ed.: unauthorized 1642]. P
D'Avenant (1606): Unfortunate Lovers. T
Digby (1603): Observations upon Religio Medici. P
Milton (1608): Doctrine and Discipline of Divorce [enlarg. 1644]. P
Prynne (1600): Sovereign Power of Parliaments. P
    Opening of the Great Seal of England. P

Gilbert Burnet b.
John Strype b.
William Browne d.?
Mercurius Aulicus, 1643–5.
Mercurius Britannicus, 1643–6.
Mercurius Civicus, 1643–6.

1644

Hammond, Henry (1605): Practical Catechism [enlarg. 1648]. P
Milton (1608): Of Education: to Mr Hartlib. P
    (Trs.) Judgement of Martin Bucer concerning Divorce. P
    Areopagitica. P
Quarles (d. 1644): Barnabas and Boanerges. P
Raleigh (d. 1618): To-day a Man, To-morrow None [cont. Letter to his Wife]. P
Williams, Roger (1604?): The Bloudy Tenent of Persecution for the Cause of Conscience. P

William Penn b.
George Sandys d.
Francis Quarles d.
William Chillingworth d.
Sir Henry Manwayring, 'Seaman's Dictionary'.
First Letters of Mme de Sévigné about this time.

Digby (1603): Treatise of Bodies and of Man's Soul. P

Fuller (1608): Good Thoughts in Bad Times. P

Howell (1594?): Epistolae Ho-elianae vol. i [ii 1647, iii 1650, iv 1655; ed. J. Jacobs 1890]. P

Milton (1608): Tetrachordon. P

Colasterion. P

Poems [Christ's Nativity; L'Allegro; Il Penseroso; Sonnets; reprts. of Comus (see 1637) and Lycidas (see 1638); Arcades; and juvenile poems in Latin, Greek, and Italian: see 1673, 1695].

Quarles (d. 1644): Solomon's Recantation. V

Ussher (1581): A Body of Divinitie.

Waller (1606): Poems [also 1664 (supposed first authorized ed.) and 1668; Second Part of Poems 1690; a collected ed. 1711; ed. Elijah Fenton 1729; ed. Thorn Drury 1893].

Wither (1588): Vox Pacifica. V

Execution of William Laud.

Battle of Naseby.

Earliest Eng. trs. of Jacob Boehme's Works by John Sparrow and others (concl. 1662).

Pierre Corneille, ' Théodore'.

Scarron, ' Jodelet'.

Grotius d.

Quevedo d.

1646

Browne (1605): Pseudodoxia Epidemica [or Vulgar Errors]. P

Crashaw (1613?): Steps to the Temple [enlarg. 1648; ed. Martin 1927]. V

Edwards, Thomas: Gangraena. P

Fuller (1608): Andronicus, or the Unfortunate Politician. P

Hall (1627): Horae Vacivae, or Essays.

Quarles (d. 1644): Shepherds Oracles. V

Judgment and Mercy for Afflicted Souls [partly pub. as Barnabas and Boanerges, 1644]. P

Shirley (1596): Poems [cont. Triumph of Beauty, a masque].

Suckling (d. 1642): Fragmenta Aurea [cont., among unpub. works, Session of the Poets, The Goblins, Letters, Account of Religion by Reason: see 1659, 1696].

Taylor (1613): Discourse Concerning Prayer. P

Vaughan, Henry (1622): Poems.

Selden, ' Uxor Ebraica'.

Jeremiah Rich and William Cartwright, ' Charactery' (see 1642).

Pierre Corneille, ' Rodogune'.

Rotrou, ' Saint Genest'.

Leibnitz b.

Bacon, Nathaniel (1593): Uniformity of Government of England from Edward III to Elizabeth [completed 1651]. P

Beaumont (d. 1616) **and Fletcher** (d. 1625): Comedies and Tragedies, ed. James Shirley [cont. thirty-four unpub. plays: see 1652, 1679].

Cleveland (1613): Character of a London Diurnall and other Poems. V

Corbet, Richard (d. 1635): Certain Elegant Poems [enlarg. 1672, 1807].

Cowley (1618): The Mistress. V

Fanshawe, Sir Richard: Trs. Pastor Fido of Guarini.

Fuller (1608): Cause and Cure of a Wounded Conscience. P

Good Thoughts in Worse Times. P

Hall, John (1627): Poems.

Hall, Joseph (1574): Hard Measures. P

May (1595): History of the Long Parliament. P

More (1614): Philosophical Poems [cont. enlarg. version of Song of the Soul, 1642].

Peacham, Henry, jnr.: Worth of a Penny [date probably misprint for 1641]. P

John Wilmot (Earl of Rochester) b.
Trs. Gomberville's ' Polexandre' by W. Browne (not the poet William Browne d. 1643?).
John Selden ed. 'Fleta' (written c. 1290).
Voiture d.
Scarron, 'Virgile Travesti'.
Mercurius Melancholicus, 1647–9.
Rotrou, 'Venceslas'.
La Calprenède,'Cléopâtre'.

1648

Beaumont, Joseph (1616): Psyche. V

Denham (1615): Cato Major [trs. Cicero]. V

Hall (1627): Satire against Presbytery. V

Emblems. V

Herrick (1591): Hesperides [incl. Noble Numbers; ed. Moorman 1915]. V

Hooker (d. 1600): Ecclesiastical Politie, bks. vi and viii [see 1594]. P

Raleigh (d. 1618): Arraignment and Conviction of ——, with a few letters. P

Stearne, John: Confirmation and Discovery of Witchcraft. P

Taylor (1613): Liberty of Prophesying. P

Wither (1588): Prosopopoeia Britannica. V

Elkanah Settle b.
Robert Barclay b.
Edward Herbert, Lord Herbert of Cherbury, d.
Society of Friends founded by George Fox between 1648 and 1650.

Cavendish, William, Duke of Newcastle: The Country Captain. The Varieties. C

D'Avenant (1606): Love and Honour. D

Donne (d. 1631): Fifty Sermons [see 1640]. P

Dryden (1631): Upon the Death of the Lord Hastings. V

Gauden, John (?): Eikon Basilike. P

Herbert, Edward, Lord Herbert of Cherbury (d. 1648): Life of Henry VIII. P

Howell (1594?): Description of the Country of Scotland. P

Lovelace (1618): Lucasta. V

Milton (1608): Tenure of Kings and Magistrates. P Eikonoklastes. P

Prynne (1600): Historical Collection of the Ancient Parliaments of England. P

R. B. (ed.): Lachrymae Musarum [poems on death of Lord Hastings by Dryden, Marvell, Herrick, and Denham].

Taylor (1613): The Great Exemplar. P

Execution of Charles I.
The Commonwealth.
William Drummond of Hawthornden d.
Richard Crashaw d.
John Ogilby trs. 'Virgil'.
Descartes, 'Traité des Passions'.
Scudéry, 'Le Grand Cyrus' (concl. 1653).

1650

Baron, Robert: Pocula Castalia. V

Baxter (1615): Saints' Everlasting Rest. P

Bradstreet, Anne (*c.* 1612): The Tenth Muse. V

Cowley (1618): The Guardian [see 1663]. C

Fuller (1608): Pisgah Sight of Palestine. P

Hall (1627): Paradoxes.

Heath, Robert: Clarastella. V

Hobbes (1588): Human Nature. P
De Corpore Politico, or Elements of Law, Moral and Politic. P

Raleigh (d. 1618): Judicious and Select Essays and Observations.

Satterstall, Wye: Picturæ Loquentes (characters). P

Taylor (1613): Rule and Exercises of Holy Living. P

Vaughan, Henry (1622): Silex Scintillans, [with pt. ii 1655]. V

Vaughan, Thomas (1622): Anthroposophia Theomagica. V

Weldon, Sir Anthony (d. 1649?): The Court & Character of King James I. P

Jeremy Collier b.
Phineas Fletcher d.
Thomas May d.
James Ussher, 'Annales Veteris Testamenti' (concl. 1654).
Mercurius Politicus, 1650–60.
Probable date of the MS. of Percy Folio: see 1765 (ed. Hales and Furnivall 1867).
Descartes d.
Pierre Corneille, 'Andromède'.

Cartwright, William (d. 1643): Comedies, Tragi-comedies, with other Poems [cont. Lady Errant, Royal Slave, The Ordinary, The Siege].

Cleveland (1613): Poems.

D'Avenant (1606): Gondibert [cont. D.'s Preface to Gondibert and Hobbes's Answer to it]. V

Denham (1615): Anatomy of Play. P

Donne (d. 1631): Essays in Divinity. P
Letters to Several Persons of Honour. P

Hobbes (1588): Leviathan. P
Philosophical Rudiments Concerning Government and Society [trs. De Cive, 1642]. P
Epistle to D'Avenant on Gondibert.

Laud (d. 1645): Sermons [see 1695].

Sherburne, Sir Edward: Salmacis. V

Stanley, Thomas: Collected Poems [original poems and translations, first pub. 1647–9–50: ed. Brydges 1814–15; ed. Guiney 1907].

Taylor (1613): Rule and Exercises of Holy Dying. P

Vaughan, Henry (1622): Olor Iscanus [collection of poems and translations]. P and V

Walton (1593): Life of Sir Henry Wotton [see below]. P

Wotton (d. 1639): Reliquiae Wottonianae, with Life of Wotton by Izaak Walton [3rd ed. enlarg. 1672; 4th ed. with further additions 1685].

Charles II crowned at Scone.
Battle of Worcester.
Nathanael Culverwel d.
William Harvey 'Exercitationes de generatione animalium' (see 1616, 1628).
John Ogilby trs. Aesop (pt. ii 1665).
Fénelon b.
Scarron, 'Roman Comique'.
Racan, 'Psaumes'.

1652

Ashmole, Elias: Theatrum Chemicum. P

Beaumont (d. 1616) **and Fletcher** (d. 1625): Wild Goose Chase. C

Benlowes, Edward: Theophila. V

Brome (d. 1652?): A Jovial Crew, or Merry Beggars. C

Culverwel (d. 1651): Of the Light of Nature. P

Donne (d. 1631): Paradoxes, Problems, Essays, Characters. P

Fanshawe, Sir Richard: Trs. Select Parts of Horace.

Greville (d. 1628): Life of Sir Philip Sidney. P

Hall (1627): Trs. Longinus on the Height of Eloquence. P

Herbert (d. 1633): Remains, ed. with Life by B. Oley [cont. A Priest to the Temple].

Heylyn (1600): Cosmographie [enlarg. through many edd. from Microcosmus, 1621].

Middleton (d. 1627): The Widow [with Jonson and Fletcher]. C

Tatham, John: The Scots Figgaries. C

Vaughan, Henry (1622): Mount of Olives. P and V

Thomas Otway b.
Nahum Tate b.
Richard Brome d.?
Dorothy Osborne's Letters, 1652–4 (first pub. 1888).
Pierre Corneille, 'Nicomède'.

1653

Basse, William (d. 1653?): Pastoráls and other Poems [ed. J. P. Collier 1870; Works ed. R. W. Bond 1893].

Brome (d. 1652?): Five New Plays [Mad Couple Well Matcht, Novella, Court Beggar, City Wit, Damoiselle].

Cleveland (1613): Poems [later important collections with additions 1659–77–87].

Hammond, Henry: Paraphrase and Annotations upon the New Testament.

Hookes, Nicholas (1628): Amanda. V

Middleton (d. 1627): Spanish Gipsie [with Rowley]. D tragi-comedy.

The Changeling [with Rowley]. T

More (1614): Antidote against Atheism. P

Conjectura Cabbalistica. P

Newcastle (1624?): Poems and Fancies [Select Poems, ed. Brydges 1813]. V

Philosophical Fancies. P

Shirley (1596): Six New Plays [the Brothers, Sisters, Doubtful Heir, Imposture, Cardinall, Court Secret].

Cupid and Death, a masque.

Taylor (1613): Two Discourses [Of Baptism, Of Prayer]. P

Eniautos . . . Sermons for all the Sundays in the Year [concl. 1656; enlarg. 1667–8]. P

Urquhart (1611): Trs. Rabelais, bks. i, ii [bk. iii 1693; 2nd ed. of bks. i, ii with introductory matter by P. A. Motteux 1694; complete version by Urquhart, Motteux, and others 1708]. P

Walton (1593): Compleat Angler [2nd ed., largely re-written, 1655; also 1661, 1668; pt. ii, being a treatise on fly-fishing by Charles Cotton 1676]. P

Cromwell Protector.
Nathaniel Lee b.?
John Oldham b.
Thomas D'Urfey b.
Roger North b.
Eng. trs. of Scudéry's 'Le Grand Cyrus' (1653–5).
Molière, 'L'Étourdi'.
Scarron, 'Don Japhet'.

1654

Chapman (d. 1634): Revenge for Honour. T

Alphonsus Emperor of Germany. T

Hobbes (1588): Of Liberty and Necessity [surreptitious]. P

Johnson, Edward (1589): History of New England. P

Orrery, Earl of (Roger Boyle) (1621): Parthenissa, pt. i [complete 1665]. P

Vaughan, Henry (1622): Flores Solitudinis [trs. religious tracts from Latin]. P

Walton, Brian (ed.): Polyglot Bible [concl. 1657].

Webster (d. 1625?): Appius and Virginia. T

John Selden d.
William Habington d.
Molière, 'Le Dépit Amoureux'.
Scudéry, 'Alaric', 'Clélie' (concl. 1660).
Cyrano, 'Le Pédant Joué'.

Cotgrave, John: English Treasury of Literature
and Language [miscellany].
  Wit's Interpreter: the English Parnassus [miscellany].

Davenport, Robert: King John and Matilda. T

Drummond (d. 1649): History of Scotland, 1423–
1524 [with Memorials of State, and other
prose works: see 1711]. P

Dugdale (1605): Monasticon Anglicanum [with
Roger Dodsworth; concl. 1673].

Fuller (1608): Church History of Britain. P
  History of Cambridge University. P
  History of Waltham Abbey. P

Hammond, William: Poems.

Heywood (d. 1641): Fortune by Land and Sea
[with Rowley]. D tragi-comedy.

Marvell (1621): First Anniversary of the Government under the Lord Protector. V

Massinger (d. 1640): Three New Plays [Bashful
Lover, Guardian, The Very Woman].

Newcastle (1624?): Philosophical and Physical
Opinions [see 1668]. P

Phillips (1631): Satyr against Hypocrites [called
Religion of the Hypocritical Presbyterians,
1661]. V

Shirley (1596): Gentleman of Venice. D tragi-comedy.
  The Polititian. T

Spottiswood, John (d. 1639): History of the
Church and State of Scotland. P

Stanley, Thomas: History of Philosophy, vol. i
[ii 1656, iii 1660, iv 1662, collected 1687]. P

Strode, William (d. 1645): The Floating Island.
D tragi-comedy.

Taylor (1613): Golden Grove [enlarged as Choyce
Manual 1677]. P

Vaughan, Henry (1622): Hermetical Physics [trs.
of Latin Tracts]. P
  Silex Scintillans, pts. i, ii [see 1650]. V

Waller (1606): Panegyric to my Lord Protector. V

Richard Blackmore b.?
Walter Charleton trs.
  Epicurus's 'Morals'.
Sir Richard Fanshawe
  trs. 'Lusiad' of Camoens.
John Davies of Kidwelly
  trs. Letters of Voiture.
Francis Junius's ed. of
  Caedmon pub. at Amsterdam.
Sir William Lower trs.
  'Polyeucte' of Pierre
  Corneille.
John Wallis, 'Arithmetica
  Infinitorum'.
Hobbes, 'Elementorum
  Philosophiae Sectio
  prima de Corpore' (Eng.
  trs. 1656: see 1658).

1656

Bunyan (1628): Some Gospel Truths opened. P

Collop, John: Poesis Rediviva. V

Cowley (1618): Poems [cont. Miscellaneous Poems,
Mistress (see 1647), Davideis, Pindarique
Odes; the last two now first pub.]

D'Avenant (1606): Siege of Rhodes made a representation by the art of perspective in scenes
[see 1663].

Denham (1615): Destruction of Troy [trs. Virgil:
with prefatory essay on Translation]. V

Gerard Langbaine b.
Joseph Hall d.
John Hall d.
John Hales d.
James Ussher d.
Milton's second marriage
  (with Catharine Woodcock).
'Parnassus Biceps'.
'Choyce Drollery'.
'Wit and Drollery'.

Drummond (d. 1649): Poems, ed. Edward Phillips [incl. many unpub. pieces: see 1711].

Dugdale (1605): Antiquities of Warwickshire. P

Ford (d. 1640?): The Sun's Darling [with Thomas Dekker]. D masque.

Harington (1611): Commonwealth of Oceana. P

Hobbes (1588): Questions concerning Liberty, Necessity and Chance. P

  Eng. trs. of Elementorum Philosophiae: De Corpore [original Latin 1655].

Massinger (d. 1640): Old Law [with Middleton and Rowley]. C

More (1614): Enthusiasmus Triumphatus. P

Newcastle (1624?): Nature's Pictures drawn by Fancy's Pencil [cont. Autobiography, reprtd. 1814: see 1667]. V

Osborne, Francis (1593): Advice to a Son [pt. ii 1658]. P

John Davies of Kidwelly trs. 'Clélie' of Scudéry.
Pascal, 'Lettres Provinciales'.
Chapelain, 'La Pucelle'.

1657

Baker, Augustine (d. 1641): Sancta Sophia [compiled out of B.'s treatises by S. Cressy]. P

Baxter (1615): Call to the Unconverted. P

Brome (d. 1652?): The Queen's Exchange. C

Carlell, Lodowick: The Fool would be a Favourite. D Osmond, the Great Turk. D

D'Avenant (1606): First Day's Entertainment at Rutland House. D show.

Hall, John (d. 1656): Hierocles upon the Golden Verses of Pythagoras, ed. with Life by John Davies of Kidwelly. V

Heylyn (1600): Ecclesia Vindicata. P

Howell (1594?): Londinopolis. P

King, Henry (1592): Poems [enlarg. 1664; Sacred Poems ed. Hannah 1843; Selected Poems ed. Tutin 1904, ed. Sparrow 1925].

Marlowe (d. 1593): Lust's Dominion [attrib. M. on the title-page; probably by Dekker, John Day, and William Haughton]. T

Middleton (d. 1627): No Wit, no Help like a Woman's. C

  Two New Plays [Women Beware Women, More Dissemblers besides Women]. C

Raleigh (d. 1618): Remains [enlarg. from collection of tracts pub. 1651, 1656]. P

Taylor, (1613): Discourse of Friendship. P Polemical and Moral Discourses. P

John Dennis b.
Matthew Tindal b.
John Norris b.
Richard Lovelace d.
William Harvey d.
Edward Sexby's tract, 'Killing no Murder'.
Joshua Poole, 'England's Parnassus'.
George Thornley trs. 'Daphnis and Chloe'.

Anon.: Whole Duty of Man [Lady Dorothy Pakington or Richard Allestree?]. P
Brathwaite (1558?): The Honest Ghost. V
Browne (1605): Hydriotaphia, or Urne-Buriall. Garden of Cyrus. P
Chamberlayne (1619): Love's Victory [called Wits led by the Nose 1678]. D tragi-comedy.
D'Avenant (1606): Cruelty of Spaniards in Peru [afterwards formed part of Playhouse to be Let, 1673]. D opera.
Dugdale (1605): History of St. Paul's Cathedral. P
Flecknoe, Richard: Enigmaticall Characters. P
Harrington (1611): Prerogative of Popular Government. P
Massinger (d. 1640): City Madam. C
May (d. 1650): The Old Couple, a comedy. D
Raleigh (d. 1618): Cabinet Council [pub. by Milton]. P
Rowley (d. 1642?): Witch of Edmonton [with Dekker and Ford]. D tragi-comedy.
Ussher (d. 1656): Annals of the World [trs. of Latin Works first pub. 1650, 1654]. P
Waller (1606): Passion of Dido for Æneas [with Sidney Godolphin]. V

Richard Cromwell Protector.
Oliver Cromwell d.
John Cleveland d.
William London, 'Catalogue of most vendible books in England' (supplement 1660).
Edward Phillips, 'New World of Words' (enlarg. ed. Kersey 1700, 1706, 1720).
Hobbes, 'Elementorum Philosophiae, sectio secunda de Homine' (see 1655).
'Wit Restor'd' (anthology).

1659

Baxter (1615): Holy Commonwealth. P
Brome (d. 1652?): Five New Plays [English Moor, Lovesick Court, Covent Garden Weeded, New Academy, Queen and Concubine].
Chamberlayne (1619): Pharonnida. V
Cleveland (d. 1658): John Cleveland revived [poems, orations, epistles, &c.]. V
D'Avenant (1606): History of Sir Francis Drake, expressed by instrumental and vocal music [afterwards formed part of Playhouse to be Let, 1673]. D opera.
Day, John: Blind Beggar of Bednal Green. C
Dryden (1631): Poem upon the Death of his late Highness Oliver Lord Protector. V
Evelyn (1620): Character of England. P
Trs. Golden Book of St. Chrysostom. P
Fuller (1608): Appeal of Injured Innocence. P
Hales (d. 1656): Golden Remains [enlarg. 1673].
Harrington (1611): Aphorisms Political [n.d.]. P
Art of Lawgiving [abridgement of Oceana]. P
Lovelace (d. 1657): Posthume Poems.

James Harrington's club, the Rota, meets in Miles's Coffee-house in Palace Yard, London, 1659–60.
John Rushworth, 'Collection of State Papers, 1618–48' (concl. 1701; 2nd ed. 1721).
William Somner's 'Dictionarium Saxonico-Latino-Anglicum'.
Molière, 'Les Précieuses ridicules'.
Pierre Corneille, 'Oedipe'.

Mayne (1604): The Amorous War. D tragi-
comedy.

Milton (1608): Treatise of Civil Power in Ecclesiastical Causes. P

Likeliest Means to remove Hirelings out of the
Church. P

More (1614): Immortality of the Soul. P

Pearson, John: Exposition of the Creed. P

Shirley (1596): Honoria and Mammon. D

Contention of Ajax and Achilles [contains The
glories of our blood and state]. D

Stillingfleet (1635): Irenicum. P

Suckling (d. 1642): Last Remains [cont. unpub.
poems, letters, and the unfinished tragedy
The Sad One: see 1646, 1696].

Waller (1606): Upon the late Storm and Death of
His Highness. V

1660

Boyle (1627): New Experiments Physico-Mech-
anical. P

Cary, Lucius, Viscount Falkland (d. 1643): Discourse of Infallibility. P

Donne (d. 1631): XXVI Sermons [see 1640]. P

Dryden (1631): Astraea Redux. V

Fuller (1608): Alarum to the Counties of England
and Wales. P

Mixt Contemplations in Better Times. P

Hall, Joseph (d. 1656): Shaking of the Olive Tree
[collection of posthumous pieces: see 1621,
1662].

Harrington (1611): Political Discourses. P

Howard, Sir Robert (1626): Poems.

Milton (1608): Ready and Easy Way to establish
a Free Commonwealth. P

Present Means and Brief Delineation of a Free
Commonwealth. P

More (1614): Grand Mystery of Godliness. P

Phillips (1631): Montelion, 1660; or the Propheti-
cal Almanack. V

Pordage, Samuel (1633): Poems. V

Smith, John (d. 1652): Select Discourses. P

Tatham, John: The Rump. C

Taylor (1613): Ductor Dubitantium. P

Worthy Communicant. P

Ussher (d. 1656): Chronologia Sacra. P

Winstanley, William: England's Worthies [rev.
1684]. P

*The Restoration: Charles
II King.*
Thomas Southerne b.
Peter Anthony Motteux b.
Sir Thomas Urquhart d.
*Patents for re-opening
theatres granted to
Thomas Killigrew (sr.)
and Sir William D'Ave-
nant: the King's and the
Duke of York's com-
panies formed.*
*Establishment of the Royal
Society (charter granted
1662).*
*Pepys (b. 1633) begins
Diary on 1 Jan. (ends
31 May 1669; first pub.
1825).*
*Imprisonment of Bunyan,
1660–72.*
*Hobbes, 'Examinatio et
Emendatio'.*
John Ogilby trs. 'Iliad'.
Scarron d.
Molière, 'Sganarelle'.
*Corneille, 'La Toison
d'or'.*
Scudéry, 'Almahide'.

Anon.: Tom Tyler and his Wife [performed *c.*
1540]. D interlude.
Boyle (1627): The Sceptical Chymist. P
Davenport, Robert: The City Night Cap. D
Dryden (1631): To His Sacred Majesty. V
Evelyn (1620): Fumifugium. P
Flecknoe, Richard: Erminia. D tragi-comedy.
Glanvill (1636): Vanity of Dogmatising [recast
as Scepsis Scientifica 1665]. P
Graunt, John: Natural and Political Observations
on the Bills of Mortality. P
Heylyn (1600): Ecclesia Restaurata. P
Mackenzie, Sir George (1636): Aretina. P
Middleton (d. 1627): Mayor of Quinborough
[acted *c.* 1596]. C
Waller (1606): St. James's Park. V
To my Lady Morton. V
Webster (d. 1625?) **and Rowley** (d. 1626): Two
New Plays [Cure for a Cuckold, The Thra-
cian Wonder]. C

Daniel Defoe b.?
*Anne Finch (Countess of
Winchilsea) b.*
Sir Samuel Garth b.
Thomas Fuller d.
*Boyle's Law of Compres-
sibility.*
*Hobbes, 'Dialogus Physi-
cus'.*
'Wit and Drollery'.
'Merry Drollery'.
*La Calprenède, 'Phara-
mond'.*
*Molière, 'Don Garcie du
Navarre', 'L'École des
maris', 'Les Fâcheux'.*

1662

The Prayer Book [final version: see 1549].
Baker, Sir Richard (d. 1645): Theatrum Redivi-
vum [reply to Prynne's Histrio-Mastix]. P
Butler (1612): Hudibras, pt. i [bears date 1663;
really end of 1662: see 1663, 1678].
Dryden (1631): To My Lord Chancellor. V
Dugdale (1605): History of Imbanking and
Draining of Fens and Marshes. P
Evelyn (1620): Sculptura. P
Fuller (d. 1661): Worthies of England. P
Glanvill (1636): Lux Orientalis. P
Hall (d. 1656): Works [fuller collection ed. J.
Pratt 1808; Peter Hall 1837; P. Wynter
1863: see 1621].
Haughton, William: Grim the Collier of Croydon
[performed *c.* 1600]. C
Hobbes (1588): Considerations upon the Reputa-
tions, Loyalty, Manners and Religion of —. P
Hooker (d. 1600): Works, ed. with Life by Gauden
[re-issued with Life by Izaak Walton 1666;
with corrections by Strype 1705; ed. Ran-
dolph 1793; Dobson 1825; Hanbury 1831;
Keble 1836; R. W. Church 1888: see 1594].
Middleton (d. 1627): Anything for a Quiet Life. C
Newcastle (1624?): Plays [21 plays: see 1668].
Petty (1623): Treatise of Taxes and Contributions. P
Rowley (d. 1626): Birth of Merlin [alleged contri-
bution by Shakespeare: see 1597]. C
Stillingfleet (1635): Origines Sacrae. P
Winstanley, William: Loyal Martyrology. P

Act of Uniformity.
*Royal Society's First
Charter.*
Richard Bentley b.
Francis Atterbury b.
Peter Heylyn d.
*Milton's third marriage
(with Elizabeth Min-
shull).*
*The series of anon. verse
almanacks and chap-
books, 'Poor Robin's Al-
manack or Complaint',
begins to appear (origi-
nator probably William
Winstanley; continued
by various hands to
1776).*
Pascal d.
*Molière, 'L'École des
femmes'.*

74

Boyle (1627): Considerations concerning the Use-fulness of Experimental Philosophy. P

Butler (1612): Hudibras, pt. ii [bears date 1664; really end of 1663: see 1662, 1678]. V

Cowley (1618): Cutter of Coleman Street [new version of The Guardian 1650]. C

Verses upon several occasions.

Davenant (1606): Siege of Rhodes, pt. i, ii [see 1656]. D opera.

Philips (1631): Pompey [trs. Corneille]. D

Shakespeare (d. 1616): Third Folio [two issues, the 2nd dated 1664: cont. Pericles (first pub. 1609) and the following spurious plays not in First Folio:—London Prodigal (first pub. 1605), Chronicle History of Thomas Lord Cromwell (1602), Sir John Oldcastle (1600), The Puritan (1607), Yorkshire Tragedy (1608), Tragedy of Locrine (1595): see 1623].

Stapylton, Sir Robert: Slighted Maid. C

Tuke, Sir Samuel: Adventures of Five Hours. C

Thomas Brown of Shifnal b.
Roger L'Estrange starts 'The Intelligencer' (concl. 1666).
Edward Somerset, Marquis of Worcester, 'Century of Inventions'.
La Calprenède d.

1664

Boyle (1627): Experiments concerning Colour. P

Cary, Henry, Viscount Falkland (d. 1633): The Marriage Night. C

Cotton (1630): Scarronides, or first Book of Virgil Travestie [enlarg. 1670]. V

Dryden (1631): Rival Ladies [with prefatory defence of rhyme in tragedy]. D tragi-comedy.

Etherege (1635?): Comical Revenge. C

Evelyn (1620): Sylva [enlarg. 1670, 1679, 1706; with other works on gardening 1729]. P

Flecknoe, Richard: Love's Kingdom, a tragi-comedy [cont. Short Discourse on the English Stage].

Jordan (1612?): A Royall Arbour of Loyall Poesie. V

Killigrew (1612): Comedies and Tragedies [cont., besides those of 1641: the Princess, The Parson's Wedding, The Pilgrim, Cicilia and Clorinda, Thomaso, Bellamira].

Killigrew, Sir William (1606?): Three Plays [Selindra, Pandora, Ormasdes; Four Plays, adding Siege of Urbin, 1666].

More (1614): Mystery of Iniquity. P

Mun, Thomas (d. 1641): England's Treasure by foreign trade [written *c.* 1630].

Patrick, Simon: Parable of the Pilgrim. P

Stapylton, Sir Robert: The Stepmother. D

Tillotson (1630): Wisdom of being religious. P

Wilson, John (1626): The Cheats. C

Waller (1606): Poems [supposed first authorized collection: see 1645].

Sir John Vanbrugh b.
Matthew Prior b.
Katherine Philips ('Matchless Orinda') d.
Francis Junius, 'Gothicum Glossarium'.
Racine, 'La Thébaide'.

Bunyan (1628): The Holy City. P

Burnet (1643): Discourse on Sir Robert Fletcher of Saltoun. P

Crowne, John: Pandion and Amphigenia. P

Head, Richard (?): The English Rogue. P

Herbert of Cherbury (d. 1648): Poems [ed. G. C. Moore-Smith 1923].

Howard, Sir Robert: Four Plays [the Surprisal, The Committee, The Vestal Virgin, and The Indian Queen, written with Dryden: cont. Preface starting controversy on dramatic poetry with Dryden].

Jordan (1612?): Pictures of Passions, Fancies, and Affections. V

Lloyd, David (1635): Statesmen and Favourites of England [ed. with additions by Charles Whitworth and called State Worthies 1766]. P

Marvell (1621): Character of Holland. V

Sprat (1635): Observations on Monsieur de Sorbier's Voyage into England [Sorbière's book was pub. in 1664]. P

Stevenson, Matthew (1627): Poems. V

Waller (1606): Upon Her Majesty's new Building at Somerset House. P

Walton (1593): Life of Richard Hooker. P

Wilson, John (1626): The Projectors. C

Charles Gildon b.
Sir Kenelm Digby d.
John Earle d.
The Great Plague.
Henry Muddiman starts 'The London Gazette' (nos. 1–23 called Oxford Gazette).
John Phillips trs. Scarron's 'Typhon'.
Robert Hooke, 'Micrographia'.
John Ogilby trs. 'Odyssey'.
Molière, 'Don Juan'.
La Rochefoucauld, 'Maximes'.
Francis Junius, ed. of the Moeso-Gothic Text of Ulphilas.

1666

Boyle (1627): Origin of Forms and Qualities. P
Hydrostatical Paradoxes. P

Bunyan (1628): Grace Abounding. P

Glanvill (1636): Philosophical Considerations concerning Witches and Witchcraft (4th ed. Blow at Modern Sadducism 1668; 5th ed. Sadducismus Triumphatus 1681]. P

Tillotson (1630): Rule of Faith. P

Waller (1606): Instructions to a Painter. V

James Shirley d.
James Howell d.
Thomas Vaughan d.
Fire of London.
Boileau, 'Satires'.
Molière,' Le Misanthrope', 'Le Médecin malgré lui'.
Furetière, 'Roman bourgeois'.

1667

Cavendish, George: Life and Death of Thomas Woolsey [see 1641]. P

Davies, John, of Kidwelly: Trs. Novels of Scarron [collected: separately 1657, 1662]. P

Denham (1615): Instructions to a Painter. V

Dryden (1631): Annus Mirabilis.
Indian Emperor [sequel to Indian Queen: see Howard 1665]. T

Flecknoe, Richard: Damoiselles a la Mode. C

Laud (d. 1645): Sum of Devotions [complete: parts in 1650, 1663]. P

Jonathan Swift b.
John Arbuthnot b.
Susannah Centlivre b.?
George Granville b.
William Whiston b.
Jeremy Taylor d.
George Wither d.
Abraham Cowley d.
Racine, 'Andromaque'.
Molière, 'Tartuffe'.

Marvell (1621): Clarendon's House-Warming [in Denham's Instructions above].

Milton (1608): Paradise Lost [in 10 books; 5th issue of 1st ed., cont. the paragraph 'Verse' defending absence of rhyme, 1668 (?); 2nd ed., rev. and rearranged in 12 books, 1674]. V

More (1614): Enchiridion Ethicum. P

Newcastle (1624?): Life of William Cavendish, Duke of Newcastle [ed. with Autobiography of the Duchess (see 1656) by M. A. Lower 1872; ed. C. H. Firth 1886]. P

Philips (d. 1664): Collected Works. V

Sprat (1635): History of the Royal Society. P

1668

Child, Sir Josiah: A New Discourse of Trade. P

Cowley (d. 1667): Works, ed. Thomas Sprat [cont. Poems of 1656 and Verses upon Several Occasions of 1663, Essays in Prose and Verse now first pub.; pt. ii of Works added 1681; 7th ed. of Works incorporating additions in successive edd. up to date 1707; Works ed. Grosart 1876–9; ed. Waller 1905–6].

D'Avenant (d. 1668): The Rivals, a comedy.

Denham (1615): Collected Poems [later edd.: 1671–6–84–1709].

Dryden (1631): Sir Martin Mar-all. C

Secret Love. D tragi-comedy.

Essay of Dramatick Poesie. P

Defence of Essay of Dramatick Poesie [in 2nd ed. of Indian Emperor: see 1667]. P

Etherege (1635?): She wou'd if she cou'd. C

Glanvill (1636): Plus Ultra, or Progress of Knowledge since Aristotle. P

Blow at Modern Sadducism [see 1666, 1681]. P

Heylyn (d. 1662): Cyprianus Anglicanus [Life of Archbishop Laud]. P

Howard, Sir Robert: The Great Favourite. D

Jordan, Thomas: Money is an Asse. C

More (1614): Divine Dialogues [best ed. 1713]. P

Newcastle (1624?): Plays never before printed [cont. five plays: see 1662].

Grounds of Natural Philosophy [altered ed. of Philosophical and Physical Opinions 1655]. P

Orrery (1621): History of Henry V. D

Tragedy of Mustapha. D

Penn (1644): Sandy Foundation Shaken. P

Truth Exalted. P

Sedley (1639?): Mulberry Garden. C

Shadwell (1642?): Sullen Lovers. C

Wilkins, John: Essay towards a Real Character and a Philosophical Language. P

Sir William D'Avenant d.
Dryden poet-laureate.
William Penn committed to the Tower (released 1669).
Term Catalogues Commence (concl. 1709; ed. Arber 1903–6).
First instalment of Robert Clavell's Catalogue of Books published from 1666 to 1700 (series completed 1700).
Roger L'Estrange trs. 'Visions' of Quevedo.
Lesage b.
La Fontaine, 'Fables', pt. i.
Molière, 'Amphitryon', 'L'Avare'.
Racine, 'Les Plaideurs'.
Grimmelshausen, 'Simplicius Simplicissimus'.

Burnet (1643): Conference between a Conformist and a Nonconformist. P

Chamberlayne, Edward: Angliae Notitiae, or Present State of England. P (Frequent editions until 1755.)

D'Avenant (d. 1668): The Man's the Master. C

Dryden (1631): The Wild Gallant. C

Orrery (1621): The Black Prince. Tryphon. T

Penn (1644): No Cross No Crown. P
  Innocency with her Open Face. P

Shadwell (1642?): Royal Shepherdess. D

Sir John Denham d.
William Prynne d.
Pepys's Diary ends on 31 May (see 1660).
University Press at Oxford housed in the Sheldonian Theatre: moved to new habitation and called Clarendon Press 1713.
Milton, 'Latin Grammar'.
John Wallis, 'Mechanica' (concl. 1671).
Racine, 'Britannicus'.
Molière, 'Monsieur de Pourceaugnac'.
Bossuet, 'Oraison funèbre de la reine d'Angleterre'.

1670

Baxter (1615): Life of Faith. P

Dryden (1631): The Tempest [altered from Shakespeare: with D'Avenant]. C
  Tyrannick Love. T

Greville, Sir Fulke (Lord Brooke) (d. 1628): Remains [complete works ed. Grosart 1870].

Milton (1608): History of Britain. P

Heylyn (d. 1662): Aerius Redivivus, or History of Presbyterianism. P

Parker, Samuel: Discourse of Ecclesiastical Polity [Defence and Continuation 1671]. P 1671]. P

Walton (1593): Life of George Herbert. P
  Lives of Donne, Wotton, Hooker, and Herbert [collected].

William Congreve b.
John Toland b.
Bernard Mandeville b.?
Laurence Echard b.?
Pascal, 'Pensées'.
Molière, 'Le Bourgeois gentilhomme', 'Les Amants magnifiques'.
Racine, 'Bérénice'.
Corneille, 'Tite et Bérénice'.
Mme de La Fayette, 'Zaïde'.
Ray, 'A Collection of English Proverbs'.

1671

Behn (1640): Forc'd Marriage. D tragi-comedy.

Bunyan (1628): Confession of my Faith. P

Collins, Samuel: Present State of Russia in a Letter to a Friend in London. P

Crowne, John: Juliana. T

Dryden (1631): An Evening's Love. C

Howard, Edward: Women's Conquest. D
  Six Days' Adventure. D

Milton (1608): Paradise Regained. Samson Agonistes. V

Settle (1648): Cambyses King of Persia. T

Shadwell (1642?): The Humorists. C

Anthony Ashley Cooper, third Earl of Shaftesbury b.
Colley Cibber b.
'Westminster Drollery'.
'Windsor Drollery'.
'Oxford Drollery'.
Molière, 'Psyché', 'Les Fourberies de Scapin'.
Corneille, 'Psyché'.
Bossuet, 'Exposition de la Foi catholique'.
Mme de Sévigné, first series of letters to Mme de Grignan.

Ashmole (1617): Institution, Laws, Ceremonies of the Order of the Garter [with Continuation by T. Walker as History of the Order of the Garter 1715]. P

Buckingham (1628) **and others**: The Rehearsal [with a 'Key' 1709]. D burlesque.

Cave, William: Primitive Christianity. P

Dryden (1631): Conquest of Granada; pt. i, ii [pt. ii called Almanzor and Almahide: cont. Essay on Heroic Plays and Essay on Dramatic Poetry of the Last Age]. T

Josselyn, John: New England's Rarities Discovered. P

Lacy, John: The Old Troop, or Monsieur Ragout. C The Dumb Lady. C

Marvell (1621): The Rehearsal Transpros'd [pt. ii 1673]. P

Phillips (1631): Maronides, or Virgil Travesty [an enlarged 2nd ed. 1673]. V

Ravenscroft, Edward: Citizen turned Gentleman [called Mamamouchi 1675]. C

Shadwell (1642): The Miser. C

Temple (1628): Observations upon the United Provinces of the Netherlands. P

Wycherley (1640?): Love in a Wood. C

Joseph Addison b.
Richard Steele b.
Jasper Mayne d.
'Covent Garden Drollery'.
Hobbes, 'Lux Mathematica'.
Cumberland's 'De Legibus Naturae Disquisitio Philosophica'.
Racine, 'Bajazet'.
Molière, 'Les Femmes Savantes'.

1673

Behn (1640): The Dutch Lover. C

Burnet (1643): Mystery of Iniquity Unveiled. P

D'Avenant (d. 1668): Collected Works [incl. unpub. poems and following unpub. plays; News from Plymouth, Fair Favourite, Distresses, The Siege, Law against Lovers, and Playhouse to be let].

Dryden (1631): Marriage à la mode. C
  The Assignation. C
  Amboyna. T

Milton (1608): Poems upon various occasions [a revision, with additions, of 1645; all the minor poems except those of 1694: see 1645].

Pordage, Samuel: Herod and Mariamne. T

Ravenscroft, Edward: Careless Lovers. D

Settle (1648): Empress of Morocco. T

Shadwell (1642?): Epsom Wells. C

Wycherley (1640?): Gentleman Dancing Master. C

John Oldmixon b.
'Holborn Drollery'.
'Norfolk Drollery'.
'London Drollery'.
Molière d.
Molière, 'Malade Imaginaire'.
Racine, 'Mithridate'.

Cotton (1630): Complete Gamester. P
D'Avenant (d. 1668): Macbeth [made into opera].
Flatman, Thomas: Poems and Songs [enlarged ed. 1686].
Hammond, Henry (d. 1660): Collected Works, ed. W. Fulman [concl. 1684; ed. Pocock 1847–50].
Hobbes (1588): Trs. Odyssey [with Iliad 1675; cont. Essay on Vertues of an Heroique Poem]. V
Howard, James: English Mounsieur. C
Josselyn, John: Two Voyages to New England. P
Milton (1608): Paradise Lost [2nd ed., in 12 books; see 1667]. V
Epistolarum Familiarium Liber unus. P
Rymer (1641): Reflections on Aristotle's Treatise of Poesie [trs. of Rapin]. P
Shadwell (1642): The Tempest [made into opera].

Isaac Watts b.
Nicholas Rowe b.
John Milton d.
Robert Herrick d.
Thomas Traherne d.
Edward Hyde, first Earl of Clarendon d.
Margaret Cavendish, Duchess of Newcastle, d.
Dryden, Shadwell, and Crowne attack Settle in 'Notes and Observations on the Empress of Morocco'.
Settle replies in 'Notes and Observations on the Empress of Morocco revised'.
Anthony à Wood, 'Historia et Antiquitates Universitatis Oxoniensis' (Eng. trs. by Wood 1791–6).
Boileau, 'Lutrin', 'Art Poétique'.
Racine, 'Iphigénie'.
Malebranche, 'Recherche de la verité'.
Giambattista Basile, 'Il Pentamerone'.

1675

Barnes, Joshua: Gerania, or the Discovery of a little sort of people called Pygmies. P
Cotton (1630): Planter's Manual. P
Burlesque upon Burlesque. V
Crowne, John: The Country Wits. C
Calisto. D opera. Andromache. T
Lee (1653?): Tragedy of Nero. T
Leigh, Richard (1649): Poems. V
Marvell (1621): Dialogue between Two Horses. V
Otway (1652): Alcibiades. T
Phillips, Edward: Theatrum Poetarum. P
Settle (1648): Love and Revenge. T
Shadwell (1642?): Psyche. D opera.
Traherne (d. 1674): Christian Ethics. P
Wycherley (1640?): Country Wife. C

William Somerville b.
Ambrose Philips b. ?
Bulstrode Whitelocke d.
Sir William Dugdale, 'Baronage of England' (concl. 1676).
William Higford (?), 'The Courtier's Calling'.
'The City Mercury' started by Roger L'Estrange (?).
John Ogilby, 'Book of Roads'.
Saint-Simon b.

Barclay, Robert (1648): Apology. P
Cotton (1630): Part II of Walton's Compleat Angler [see 1653]. P
Dryden (1631): Aureng-Zebe. T
Etherege (1635?): Man of Mode. C
Glanvill (1636): Essays on Several Important Subjects. P
Lee (1653?): Sophonisba. T
  Gloriana. T
Otway (1652): Don Carlos. T
Settle (1648): Conquest of China. T
Shadwell (1642?): The Libertine. C
  The Virtuoso. C

John Philips b.
Benjamin Hoadly b.
Sir Matthew Hale d.

1677

Banks, John: Rival Kings. T
Behn (1640): The Rover [see 1681]. C
  The Debauchee. C
  The Town-Fopp. C. Abdelazer. T
Cavendish, William, Duke of Newcastle (d. 1676): Triumphant Widow. C
  Humorous Lovers. C
Cleveland (d. 1658): Clevelandi Vindiciae. V
Crowne, John: Destruction of Jerusalem. T
Davenant, Charles: Circe. D
Dryden (1631): State of Innocence. D opera.
D'Urfey (1653): Madam Fickle. C
  Fond Husband, or The Plotting Sisters. C
Hales (d. 1656): Several Tracts. P
  Sermons preached at Eton. P
Hubbard, William (c. 1621): Troubles with the Indians. P
Lee (1653?): Rival Queens. T
Mather, Increase (1639): The Troubles that have happened in New England. P
Otway (1652): Titus and Berenice. Cheats of Scapin [adapt. Racine and Molière]. D
Plot, Robert (1640): Natural History of Oxfordshire. P
Ravenscroft, Edward: Scaramouch. C
  King Edgar and Alfreda. D tragi-comedy.
  Wrangling Lovers. C
Sedley (1639?): Antony and Cleopatra. T
Settle (1648): Ibrahim, the Illustrious Bassa. T
  Pastor Fido. D pastoral.
Tate, Nahum (1652): Poems. V
Waller (1606): Of the Lady Mary. V
Webster, John (1610): Displaying of Supposed Witchcraft. P
Wycherley (1640?): The Plain Dealer. C

James Harrington d.
Isaac Barrow d.
William Cave, 'Apostolici or History of Martyrdoms'.
John Phillips's trs. of La Calprenède's 'Pharamond', Scudéry's 'Almahide', and Six Voyages of Tavernier's 'Voyages'.
Racine, 'Phèdre'.
Spinoza d.
Spinoza, 'Ethics'.

Barclay (1648): Apology for the True Christian Divinity. P
Barrow (d. 1677): Sermons on Various Occasions.
Behn (1640): Sir Patient Fancy. C
Bunyan (1628): Pilgrim's Progress, pt. i [ii 1684]. P
Butler (1612): Hudibras, pt. iii [see 1662, 1663]. V
Calderwood, David (d. 1650): History of the Church of Scotland. P
Cudworth (1617): True Intellectual System of the Universe. P
Dryden (1631): All for Love. T
D'Urfey (1653): Fool turn'd Critick. C
Trick for Trick. C
Hobbes (1588): Decameron Physiologicum. P
Lee (1653?): Mithridates. T
Marvell (d. 1678): Advice to a Painter [n.d.]. V
Otway (1652): Friendship in Fashion. C
Pordage, Samuel: Siege of Babylon. T
Ravenscroft, Edward: English Lawyer. C
Rymer (1641): Tragedies of the Last Age Considered. P
Edgar, an Heroick Tragedy. T
Shadwell (1642?): Timon of Athens [adapt. Shakespeare]. T
Spelman, Sir John (d. 1643): Life of Alfred the Great [Latin trans. ed., with additions, Hearne 1709]. P
Tate, Nahum: Brutus of Alba. T
Vaughan, Henry (1622): Thalia Rediviva. V
Walton (1593): Life of Dr. Sanderson. P

The Popish Plot.
Henry St. John (Viscount Bolingbroke) b.
George Farquhar b.
Andrew Marvell d.
Henry Cave starts 'The Pacquet of Advice from Rome' (weekly 1678–83).
Narcissus Luttrell's 'Brief Historical Relations' begun (concl. 1714; pub. 1857).
Bossuet, 'Politique', c. 1678.
La Fontaine, 'Fables', pt. ii 1678–9.
Mme de La Fayette,' Princesse de Clèves'.

1679

Bancroft, John: Tragedy of Sertorius. T
Banks, John: Destruction of Troy. T
Beaumont (d. 1616) and Fletcher (d. 1625): Fifty Comedies and Tragedies [cont. all plays and masques pub. in 1647 and 1652 and others previously pub. but not collected. Works, ed. Theobald, Seward, and Sympson 1750; Colman 1778; Weber 1812 (The Faithful Friend first appears here); Darley 1840; Dyce 1843–6; A. H. Bullen and others 1904 ff. (variorum ed.); Glover and Waller 1905 ff.].
Behn (1640): The Feign'd Courtezans. C
Burnet (1643): History of the Reformation, pt. i [ii 1681; iii 1714; ed. Pococke 1865]. P
Crowne, John: Ambitious Statesman. D
Dryden (1631): Oedipus [with Nat. Lee]. T
Troilus and Cressida [adapt. Shakespeare; with Preface concerning grounds of criticism in Tragedy]. T

Thomas Parnell b.
Charles Johnson b.
Thomas Hobbes d.
Roger Boyle, Earl of Orrery, d.
On 18 Dec. Dryden assaulted by hired men in Rose Alley, Covent Garden (D. wrongly supposed to have been author of Mulgrave's Essay on Satyr in which Rochester had been satirized).
Collected ed. of the ' Year Books'.
Benjamin Harris starts 'The Domestic Intelligencer'.
Licensing Act expires.

D'Urfey (1653): Squire Oldsapp. C
Oldham (1653): Garnet's Ghost. V
Shadwell (1642?): A True Widow. C
South (1634): Sermons [concl. in six volumes, 1715; another vol. with memoirs and account of Travel in Poland with Rochester 1717; five more in 1744]. P

1680

Barrow (d. 1677): Treatise of the Pope's Supremacy, ed. John Tillotson. P
Blount, Charles: Two First Books of Apollonius Tyaneus. P
  Great is Diana of the Ephesians. P
Bunyan (1628): Life and Death of Mr. Badman. P
Burnet (1643): Passages of the Life and Death of the Earl of Rochester. P
Dillon, Wentworth, Earl of Roscommon (1633?): trs. Horace's Art of Poetry. V
Dryden (1631): The Kind Keeper. C
  Trs. Ovid's Epistles [with others]. V
D'Urfey (1653): The Virtuous Wife. C
Filmer, Sir Robert (d. 1653): Patriarcha, or the Power of Kings [cont. other treatises]. P
Hobbes (d. 1679): Historical Narrative concerning Heresy. P
Lee (1653?): Caesar Borgia. T
  Theodosius. T
L'Estrange (1616): Trs. Select Colloquies of Erasmus [enlarg. 1689]. P
Otway (1652): History and Fall of Caius Marius. T
  The Orphan. T
  Poet's Complaint of his Muse. V
Radcliffe, Alexander: Ovid Travestie. V
  Bacchanalia Caelestia. V
Rochester (d. 1680): Poems by the E—— of R—— [surreptitious].
Settle (1648): Female Prelate. T
  Fatal Love. T
Shadwell (1642?): Woman Captain. C
Tate, Nahum: Loyal General. T
Temple (1628): Miscellanea, pt. i [cont., among others, Essay on Government, Survey of the Constitution: see 1692, 1701]. P

Samuel Butler d.
John Wilmot, Earl of Rochester, d.
Joseph Glanvill d.
La Rochefoucauld d.
Fénelon, 'Dialogues sur l'Eloquence' (concl. 1690).
'A compleat catalogue of all the stitch'd books and single sheets printed since the first discovery of the Popish Plot.'

Behn (1640): The Rover, pt. ii [see 1677]. C
Cotton (1630): Wonders of the Peak. V
Cowley (d. 1667): Collected Works, pt. ii [see 1668].
Crowne, John: Henry the Sixth, pt. i. T
   Thyestes. T
Dryden (1631): Absalom and Achitophel, pt. i
   [see 1682]. V.   Spanish Friar. C
D'Urfey (1653): Sir Barnaby Whigg. C
Glanvill (d. 1680): Sadducismus Triumphatus [see
   1666, 1668]. P
Heylyn (d. 1662): Historical and Miscellaneous
   Tracts. P
Hobbes (d. 1679): Behemoth [first authoritative
   ed.; surreptitious ed. 1679]. P
   Dialogue between a Philosopher and a Student
   of Common Law. P
   Art of Rhetoric. P
Lee (1653?): Lucius Junius Brutus. T
Marvell (d. 1678): Miscellaneous Poems [later edd:
   Cooke 1726; with unpub. letters, prose
   tracts, and poems 1776 (ed. Thompson);
   Works ed. Grosart 1872–5; Poems and Satires
   ed. Aitken 1892; Poems and Letters ed. Mar-
   goliouth 1927].
Oldham (1653): Satyrs upon the Jesuits. Satire
   against Virtue. V [unauthorized edd. of parts
   of it 1679, 1680].
   Horace's Art of Poetry imitated. V
Otway (1652): The Souldiers Fortune. C
Tate, (1652): History of King Richard the
   Second. T
   King Lear [adapt. Shakespeare]. T

*Roger L'Estrange starts
'The Observator' (13
Apr. 1681 to 9 March
1687).*
*Bossuet, 'Histoire Uni-
verselle'.*
Calderon d.
*Thomas Burnet, 'Telluris
Theoria Sacra' (Eng-
lish Version, 1684–89).*
*Stair, 'Institutions of the
Law of Scotland'.*

1682

Banks, John: Unhappy Favourite. T
   Virtue Betray'd. T
Behn (1640): The Roundheads. C
   The City-Heiress. C.   The False Count. C
Bunyan (1628): The Holy War. P
Burnet (1643): Life and Death of Sir Matthew
   Hale. P
Coppinger, Matthew: Poems.
Dryden (1631): The Medall. V
   Religio Laici. V.   Mac Flecknoe. V
   Absalom and Achitophel, pt. ii [with Nahum
   Tate: see 1681]. V
D'Urfey (1653): The Injur'd Princess. T
   The Royalist. D tragi-comedy.
   Butler's Ghost, or Hudibras, the fourth part. V
   Wit and Mirth, or Pills to purge Melancholy [an-
   thology of poems and songs; other volumes
   1699, 1700, 1706, 1710; final ed. 1719–20].

Sir Thomas Browne d.
*William Cave, 'Eccle-
siastici' (writings and
Lives of Fathers of the
Church).*
'Wit and Drollery.'
*Thomas Creech trs. Lu-
cretius.*
*Nehemiah Grew, 'Ana-
tomy of Plants'.*
*John Ray, 'Methodus
Plantarum Nova'.*
*John Nalson, 'Impartial
Collection of the Great
Affairs of State'.*
*Sir Simonds D'Ewes,
'Journal of all the Par-
liaments during the reign
of Queen Elizabeth'.*

Hobbes (d. 1679): Seven Philosophical Problems [trs. Problemata Physica, 1662]. P
Milton (d. 1674): Brief History of Muscovia. P
Otway (1652): Venice Preserv'd. T
Petty (1623): Essay concerning multiplication of Mankind; together with an Essay on Political Arithmetick [see 1690]. P
Pordage, Samuel: Azaria and Hushai. V
  Medal Revers'd. V
Radcliffe, Alexander: The Ramble. V
Ravenscroft, Edward: London Cuckolds. C
Settle (1648): Absalom Senior, or Achitophel Transpros'd. V
  Heir of Morocco. D
Shadwell (1642?): Lancashire Witches, with First part of Tegue O Divelly [see 1690]. C
  (?) Medall of John Bayes. V
Sheffield, John, Duke of Buckingham : An Essay on Poetry. V
Southerne (1660): The Loyal Brother. T
Tate, Nahum: Ingratitude of a Commonwealth, or Fall of Coriolanus. T
Whitelocke (d. 1675): Memorials of English Affairs from the beginning of the Reign of Charles I to the Restoration [enlarg. 1732; this reprtd. Oxford, 1853].

1683

Ayres, Philip (1638): Emblemata Amatoria. Emblems of Love. V
Barrow (d. 1677): Works, ed. John Tillotson [concl. 1687; ed. Napier 1859].
Chalkhill, John: Thealma and Clearchus [cont. Preface by Izaak Walton dated 1678]. V
Crowne, John: City Politiques. C
Dryden (1631): Duke of Guise [with Nat. Lee]. T
  Vindication of the Duke of Guise. P
  Trs. Plutarch [with others]. P
Mason, John (1646): Songs of Praise. V
Oldham (d. 1683): Poems and Translations [Remains in Verse and Prose 1684; Works ed. E. Thompson 1770; Bell 1854].
Shipman, Thomas (1632): Carolina. V

Siege of Vienna by the Turks.
Rye House Plot.
Algernon Sidney and Lord Russell executed.
Conyers Middleton b.
Edward Young b.
Izaak Walton d.
John Oldham d.
Thomas Killigrew senr. d.
Benjamin Whichcote d.
Pepys's Narrative of Voyage to Tangiers written (called The Second Diary: first published 1840).

Banks, John: IslandQueens[laterAlbionQueens].T
Browne (d. 1682): Miscellany Tracts, ed. Tenison.
Bunyan (1628): Pilgrim's Progress, pt. ii [see 1678]. P
Burnet (1643): Trs. More's Utopia. P
Creech, Thomas: Trs. Horace. V
　　Trs. Theocritus. V
Dillon, Wentworth, Earl of Roscommon (1633?): Essay on Translated Verse. V
Dryden (1631): Miscellany Poems [by various writers: pub. by Jacob Tonson]. See 1709. V
　　Trs. History of the League. P
Lacy, John (d. 1681): Sir Hercules Buffoon. C
Lee (1653?): Constantine the Great. T
Mather, Increase (1639): Illustrious Providences. P
Otway (1652): The Atheist. C
Southerne (1660): The Disappointment. C

Robert Leighton d.
' The Turkish Spy' begins (trs. from Italian of Marana by William Bradshaw or R. Midgeley?).
Corneille d.
Esquemeling, 'History of the Bucaniers of America' (trs. 2nd volume by Basil Ringrose, 1683).

1685

Cotton (1630): Trs. Montaigne's Essays. P
Crowne, John: Sir Courtly Nice. C
Dryden (1631): Albion and Albanius. D opera.
　　Threnodia Augustalis. V
　　Ed. Sylvae, or the second part of Poetical Miscellanies [see 1684].
Otway (d. 1685): Windsor Castle. V
Rochester (d. 1680): Valentinian. T
Shakespeare (d. 1616): Fourth Folio [contents same as second issue of Folio III, 1663–4].
Sprat (1635): A true Declaration of the Horrid Conspiracy. P
Stillingfleet (1635): Origines Britannicae. P
Tate, Nahum: A Duke and no Duke. D
Waller (1606): Divine Poems. V
Wesley, Samuel (1662): Maggots. V

Accession of James II.
Edict of Nantes revoked.
Insurrection of Monmouth.
John Gay b.
George Berkeley b.
Aaron Hill b.
New Licensing Act (for 10 years).
Thomas Otway d.
Wentworth Dillon, Earl of Roscommon, d.
Fontenelle, ' Dialogues des Morts' and ' Discours sur la Pluralité des Mondes'.

1686

Browne (d. 1682): Works (folio). P
Bunyan (1628): Book for Boys and Girls [abridged 1701 as Divine Emblems]. V
Burnet (1643): Some Letters containing an Account of Switzerland and Italy. P
Compton, Henry (1632): Episcopalia. P
Dryden (1631): To the Memory of Mrs. Anne Killigrew. V
D'Urfey (1653): Commonwealth of Women. D
　　Banditti. D
Halifax (1633): Letter to a Dissenter. P
Killigrew, Anne (d. 1685): Poems.
Parr, Richard: Life of James Ussher. P
Plot, Robert (1640): Natural History of Staffordshire. P

William Law b.
Allan Ramsay b.
Thomas Tickell b.
Sir William Dugdale d.
John Ray, ' Historia Plantarum' (concl. 1704).

Ayres, Philip (1638): Lyric Poems made in imitation of the Italians. V

Behn (1640): Lucky Chance. C
Emperor of the Moon. C

Cleveland (d. 1658): Works [ed. Berdan 1903].

Clifford, Martin (d. 1677): Notes upon Mr. Dryden's Poems in Four Letters [with Reflections on Hind and Panther by Thomas Brown of Shifnal].

Dryden (1631): Song for St. Cecilia's Day. V
Hind and the Panther. V

Langbaine, Gerard (1656): Momus Triumphans [2nd ed. 1687 entitled A New Catalogue of English Plays]. P

Norris (1657): Miscellanies. P

Phillips (1631): History of Don Quixote. P

Prior (1664) and Montague, Charles: Hind and the Panther Transvers'd to the Story of the Country Mouse and the City Mouse. V

Sedley (1639?): Bellamira. C

Tate, Nahum: The Island Princess. D

Winstanley, William: Lives of the English Poets. P

Declaration of Indulgence.
George Villiers, Duke of Buckingham, d.
Henry More d.
Edmund Waller d.
Sir William Petty d.
Newton, 'Principia' (3rd ed. rev. 1726; see 1727).
John Wallis, 'Institutio Logicae'.
Bossuet, 'Oraison funèbre de Condé'.
Fénelon, 'Education des Filles'.

1688

Barnes, Joshua: Life of Edward III. P

Boyle (1627): Disquisition Concerning Causes of Natural Things. P

Crowne, John: Darius, King of Persia. T

Dryden (1631): Britannia Rediviva. V

D'Urfey (1653): A Fool's Preferment. C

Halifax (1633): Character of a Trimmer [circulated in MS. in 1685]. P
A Lady's New Year Gift, or Advice to a Daughter. P
Anatomy of an Equivalent. P

Pecock (d. 1460?): Book of Faith. P

Shadwell (1642?): Squire of Alsatia. C

The Revolution.
Alexander Pope b.
Lewis Theobald b.
John Bunyan d.
Ralph Cudworth d.
Shadwell poet-laureate.
William Cave, 'Scriptorum Ecclesiasticorum Historia Literaria'.
La Bruyère, 'Caractères'.
Bossuet, 'Variations des Eglises protestantes'.
Perrault, 'Parallèles des anciens et des modernes' (concl. 1697).

1689

Cotton (d. 1687): Collected Poems [another ed. called Genuine Works 1715].

Lee (1653?): Princess of Cleve. T

Locke (1632): First Letter on Toleration [see 1690, 1692]. P

Marvell (d. 1678): Poems on Affairs of State. V

Selden (d. 1654): Table Talk [ed. Singer 1847; David 1854; Reynolds 1892; Gollancz 1899].

Shadwell (1642?): Bury Fair. C

Sherlock, William: Practical Discourse Concerning Death. P

Accession of William and Mary.
Toleration Act.
Advocates' Library founded.
Samuel Richardson b.
Lady Mary Wortley Montagu b.
Aphra Behn d.
William Chamberlayne d.
Sir John Reresby d.
Hickes, 'Anglo-Saxon Moeso-Gothic Grammar'.
Montesquieu b.
Racine, 'Esther'.

Behn (d. 1689): Widow Ranter. C
Browne (d. 1682): Letter to a Friend upon the Death of his Intimate Friend. P
Crowne, John: English Friar. C
Dryden (1631): Don Sebastian. T
   Amphitryon. C
Lee (1653?): Massacre of Paris. T
Locke (1632): Two Treatises on Government. P
   Essay concerning Human Understanding [enlarg. 1694-5-1700]. P
   Second Letter on Toleration [see 1689, 1692]. P
Norris (1657): Christian Blessedness. P
Orrery (d. 1679): Mr. Anthony. C
Petty (d. 1687): Political Arithmetick. P
Shadwell (1642?): Amorous Bigotte, with Second Part of Tegue O Divelly [see 1682]. C
Waller (d. 1687): Poems, pt. ii [see 1645, 1664].

Robert Barclay d.
John Phillips starts journal 'Present State of Europe' (concl. 1706: a retrospective vol. entitled 'General History of Europe', added 1692)
John Dunton starts 'The Athenian Gazette' (concl. 1696).
Sir Thomas Pope Blount's 'Censura Celebriorum Authorum'.
Boursault, 'Fables d'Æsope'.
Furetière, 'Dictionnaire'.

1691

Congreve (1670): Incognita. P
Dryden (1631): King Arthur. D opera.
D'Urfey (1653): Love for Money. C
Langbaine (1656): Account of the English Dramatick Poets [ed. Gildon under title Lives and Characters of English Dramatic Poets, 1699]. P
Ray (1627): The Wisdom of God Manifested in the Works of the Creation. P
Settle (1648): Distress'd Innocence. T
Shadwell (1642?): The Scowrers. C
Southerne (1660): Sir Anthony Love. C
Wharton, Henry: Anglia Sacra [lives of Archbishops]. P
Wilson, John (1626): Belphegor. D
Wood (1632): Athenae Oxonienses [and Fasti; ii '92; enlarged 1721; ed. Bliss 1813-20]. P

Thomas Amory b.?
Sir George Etherege d.
George Fox d.
Richard Baxter d.
Robert Boyle d.
Boyle Lectures founded.
Racine, 'Athalie'.
Perrault, 'Contes' (concl. 1697).

1692

Bentley (1662): Boyle Lectures [on Folly of Atheism; delivered and pub. 1692-3].
Blount, Sir Thomas Pope (1649): Essays on Several Subjects. P
Bunyan (d. 1688): Works, ed. C. Doe [incomplete; first complete ed., Wilson, 1736; ed. Whitefield 1767; Hogg 1780; Stebbing 1859].
Burnet (1643): Discourse of Pastoral Care. P
Dryden (1631): Eleonora. V
   Cleomenes. T
   ? Trs. Miscellaneous Essays of Saint-Évremond, with character of Saint-Évremond.
Jonson (d. 1637): Second Folio [see 1616, 1640; adds New Inn (see 1631) to Folio I].

Joseph Butler b.
Thomas Shadwell d.
Nathaniel Lee d.
Elias Ashmole d.
Nahum Tate poet-laureate.
Edmund Gibson edits 'Anglo-Saxon Chronicle'.

Leighton, Robert (d. 1684): Works, ed. Fall [concl.
 1708; ed. Pearson 1825; Aikman 1835; West
 1875].

L'Estrange (1616): Fables of Æsop and other
 Mythologists [pt. ii 1699]. P

Locke (1632): Third Letter on Toleration [see
 1689, 1690]. P

 Considerations of the Consequences of Lower-
 ing the Interest and Raising the Value of
 Money [see 1695]. P

Motteux (1660): ed. Gentleman's Journal, or
 the Monthly Miscellany [concl. 1693; con-
 tained poems, essays, short stories, &c., by
 various writers].

Settle (1648): The Fairy Queen. D opera.

Southerne (1660): The Wives' Excuse. C

Temple (1628): Miscellanea, pt. ii [cont., among
 other essays, Ancient and Modern Learning,
 which started the Phalaris Controversy].

Walsh, William (1663): Poems.

Phalaris Controversy: Temple in above essay
 draws attention to Phalaris; Wotton refutes
 him in *Reflections of Ancient and Modern
 Learning* (1694); Boyle edits Epistles of Phalaris (1695) with animadversions on Bentley;
 Bentley refutes Temple and reviews Boyle's
 Phalaris in *A Dissertation on the Epistles of
 Phalaris* in 2nd ed. of Wotton's *Reflections*
 (1697); Boyle, Atterbury, and others reply
 in *Bentley's Dissertation Examined* (1698);
 Bentley's *Dissertation upon Epistles of Phalaris* (1699).

1693

Congreve (1670): Old Bachelor. C

Dennis (1657): Impartial Critic [reply to Rymer].P

Dryden (1631): Examen Poeticum, being the third
 part of Miscellany Poems [see 1684]. V

 Trs. Juvenal (assisted by others) and Persius
 [prefaced by D.'s Discourse on Satire]. V

D'Urfey (1653): Richmond Heiress. C

Hacket, John (d. 1670): Scrinia Reserata. P

Locke (1632): Thoughts concerning Education. P

Mather, Cotton (1663): Wonders of the Invisible
 World. P

Orrery, Earl of (Roger Boyle) (d. 1679): Guzman.
 C

Penn (1644): Some Fruits of Solitude [pt. ii,
 More Fruits of Solitude, 1782]. P

Rymer, Thomas (1641): A Short View of Tragedy. P

Shadwell (d. 1692): The Volunteers. C

Southerne (1660): Maid's Last Prayer. C

Urquhart (d. 1660), Motteux (1660), and others:
 Trs. Rabelais, bk. iii [see 1653]. P

George Lillo b.
*John Ray, 'Methodus
 Animalium'.*
*La Fontaine, 'Fables', pt.
 iii, 1693-4.*
Mme de La Fayette d.

Addison (1672): Trs. Fourth Georgic; Account of the Greatest English Poets; Song for St. Cecilia's Day; trs. Ovid's Salmacis [in Annual Miscellany, ed. Dryden]. V

Banks, John: Innocent Usurper. T

Blount, Sir Thomas Pope (1649): De Re Poetica. P

Burnaby, William: Trs. Satyricon of Petronius. P

Burnet (1643): Four Discourses. P

Burthogge, Richard (d. 1694?): Essay upon Reason and the Nature of Spirits. P

Congreve (1670): Double Dealer. C

Crowne, John: Married Beau. C
  Regulus. T

Dryden (1631): Love Triumphant. D
  Annual Miscellany, being the fourth part of Miscellany Poems [see 1684].
  To Congreve. V

D'Urfey (1653): Comical History of Don Quixote, pts. i, ii [pt. iii, 1696]. C

Echard, Laurence (1670?), and others: Trs. Plautus and Terence. V

Fox (d. 1691): Journal, ed. Ellwood, Preface by Penn [original MS. pub. 1911]. P

Milton (d. 1674): Letters of State written to Princes and Republics of Europe, 1649–59, trs. with Life by E. Phillips [cont. unpub. Sonnets to Cromwell, Fairfax, Vane, Skinner].

Settle (1648): Ambitious Slave. T

Southerne (1660): Fatal Marriage. T

Strype (1643): Memorials of Thomas Cranmer. P

Wotton, William: Reflections on Ancient and Modern Learning. P

Wright, James (1643): Country Conversations. P

Death of Queen Mary; William III reigns alone.
Bank of England founded.
Philip Dormer Stanhope, fourth Earl of Chesterfield, b.
Francis Hutcheson b.
John Tillotson d.
Voltaire b.
Racine, 'Cantiques'.
Bossuet, 'Réflexions sur la Comedie'.
Boileau, 'Réflexions sur Longin'.
Dictionary of the French Academy.

1695

Addison (1672): A Poem to his Majesty.

Blackmore (*c.* 1655): Prince Arthur [enlarg. 1697]. V

Blount, Charles (d. 1693): Miscellaneous Works, ed. Charles Gildon.

Burnet (1643): Essay on Memory of Queen Mary. P

Congreve (1670): Love for Love. C

Dryden (1631): Trs. Du Fresnoy's De Arte Graphica [with Preface on the Parallel between Painting and Poetry]. P

Henry Vaughan d.
George Savile, Marquis of Halifax, d.
Anthony à Wood d.
Dorothy Osborne, Lady Temple, d.
Licensing Act lapses.
George Ridpath starts 'The Flying Post' (tri-weekly; concl. 1714).
Abel Roper starts 'The Post Boy' (tri-weekly; concl. 1710).

Laud (d. 1645): Collected Works, ed. Henry Wharton [concl. 1700; ed. Scott and Bliss 1847–60].

Locke (1632): Reasonableness of Christianity. P
Vindication of the Reasonableness of Christianity. P
Further Considerations concerning Raising the Value of Money [see 1692]. P

Milton (d. 1674): Poetical Works ed. Patrick Hume [1st annotated ed.: later edd.: Bentley 1732, Newton 1749–50, Todd 1801, '08, '26, Masson 1877, '90, Beeching 1900].

Tanner, Thomas: Notitia Monastica [enlarged ed. by John Tanner 1744; reprtd. with additions by Nasmith 1787].

Temple (1628): Introduction to the History of England. P

Tillotson (d. 1694): Works, ed. R. Barker [concl. 1704; ed. Birch 1752].

*Charles Boyle ed. of
'Epistles of Phalaris'
(see 1692 note).
Edmund Gibson trs.
Camden's 'Britannia'.
La Fontaine d.*

1696

Aubrey, John: Miscellanies. P
Banks, John: Cyrus the Great. T
Baxter (d. 1691): Reliquiae Baxterianae, ed. from B.'s MSS. by Matthew Sylvester.
Behn (d. 1689): Younger Brother. C
Brady, Nicholas, and Tate, Nahum: Trs. Psalms [called the New Version; see 1562]. V
Cibber, Colley (1671): Love's Last Shift. C
Dennis (1657): Letters written between Dryden, Wycherley, Congreve, and Dennis; with Select Letters of Voiture. P
Dryden (1631): Ode on Henry Purcell. V
Granville, George, Lord Lansdowne (1667): The She-gallants. C
Leslie, Charles: Snake in the Grass. P
Motteux (1660): Love's a Jest. C
Oldmixon, John (1673): Poems on Several Occasions. V
Penn (1644): Primitive Christianity Revived. P
Rowe, Mrs. Elizabeth (1674): Poems on Several Occasions by Philomela. P
Southerne (1660): Oroonoko. T
Suckling (d. 1642): Works, first collected [ed. W. C. Hazlitt 1874; Thompson 1910].
Toland (1670): Christianity not Mysterious. P
Whiston, William (1667): New Theory of Earth. P

*Henry Home(Lord Kames)
b.
William Oldys b.
John Wilson d.
Edward Phillips d.?
Mme de Sévigné d.
Regnard, 'Le Joueur'.
Bayle, 'Dictionnaire his-
torique et critique'.*

Bentley (1662): Dissertation upon Epistles of Phalaris [in 2nd ed. of William Wotton's Reflections upon Ancient and Modern Learning: refutes Temple and reviews Boyle's Phalaris. See 1692, 95].

Cibber, Colley (1671): Woman's Wit. C

Collier (1650): Essays. P

Congreve (1670): Mourning Bride. T

Dampier, William (1652): Voyages [concl. 1709]. P

Defoe (1661 ?): Essay upon Projects. P

Dryden (1631): Alexander's Feast. V
Trs. Virgil. V

Evelyn (1620): Numismata. P

Norris (1657): Account of Reason and Faith in Relation to Mysteries of Christianity. P

Prideaux, Humphrey (1648): Life of Mahomet. P

Ravenscroft (d. 1697): The Anatomist. C

Vanbrugh (1664): Relapse. C
Provok'd Wife. C
Æsop. C

Charles Macklin b. ?
William Hogarth b.
Edward Ravenscroft d.
Bossuet, 'États d'oraison'.
Fénelon, 'Maximes des Saints'.

1698

Behn (d. 1689): Histories and Novels [collected]. Poetical Remains, ed. Charles Gildon.

Boyle, Charles, Atterbury, Francis, and others: Dr. Bentley's Dissertations upon the Epistles of Phalaris Examined [see 1697]. P

Collier (1650): Short View of the Immorality and Profaneness of the English Stage [see below]. P

Crowne, John: Caligula. T

Defoe (1661): Occasional Conformity of Dissenters. P

Fletcher, Andrew (1655): Discourse of Government relating to Militias. P
Two Discourses concerning Scotland. P

Granville (1667): Heroick Love. T

Lacy, John (d. 1681): Sauny the Scott. C

Leslie, Charles (1650): Short and Easy Method with the Deists. P

Ludlow, Edmund (d. 1692): Memoirs [concl. 1699; ed. Firth 1894].

Milton (d. 1674): Collected Prose Works, English and Latin, ed. with Life by John Toland [an anon. ed. of Eng. prose works in 1697].

Motteux (1660): Beauty in Distress. T

Sidney, Algernon (d. 1683): Discourses concerning Government. P

William Warburton b.
Edward Ward's 'London Spy' (monthly from Nov.; collected 1703).
'Society for Promoting Christian Knowledge' founded.
Metastasio b.

Whichcote (d. 1683): Select Sermons, ed. with Preface by Shaftesbury.

Jeremy Collier Controversy: John Dennis's *Usefulness of the Stage* and Filmer's *Defence of Dramatic Poetry*, 1698; Thomas D'Urfey's *Campaignes*, 1698; Congreve's *Amendments of Mr. Collier's False Citations* and Vanbrugh's *Vindication of the Relapse and Provok'd Wife*, 1699; Collier's reply to Congreve and Vanbrugh, *A Defence of the Short View*, 1699; John Drake's *Ancient and Modern Stages Surveyed*, 1699, and Collier's reply to it, *A Second Defence of the Short View*, 1700; Dryden's reply to Collier in Preface to *Fables* and in Epilogue to Vanbrugh's *Pilgrim*, 1700; Filmer's *Defence of Plays*, 1707, and Collier's reply to it, *A Further Defence of the Short View*, 1708.

1699

Bentley (1662): Dissertation upon the Epistles of Phalaris [concludes the controversy: see 1692]. P

Brown, Thomas (1663): Collection of Miscellany Poems, Letters, etc.

Burnet (1643): Exposition of the Thirty-nine Articles. P

Cibber, Colley (1671): Xerxes. T

Dennis (1657): Rinaldo and Armida. T

Evelyn (1620): Acetaria. P

Fairfax, Thomas, Lord Fairfax (d. 1671): Memorials, written by himself, ed. B. Fairfax [incomplete: complete, ed. Lodge, 1808].

Farquhar (1678): Love and a Bottle. C
Constant Couple. C

Garth (1661): Dispensary. V

King, William (1663): A Journey to London in 1698. P
Dialogues of the Dead. P

Toland (1670): Amyntor. P

Traherne (d. 1674): Serious and Patheticall Contemplation of the Mercies of God. P

Robert Blair b.
Joseph Spence b.
Edward Stillingfleet d.
Sir William Temple d.
Joseph Beaumont d.
'History of the Works of the Learned', 1699–1711.
Racine d.
Fénelon, 'Télémaque'.

Blackmore (*c.* 1655): Satyr against Wit. V
Brown (1663): Amusements Serious and Comical.
 P and V
Congreve (1670): Way of the World. C
Dennis (1657): Iphigenia. T
Dryden (d. 1700): Fables. V
 A Secular Masque. V
Halifax (d. 1695): Miscellanies [Advice to a
 Daughter, Character of a Trimmer, Anatomy
 of an Equivalent, Letter to a Dissenter,
 Maxims of State, etc.].
Harington (d. 1677): Collected Works, ed. with
 Life by John Toland [enlarged ed. Millar
 1737].
Motteux (1660): Trs. Don Quixote, vol. i (vol. ii,
 1701, vol. iii, 1703).
Pomfret, John (1667): The Choice. V
Southerne (1660): Fate of Capua. T
Tate, Nahum (1652): Panacea; a Poem on Tea.
Temple (d. 1699): Letters, ed. Swift, vols. i–ii
 [iii, 1703].
Vanbrugh (1664): Pilgrim [altered from Fletcher]. C

James Thomson b.
John Dyer b.?
John Dryden d.
Fénelon, 'Dialogues des
 morts'.
Gottsched b.

1701

Cibber, Colley (1671): Love makes a Man. C
Congreve (1670): Judgement of Paris. D masque.
Defoe (1661 ?): True-born Englishman. V
Dennis (1657): Advancement of Modern Poetry. P
Dryden (d. 1700): Collected Plays [later edd.:
 Congreve 1717, Scott 1808, Saintsbury 1882].
 Collected Poems [later edd.: Brougham 1743,
 Derrick 1760, Warton 1811, Christie 1870,
 Sargeaunt 1910].
Farquhar (1678): Sir Harry Wildair. C
Gildon (1665): Examen Miscellaneum. P
 A New Miscellany of Poems [incl. works by
 Dorset, Sedley, Fleetwood, Sheppard, &c.].
Norris, John (1657): Ideal and Intelligible World,
 pt. i (ii, 1704). P
Philips, John (1676): The Splendid Shilling. V
Rowe (1674): Ambitious Stepmother. T
 Tamerlane. T
Settle (1648): Virgin Prophetess. T
Steele (1672): Christian Hero. P
 The Funeral. C
Swift (1667): Contests in Athens and Rome. P
Temple (d. 1699): Miscellanea, pt. iii ed. Swift
 [see 1680, 1692].
Whichcote (d. 1683): Several Discourses. P

Act of Settlement.
James II d.
Sir Charles Sedley d.
Jeremy Collier, 'Histori-
 cal, Geographical, Gene-
 alogical, and Poetical
 Dictionary' (concl.
 1721).

Bacon (d. 1626): Letters written during the reign of James II, ed. R. Stephens [see 1734].
Brown, Thomas (1663): Letters from the Dead to the Living. P
Bysshe, Edward: Art of English Poetry [pts. ii–iii pub. as British Parnassus, 1734]. P
Clarendon (d. 1674): History of the Rebellion [concl. 1704; later edd.: Bandinel 1826, Macray 1888: see 1759]. P
Defoe (1661 ?): Shortest Way with Dissenters. P
Echard (1670 ?): General Ecclesiastical History. P
Farquhar (1678): The Inconstant. C
Gildon (1665): Comparison between the Two Stages. P
King, William (1650): De Origine Mali. P
Mather, Cotton (1663): Magnalia Christi Americana. P
Pomfret, John (d. 1702): Collected Poems.
Raleigh (d. 1618): Three Discourses, pub. by Philip Raleigh. P
Sedley (d. 1701): Poetical Works and Speeches [collected; other edd. 1707, 1776].
Shaftesbury (1671): Paradoxes of State. P
Vanbrugh (1664): False Friend. D

Accession of Queen Anne.
Philip Doddridge b.
'The Daily Courant' (first daily paper) in March (concl. 1735).
'Observator', 1702–12.
'Poems on Affairs of State', 1702–7 (one of the principal edd.).

1703

Addison (1672): Letter from Italy to Lord Halifax. V
Boyer, Abel (1667): History of the Reign of Queen Anne [concl. 1720]. P
Cibber, Colley (1671): She would and She would not. C
Defoe (1661 ?): Hymn to the Pillory. V
Farquhar (1678): Twin-Rivals. C
Rowe (1674): Fair Penitent. T
Whichcote (d. 1683): Moral and Religious Aphorisms, ed. Jeffrey (enlarg. 1753).

John Wesley b.
Henry Brooke b.?
Robert Dodsley b.
Gilbert West b.
Samuel Pepys d.
George Hickes, 'Thesaurus'.
Edward Ward, 'London Spy' (collected: see 1698).
Thomas Hearne, 'Reliquiae Bodleianae'.
Perrault d.

1704

Brown, Thomas (d. 1704): Dialogues [collected]. P
Burnet (1643): Tracts and Discourses [collected]. P
Defoe (1661 ?): The Review [1704–13]. P
    The Consolidator.
Fletcher, Andrew (1655): Account of a Conversation concerning a Right Regulation of Governments. P
Steele (1672): Lying Lover. C
Swift (1667): Tale of a Tub, Battle of the Books. P
Tonson, Jacob (pub.): Poetical Miscellanies [5th pt. of Miscellanies, begun by Dryden, 1684].
Wycherley (1640 ?): Miscellany Poems.

Battle of Blenheim.
Roger L'Estrange d.
John Locke d.
Thomas Brown of Shifna d.
Robert Nelson, 'Companion for Festivals and Fasts'.
First Eng. trs. of Newton's 'Optics', incl. 'Fluxions'.
Thomas Rymer and Robert Sanderson (ed.), 'Foedera' (concl. 1735: see also 1725).

Addison (1672): The Campaign. V
  Remarks on Italy. P
Blackmore (*c.* 1655): Eliza. V
Centlivre, Susannah (1667?): The Gamester. C
Cibber, Colley (1671): Careless Husband. C
Clarke (1675): Being and Attributes of God. P
Coppinger, Matthew: A Session of the Poets. V
Dunton, John (1659): Life and Errors. P
King William (1663): Miscellanies (n.d.).
Farquhar (1678): Stage-Coach [with Motteux]. C
Locke (d. 1704): On the Epistles of St. Paul. P
Mandeville (1670?): Grumbling Hive [repub. in
  Fable of the Bees, 1714, 1723]. V
Philips, John (1676): Blenheim. V
Steele (1672): Tender Husband. C
Vanbrugh (1664): The Confederacy. C
Ward, Edward (1667): Hudibras Redivivus. V

Abraham Tucker b.
David Mallet b.?

1706

Centlivre, Susannah (1667?): Love at a Venture. C
  Basset Table. C
Defoe (1661?): Apparition of Mrs. Veal. P
  Jure Divino. V
Dennis (1657): On the Operas after Italian
  Manner. P
Farquhar (1678): Recruiting Officer. C
Hughes, John (1677): History of England. P
Kennett, White (1660): History of England. P
Locke (d. 1704): Posthumous Works [cont.
  Conduct of the Understanding, Discourse of
  Miracles, Fourth Letter on Toleration].
Philips, John (1676): Cerealia. V
Rowe (1674): Ulysses. T
Tindal (1657): Rights of the Christian Church. P
Vanbrugh (1664): The Mistake. C
Watts (1674): Horæ Lyricæ. V

Union with Scotland.
Act of Succession.
Benjamin Franklin b.
John Evelyn d.
John Phillips d.
James Watson, 'Choice
  Collection of Scottish
  Poems'.

1707

Addison (1672): Fair Rosamond. D opera.
Brown, Thomas (d. 1704): Works [concl. 1708.
  Remains 1721: complete ed. 1760].
Echard (1670?): History of England, vol. i [ii–iii
  1718]. P
Farquhar (1678): Beaux' Stratagem. C
Philips, John (1676): Ode to Bolingbroke. V
Prior (1664): Poems on Several Occasions [un-
  authorized, see 1709].
Rowe (1674): Royal Convert. T
Tickell (1686): Oxford. V
Watts (1674): Hymns.

Henry Fielding b.
Charles Wesley b.
George Farquhar d.
Newton, 'Arithmetica
  Universalis'.
'The Muses Mercury',
  1707–8.
Lesage, 'Diable boiteux'.

Bingham, Joseph (1668): Origines Ecclesiasticae [concl. 1722]. P

Cibber, Colley (1671): Lady's Last Stake [n.d.]. C

Collier (1650): Ecclesiastical History of Great Britain, vol. i (ii 1714; ed. Barham 1840, Lathbury 1852). P

Downes, John (*fl.* 1662–1710): Roscius Anglicanus. P

Henry, Matthew (1662): Exposition of the Testaments (concl. 1710). P

King, William (1663): Art of Cookery [n.d.]. V

Locke (d. 1704): Letters [ed. Forster 1830].

Ockley, Simon (1678): History of the Saracens, vol. i (ii 1718, iii 1757). P

Motteux, Urquhart, and others: Trs. of Rabelais [complete: see 1653, 1693]. P

Philips, John (1676): Cyder. V

Shaftesbury, Anthony Ashley Cooper, Third Earl of (1671): Letter concerning Enthusiasm. P

Swift (1667): Predictions for 1708. P

  Elegy upon Partridge. V

John Hughes trs. of Fontenelle's 'Dialogues of the Dead'.

1709

Berkeley (1685): New Theory of Vision. P

Centlivre, Susannah (1667 ?): The Busybody. C

Defoe (1661 ?): History of the Union of Great Britain. P

Dennis (1657): Appius and Virginia. T

King, William (1663): The Art of Love. V

Manley, Mary (1663): New Atalantis. P

Philips, Ambrose (1675 ?): Pastorals [in Poeticall Miscellanies, the sixth part]. V

  Epistle to Earl of Dorset. V

Pope (1688): Pastorals [in Poetical Miscellanies, the sixth part]. **V**

Prior (1664): Poems on Several Occasions [see 1707; enlarg. 1718].

Steele (1672): The Tatler [April 1709–Jan. 1711].

Strype (1643): Annals of the Reformation [concl. 1731]. P

Swift (1667): Project for the Advancement of Religion. P

  Letter concerning Sacramental Test. P

  Baucis and Philemon. V

Temple (d. 1699): Memoirs, pt. iii ed. Swift.

Tonson, Jacob (pub.): Poetical Miscellanies [6th pt. of Miscellanies begun by Dryden, 1684].

Whitelocke (d. 1675): Memorials of English Affairs. P

First Copyright Act imposes penalties for infringement and fixes term of copyright at 14 years, renewable, if the author is still alive, for another 14 years. See 1774, 1842.
Samuel Johnson b.
George Lyttelton b.
John Armstrong b.
Arthur Collins, 'Peerage of England' (with add. 1710–11, 1717; first complete ed. 1735; standard ed. Brydges 1812).
Thomas Hearne's ed. of Spelman's 'Life of Alfred' with additions (see 1678).
A. Hall's ed. of Leland's 'De Scriptoribus Britannicis'.
Nicholas Rowe's ed. of Shakespeare (concl. 1710; stage ed. 1714).
Lesage, 'Turcaret'.

Berkeley (1685): Principles of Human Knowledge. P

Burnet (1643): Exposition of Church Catechism. P

Centlivre, Susannah (1667 ?): The Man's bewitched [n.d.]. D

Congreve (1670): Collected Works [ed. Leigh Hunt 1840].

Gildon (1665): Life of Betterton. P

Granville (1667): The British Enchanters [an opera].

Hill (1685): Elfrid [rewritten as Athelwold, 1732]. T

Manley, Mary (1663): Memoirs of Europe [afterwards printed as vols. 3 and 4 of New Atlantis: see 1709]. P

King, William (1663): Historical Account of Heathen Gods and Heroes. P

Stillingfleet (d. 1699): Works, with Life by Richard Bentley.

Swift (1667): Meditation upon a Broomstick. P

Thomas Reid b.
Addison starts 'The Whig Examiner' (Sept. and Oct.).
'The Examiner' (1710–12) started by Bolingbroke, Swift, Prior, and others.
Thomas Hearne's ed. of Leland's 'Itinerary' (concl. 1712).
Bayle's Historical and Critical Dict.; first ed. in English.
Leibnitz, 'Théodicée'.

1711

Addison (1672): The Spectator [1 Mar. 1711–6 Dec. 1712; coll. 1714, ed. G. Smith 1907].

Alexander (d. 1640): Anacrisis: or a censure of some poets [in Works of Drummond below]. P

Atterbury (1662): Representation of the State of Religion. P

Blackmore (c. 1655): Nature of Man. V

Centlivre, Susannah (1667?): Mar-plot. C

Dennis (1657): On the Genius and Writings of Shakespeare. P

  Essay upon Public Spirit. P

Drummond (d. 1649): Collected Works, ed. Sage and Ruddiman [cont. imperfect version of D.'s Conversations with Ben Jonson. See 1842].

Pope (1688): Essay on Criticism. V

Shaftesbury (1671): Characteristics of Men and Manners [collection of treatises pub. from 1708 onwards: 2nd ed. enlarg. 1714; Baskerville ed. 1773]. P

Swift (1667): Miscellanies [cont. An Argument against abolishing Christianity].

  Conduct of the Allies. P

Waller (d. 1687): Collected Works [later edd.: Elijah Fenton 1729; Thorn Drury 1893].

Whiston (1667): Primitive Christianity Revived [concl. 1712]. P

David Hume b.
John Norris d.
Abel Boyer, 'Political State of Great Britain' (monthly: completed 1729).
Richard Bentley's ed. of Horace.
Joseph Trapp, 'Praelectiones Poeticae' (vol. ii, 1715).
Boileau d.
Crébillon, 'Rhadamiste et Zénobie'.

Arbuthnot (1667): Art of Political Lying. P
  History of John Bull. P
Berkeley (1685): Passive Obedience. P
Blackmore (*c.* 1655): Creation. V
Browne (d. 1682): Posthumous Works [see 1716].
Clarke, Samuel (1675): Scripture Doctrine of
  Trinity. P
Gay (1685): The Mohocks. D
Granville (1667): Poems upon Several Occasions.
  V

Hughes, John (1677): Calypso and Telemachus. D
Motteux (1660): Trs. of Don Quixote. P
Oldmixon (1673): Secret History of Europe. P
Philips, Ambrose (1675 ?): Distressed Mother. T
Pope (1688): Rape of the Lock [in Miscellaneous
  Poems and Translations: rev. 1714, 1717]. V
  To a Young Lady, with the Works of Voiture
  [in Miscellaneous Poems as above: enlarged
  ed. 1714]. V
  Messiah [in Spectator, 14 May]. V
Swift (1667): Advice to Members of the October
  Club. P
  Some Remarks on the Barrier Treaty. P
  Proposal for Correcting the English Language.
  P
Tickell (1686): To the Lord Privy Seal [1713]. V

The Stamp Act.
Richard Glover b.
Edward Moore b.
*Woodes Rogers, ' A Cruis-
  ing Voyage round the
  World '.*
Rousseau b.
*Fénelon, ' Existence de
  Dieu '.*
*Fontenelle, ' Éloge des
  Académiciens '.*

1713

Addison (1672): Cato. T
Bentley (1662): Remarks upon a Discourse of
  Free-thinking [see Collins below]. P
Berkeley (1685): Dialogues between Hylas and
  Philonous. P
Carey, Henry: Poems on Several Occasions [see
  1729].
Collier, Arthur (1680): Clavis Universalis. P
Collins, Anthony (1676): Discourse of Free-
  thinking. P
Dennis (1657): Remarks upon Cato. P
Gay (1685): Rural Sports. V
  Wife of Bath [revised 1730]. C
Parnell (1679): Essay on different Styles of
  Poetry. V
Pope (1688): Windsor Forest. V
  Ode for Musick [Ode on St. Cecilia's Day]. V
Steele (1672): The Guardian [12 Mar.-1 Oct.].
  The Englishman [6 Oct. 1713-11 Feb. 1714].
Swift (1667): Importance of the Guardian con-
  sidered. P
Winchilsea, Countess of: Miscellany Poems
  [enlarg. ed. M. Reynolds 1903].

Treaty of Utrecht.
Laurence Sterne b.
Diderot b.
*Anthony Cooper, third
  Earl of Shaftesbury, d.*
Thomas Rymer d.
Thomas Sprat d.
*Swift Dean of St. Pat-
  rick's.*
*In this year Pope, Swift,
  Arbuthnot,Gay,Parnell,
  Congreve, Lord Oxford,
  and Atterbury form the
  Scriblerus Club (see
  1741).*
*Anthony Hamilton, 'Mé-
  moires du comte de
  Grammont' (see 1714).*

Centlivre, Susannah (1667 ?): The Wonder! A Woman Keeps a Secret. C

Ellwood, Thomas (d. 1713): History of the Life of Thomas Ellwood, written by his own hand [with a Supplement by Joseph Wyeth]. P

Gay (1685): The Fan. V

The Shepherd's Week. V

Locke (d. 1704): Collected Works [later edd.: 1768–91–1801–12–23].

Mandeville (1670 ?): Fable of the Bees [with An Inquiry into the Origin of Moral Virtue: see 1705, 1723]. P and V

Rowe (1674): Jane Shore. T

Steele (1672): The Crisis. P   The Ladies' Library. P

Swift (1667): Public Spirit of the Whigs. P

Young (1683): Force of Religion. V

Accession of George I.
William Shenstone b.
George Whitefield b.
James Hervey b.
James Burnett (Lord Monboddo) b.
Abel Boyer's trs. of 'Memoirs of Count Grammont' (see 1713).
Narcissus Luttrell's 'Brief Relation' ends (see 1678, 1857).
La Motte, 'Iliade'.
Leibnitz, 'Monadologie'.

1715

Bullock, Christopher (1690?): Woman's Revenge. C

Cibber, Colley (1671): Hob, or the Country Wake. C

Cotton (d. 1687): Collected Works.

Defoe (1661 ?): Appeal to Honour and Justice. P

Garth (1661): Claremont. V

Gay (1685): What d'ye call it [n.d.]. D burlesque.

Johnson, Charles (1679): Country Lasses. C

Pope (1688): Iliad vol. i, with prefatory essay by Thomas Parnell [ii 1716, iii 1717, iv 1718, v–vi 1720]. V Key to the Lock. V Temple of Fame. V

Rowe (1674): Lady Jane Grey. T

Tickell (1686): Iliad [bk. i only]. V

Watts (1674): Divine Songs for Children. V

First Jacobite Rebellion.
Richard Graves b.
Richard Jago b.
William Whitehead b.
John Brown b.
Gilbert Burnet d.
Nahum Tate d.
Nicholas Rowe poet-laureate.
John Hughes's ed. of Spenser.
Thomas Hearne's ed. of Leland's 'Collectanea'.
Society of Antiquaries revived.
Louis XIV d.
Lesage, 'Gil Blas' (concl. 1735).

1716

Addison (1672): The Drummer. C

The Freeholder [23 Dec. 1715–9 June 1716].

Blackmore (*c.* 1655): Essays. P

Poems on Various Subjects.

Browne (d. 1682): Christian Morals, ed. J. Jeffrey. P

Gay (1685): Trivia [n.d.]. V

Hill (1685): Fatal Vision. T

Gideon, bk. i, ii [iii–iv 1749]. V

Pope (1688): Epistle to Jervas [in ed. of Du Fresnoy's Art of Painting]. V

Horrid and Barbarous Revenge . . . on Curll. P

Pope, Gay, and Wortley Montagu: Court Poems [see 1747]. V

Prideaux, Humphrey (1648): Old and New Testament connected in the History of Jews. P

Shaftesbury (d. 1713): Letters to a Student at the University. P

Septennial Act.
Thomas Gray b.
William Wycherley d.
Thomas Hearne's ed. of 'Old English Chronicles' between 1716 and 1735.
'Historical Register', 1716–38.
Daniel Defoe, 'Mercurius Politicus', 1716–20.
Leibnitz d.
Fénelon, 'Lettre à l'Académie'.

Ashmole, Elias (d. 1698): Memoirs, drawn up by himself. P
Duke, Richard (d. 1711): Poems upon Several Subjects [in Roscommon's Poetical Works].
Fenton, Elijah (1683): Poems on Several Occasions.
Garth, Samuel (1661): Ed. Ovid's Metamorphoses, trs. by eminent hands [Dryden, Addison, Tate, Croxall, Gay, Garth]. V
Gay, Pope, and Arbuthnot: Three Hours after Marriage. C
Hoadly (1676): Nature of the Kingdom of Christ. P
Law (1686): Letters I and II to the Bishop of Bangor [i.e. Hoadly above. Letter III 1719]. P
Parnell (1679): Homer's Battle of the Frogs and Mice. V
Pope (1688): Collected Works [cont. the unpub. Elegy to the Memory of an Unfortunate Lady, and Eloisa to Abelard. Continued 1735–36–42. Later edd.: Warburton 1751, Wakefield 1794, Warton 1797, Bowles 1806, Carruthers 1858, Ward 1869, Elwin and Courthope 1871–89].
Tickell (1686): Epistle from a Lady in England. V

Horace Walpole b.
David Garrick b.
Richard Owen Cambridge b.
Congreve's ed. of Dryden.
The Bangorian Controversy, 1717–20.

1718

Centlivre, Susannah (1667?): Bold Stroke for a Wife. C
Cibber, Colley (1671): The Non-juror. C
Gildon (1665): Complete Art of Poetry. P
Prior (1664): Poems [cont., among unpub. works, Alma, and Solomon on the Vanity of the World: see 1709].
Ramsay (1686): Christ's Kirk on the Green. V
Rowe (d. 1718): Trs. of Lucan. V

Nicholas Rowe d.
Thomas Parnell d.
William Penn d.
Peter Anthony Motteux d.
Eusden poet-laureate.
Joseph Trapp, trs. of Æneid, vol. i (vol. ii, 1720; complete, with notes, 1731, 1735).
Society of Antiquaries re-founded.
Voltaire, 'Œdipe'.
Massillon, 'Petit Carême'.

1719

Addison (d. 1719): The Old Whig. P
Defoe (1661?): Robinson Crusoe. P
 Further Adventures of Robinson Crusoe. P
Jacob, Giles (1686): Poetical Register [2nd vol. 1720]. P
Southerne (1660): Spartan Dame. T
Watts (1674): Psalms of David. V
Young (1683): Busiris. T
 Letter to Mr. Tickell [on Addison's death]. V

Giuseppe Baretti b.
Joseph Addison d.
Samuel Garth d.
'Daily Post' (ran till 1746).
La Motte, 'Fables'.
Voltaire, 'Lettres sur Œdipe'.

Clarendon (d. 1674): History of the Rebellion in Ireland. P

Croxall, Samuel: Fair Circassian. V

  Select Collection of Novels [concl. 1722; enlarg. 1729]. P

Defoe (1661 ?): Memoirs of a Cavalier. P

  Captain Singleton. P

  Duncan Campbell. P

Gay (1685): Collected Poems.

Hill (1685): The Creation. V

Hughes (d. 1720): Siege of Damascus. T

Pope (1688) and others: New Miscellany of Original Poems ['Hammond's Miscellany', incl. P.'s Verses to Lady M. W. Montagu].

Prior (1664): The Conversation. P

Ramsay, (1686): Poems [8vo, see 1721].

Swift, (1667): Proposal for the Universal use of Irish Manufactures. P

South Sea Bubble.
Gilbert White b.
Richard Hurd b.
Samuel Foote b.
Charlotte Lennox b.
Mrs. Elizabeth Montagu b.
John Hughes d.
Countess of Winchilsea d.
Arthur Collins, 'Baronetage of England' (final ed. Wotton 1741).
Stow's 'Survey of London' ed. and enlarged by Strype.
Marivaux, 'Arlequin poli par l'amour'.

1721

Addison (d. 1719): Works, ed. with prefatory elegy by Thomas Tickell [cont. unpub. essays on Ancient Medals and Evidences of Christian Religion. Later edd.: Baskerville 1761, Hurd 1811, Greene 1856].

Gildon (1665): Laws of Poetry. P

Pope (1688): To Mr. Addison [in A.'s Works above]. V

  To Robert, Earl of Oxford. V

Ramsay (1686): Poems [4to, see 1720; vol. ii 1727].

Shaftesbury (d. 1713): Letters to Robert Molesworth. P

Strype (1643): Ecclesiastical Memorials. P

Swift (1667): Letter to a Young Gentleman lately entered into Holy Orders. P

  Letter of Advice to a Young Poet. P

Young (1683): The Revenge. T

William Collins b.
Tobias Smollett b.
Thomas Francklin b.
Mark Akenside b.
William Robertson b.
Matthew Prior d.
Nathan Bailey, 'Universal Etymological English Dictionary' (Suppl. vol. 1727; enlarged as 'Dictionarium Britannicum', 1730).
John Urry's ed. of Chaucer.
Montesquieu, 'Lettres persanes'.

1722

Bolton, Edmund (d. 1633 ?): Hypercritica [in Anthony Hall's Nicolai Triveti Annalium Continuatio]. P

Buckingham, Duke of (John Sheffield: d. 1721): Works, ed. Pope.

Croxall, Samuel: Fables of Æsop and others. P

John Burgoyne b.
John Home b.
Thomas Leland b.
Christopher Smart b.
Joseph Warton b.
John Toland d.

Defoe (1661 ?): Journal of the Plague Year. P
  Moll Flanders. P
  Colonel Jacque. P
  History of Peter the Great. P
Parnell (d. 1718): Poems, ed. with Epistle to
  Lord Oxford by Pope [later edd.: Goldsmith
  1770, Mitford 1833, Aitken 1894: see 1758].
Philips, Ambrose (1675 ?): The Briton. T
Tickell (1686): To Sir Godfrey Kneller. V
  Kensington Gardens. V

1723

Blackmore (*c.* 1655): Alfred. V
Burnet (d. 1715): History of my own time, vol. i
  [ii 1734; whole work 1735; ed. Routh 1823,
  1833; (reign of Charles II only) Airy 1897–
  1900; Supplement to the History, from
  unpub. memoirs, letters, etc., ed. Foxcroft
  1902]. P
Centlivre, Susannah (d. 1723): The Artifice. C
Fenton, Elijah (1683): Mariamne. T
Law (1686): Remarks on the Fable of the Bees. P
Mandeville (1670 ?): Fable of the Bees, 2nd ed.
  with Essay on Charity, and Search into the
  Nature of Society [see 1705, 1714]. P and V
Philips, Ambrose (1675 ?): Humphrey, Duke of
  Gloucester. T
Prior (d. 1721): Down Hall. V
Steele (1672): Conscious Lovers. C

Adam Smith b.
Sir William Blackstone b.
Sir Joshua Reynolds b.
Richard Price b.
Thomas D'Urfey d.
Susannah Centlivre d.
*David Mallet, 'William
  and Margaret' (repub.
  in Ramsay's 'Tea Table
  Miscellany', 1724, and
  Percy's 'Reliques',
  1765).*
Voltaire, 'Henriade'.

1724

Boyle (d. 1679): State Letters.
Collins, Anthony (1676): Grounds of the Christian
  Religion. P
Defoe (1661 ?): Roxana. P
  Tour through Great Britain (concl. 1726). P
Johnson, Charles (fl. 1724–34): General History
  of the Robberies & Murders of the most
  Notorious Pyrates. P
Oldmixon (1673): Critical History of England
  [with Essay on Criticism prefixed; concl.
  1726]. P
Ramsay (1686): Ever Green. V
  Tea-table Miscellany, vol. i [ii 1726, iii
  1727(?)]. V
Savage, Richard: Sir Thomas Overbury. T
Swift (1667): Drapier's Letters. P

William Gilpin b.
Frances Brooke b.
Elkanah Settle d.
Charles Gildon d.
*Thomas Cooke's trs. of
  Bion and Moschus.*
*William Stukeley's 'Itine-
  rarium Curiosum'.*
Kant b.
Klopstock b.

Cooke, Thomas (1703): Battle of the Poets [enlarg. as Tales, Epistles, Odes, 1729]. V

Defoe (1661?): Complete English Tradesman [concl. 1727]. P

　A New Voyage round the World. P

　Account of Jonathan Wild. P

Hutcheson, Francis (1694): Original of our ideas of Beauty and Virtue. P

Mandeville, Sir John: Travels [first Eng. version from the Cottonian MS.: see 1499, 1889]. P

Pope (1688): Ed. of Shakespeare [2nd ed. accepting some of Theobald's corrections 1728: see 1726].

　Odyssey, vols. i–iii [iv–v 1726; with William Broome and Elijah Fenton]. V

Ramsay (1686): Gentle Shepherd. D

Tindal, Nicholas (1688): Trs. of Rapin's History of England [concl. 1731; continuation of same 1744–5; continued by Smollett 1785–9].

Watts (1674): Logic. P

Young (1683): Universal Passion [seven Satires collected as Love of Fame 1728]. V

William Kenrick b.?
William Mason b.
Stephen Whatley, 'Acta Regia' (from Rapin's abridgement of Rymer's 'Foedera'; concl. 1727).

1726

Atterbury (1662): Sermons, 2 vols. P

Bolingbroke (1678): The Craftsman [concl. 1736: collected reprint 1731–7; editor Nicholas Amhurst as 'Caleb d'Anvers'].

Butler (1692): Fifteen Sermons.

Dennis (1657): The Stage defended [reply to Law below]. P

Hill (1685): Fatal Extravagance. T

Law (1686): Treatise upon Christian Perfection. P

　Unlawfulness of Stage Entertainments. P

Penn (d. 1718): Works, ed. J. Besse.

Pope (1688) and others: Miscellanea, in 2 vols. ['Curll's Miscellany', incl. P.'s Letters to Henry Cromwell].

Shelvocke, George (fl. 1690–1728): A Voyage round the World. P

Swift (1667): Cadenus and Vanessa. V

　Gulliver's Travels [pt. i Lilliput; ii Brobdingnag; iii Laputa; iv Houyhnhnms]. P

Theobald (1688): Shakespeare Restored (criticism of Pope's Shakespeare). P

Thomson (1700): Winter. V

Charles Burney b.
Maurice Morgann b.
Thomas Pennant b.
Sir John Vanbrugh d.
Jeremy Collier d.
'The Craftsman', 1726–47 (?).
Voltaire begins his three years' stay in England.

Bolingbroke (1672): The Occasional Writer [in The Craftsman]. P

Defoe (1661 ?): History and Reality of Apparitions. P

Dorrington, Edward (?): The Hermit, or Adventures of Philip Quarll. P

Dyer (1700 ?): Grongar Hill [early version as An Irregular Ode in Miscellaneous Poems, 1726; rev. version in D. Lewis's Miscellaneous Poems, 1726]. V

Gay (1685): Fables, series i (ii 1738; complete 1750). V

Harte, Walter (1709): Poems on Several Occasions.

Pope (1688), **Swift, Arbuthnot,** and others: Miscellanies i, ii [vol. i by Swift; vol. ii cont. Pope's Imitation of English Poets; vol. iii cont. Pope's Treatise on Bathos 1728; vol. iv 1732; vol. v 1735; 'Motte's Miscellanies'].

Somerville (1675): Poems, Translations, Fables and Tales. V

Thomson (1700): Summer. V

Warburton (1698): Inquiry into Prodigies, Miracles. P

Accession of George II.
Arthur Murphy b.
John Wilkes b.
John Hoole b.
Sir Isaac Newton d.
First Eng. trs. of Newton's 'Principia' (see 1687) by Motte.
Thomas Wotton, 'English Baronetage' (enlarged 1741; ed. Johnson and Kimber 1771).
Destouches, 'Le Philosophe marié'.

1728

Carleton, Captain George: Memoirs (? by Defoe).

Cibber, Colley (1671): Provok'd Husband [from Vanbrugh's Journey to London]. C

Fielding (1707): Love in Several Masques. C

Gay (1685): Beggar's Opera. D opera.

Hutcheson, Francis (1694): Nature and Conduct of the Passions and Affections. P

Law (1686): Serious Call to Devout and Holy Life. P

Pope (1688): Dunciad i–iii [rev. ed. as Dunciad Variorum 1729; bk. iv entitled New Dunciad 1742; bks. i–iv in final form 1743; another ed. with add. 1749]. V

Ramsay (1686): Poems [incl. Gentle Shepherd and Nuptials of Duke of Hamilton: see 1721].

Rowe, Mrs. Elizabeth (1674): Friendship in Death. P

Savage, Richard: Nature in Perfection. V
    The Bastard. V

Swift (1667): Short View of the State of Ireland. P

Thomson (1700): Spring. V

Wycherley (d. 1716): Posthumous Works in Prose and Verse, ed. Theobald.

Young (1683): Ocean: an ode. V
    Vindication of Providence. P

Thomas Warton, jnr., b.
Robert Bage b.
Thomas Cooke, trs. of Hesiod.
Ephraim Chambers, 'Cyclopaedia'.
'Intelligencer' (Swift, &c.), 1728–9.

Carey, Henry: Poems on Several Occasions [3rd ed., enlarg.; cont. Namby-Pamby and Sally in Our Alley: see 1713].

Cibber, Colley (1671): Damon and Phillida. D opera.

Gay (1685): Polly, an opera.

Johnson, Charles (1679): Village Opera. D

Oldmixon (1673): History of England [concl. 1739].

Savage, Richard: The Wanderer. V

Swift (1667): Modest Proposal for preventing the Children of the Poor People from being a Burthen to their Parents. P

Thomson (1700): Britannia. V
Poem to the Memory of Congreve. V

Edmund Burke b.
Thomas Percy b.
Clara Reeve b.
Richard Steele d.
William Congreve d.
Sir Richard Blackmore d.
Anthony Collins d.
First Eng. trs. of Perrault's 'Contes' by Robert Samber.
Elijah Fenton's ed. of Waller's Works.
Lessing b.
Moses Mendelssohn b.

1730

Bacon (d. 1626): Works, ed. Blackbourne [first collected ed.; cont. some unpub. legal tracts: see 1740, 1765].

Bolingbroke (1678): Remarks upon the History of England [in The Craftsman 1730–1]. P

Fielding (1707): Temple Beau. C
Author's Farce, Pleasures of the Town. C
Rape upon Rape, Coffee House Politician. C
Tom Thumb [enlarg. 1731]. Burlesque.

Thomson (1700): The Seasons. A hymn on the seasons and other poems [Autumn first appears in this vol.].
Sophonisba. T

Tindal, Matthew (1657): Christianity as old as the Creation. P

Watts (1674): Catechisms. P

Oliver Goldsmith b.
Laurence Echard d.
Colley Cibber poet-laureate.
John Martyn and Richard Russell start 'The Grub Street Journal' (1730–7; Pope probably contributed to it).
Voltaire, 'Brutus' and 'Préface de Brutus'.　•
Marivaux, 'Le jeu de l'amour et du hasard'.
Gottsched, 'Critische Dichtkunst'.

1731

Cudworth (d. 1688): Eternal and Immutable Morality. P

Johnson (1709): Latin Trs. of Pope's Messiah [in J. Husbands' Miscellany of Poems].

Law (1686): The Case of Reason [reply to Tindal: see 1730]. P

Lillo (1693): The London Merchant. T

Mallet (1705): Eurydice. T

Pope (1688): Of Taste: an Epistle to the Earl of Burlington [later called Of False Taste: fourth moral essay: see 1732]. V

William Cowper b.
Erasmus Darwin b.
Charles Churchill b.
Daniel Defoe d.
Edward Cave starts 'The Gentleman's Magazine' (monthly to 1907).
'Daily Advertiser' started.
Marivaux, 'Marianne' (concl. 1742).

Berkeley (1685): Alciphron. P
Dodsley (1703): Muse in Livery. V
Fielding (1707): Covent Garden Tragedy. D
    Modern Husband. C
    Mock Doctor. C
Hill (1685): Athelwold [see 1710]. T
King, William (1685): The Toast. V
Lyttelton (1709): Progress of Love. V
Neal, Daniel (1678): History of the Puritans, vol.
    i [ii 1733, iii 1736, iv 1738]. P
Pope (1688): Of the Use of Riches; an epistle to
    Lord Bathurst [third moral essay]. V
Watts (1674): Scripture History. P

George Colman, senr., b.
William Falconer b.
Richard Cumberland b.
John Gay d.
Francis Atterbury d.
Richard Bentley's ed. of
   'Paradise Lost'.
'The London Magazine'
   or 'Gentleman's Monthly
   Intelligencer' appears.
'Poor Richard's Almanac'
   (ed. B. Franklin), 1732–
   57.
Voltaire, ' Zaïre'.
Destouches, ' Le Glorieux'.

1733

Bolingbroke (1678): Dissertation upon Parties [in
    The Craftsman: reprtd. 1735]. P
Fielding (1707): The Miser. C
Gay (1685): Achilles, an opera.
Johnson, Charles (1679): Caelia, or the perjured
    lover. D
Pope (1688): Essay on Man [The Universal
    Prayer added, and also pub. separately,
    1738]. V
    Of the Knowledge and Characters of Men:
    an epistle to Viscount Cobham [first moral
    essay]. V
    First Satire of bk. ii of Horace imitated. V
    The Impertinent. V
Swift (1667): Life and genuine Character of Dr.
    Swift. P
    On Poetry: a Rapsody.

Joseph Priestley b.
Matthew Tindal d.
Wieland b.
'The Bee', Feb. 1733–
   June 1735.
Voltaire, 'English Letters'.
Prévost, 'Manon Lescaut'.

1734

Atterbury (d. 1732): Sermons, 2 vols. P
Bacon (d. 1626): Letters and Remains, collected
    by R. Stephens [see 1702].
Carey, Henry: Chrononhotonthologos [n.d.]. D
    burlesque.
Fielding (1707): Don Quixote in England. C
Johnson, Charles (fl. 1724–34): General History
    of the Lives & Adventures of the most
    Famous Highwaymen.
Pope (1688): Second Satire of bk. ii of Horace. V
Reresby, Sir John (d. 1689): Memoirs [ed. Cart-
    wright 1875, Ivatt 1904: see 1813].
Sale, George (1697?): Trs. of the Koran.
Theobald, Lewis: Ed. of Shakespeare.

Roger North d.
John Dennis d.
First Eng. trs. (anon.) of
   La Fontaine's Fables.
'General Advertiser'
   started (from 1752 as
   'Public Advertiser').
Montesquieu, 'Grandeur
   et Decadence des Ro-
   mains'.
Thomas Cooke, trs. of
   Terence.

Berkeley (1685): The Querist, pt. i (ii 1736, iii 1737). P

Brooke, Henry (1703 ?): Universal Beauty. V

Dodsley (1703): The Toy Shop. D

Beauty, or The Art of Charming. V

Hughes (d. 1720): Collected Poems, with Select Essays in Prose.

Johnson (1709): Voyage to Abyssinia [trs. Jerome Lobo]. P

Lillo (1693): Christian Hero. T

Lyttelton (1709): Letters from a Persian in England. P

Pope (1688): Characters of Women [second moral essay]. V

Epistle to Arbuthnot. V

Satires of Donne versified.

Correspondence [pub. Curll; unacknowledged, though really manipulated by Pope: see 1726, 1737].

Collected Works, vol. ii, see 1717.

Savage, Richard: Progress of a Divine. V

Somerville (1675): The Chace. V

Swift (1667): Collected Works, ed. Faulkner [4 vols., 6 vols. 1738, 8 vols. 1746].

Thomson (1700): Italy [Liberty, pt. i]. V

Greece [Liberty, pt. ii]. V

Rome [Liberty, pt. iii]. V

James Beattie b.
John Arbuthnot d.
John Wesley, 'Journals' (concl. 1790).
'Daily Gazetteer', 1735–48.
La Chaussée, 'Préjugé à la mode'.
Marivaux, 'Paysan parvenu'.

1736

Armstrong (1709): Œconomy of Love. V

Browne, Isaac Hawkins (1705): A Pipe of Tobacco. V

Butler (1692): Analogy of Religion. P

Carey, Henry: The Honest Yorkshireman. D ballad-farce.

Carte, Thomas: Life of James, Duke of Ormond. P

Duck, Stephen: Poems on Several Occasions.

Fielding (1707): Pasquin. D farce.

Historical Register for 1736. D farce.

Hill (1685): Zara [from Voltaire]. D

Alzira [from Voltaire]. D

Oldys (1696): Life of Sir Walter Raleigh [in ed. of R.'s History of the World]. P

Pope (1688): Bounce to Fop. V

Thomson (1700): Britain [Liberty, pt. iv]. V

The Prospect [Liberty, pt. v]. V

Liberty, a poem [composed of pts. pub. 1735–6].

Warburton (1698): Alliance between Church and State. P

Robert Jephson b.
James Macpherson b.
George Steevens b.
Newton, 'Method of Fluxions'.
Voltaire, 'Le Mondain' and 'Enfant prodigue'.

Carey, Henry: Dragon of Wantley. D burlesque opera.

Dodsley (1703): King and Miller of Mansfield. D

Edwards, Jonathan (1703): The Surprising Work of God in the Conversion of Many Hundred Souls. P

Fletcher, Andrew (d. 1716): Political Works. P

Glover (1712): Leonidas. V

Green, Matthew (d. 1737): The Spleen. V

Hill (1685): Tears of the Muses. V

Lillo (1693): Fatal Curiosity. T

Oldys (1696): British Librarian. P

Pope (1688): Epistle VI of bk. i of Horace imitated. V

Epistle I of bk. i of Horace imitated. V

Epistles I and II of bk. ii of Horace imitated. V
Ode to Venus. V

Letters [Works in Prose; first acknowledged and authenticated ed.: see 1726, 1735].

Shenstone (1714): Poems on Various Occasions [cont. first draft of The Schoolmistress].

Thomson (1700): Poem to memory of Lord Talbot.

Warburton (1698): Divine Legation of Moses [concl. 1741]. P

Wesley, John (1703): Psalms and Hymns.

Edward Gibbon b.
Thomas Paine b.
John Strype d.
Alexander Cruden, 'Biblical Concordance'.
David Wilkins, 'Concilia'.
Thomas Cooke's trs. of Cicero's 'De Natura Deorum'.
William Oldys, 'British Librarian' (Jan.–June).

1738

Akenside (1721): A British Philippic. V

Edwards, Jonathan (1703): Discourses on Various Important Subjects. P

Gay (1685): Fables, ii [i 1727; complete 1750]. V

Hooke, Nathaniel: Roman History [concl. 1771]. P

Johnson (1709): London [in imitation of Juvenal, Sat. iii]. V

Pope (1688): Universal Prayer. V

One Thousand Seven Hundred and Thirty-Eight [two dialogues]. V

Swift (1667): Collection of Genteel Conversation. P

Thomson (1700): Agamemnon. T

Watts (1674): World to Come. P

John Wolcot ('Peter Pindar') b.
George Whitefield, 'Journals' (concl. 1741).
Thomas Birch's ed. of Milton's Prose Works (also 1753).
Voltaire, 'Discours sur l'homme'.
Piron, 'La Métromanie'.

Addison (d. 1719): Ancient and Modern Learning [doubtful if by A.]. P

Boyse, Samuel (1708): The Deity. V

Brooke, Henry (1703 ?): Gustavus Vasa [sometimes called The Patriot]. T

Carey, Henry: Nancy [called The Pressgang 1755, The True Blue 1787]: D musical interlude.

Glover (1712): London, or the Progress of Commerce. V

Admiral Hosier's Ghost. V

Hume (1711): Treatise of Human Nature [concl. 1740]. P

Johnson (1709): Marmor Norfolciense. P

Compleat Vindication of Licensers of the Stage [an attack on the censorship provoked by the prohibition of Brooke's Gustavus Vasa]. P

Mallet (1705 ?): Mustapha. T

Smith, William: Trs. of Longinus on the Sublime. P

Swift (1667): Verses on the Death of Dr. Swift.

Thomson (1700): Edward and Eleanore. D T

Wesley, John (1703): Journal [23 parts, till 1791; ed. Curnock, 1909–16].

West (1703): A Canto of the Faery Queen [imitation of Spenser].

Hugh Kelly b.
George Lillo d.
'Scots Magazine' started.
William Warburton, 'Commentary on Pope's Essay on Man' (remodelled 1741).
Henry Fielding and James Ralph start 'The Champion'.
The Letters and Despatches, 1611–40, of Thomas Wentworth, Earl of Strafford, ed. W. Knowler.

1740

Bacon (d. 1626): Works, ed. with Life by D. Mallet [see 1730, 1765].

Cibber, Colley (1671): Apology for his Life. P

Dyer (1700 ?): Ruins of Rome. V

Law (1686): Appeal to all that doubt. P

Lillo (1693): Elmerick. T

North, Roger (d. 1734): Examen, or An Enquiry into the Credit & Veracity of a pretended complete History. P

Pitt, Christopher (1699): Trs. of Æneid. V

Prior (d. 1721): Miscellaneous Works, ed. Adrian Drift [Poems ed. Evans 1779, Mitford 1835, 1892. Complete Works, incl. for the first time Dialogues of the Dead, ed. A. R. Waller 1905–7].

Richardson (1689): Pamela or Virtue Rewarded. P

Somerville (1675): Hobbinol. V

Thomson (1700) and Mallet (1705): Alfred [new version by Mallet 1751; cont. Rule Britannia]. D masque.

Whitefield, George: Short Account of God's dealings with George Whitefield [see 1747]. P

Christian History [concl. 1747]. P

James Boswell b.
Thomas Tickell d.
William Stukeley's 'Stonehenge'.
Saint-Simon, 'Mémoires', 1740 ff.

Arbuthnot, Pope, Gay, Parnell, and others: Memoirs of Scriblerus [in the 4to ed. of Pope's Works: mostly by Arbuthnot].

Betterton, Thomas (d. 1710): History of the English Stage [doubtful if by B.]. P

Dodsley (1703): Blind Beggar of Bethnal Green. D

Public Register [3 Jan.–13 June].

Fielding (1707): Shamela. P

Francklin (1721): Of the Nature of the Gods [trs. Cicero].

Hume (1711): Essays Moral and Political [concl. 1742].

Middleton (1683): Life of Cicero. P

Ogle, George (1704): Tales of Chaucer modernized by several hands [Dryden, Pope, and others].

Pope (1688): Works in Prose, vol. ii.

Richardson (1689): Familiar Letters. P

Shenstone (1714): Judgment of Hercules. V

Watts (1674): Improvement of the Mind. P

William Combe b.
Arthur Young b.
Sarah Trimmer b.
Edmond Malone b.
Laclos b.
La Chaussée, 'Mélanide'.

1742

Campbell, John (1708): Lives of the Admirals, vol. i, ii [iii and iv 1744]. P

Cibber (1671): Letters to Mr. Pope. P

Collins (1721): Persian Eclogues [repub. as Oriental Eclogues 1757]. V

Cooke (1703): Bays' Miscellany [including revised ed. of Battle of the Poets]. V

Fielding (1707): Joseph Andrews. P

North (d. 1734): Life of Francis North [see 1744]. P

Pope (1688): New Dunciad [bk. iv of Dunciad: see 1728]. V

Blast upon Bays. P

Shenstone (1714): Schoolmistress [revised; see 1737]. V

Somerville (d. 1742): Field Sports. V

Thurloe, John (d. 1668): Collection of State Papers, ed. Birch, 7 vols. P

West (1703): Order of the Garter [altered by Garrick 1771]. D

Young (1683): The Complaint, or Night Thoughts i–iv [v 1743, vi–vii 1744, viii–ix 1745]. V

William Somerville d.
Richard Bentley d.
John Oldmixon d.
Memorials of Sarah, Duchess of Marlborough, ed. Nathaniel Hooke.
Voltaire, 'Mahomet'.

Blair (1699): The Grave. V
Collins (1721): Verses on Hanmer's Shakespeare.
Fielding (1707): Miscellanies [cont. Jonathan Wild P, Journey from this World to the Next P, Eurydice D, The Wedding Day D, Essay on Nothing P, and other works].
Francis, Philip (1708?): Trs. Odes, Epodes, and Carmen Seculare of Horace [see 1746]. V
Gay (d. 1732): The Distress'd Wife. C
Hammond, James (d. 1742): Love Elegies. V
Hanmer (1677): Ed. of Shakespeare.
Hill (1685): Fancid. V
Milton (d. 1674): Letters and Papers of State addressed to Oliver Cromwell, ed. John Nickolls, jnr. [see 1694].
Pococke, Richard (1704): Description of the East and some other Countries [concl. 1745]. P
Pope (1688): The Dunciad [final form]. V

Anna Barbauld (née Aikin) b.
Hannah Cowley b.
William Paley b.
Henry Carey d.
Richard Savage d.
'Old England', 1743–53.
William Oldys, 'Catalogus bibliothecae Harleianae' (with contribution by Samuel Johnson; concl. 1744).
Cooke's trs. of Amphitruo of Plautus.

1744

Akenside (1721): Epistle to Curio. V
Pleasures of Imagination (rev. ed. 1772). V
Armstrong (1709): Art of Preserving Health. V
Berkeley (1685): Philosophical Reflections concerning Tar-water [later called Siris]. P
Collins (1721): Dirge in Cymbeline. V
Denham (d. 1669): Psalms of David [with an essay on earlier metrical versions]. V
Dodsley (1709): Collection of Old Plays [ed. Reed 1780, Collier 1825–8, W. C. Hazlitt 1874–6].
Fielding, Sarah (1710): David Simple. P
Johnson (1709): Life of John Philip Barretier. P
Life of Richard Savage. P
Moore, Edward (1712), and Brooke (1703?): Fables for the Female Sex.
North (d. 1734): Lives of Dudley North and John North [see 1742, 1890].
Warton, Joseph (1722): The Enthusiast. V

Alexander Pope d.
Lewis Theobald d.
William Oldys, 'Harleian Miscellany' (with Introduction by Samuel Johnson; concl. 1746).
Zachary Grey's ed. of 'Hudibras' (Supplement, cont. critical, historical, and explanatory notes, 1752).

1745

Akenside (1721): Odes on Several Subjects.
Carew, Bampfylde-Moore (1690): Life & Adventures. P
Doddridge (1702): Rise and Progress of Religion in the Soul. P
Johnson (1709): Observations on Macbeth [with Proposals for a new edition of Shakespeare]. P
Swift (1667): Directions to Servants. P
Thomson (1700): Tancred and Sigismunda. T

Second Jacobite Rebellion.
William Hayley b.
Henry Mackenzie b.
Hannah More b.
Thomas Holcroft b.
Henry James Pye b.
Jonathan Swift d.
Fielding starts 'The True Patriot' (concl. 1746).
Voltaire, 'Mérope'.
Gresset, 'Le Méchant'.

Blacklock, Thomas (1721, the blind poet): Poems.
Collier, John ('Tim Bobbin'): View of Lancashire Dialect. V
Collins (1721): Odes [To Evening, How Sleep the Brave, On Death of Colonel Ross, &c.].
Edwards, Jonathan (1703): A Treatise concerning Religious Affections. P
Francis, Philip: Trs. Satires, Epistles, and Art of Poetry of Horace [see 1743]. V
Hervey, James (1714): Meditations and Contemplations, vol. i (ii 1747). P
Pope (d. 1744): Verses on the Duchess of Marlborough. V
  Character of the Duchess of Buckinghamshire. V
Upton, John (1707): Critical Observations on Shakespeare [2nd ed. with attack on Warburton 1748].
Walpole (1717): The Beauties. V
Warton, Joseph (1722): Odes.

Thomas Southerne d.
Robert Blair d.
Francis Hutcheson d.
Robert Dodsley starts 'The Museum' (concl. 1747).

1747

Birch, Thomas (1705): Lives [in Heads of Illustrious Persons engraved by Houbraken and Vertue; concl. 1752]. P
Carte, Thomas: History of England [concl. 1755].
Garrick (1717): Miss in her Teens. D farce.
Glasse, Hannah (fl. 1747): The Art of Cookery made Plain & Easy. P
Gray (1716): Ode on Eton College. V
Hoadly, Benjamin (1706): Suspicious Husband. C
Johnson (1709): Prologue [and Epilogue] at the Opening of the Theatre in Drury Lane. V
  Plan of a Dictionary of the English Language. P
Lyttelton (1709): Monody to the Memory of a Lady [his wife]. V
Mallet (1705?): Amyntor and Theodora. V
Mason (1724): Musaeus (elegy on Pope). V
Montagu, Lady Mary Wortley (1689): Town Eclogues [unauthorized ed. as Court Poems 1716]. V
Pococke, Richard (1704): Tours in Scotland. P
Sterne (1713): The Case of Elijah. P
Warburton, William: Ed. of Shakespeare.
Warton, Thomas (1728): Pleasures of Melancholy. V
West (1703): Observations on the Resurrection. P
Whitefield (1714): Full Account of God's Dealings with George Whitefield. P

Uvedale Price b.
Anna Seward b.
Fielding starts 'The Jacobite's Journal' (concl. 1748).
'Biographia Britannica' (concl. 1766; 2nd ed. 1778–93).
Spence, 'Polymetis'.
Voltaire, 'Zadig'.
Lesage d.

Akenside (1721) : Ode to the Earl of Huntingdon. V
Anson, George (1697) : Voyage Round the World. P
Bower, Archibald (1686): History of the Popes [concl. 1758]. P
Collins (1721): Odes (revised) in Dodsley's Collection [see 1746].
Dodsley (1703): Collection of Poems, vols. i–iii (iv 1755, v–vi 1758).
The Preceptor. P
Edwards, Thomas (1699): Canons of Criticism [attack on Warburton's Shakespeare]. P
Gray (1716): Ode to Spring. On Death of a Favourite Cat [in vol. ii of Dodsley's Collection above]. V
Hume (1711): Philosophical Essays concerning Human Understanding [cont., among others, Essay upon Miracles]. P
Richardson (1689): Clarissa Harlowe. P
Smollett (1721): Roderick Random. P
Thomson (1700): Castle of Indolence. V
Whalley, Peter (1722): Enquiry into the Learning of Shakespeare. P

Jeremy Bentham b.
James Thomson d.
Isaac Watts d.
Somers Tracts (so called after Sir John Somers, 1651–1716) first published (concl. 1752; ed. Scott 1809).
Thomas Tanner, 'Bibliotheca Britannico-Hibernica'.
Montesquieu, 'Esprit des Lois'.
Klopstock, 'Der Messias' (concl. 1773),

1749

Ames, Joseph (1689): Typographical Antiquities [ed. Herbert 1785, Dibdin 1805]. P
Bolingbroke (1678): On the Spirit of Patriotism. P
Idea of a Patriot King. P
State of Parties at the Accession of George I. P
Chetwood, William: General History of the Stage. P
Collins (1721): On the Death of Thomson. V
Fielding (1707): Tom Jones. P
The Case of Bosavern Penlez. P
A Charge to the Grand Jury. P
Hartley, David (1705): Observations on Man. P
Hill (1685): Mérope [from Voltaire]. T
Johnson (1709): Vanity of Human Wishes [in imitation of Satire x of Juvenal]. V
Irene: a tragedy.
Law (1686): Spirit of Prayer, pt. i (ii. 1750). P
Middleton (1683): Free Inquiry into Miraculous Powers. P
Smollett (1721): Trs. of Gil Blas. P
Thomson (d. 1748): Coriolanus. T
Warton, Thomas (1728): Triumph of Isis. V
West (1703): Trs. of Odes of Pindar. V

Charlotte Smith b.
Ambrose Philips d.
'The Monthly Review, or the Literary Journal' (concl. 1845).
Thomas Francklin's trs. of Epistles of Phalaris.
T. Newton's ed. of Milton's Poetical Works (concl. 1750).
Johann Wolfgang von Goethe b.
Buffon, 'Histoire Naturelle'.
Voltaire, 'Nanine'.
Diderot, 'Lettre sur les aveugles'.

Campbell, John (1708): Political State of Europe. P
Dodsley (1703): Œconomy of Human Life. P
Fielding (1707): Intriguing Chambermaid. D
Halifax (d. 1695): Character of Charles II. P
Hobbes (d. 1679): Works, ed. J. Campbell [ed. Molesworth 1839–45].
Johnson (1709): Prologue at Representation of Comus. V
    The Rambler [bi-weekly from 20 Mar. 1750 to 14 Mar. 1752]. P
    Preface and Postscript to An Essay on Milton's Use and Imitation of Moderns by William Lauder. P
Smart (1722): Eternity of Supreme Being. V
Sterne (1713): Abuses of Conscience. P
Thomson (d. 1748): Poems on Several Occasions.
Whitehead (1715): Roman Father. T

Richard Payne Knight b.
Sophia Lee b.
Aaron Hill d.
Elijah Fenton d.
The Blue-stocking parties begin.
Moses Browne's ed. of Walton's 'Compleat Angler' with alterations 'to suit the taste of the age'.
'The Student', 1750–1.
Rousseau, 'Discours sur les lettres'.

1751

Arbuthnot (d. 1735): Miscellaneous Works [collected; enlarg. ed. 1770].
Cambridge (1717): Scribleriad. V
Fielding (1707): Late Increase of Robbers. P
    Amelia. P
Gray (1716): Elegy wrote in a Country Churchyard [3rd ed. 1751 contains Redbreast stanza, omitted again in 1753]. V
Hume (1711): Enquiry concerning Principles of Morals. P
Kames (1696): Principles of Morality and Natural Religion. P
Paltock (1697): Peter Wilkins. P
Raleigh (d. 1618): Works, ed. with Life by Thomas Birch [Oxford ed. 1829].
Smollett (1721): Peregrine Pickle. P
West (1703): Education, a poem.

Richard Brinsley Sheridan b.
Henry St. John, Viscount Bolingbroke, d.
Philip Doddridge d.
'L'Encyclopédie' (1751–80).
D'Alembert,' Discours préliminaire de l'encyclopédie'.
Voltaire, 'Siècle de Louis XIV'.
Warburton, ed. Pope.

1752

Birch, Thomas (1705): Life of Archbishop Tillotson. P
Bolingbroke (d.1751): Study and Uses of History. P
    Reflections concerning Moral Principles. P
Hume (1711): Political Discourses. P
Law (1686): Way to Divine Knowledge. P
Lennox (1720): Female Quixote. P
Mason (1724): Elfrida. D
Smart (1722): Poems [incl. Hop Garden].

The calendar changed.
Thomas Chatterton b.
Frances Burney b.
Joseph Butler d.
Samuel Croxall d.
William Whitson d.
Fielding starts 'The Covent Garden Journal' (Jan.–Nov.).
William Dodd, 'Beauties of Shakespeare'.

Bolingbroke (d. 1751): Letter to Sir William Wyndham, Reflections on the State of the Nation, Introductory Letter to Pope. P

Cibber, Theophilus (1703): Lives of the Poets [really by Robert Shiels]. P

Lives of Actors and Actresses. P

Dodsley (1703): Public Virtue. V

Foote (1720): Englishman in Paris. C

Glover (1712): Boadicea. T

Gray (1716): Hymn to Adversity, &c. [in Designs by Bentley for Six Poems by Gray].

Hill (d. 1750): Works [correspondence and poems: see 1760].

Jones, Henry (1721): Earl of Essex. T

Law (1686): Collected Works.

Lennox (1720): Shakespear Illustrated. P

Moore (1712): The Gamester [with David Garrick]. T

Smart (1722): Hilliad. V

Smollett (1721): Ferdinand Count Fathom. P

Warton, Joseph (1722), **and Pitt, Christopher**: Ed. of Virgil with Eng. trs. in verse.

Young (1683): The Brothers. T

Elizabeth Inchbald b.
Dugald Stewart b.
William Roscoe b.
George Berkeley d.
Dodsley starts 'The World' (concl. 1757).
Hawkesworth, Johnson, Joseph Warton, and others start 'The Adventurer' (concl. 1754).
The Union, or Select Scots and English Poems.
Construction of Horace Walpole's house at Strawberry Hill started.
Charter of the British Museum.
Voltaire, 'Essai sur les mœurs' (1753–5).
William Smith, trs. Thucydides' Peloponnesian War.

1754

Birch, Thomas (1705): Memoirs of Reign of Queen Elizabeth. P

Bolingbroke (d. 1751): Collected Works, ed. David Mallet.

Butler (d. 1680): Genuine Remains. P and V

Edwards, Jonathan (1703): Freedom of Will. P

Gay (d. 1732): Rehearsal at Goatham. D farce.

Grey, Zachary: Notes on Shakespeare.

Hume (1711): History of England [The Stuarts, concl. 1757; Tudors 1759; Early History 1762].

Richardson (1689): Sir Charles Grandison (dated 1754; but vols. 1–4 appeared before Sep. 1753). P.

Warton, Thomas (1728): Observations on the Fairie Queene [2nd ed. corrected 1762]. P

Whitehead (1715): Creusa, Queen of Athens. T

Young (1683): Centaur not fabulous. P

George Crabbe b.
Henry Fielding d.
George Colman and Bonnell Thornton, 'The Connoisseur', Jan. 1754–Sept. 1756.
Chesterfield's Papers in 'The World' on Johnson's 'Dictionary'.
Erskine, 'Principles of the Law of Scotland'.
Diderot, 'L'Interprétation de la nature'.
Condillac, 'Traité des sensations'.

1755

Amory, Thomas (1691 ?): Memoirs of Several Ladies of Great Britain. P

Brown, John (1715): Barbarossa. T

Doddridge (d. 1751): Hymns.

Dodsley (1703): Collection of Poems, vol. iv [see 1748].

'The Monitor' started (concl. 1763).
Mary Barber's anthology, 'Poems by Eminent Ladies'.
'Edinburgh Review', 1755–6.

Fielding (d. 1754): Voyage to Lisbon. P
Grainger, James (1721 ?): Ode on Solitude. V
Hervey, James (1714): Theron and Aspasio. P
Hutcheson (d. 1746): System of Moral Philosophy. P
Johnson (1709): English Dictionary [abridged
    1756; revised 1773].
Smollett (1721): Trs. of Don Quixote. P
Swift (d. 1745): Collected Works, ed. Hawkes-
    worth.

Montesquieu d.
Voltaire, 'Orpheline de la
    Chine'.
Rousseau, 'Discours sur
    Inégalité'.
Lessing, 'Miss Sara
    Sampson'.
Winckelmann, 'Gedanken
    über die Nachahmung
    der griechischen Werke'.

1756

Amory, Thomas (1691 ?): Life of John Buncle,
    vol. i (ii 1766). P
Brown, John (1715): Athelstane. T
Burke (1729): Vindication of Natural Society. P
    Origin of our Ideas of the Sublime and Beauti-
    ful [2nd ed. cont. Discourse concerning
    Taste 1757]. P
Butler, Alban (1711): Lives of the Saints, vol. i
    [later vols. 1757–8–9].
Foote (1720): Englishman returned from Paris. D
Johnson (1709): Life of Sir Thomas Browne [in
    ed. of Christian Morals: see 1716]. P
    Proposals for the Dramatick Works of Shake-
    speare. P
Mason (1724): Odes.
Moore (1712): Poems, Fables, and Plays [col-
    lected].
Smollett (1721): Compendium of Authentic
    Voyages. P
Warton, Joseph (1722): Genius and Writings of
    Pope, vol. i [ii 1782]. P

William Godwin b.
William Gifford b.
Robert and James Dodsley,
    'Theatrical Records'.
John Shebbeare's 'Letters
    on the English Nation'
    begin to appear.
Smollett's 'Critical Re-
    view'.
Christopher Smart's trs.
    of Horace.
'Literary Magazine',
    1756–8.
Mirabeau, 'Ami des
    hommes'.
Voltaire, 'Loi naturelle',
    'Désastre de Lisbonne'.

1757

Brown, John (1715): Estimate of Manners and
    Principles of the Times. P
Burke (1729): An Account of the European
    Settlements in America [probably written
    by William Burke, revised and added to by
    Edmund Burke]. P
Collins (1721): Oriental Eclogues [see 1742].
Dyer (1700 ?): The Fleece. V
Gray (1716): Odes [Progress of Poesy, The Bard]. V
Home (1722): Douglas. T
Hume (1711): Four Dissertations [Natural
    History of Religion, Of the Passions, Of
    Tragedy, Of Standard of Taste]. P
Price (1723): Principal Questions in Morals. P
Smollett (1721): History of England [concl. 1758:
    see 1763]. P
Wilkie (1721): Epigoniad. V

William Blake b.
Colley Cibber d.
Edward Moore d.
William Whitehead poet-
    laureate.
Horace Walpole sets up
    Strawberry Hill Press.
'London Chronicle' started.
Diderot, 'Fils Naturel'.
Klopstock, 'Der Tod
    Adams'.

Akenside (1721): Ode to the Country Gentlemen of England. V

Armstrong (1709): Sketches. P

Dodsley (1703): Cleone. T
Collection of Poems, vols. v–vi [see 1748].

Gibbon (1737): Essai sur l'étude de la littérature [at Lausanne, Eng. ed. 1764]. P

Goldsmith (1730): Memoirs of a Protestant [trs. Jean Marteilhe of Bergerac]. P

Johnson (1709): The Idler [in the Universal Chronicle, 15 Ap. 1758 to 5 Ap. 1760; collected 1761].

Lowth (1710): Life of William of Wykeham. P

Murphy (1727): The Upholsterer. D

Parnell (d. 1718): Posthumous Works [cont. unpub. poems: see 1722].

Swift (d. 1745): Four Last Years of the Queen. P

Walpole (1717): Catalogue of Royal and Noble Authors [rev. 1759]. P

John Dyer d.
Allan Ramsay d.
James Hervey d.
Elizabeth Carter's trs. of Epictetus.
John Upton's ed. of 'Faerie Queene'.
Diderot, 'Père de famille'.
Voltaire, 'Pauvre Diable'.
Helvétius, 'De l'esprit'.

1759

Butler (d. 1680): Remains in Verse and Prose, ed. R. Thyer [incl. Elephant in the Moon V, Characters P].

Clarendon (d. 1674): Life, being a Continuation of the History of the Rebellion [see 1702]. P

Gerard, Alexander (1723): Essay on Taste. P

Goldsmith (1730): Present State of Polite Learning [rev. 1774]. P
The Bee [6 Oct.–24 Nov.]. P

Hurd (1720): Moral and Political Dialogues [enlarg. 1762]. P

Johnson (1709): Rasselas. P

Mason (1724): Caractacus. D

Murphy (1727): Orphan of China [from Voltaire]. T

Robertson (1721): History of Scotland. P

Smith, Adam (1723): Theory of Moral Sentiments. P

Townley (1714): High Life below Stairs. C

Wilkes, Thomas: General View of the Stage. P

Young (1683): Conjectures on Original Composition. P

Robert Burns b.
Mary Wollstonecraft b.
William Beckford b.
William Collins d.
British Museum opens.
Annual Register, vol. i (pub. Dodsley. Burke in charge till 1788).
'The Public Ledger' (daily) started.
Thomas Francklin's trs. of Sophocles.
Thomas Coxeter's ed. of Massinger.
Voltaire, 'Candide'.
Schiller b.
Lessing, 'Philotas'.
Lessing and others, 'Die Litteraturbriefe', 1759–65.

Colman, senr. (1732): Polly Honeycombe. D
Foote (1720): The Minor. C
Goldsmith (1730): Citizen of the World [in The Public Ledger, 24 Jan. 1760 to 14 Aug. 1761; collected 1762].
Hamilton, William, of Bangour (d. 1754): Poems [first authoritative collection].
Hill (d. 1750): Collected Works [see 1753]. D
Johnstone, Charles (1719?): Chrysal, or Adventures of a Guinea. P
Lloyd (1733): The Actor. V
Lyttelton (1709): Dialogues of the Dead [see 1765]. P
Macpherson (1736): Fragments of Ancient Poetry [first publication of Ossian: see 1762–3].
Murphy (1727): The Way to Keep Him. C
Sterne (1713): Tristram Shandy, vols. i–ii [iii–vi 1761–2; vii–viii 1765; ix 1767; collected 1767]. P
  Sermons of Yorick [concl. 1769]. P

Accession of George III.
Smollett, 'British Magazine'.
Newbery's 'Public Ledger'.
Baretti, 'Italian and English Dictionary'.
Francis Fawkes's trs. of Anacreon, Sappho, Bion, and others.
Capell, 'Prolusions, or Select Pieces of English Poetry'.
Voltaire, 'Tancrède'.
Diderot, 'La Religieuse'.
Palissot, 'Les Philosophes'.

1761

Armstrong (1709): Day: an Epistle to John Wilkes. V
Ascham (d. 1568): English Works, ed. J. Bennet [really S. Johnson; ed. Aldis Wright, 1904].
Brooke (1703?): Earl of Essex. T
Churchill (1731): Rosciad. V
  The Apology. V
Colman, senr. (1732): Jealous Wife. C
Dodsley (1703): Fugitive Pieces by Several Authors [ed. Joseph Spence]. P
Glover (1712): Medea. T
Johnson (1709): Life of Roger Ascham [in English Works of Ascham, nominally ed. J. Bennet].
Murphy (1727): All in the Wrong. C
  The Old Maid. C
Sheridan, Frances (1724): Memoirs of Miss Sidney Bidulph. P
Victor, Benjamin: History of the Theatres of London and Dublin. P

Samuel Richardson d.
William Law d.
Meeting of Johnson and Goldsmith.
'St. James's Chronicle' started.
Thomas Percy, 'Hau Kiou Choaan' (from Portuguese trs. of a Chinese romance).
Francklin, Smollett, and others, trs. of Works of Voltaire (concl. 1774).
Kotzebue b.
Rousseau, 'Nouvelle Héloïse'.

Campbell (1719): Dissertation on Miracles. P
Carter, Elizabeth (1717): Poems.
Churchill (1731): Night. V
  The Ghost, bks. i–iii (iv 1763). V
Falconer, William (1732): The Shipwreck. V
Fielding (d. 1764): Works, ed. with Life by
  Arthur Murphy.
Goldsmith (1730): Citizen of the World [see 1760]. P
  Life of Richard Nash. P
  Mystery Revealed. P.   Art of Poetry. P
Hurd (1720): Letters on Chivalry and Romance.
Kames (1696): Elements of Criticism. P
Macpherson (1736): Fingal, and Other Poems by
  'Ossian' [see 1760, 1763]. V
Smollett (1721): Sir Lancelot Greaves. P
Stevenson, John Hall- (1718): Crazy Tales. V
Walpole (1717): Anecdotes of Painting [concl.
  1780].
Whitehead (1715): School for Lovers. C
  A Charge to the Poets. V
Young (1683): Resignation. V

George Colman jnr. b.
William Lisle Bowles b.
Helen Maria Williams b.
William Cobbett b.
Joanna Baillie b.
Lady Mary Wortley Mon-
  tagu d.
Johnson granted a pension.
'The Briton' (ed. Smollett),
  1762–3.
'The North Briton' (ed.
  Wilkes and Churchill),
  1762–3.
'The Auditor' (ed. Mur-
  phy), 1762–3.
John Parkhurst, 'Hebrew
  and English Lexicon'.
Robert Lowth, 'Introduc-
  tion to English Gram-
  mar'.
Wieland's translations of
  Shakespeare (till 1766).
André Chénier b.
Rousseau, 'Contrat Social';
  'Émile'.
Fichte b.
Diderot, 'Neveu de
  Rameau'.

1763

Bickerstaffe, Isaac: Love in a Village. D
Blair, Hugh (1718): On the Poems of Ossian. P
Brooke, Frances (1724): Lady Julia Mandeville. P
Brown (1715): Dissertation on Poetry and Music. P
Burke (1729): History of the Late War [repub.
  from The Annual Register, 1759–63]. P
Churchill (1731): Prophecy of Famine; Epistle to
  Hogarth, The Conference, The Duellist,
  The Author. V
  Collected Poems [vol. ii 1766].
Colman, senr. (1732): The Deuce is in him. D
Foote (1720): The Mayor of Garratt. C
Goldsmith (1730): Brookes's Natural History. P
Hoole (1727): Trs. Jerusalem Delivered. V
Johnson (1709): On Life and Writings of Collins
  [in The Poetical Calendar]. P
Keate, George (1729): The Alps. V
Macpherson (1736): Temora, with Other Poems
  by 'Ossian' [see 1760, 1762]. V
Mallet (1705?): Elvira. T
Mason (1724): Elegies. V
Montagu (d. 1762): Letters [unauthorized ed.;
  a fourth vol. 1767: see 1803].
Murphy (1727): The Citizen. D
Orme, Robert (1728): History of Military Trans-
  actions of the British in Indostan. P

Samuel Rogers b.
William Shenstone d.
Prosecution of John
  Wilkes for having at-
  tacked the government in
  No. 45 of 'The North
  Briton'.
Meeting of Johnson and
  Boswell.
Fawkes and Woty, 'The
  Poetical Calendar', 12
  vols.
Voltaire, 'Traité sur la
  Tolérance'.
Jean-Paul Richter b.

Percy (1729): Five Pieces of Runic Poetry.
Shebbeare (1709): History of the Sumatrans. P
Smart (1722): Song to David. V
Smollett (1721): Continuation of History of England [concl. 1765: see 1757]. P

1764

Baker, David Erskine (1730): Companion to the Play-house [ed. Reed as Biographia Dramatica 1782; ed. Stephen Jones 1812]. P
'Candor' [Sir Philip Francis?]: A Letter to the Public Advertiser. P
  Letter concerning Libels, Warrants [in Public Advertiser] P
Churchill (1731): Gotham, The Candidate, Independence, The Times, The Farewell. V
Falconer, William (1732): The Demagogue. V
Goldsmith (1730): History of England in a series of Letters (2 vols.; see 1771). P
  The Traveller [1765]. V
Grainger, James (1721?): Sugar-cane. V
Herbert, Edward, Lord Herbert of Cherbury (d. 1648): Autobiography [ed. S. Lee 1886].
Murphy (1727): What we must all come to [as Three Weeks after Marriage, 1776]. C
  No one's enemy but his own [from Voltaire]. D
Reid (1710): Enquiry into the Human Mind. P
Shenstone (d. 1763): Works in Verse and Prose [Letters added 1769].
Smollett (1721): Present State of all Nations. P
Wilson, John (1720): Earl Douglas. D
  The Clyde. V

Thomas Morton b.?
Ann Radcliffe b.
Charles Churchill d.
Robert Dodsley d.
Thomas Warton jnr., 'Oxford Sausage' (anthology).
Evan Evans, 'Specimens of the Poetry of the Ancient Welsh Bards'.
George Ward and Thomas Langcake, trs. of Works of Jacob Boehme (concl. 1781).
Frances Brooke, trs. of Riccombini's 'Lady Juliet Catesby'.
John Entick, 'Spelling Dictionary'.
Rousseau, 'Émile'.
Voltaire, 'Dictionnaire philosophique'.
Sedaine, 'Le Philosophe sans le savoir'.
Winckelmann, 'Geschichte der Kunst des Altertums'.

1765

Bacon (d. 1626): Works, with unpub. Letters and Speeches, ed. Birch [later edd.: Montagu 1825; Ellis, Spedding, & Heath 1857-74].
Beattie (1735): Judgment of Paris. V
Bickerstaffe, Isaac: Maid of the Mill. D
Blackstone (1723): Commentaries on Laws of England [concl. 1769].
Bunyan (d. 1688): Relation of his Imprisonment. P
Collins (d. 1759): Poetical Works (collected).
Colman, senr. (1732): Trs. of Terence. V
Dulany, Daniel (1721): Taxes on Colonies. P
Goldsmith (1730): Essays [collected].
  Edwin and Angelina [privately printed: included in Vicar of Wakefield 1766]. V
Heath (1704): Revisal of Shakespeare's Text. P
Johnson (1709): Ed. of Shakespeare [new ed. Steevens 1773, Reed 1785].
Lyttelton (1709): Four New Dialogues of the Dead [see 1760]. P

Sir James Mackintosh b.
Edward Young d.
David Mallet d.
William Cole of Bletchley, Diary, 1765-7 (pub. 1931).
Leibnitz, 'Nouveaux Essais'.

Percy (1729): Reliques of Ancient English Poetry [later edd.: 1767–75–94–1812; ed. Wheatley 1876–7, Schröer, 1893].
Smart (1722): Translation of Psalms of David. V
Walpole (1717): Castle of Otranto. P
Wesley, John (1703): Journal (publication continued until 1790; in 4 vols. 1827). P

1766

Anstey, Christopher (1724): New Bath Guide. V
Brooke, Henry (1703?): Fool of Quality. P
Burke (1729): Short Account of a Short Administration. P
Colman, senr. (1732): Clandestine Marriage [with Garrick]. C
Francklin (1721): Earl of Warwick. T
Goldsmith (1730): Vicar of Wakefield. P
Graves (1715): The Festoon. V
Griffith, Elizabeth (1720?): A Double Mistake. C
Johnson (1709): Miscellaneous Pieces [in Anna Williams's Miscellanies].
Smollett (1721): Travels through France and Italy. P
Steevens (1736): Shakespeare Quartos [see 1773].
Swift (d. 1745): Letters, ed. Hawkesworth [cont. Letters 1, 41–65 of Journal to Stella: see 1768].
Tyrwhitt (1730): Observations on Passages of Shakespeare. P

Thomas Robert Malthus b.
Isaac D'Israeli b.
Robert Bloomfield b.
Mme de Staël b.
The Old Pretender d.
Letters to 'The Public Advertiser' signed 'Anti-Sejanus' (James Scott).
Smollett, 'The British Magazine' (concl. 1767).
Rousseau in England.
Lessing, 'Laokoon'.
Wieland, 'Agathon' (concl. 1767).

1767

Clarendon (d. 1674): State Papers, ed. Scrope and Monkhouse [selection only: see 1872].
Colman, senr. (1732): English Merchant [from Voltaire]. C
Farmer (1735): Essay on the Learning of Shakespeare. P
Ferguson, Adam (1723): History of Civil Society. P
Goldsmith (1730): Poems for Young Ladies. Beauties of English Poesy.
Hoole (1727): Trs. of Dramas of Metastasio. V
Jago (1715): Edge Hill. V
Kelly (1739): Memoirs of a Magdalen. P
Lyttelton (1709): History of Henry II. P
Mickle (1735): The Concubine [reissued as Sir Martin 1778]. V
Murphy (1727): School for Guardians. C
Sheridan, Frances (1724): History of Nourjahad. P
Thornton, Bonnell (1724): The Battle of the Whigs. V
　Trs. Plautus. V

Maria Edgeworth b.
John Byrom, 'Universal English Shorthand'.
Beaumarchais, 'Eugénie'.
Lessing, 'Minna von Barnhelm. Hamburgische Dramaturgie' (1767–9).
Herder, 'Fragmente' (which begins the Sturm und Drang period, ending with Schiller's 'Don Carlos', 1787).

Adams, John (1735): Canon and Feudal Law. P
Baretti (1719): Account of Italy. P
Bickerstaffe, Isaac: The Padlock. D
　Lionel and Clarissa [School for Fathers 1773]. D
Boswell (1740): Account of Corsica. P
Browne, Isaac Hawkins (d. 1760): Coll. Poems.
Capell (1713): Ed. of Shakespeare.
Foote (1720): Devil upon two Sticks. C
Goldsmith (1730): Good-natur'd Man. C
Gray (1716): Poems [cont. unpub. Fatal Sisters,
　Descent of Odin, Triumphs of Owen].
Hoole (1727): Cyrus. T
Kelly (1739): False Delicacy [with Garrick]. C
Montagu, Lady Mary Wortley (d. 1762): Poetical
　Works, ed. Reed.
Murphy (1727): Zenobia. T
Percy (1729): Ed. of Household Book of the Earl
　of Northumberland in 1512.
Priestley (1733): First Principles of Government. P
Ross, Alexander (1699): Fortunate Shepherdess. V
Sterne (d. 1768): Sentimental Journey through
　France and Italy. P
Swift (d. 1745): Letters, ed. Deane Swift [cont.
　Letters 2–40 of Journal to Stella: see 1766].
Tucker (1705): Light of Nature pursued, vols.
　i–iv [v–vii 1778]. P
Walpole (1717): Mysterious Mother. T
　Historic Doubts on Richard III. P

Sharon Turner b.
Laurence Sterne d.
Joseph Spence d.
Royal Academy founded.
'Encyclopaedia Britannica', 1st ed. (concl. 1771; ed. William Smellie).
Chateaubriand b.

1769

Burke (1729): Observations on 'The Present
　State of the Nation'. P
Chatterton (1752): Elinoure and Juga [in Town
　and Country Magazine for May]. V
Colman, senr. (1732): Oxonian in Town. C
Goldsmith (1730): Roman History. P
Granger (1723): Biographical History of England
　[supplement 1774 ; continued by Noble 1806].
Gray (1716): Installation Ode. V
Griffith, Elizabeth (1720?): School for Rakes
　[from Beaumarchais's Eugénie]. C
Lennox (1720): The Sister. C
Montagu (1720): Essay on Shakespeare. P
Reynolds (1723): Discourses to the Royal
　Academy [see 1797].
Robertson (1721): History of Charles V. P
Smollett (1721): Adventures of an Atom [1749]. P
Sterne (1713): Political Romance addressed to
　—— Esq. of York [History of a Warm
　Watch Coat]. P

Amelia Opie b.
John Hookham Frere b.
William Falconer d.
Shakespeare Jubilee at Stratford-on-Avon (conducted by Garrick).
The Letters of 'Junius' appear in 'The Public Advertiser', 1769–71.
'The Morning Chronicle'.
'Town and Country Magazine'.
John Parkhurst, 'Greek and English Lexicon to the New Testament' (ed. H. J. Rose 1829).
David Herd, 'Ancient and Modern Scottish Songs' (enlarg. 1776).
William Falconer, 'Marine Dictionary'.
Napoleon b.
Voltaire, 'Les Guèbres'.
Klopstock, 'Hermanns Schlacht'.

Armstrong (1709): Miscellanies. P and V
Baretti (1719): Journey from London to Genoa. P
Beattie (1735): Essay on Truth. P
Bruce, Michael (d. 1767): Poems, ed. John Logan.
Burke (1729): Thoughts on the Present Discontents. P
Cumberland (1732): The Brothers. C
Dalrymple, Sir David (1726): Ed. of Ancient Scottish Poems from the MS. of George Bannatyne, 1568.
Goldsmith (1730): Deserted Village. V
    Life of Thomas Parnell. P
    Life of Viscount Bolingbroke. P
Hoole (1727): Timanthes. T
Johnson (1709): False Alarm. P
Kelly (1739): A Word to the Wise. C
Mickle (1735): Voltaire in the Shades. V
Percy (1729): Northern Antiquities [trs. of M. Mallet's Introduction to L'Histoire de Dannemarc]. P
Young (1741): A Six Months' Tour through the North of England. P

William Wordsworth b.
James Hogg b.
Mark Akenside d.
George Whitefield d.
Thomas Chatterton d.
The popular children's book 'London Cries' (anon.).
John and William Langhorne, trs. of Plutarch.
'Archaeologia' first pub.
Hölderlin b.

1771

Beattie (1735): Minstrel, bk. i [ii 1774]. V
Burney, Charles (1726): Present State of Music in France and Italy. P
Cumberland (1732): West Indian. C
Dalrymple, Sir John (1726): Memoirs of Great Britain. P
Fletcher, John William (1729): Checks to Antinomianism. P
Goldsmith (1730): History of England [4 vols., distinct from History, 1764]. P
Griffith, Elizabeth (1720?): History of Lady Barton. P
Henry, Robert (1718): History of England [concl. 1793]. P
Hull, Thomas (1728): History of Sir William Harrington. P
Johnson (1709): Thoughts on Falkland's Islands. P
Mackenzie (1745): Man of Feeling. P
Pennant (1726): Tour in Scotland [supplement 1772]. P
Smollett (1721): Humphry Clinker. P
Wesley, John (1703): Collected Prose Works [concl. 1774].

Walter Scott b.
John Lingard b.
James Montgomery b.
Robert Owen b.
Thomas Gray d.
Tobias Smollett d.
Christopher Smart d.
Richard Price's pamphlet, 'Appeal to the Public on National Debt'.
Klopstock, 'Oden'.

Akenside (d. 1770): Poems (collected).
Brooke, Henry (1703 ?): Redemption. V
Chatterton (d. 1770): Execution of Sir Charles Bawdin. V
Cumberland (1732): Fashionable Lover. C
Ferguson, Adam (1723): Institutes of Moral Philosophy. P
Goldsmith (1730): Threnodia Augustalis. V
Graves (1715): Spiritual Quixote. P
Hurd (1720): Study of Prophecies. P
Jones, Sir William (1746): Poems consisting chiefly of Translations from the Asiatick Languages. V
'Junius': Letters [first auth. collection: see 1768; later edd.: Good 1812, Wade 1850].
Mason (1724): English Garden, bk. i [ii 1777, iii 1779, iv 1782]. V
Murphy (1727): Grecian Daughter. T
Trumbull, John (1750): The Progress of Dulness. V

Samuel Taylor Coleridge b.
Henry Francis Cary b.
Pierce Egan b.
David Ricardo b.
'The Morning Post' (daily) started.
Swedenborg d.
Hardenberg ('Novalis') b.
Lessing, 'Emilia Galotti'.
Edward Lye, 'Dict. Saxonico-Latinum'.

1773

Barbauld (1743): Poems.
Barbauld and Aikin, John: Miscellaneous Pieces in Prose.
Byrom (d. 1763): Collected Poems.
Chapone, Hester (1727): Letters on the Improvement of the Mind. P
Cook (1728): Voyage round the World in the Years 1768–71 [in Hawkesworth below: see 1777, 1784].
Fergusson, Robert (1750): Poems [Part II '79].
Goldsmith (1730): She Stoops to Conquer. C
Hawkesworth (1715 ?): Voyages in the Southern Hemisphere. P
Hoole (1727): Trs. Orlando Furioso [concl. 1783]. V
Leland (1722): History of Ireland. P
Mackenzie (1745): Man of the World. P
Prince of Tunis. T
Macpherson (1736): Trs. Iliad. P
Mason (1724): Epistle to Chambers [and other anon. poems, concl. 1782].
Monboddo (1714): Origin and Progress of Language. P
More (1745): Search after Happiness. D pastoral.
Steevens (1736): Ed. of Shakespeare [with Johnson, and embodying contributions by Malone and Farmer: see 1766].
Strutt (1749): Regal and Ecclesiastical Antiquities of England. P

Francis Jeffrey b.
James Mill b.
Charles Apperley ('Nimrod') b.
Philip Dormer Stanhope, Earl of Chesterfield, d.
George Lyttelton d.
'The Newgate Calendar' about this date.
'Edinburgh Review', 1773–99.
Grose, 'Antiquities of England and Wales'.
Erskine, 'Institutes of the Law of Scotland'.
Tieck b.
Herder and Goethe, 'Von deutscher Art und Kunst'.
Bürger, 'Lenore'.
Goethe, 'Götz von Berlichingen'.

Barbauld (1743): Early Lessons for Children.
Brooke, Henry (1703 ?): Juliet Grenville. P
Burgoyne (1722): Maid of the Oaks. D
Burke (1729): Speech on American Taxation. P
Campbell, John (1708): Political Survey of England. P
Chesterfield (d. 1773): Letters to his Natural Son [ed. Mahon 1845, Dobrée 1932: see 1890]. P
Colman, senr. (1732): Man of Business. C
Goldsmith (d. 1774): Retaliation. V
  Grecian History. P
  History of Earth and Animated Nature. P
Hull, Thomas (1728): Henry II. T
Johnson (1709): The Patriot. P
Kames (1696): Sketches of the History of Man. P
Kelly (1739): School for Wives. C
More (1745): Inflexible Captive [from Metastasio]. D
Pennant, Thomas (1726): Tour in Scotland and Voyage to the Hebrides. P
Priestley (1733): Experiments on Different Kinds of Air [vol. ii 1775, vol. iii 1777, vol. iv 1779, vol. v 1780, vol. vi 1786].
Richardson, William (1743): A Philosophical Analysis of some of Shakespeare's Remarkable Characters. P
Strutt, Joseph (1749): Manners, Customs, etc. of People of England [concl. 1776]. P
Walpole (1717): Description of Strawberry Hill [enlarg. 1784]. P
Warton, Thomas (1728): History of English Poetry, vol. i [ii 1778, iii 1781; ed. R. Price 1824; W. C. Hazlitt 1874]. P

Decision of the House of Lords in the case of Donaldson v. Becket destroys the doctrine of perpetual copyright. See 1709.
Robert Southey b.
Oliver Goldsmith d.
Abraham Tucker d.
Goethe,   'Werther' 'Clavigo'.
Wieland, 'Abderiten'.
Herder, 'Älteste Urkunde'.

1775

Burke (1729): Speech on Conciliation with America. P
Crabbe (1754): Inebriety. V
Cumberland (1732): Choleric Man. D
De Lolme, John Louis: Constitution of England [trs. Fr.] P
Fletcher, John William (1729): Zelotus and Honestus. P
Francklin (1721): Matilda. T
Garrick (1717): Bon Ton. C
Gray (d. 1771): Poems ed. W. Mason, with Letters & Memoir [Works ed. Mathias 1814; ed. Mitford 1814–16 and 1835–53; Letters ed. Tovey 1900–12, ed. Toynbee and Whibley 1935].

War of American Independence.
Jane Austen b.
Charles Lamb b.
Walter Savage Landor b.
Matthew Gregory Lewis b.
Thomas Tyrwhitt, ed. of Canterbury Tales (concl. 1778).
Beaumarchais, 'Barbier de Seville'.

Griffith, Elizabeth (1720?): Morality of Shakespeare's Drama. P
Jephson (1736): Braganza. T
Johnson (1709): Journey to Western Islands of Scotland [in 1773; see Boswell 1785]. P
    Taxation no Tyranny. P
Luxborough, Lady (d. 1756): Letters to William Shenstone [see 1778].
Macpherson (1736): History of Great Britain. P
    Original Papers containing the Secret History of Great Britain. P
Savage (d. 1743): Collected Works, with Life by Johnson.
Sheridan (1751): The Rivals. C
Sterne (d. 1768): Letters from Yorick to Eliza. P
    Twelve Letters to his Friends [with History of a Watch Coat].
    Letters to his Friends, ed. with Memoir by L. Sterne de Medalle (ed. Curtis 1935).
Woolman, John (d. 1772): Journal. P

1776

Beattie (1735): Essays [on Poetry and Music, &c.]. P
Bentham (1748): Fragment on Government. P
Burney, Charles (1726): History of Music, vol. i (ii 1782, iii–iv 1789). P
Campbell, George (1719): Philosophy of Rhetoric. P
Cowley, Hannah (1743): The Runaway. C
Dalrymple, Sir David (1726): Annals of Scotland [concl. 1779]. P
Gibbon (1737): Decline and Fall of the Roman Empire, vol. i [ii–iii 1781, iv–vi 1788; ed. Milman 1838–9, Bury 1896–1900]. P
Goldsmith (d. 1774): Haunch of Venison. V
    Experimental Philosophy. V
Graves (1715): Euphrosyne. V
Griffith, Elizabeth (1720?): Lady Juliana Harley. P
    Trs. of Beaumarchais's Barbier de Séville.
Hawkins (1719): History of Music. P
Mickle, William (1735): Trs. Lusiad of Camoens. V
More (1745): Sir Eldred of the Bower. V
Murphy (1727): Three Weeks after Marriage [see 1764]. C
Paine (1737): Common Sense. P
    The Crisis [completed 1783]. P
Price (1723): Nature of Civil Liberty. P
Smith, Adam (1723): Wealth of Nations [3rd ed. enlarged and corrected 1784]. P
Smollett (d. 1771): Trs. Télémaque of Fénelon.
Trumbull, John (1750): M'Fingal [completed 1782]. V

Declaration of American Independence.
Stamp Duty increased to three halfpence.
David Hume d.
John Bell's 'British Theatre' (1776–8; supplement 1784; another ed. 1791–7).
Condorcet, 'Pensées de Pascal'.
Voltaire, 'Lettre à l'Académie sur Shakespeare'.
Goethe, 'Stella'.
Klinger, 'Die Zwillinge'; 'Sturm und Drang'.
Lenz, 'Die Soldaten'.
Heinrich Wagner, 'Die Kindermörderin'.

Blair, Hugh (1718): Sermons [concl. 1801].
Burke (1729): Letter to the Sheriffs of Bristol. P
Chatterton (d. 1770): Poems, supposed to have been written by Thomas Rowley in the fifteenth cent., ed. T. Tyrwhitt [3rd ed., with Appendix, 1778; vindication of Appendix 1782; ed. Sharpe 1794, Skeat 1872, Hare 1911].
Chesterfield (d. 1773): Miscellaneous Works, with Life by M. Maty [Supplement 1778: see 1817, 1890].
Combe (1741): Diaboliad, Diabolady, Anti-Diabolady. V
Cook (1728): Voyage Towards the South Pole and Round the World in the Years 1772–5 [see 1773, 1784].
Hume (d. 1776): Two Essays [Suicide, Immortality of the Soul]. P
  His Own Life [prefixed to the History]. P
Johnson (1709): The Convict's Address to his Unhappy Brethren [nominally by William Dodd]. P
Mackenzie (1745): Julia de Roubigné. P
More (1745): Percy, a Tragedy.
Morgann (1726): Essay on the Character of Falstaff. P
Reeve, Clara (1729): Champion of Virtue [called Old English Baron, 1778]. P
Robertson (1721): History of America. P
Roscoe (1753): Mount Pleasant. V
Strutt, Joseph (1749): Chronicle of England [concl. 1778].
Warton, Thomas (1728): Poems [later edd. 1791, Mant 1802].
Watson (1730 ?): History of Philip II of Spain. P

Henry Hallam b.
Thomas Campbell b.
Samuel Foote d.
Hugh Kelly d.
'Encyclopaedia Britannica', 2nd ed. (concl. 1783).

1778

Burke (1729): Letters to Two Gentlemen in Bristol. P
Burney, Frances (1752): Evelina. P
Carver, Jonathan (1732): Travels. P
Chatterton (d. 1770): Miscellanies in Prose and Verse, ed. Broughton [Supplement 1784].
Ellis, George (1753): Poetical Tales by Gregory Gander. V
Fielding (d. 1754): The Fathers. C

William Hazlitt b.
John Brown, 'Self-Interpreting Bible'.
Voltaire d.
Rousseau d.
Herder, 'Volkslieder'.
Wieland, 'Rosamund'.
Maler Müller, 'Fausts Leben dramatisiert'.

Foote (1720): Trip to Calais. C
    The Nabob. C
Lowth, Robert: Trs. of Isaiah. P
More (1745): Essays on Various Subjects for
    Young Ladies.
Pennant (1726): Tour in Wales [concl. 1781]. P
Shenstone and others: Select Letters between
    Lady Luxborough (see 1775), Shenstone,
    Dodsley, and others, ed. T. Hull.
Tickell, Richard (1751): Anticipation. D
Warton, Thomas (1728): History of English
    Poetry, vol. ii [see 1774, 1781].

1779

Cowley, Hannah (1743): Albina. T
    Who's the Dupe? D farce.
Cowper (1731): Olney Hymns [with John New-
    ton].
Gibbon (1737): Vindication of Some Passages in
    the 15th and 16th chapters of the Decline
    and Fall.
Graves (1715): Columella. P
Hume (d. 1776): Dialogues concerning Natural
    Religion. P
Johnson (1709): Prefaces, Biographical and
    Critical, to Works of the English Poets
    [concl. 1781; the Prefaces issued as Lives of
    the Poets, 1781, new ed. 1783; ed. Peter
    Cunningham 1854; Birkbeck Hill 1905].
Knox (1752): Essays Moral and Literary. P
Monboddo (1714): Ancient Metaphysics. P
More (1745): Fatal Falsehood. T
Russell, William (1741): History of Modern Eur-
    ope [concl. 1786]. P

Thomas Moore b.
'Horace' Smith b.
John Galt b.
David Garrick d.
William Warburton d.
John Armstrong d.
'The Mirror' (Henry
    Mackenzie and others),
    1779–80.
Lessing, 'Nathan der
    Weise'.

1780

Burke (1729): Speech on Economic Reform and
    Independence of Parliament. P
    Speeches at the Guildhall in Bristol. P
Combe (1741): Letters of the late Lord Lyttelton
    [probably forged; 2nd vol. 1782]. P
Crabbe (1754): The Candidate. V
Davies, Thomas (1712?): Memoirs of Garrick. P
Lee, Sophia (1750): Chapter of Accidents. C
Madan, Martin (1726): Thelyphthora [see Cowper
    1781]. P
Paine (1737): Public Good. P
Young, Arthur (1741): Tour in Ireland. P

Beginning   of   Sunday
    Schools.
Gordon Riots in June.
Sir William Blackstone d.
'Sunday Monitor' (first
    Sunday paper).
'The Morning Herald'
    (daily) started.
Nichols, 'Select Collection
    of Poems' (concl. 1782).
Francklin's trs. of Lucian.
Wieland, 'Oberon'.
Frederick the Great, 'De
    la littérature alle-
    mande'.
Lessing, 'Erziehung des
    Menschengeschlechts'.

Bage (1728): Mount Henneth. P
Barbauld (1743): Hymns in Prose for Children.
Beckford, Peter (1740): Thoughts on Hunting. P
Brooke, Frances (1724): Siege of Sinope. T
Burgoyne (1722): Lord of the Manor. D opera.
Cowper (1731): Anti-Thelyphthora [see Madan 1780]. V
Crabbe (1754): Library. V
Gibbon (1737): Decline and Fall, ii–iii [see 1776]. P
Hayley (1745): Triumphs of Temper. V
   Essay on Painting. P
Holcroft (1745): Duplicity. C
Jefferson, Thomas (1743): The Rights of British America. P
Jephson (1736): Count of Narbonne. T
Johnson (1709): Beauties of Johnson.
Knox (1752): Liberal Education. P
Logan, John (1748): Poems.
Sheridan (1751): The Critic. C
   Trip to Scarborough. C
Tickell (1751): Carnival of Venice. D opera.
Walker, John (1732): Elements of Elocution. P
Warton, Thomas (1728): History of English Poetry, iii [see 1774, 1778]. P
Watson, Richard: Chemical Essays [concl. 1787]. P

Ebenezer Elliott b.
Lucy Aikin b.
Richard Jago d.
Rousseau, 'Confessions' (concl. 1788).
Lessing d.
Schiller, 'Die Räuber'.
Kant, 'Kritik der reinen Vernunft'.

1782

Burke (1729): Letter to a Peer of Ireland on Penal Laws. P
Burney, Frances (1752): Cecilia. P
Cowley (1743): Belle's Stratagem. C
Cowper (1731): Poems [Table Talk, Progress of Error, Expostulation, Charity, Consolation, &c.: see 1785].
   John Gilpin [in Public Advertiser, 14 Nov.].
Gilpin (1724): Observations on the Wye and South Wales. P
Hayley (1745): Essay on Epic Poetry in Five Epistles to Mason. V
More (1745): Sacred Dramas. V
Nichols, John (1745): Biographical and Literary Anecdotes of William Bowyer [see 1812, 1817, 1831]. P
Pennant (1726): Journey from Chester to London. P
Priestley (1733): Corruptions of Christianity. P
Scott, John (1730): Poetical Works.
Trimmer (1741): Easy Introduction to the Knowledge of Nature. P
Warton, Joseph (1722): Genius and Writings of Pope, vol. ii [see 1756]. P
Wolcot (1738): Lyric Odes to Royal Academicians.

Charles Robert Maturin b.
Susan Ferrier b.
Henry Home, Lord Kames, d.
John Bell, 'British Poets'.
'Biographia Dramatica', ed. Isaac Reed (see 1764, 1812).
Michel-Guillaume Jean de Crèvecœur, 'Letters of an American Farmer'.
'European Magazine' started.
Delille, 'Les Jardins'.
Lamennais b.
Delille, 'Les Jardins'.
Laclos, 'Liaisons dangereuses'.

Beattie (1735): Dissertations Moral and Critical. P

Beckford, William (1759): Dreams, Waking Thoughts and Incidents, in a Series of Letters from Various Parts of Europe [suppressed: see 1834]. P

Blair, Hugh (1718): Lectures on Rhetoric. P

Blake (1757): Poetical Sketches. V

Brooke (1724): Rosina. D opera.

Capell, Edward (1713): Notes on Shakespeare. P

Cowley (1743): Bold Stroke for a Husband. C

Crabbe (1754): The Village. V

Davies, Thomas (1712?): Dramatic Miscellanies. P

Day, Thomas (1748): Sandford and Merton [concl. 1789]. P

James I of Scotland (d. 1437): The Kingis Quair, ed. Lord Woodhouselee. V

Logan, John (1748): Runnamede. T

Reeve, Clara (1729): The Two Mentors. P

Richardson, William (1743): Essays on Shakespeare's Dramatic Characters. P

Sheridan (1751): School for Scandal [first Eng. ed.: earlier Dublin edd.: 1777, 1781, 1782]. C
Duenna [songs, duets, &c. first pub. 1775]. D

Webster, Noah (1758): Spelling Book.

Williams, Helen Maria (1762): Ode on the Peace. V

Peace of Versailles.
Pitt's first ministry 1783–1802.
Fox's India Bill.
Washington Irving b.
Reginald Heber b.
Henry Brooke d.
Joseph Ritson, 'Collection of English Songs'.
Vicesimus Knox, 'Elegant Extracts' (prose: see 1789).
Stendhal b.
Schiller, 'Fiesco'.
Jean Paul, 'Grönländische Prozesse'.

1784

Astle, Thomas (1735): Origin and Progress of Writing. P

Bage (1728): Barham Downs. P

Berkeley (d. 1753): Collected Works [cont. unpub. Commonplace Book: ed. Campbell Fraser 1871, 1901].

Burke (1729): Speech on Fox's India Bill. P
Representation to His Majesty. P

Colman, jnr. (1762): Two to One. C

Cook (d. 1779): Voyage to the Pacific Ocean in the Years 1776–80 [with Capt. James King: see 1773, 1777].

Cowley (1743): More Ways than One. C

Dodington, Bubb, Lord Melcombe (d. 1762): Diary, 1748–61, ed. H. P. Wyndham.

Jago (d. 1781): Collected Poems.

Jefferson, Thomas (1743): Notes on the State of Virginia. P

Macklin (1697?): Love à la mode. C

Mitford, William (1744): History of Greece, vol. i (ii 1790; complete 1810). P

Swift (d. 1745): Works, ed. Thomas Sheridan [ed. Nichols 1801, Scott 1814, 1824].

Williams, Helen Maria (1762): Peru, a poem.

Leigh Hunt b.
James Sheridan Knowles b.
Bernard Barton b.
Samuel Johnson d.
Thomas Francklin d.
Arthur Young starts 'The Annals of Agriculture'.
Thomas Evans's 'Old Ballads'.
Diderot d.
Beaumarchais, 'Mariage de Figaro'.
Bernardin de Saint Pierre, 'Études de la nature'.
Ducis, 'Macbeth'.
Schiller, 'Kabale und Liebe'.
Herder, 'Ideen zur Philosophie der Geschichte der Menschheit' (concl. 1791).
Klopstock, 'Hermann und die Fürsten'.

Boswell (1740): Tour to the Hebrides.(with Johnson, 1773: see 1775). P

Burke (1729): Speech on Nabob of Arcot's Debts. P

Cowper (1731): Poems [vol. ii, see 1782; Task, Tirocinium, Epistle to Joseph Hill, John Gilpin].

Crabbe (1754): The Newspaper. V

Dwight, Timothy (1752): The Conquest of Canaan. V

Graves (1715): Eugenius. P

Hayley (1745): Essay on Old Maids. V

Holcroft (1745): Follies of a Day [from Mariage de Figaro]. C

Tales of the Castle [from Les Veillées du Château by Comtesse de Genlis].

Inchbald (1753): Appearance is against them. D

Johnson (d. 1784): Prayers and Meditations. P

Poetical Works [collected].

Mackenzie (1745): The Lounger [Feb. 1785–Jan. 1787].

Paley (1743): Moral and Political Philosophy. P

Raspe, Rudolf (1737): Baron Munchausen's Travels. P

Reeve, Clara (1729): Progress of Romance. P

Reid (1710): Essay on the Intellectual Powers of Man. P

Smith, Charlotte (1749): Trs. Manon Lescaut.

Warton, Thomas (1728): Ed. Milton's Minor Poems.

Whateley, Thomas (d. 1772): Remarks on Some Characters of Shakespeare. P

Wolcot (1738): Lousiad [compl. 1795]. V

Lyric Odes for 1785.

Thomas De Quincey b.

Thomas Love Peacock b.

John Wilson ('Christopher North') b.

Henry Kirke White b.

Thomas Leland d.

William Whitehead d.

Richard Glover d.

Thomas Warton, jnr., poet-laureate.

The 'Rolliad' satires begin (see 1791).

Francis Grose's 'Dictionary of the vulgar tongue' (reissued as 'Lexicon Balatronicum' 1811).

William Herbert's ed. of Joseph Ames's 'Typographical Antiquities' (see 1749, 1810).

Joseph Strutt, 'Biographical Dictionary of Engravers' (concl. 1786).

John Walter starts 'The Daily Universal Register' (became 'The Times' 1788).

Richard Cumberland starts 'The Observer'.

Moritz, 'Anton Reiser' (concl. 1790).

1786

Beckford, William (1759): Vathek [first Eng. trs., perhaps by S. Henley: see 1787]. P

Burgoyne (1722): The Heiress. C

Richard Cœur-de-Lion. D opera.

Burke (1729): Articles of Charge against Warren Hastings. P

Burns (1759): Poems Chiefly in Scottish Dialect [Kilmarnock: see 1787].

Canning, George: The Microcosm [with J. Hookham Frere and J. and R. Smith].

Freneau, Philip (1752): Poems. V

Gilpin (1724): Observations on Cumberland and Westmorland. P

Graves (1715): Lucubrations. P

John Pinkerton, 'Ancient Scottish Poems'.

Samuel Taylor, 'Universal System of Stenography' (adapted by Isaac Pitman in 'Stenographic Shorthand', 1837).

Frederick the Great d.

Inchbald (1753): I'll tell you what. D
Macklin (1697?): Man of the World [rev. version of True-born Scotsman]. D
Moore, John (1729): Zeluco. P
Murphy (1727): The Choice, News from Parnassus [in Dramatic Works].
Piozzi, Hester Lynch (Thrale) (1741): Anecdotes of Samuel Johnson. P
Rogers (1763): Ode to Superstition and Other Poems.
Smith, Charlotte (1749): Romance of Real Life.
Tooke, Horne (1736): Diversions of Purley, pt. i (ii 1798, 1805). P
Trimmer (1741): Fabulous Histories [later called History of the Robins]. P
Œconomy of Charity. P
Williams, Helen Maria (1762): Poems [collected].
Wolcot (1738): Bozzy and Piozzi. V
Farewell Odes to Academicians. V
Congratulatory Epistle to James Boswell. V

1787

Adams, John (1735): Defence of the Constitution. P
Bage (1728): Fair Syrian. P
Barlow, Joel (1754): The Vision of Columbus. V
Beattie (1735): Scotticisms. P
Burns (1759): Poems chiefly in Scottish Dialect [Edinburgh and London: see 1786].
Songs [in James Johnson's Scots Musical Museum, i–vi 1787–1804].
Colman, jnr. (1762): Inkle and Yarico. D musical comedy.
Cowley (1743): Scottish Village. V
Glover (d. 1785): Athenaid. V
Hamilton, Alexander (1757): The Federalist. P
Hawkins, Sir John (1719): Life of Johnson. P
Jephson, Robert (1736): Julia, or the Italian Lover. T
Johnson (d. 1784): Works, ed. Sir John Hawkins [ed. Murphy 1792].
Paston Letters: Original Letters, Written during the Reigns of Henry VI, Edward IV, and Richard III by various Persons of Rank or Consequence [ed. John Fenn, concl. 1823].
Pye (1745): Poems [collected].
Wolcot (1738): Ode upon Ode. V
Instructions to a Celebrated Laureat. V
Wollstonecraft (1759): Thoughts on Education of Daughters. P

American Constitution signed.
Mary Mitford b.
Bryan Walter Procter ('Barry Cornwall') b.
Sheridan's Speech against Warren Hastings.
Correspondence begins in 'The World' between Robert Merry ('Della Crusca') and Hannah Cowley ('Anna Matilda').
James Johnson, 'Scots Museum' (concl. 1803).
Henry Headley, 'Select Beauties of Ancient English Poetry'.
Thomas Monro, 'Olla Podrida' (weekly).
Beckford's 'Vathek' in original Fr. in Paris (see 1786).
Bernardin de Saint Pierre, 'Paul et Virginie'.
Goethe, 'Iphigenie auf Tauris'.
Schiller, 'Don Carlos'.
Klopstock, 'Hermanns Tod'.
Herder, 'Gott'.

Bage (1728): James Wallace. P
Brooke (1724): Marian. D opera.
Collins (d. 1759): Ode on Popular Superstitions
of the Highlands. V
Crowe, William (1745): Lewesdon Hill. V
Gibbon (1737): Decline and Fall, iv–vi [see 1776,
1781].
Graves (1715): Recollection of the Life of William
Shenstone. P
Holcroft (1745): Life of Baron Frederic Trenck
[from German]. P
Inchbald (1753): Such things are. C
Child of Nature. D
Johnson (d. 1784): Sermons.
Letters to and from Mrs. Thrale (Piozzi).
Knox (1752): Winter Evenings. P
More (1745): Slavery, a Poem.
Thoughts on the Importance of the Manners
of the Great. P
Reeve, Clara (1729): The Exiles. P
Reid (1710): Essay on the Active Powers of Man.
P
Smith, Charlotte (1749): Emmeline. P
Whitehead (d. 1785): Collected Poems, ed.
William Mason.
Wollstonecraft (1759): Original Stories from Real
Life. P

The Young Pretender d.
George Gordon Byron,
Lord Byron b.
Richard Harris Barham b.
Sir William Hamilton b.
Thomas Amory d.
Charles Wesley d.
Trial of Warren Hastings,
1788–95.
'Encyclopaedia Britan-
nica', 3rd ed. (concl.
1797).
'The Times' started (see
1785).
Thomas Scott, 'Holy
Bible with Notes' (concl.
1792).
Linnean Society founded.
Barthélemy, 'Voyage du
jeune Anacharsis en
Grèce'.
Goethe, 'Egmont'.
Kant, 'Kritik der prak-
tischen Vernunft'.
Schiller, 'Abfall der Nie-
derlande'.

1789

Bentham (1748): Principles of Morals and Legisla-
tion [prtd. 1780]. P
Blake (1757): Songs of Innocence. V
Book of Thel. V
Bowles (1762): Sonnets.
Verses to John Howard.
Cobb, James (1756): Haunted Tower. D opera.
Cumberland (1732): Arundel. P
Darwin, Erasmus (1731): Loves of the Plants
[pt. 2 of Botanic Garden: see 1792]. V
Gilpin (1724): Observations on the Highlands of
Scotland. P
Macneill, Hector: The Harp. V
Phillip (1738): The Voyage of Governor Phillip
to Botany Bay. P
Radcliffe (1764): Castles of Athlin and Dunbayne. P
Ramsay, David (1749): History of the American
Revolution. P

French Revolution.
Frances Brooke d.
Dr. Richard Price's ser-
mon 'On the love of our
country' draws Burke
into controversy over the
French Revolution.
Bell's 'British Album'
with verses by Hannah
Cowley, Robert Merry,
and others.
'The Mail' (thrice weekly)
started.
Vicesimus Knox, 'Elegant
Extracts' (poetry: see
1783).
Schiller, 'Die Künstler'.

Reynolds, Frederic (1764): The Dramatist. C
Tench (*c.* 1758): A Narrative of the Expedition
to Botany Bay. P
Twining, Thomas: Aristotle's Treatise on Poetry. P
Wakefield, Gilbert: Silva Critica [concl. 1795]. P
White (1720): Natural History of Selborne. P

President U.S.A.
Washington.

1790

Alison, Archibald (1757): Essay on Taste. P
Baillie (1762): Fugitive Verses.
Beattie (1735): Elements of Moral Science [vol. ii
1793]. P
Bewick, Thomas (1753): General History of
Quadrupeds. P
Blake (1757): Marriage of Heaven and Hell [n.d.].
Bruce, James (1730): Travels to Discover the
Source of the Nile. P
Burke (1729): Reflections on the French Revolu-
tion. P
Speech on Army Estimates. P
Graves (1715): Plexippus. P
Johnson (d. 1784): Letter to Chesterfield. P
Conversation between George III and Johnson.
[Parts of Boswell's 'Life': see 1791].
Malone, Edmond: Ed. of Shakespeare [see 1821].
Merry, Robert: Laurel of Liberty. V
More (1745): Estimate of the Religion of the
Fashionable World. P
Paley (1743): Horæ Paulinæ. P
Pennant (1726): London. P
Radcliffe (1764): A Sicilian Romance. P
Sayers, Frank: Dramatic Sketches of Northern
Mythology [enlarg. 1792].
Smith, Charlotte (1749): Ethelinde. P
Smollett (d. 1771): Collected Works [later edd.:
Anderson 1796, Moore 1797, Roscoe 1841,
Cruikshank 1845, Herbert 1870, Henley
1899–1901].
Turner, Sharon (1768): History of the Anglo-
Saxons. P
Williams, Helen Maria (1762): Julia. P
Letters written in France. P
Wilson, Alexander: Poems.
Wollstonecraft (1759): Morality for Children [trs.
Salzmann]. P

John Austin b.
Benjamin Franklin d.
Adam Smith d.
Thomas Warton, jnr., d.
Henry James Pye poet-
laureate.
Wordsworth's first Con-
tinental tour.
George Ellis, 'Specimens
of Early English Poets'
(see 1801).
'The Bee', Dec. 1790–Jan.
1794.
Goethe, 'Torquato Tasso',
'Faust, ein Fragment'.
Kant, 'Kritik der Ur-
theilskraft'.
Lamartine b.
Schiller, 'Geschichte des
dreissigjährigen
Krieges' (concl. 1792).
Goethe, 'Metamorphose
der Pflanzen'.

Bentham (1748): Panopticon. P
Boswell (1740): Life of Johnson [ed. 2, 1793, ed. 3, 1799; ed. Croker 1831, Birkbeck Hill 1887, Hill, revised L. F. Powell 1934].
Burke (1729): Letter to a Member of the National Assembly. P
  Appeal from the New to the Old Whigs. P
Burns (1759): Tam o' Shanter [in Edinburgh Herald, 18 Mar. and in Grose's Antiquities of Scotland, April]. V
Cowper (1731): Trs. Iliad and Odyssey. V
D'Israeli (1766): Curiosities of Literature, vol. i [ii 1793, iii 1817, iv–v 1823, vi 1834]. P
Ellis, Laurence, Richardson, Tickell, Fitzpatrick: The Rolliad [complete: originally in Morning Herald and in Daily Advertiser from 1784]. V
Franklin, Benjamin (d. 1790): Autobiography, pt. 2 [in French: English version 1817, 1868].
Gilpin (1724): Remarks on Forest Scenery illustrated in the Scenes of New Forest. P
Inchbald (1753): A Simple Story. P
Mackintosh (1765): Vindiciæ Gallicæ. P
Merry, Robert: Lorenzo. T
Paine (1737): Rights of Man, pt. i (ii 1792). P
Radcliffe (1764): Romance of the Forest. P
Reeve, Clara (1729): School for Widows. P
Robertson, William: Disquisition concerning the Knowledge the Ancients had of India. P
Warton, Thomas (d. 1790): Poems on Various Subjects [see 1777].

Henry Hart Milman b.
Michael Faraday b.
John Wesley d.
Richard Price d.
'The Observer' (Sundays only) started.
'Mother Goose's Melody' (anon.).
Joseph Ritson's 'Ancient Popular Poetry' (anthology).
Francis Grose's 'Antiquities of Scotland'.
G. Chalmers ('Francis Oldys'), 'Life of Thomas Paine'.
Volney, 'Les Ruines'.

1792

Aikin, John, and Barbauld, Anna: Evenings at Home. P and V
Bage (1728): Man as he is. P
Blake (1757): Song of Liberty [n.d.].
Bligh, Adm. William (1754): Voyage to the South Sea in the Bounty. P
Brackenridge, Hugh Henry (1748): Modern Chivalry [additions in 1804–5, 1815]. P
Burke (1729): Letter to Sir Hercules Langrishe. P
  Speeches on Impeachment of Warren Hastings. P
    Collected Works [concl. 1827; later edd.: Laurence and King 1803–27; 1839; with correspondence 1852; 1854–5, 1865–7].

Percy Bysshe Shelley b.
John Keble b.
Frederick Marryat b.
Edward John Trelawny b.
Augustus Hare b.
Sir Archibald Alison b.
Sir Joshua Reynolds d.
John Burgoyne d.
Wordsworth in France.
Pitt's attack on slave trade.
Southey expelled from Westminster for article on corporal punishment in 'The Flagellant'.
Robert Anderson's 'Poets of Great Britain' (concl. 1807).

Darwin (1731): Economy of Vegetation [pt. i of
  Botanic Garden: see 1789]. V
Gilpin (1724): Essays on Picturesque Beauty. P
Gookin, Daniel (d. 1687): Historical Collections of
  the Indians in New England. P
Holcroft (1745): Anna St. Ives. P
  Road to Ruin. C
Hoole, John (1727): Trs. Tasso's Rinaldo. V
Morton (1764?): Columbus. D
Rogers (1763): Pleasures of Memory, with Other
  Poems.
Smith, Charlotte (1749): Desmond. P
Stewart (1753): Philosophy of the Human Mind,
  vol. i [ii 1814, iii 1827]. P
Trimmer (1741): Reflections upon Education of
  Children in Charity Schools. P
Williams, Helen Maria (1762): Letters from
  France containing Anecdotes Relative to the
  Revolution [concl. 1796]. P
Wollstonecraft (1759): Vindication of the Rights
  of Woman. P
Young, Arthur (1741): Travels in France. P

*Joseph Ritson's 'Ancient
  Songs' (anthology).*
'The Sun' (daily) started.

1793

Blake (1757): Gates of Paradise.
  Vision of the Daughters of Albion (Prophetic
  Books). V
  America (Prophetic Books). V
Burns (1759): Songs [in George Thomson's Select
  Scottish Airs, i–vi 1793–1841].
  Poems [enlarged ed.: another 1794; see 1787].
Colman, jnr. (1762): The Mountaineers. D
D'Israeli (1766): Dissertation on Anecdotes. P
Godwin (1756): Political Justice. P
Graves (1715): Reveries of Solitude. P and V
Inchbald (1753): Everyone has his fault. D
More (1745): Village Politics. P
Sayers, Frank (1763): Disquisitions, Metaphysical
  and Literary. P
Smith, Charlotte (1749): Old Manor House. P
Stewart (1753): Outlines of Moral Philosophy. P
Whitehead, John (1740?): Life of John Wesley,
  vol. i [ii 1796]. P
Wordsworth (1770): An Evening Walk. V
  Descriptive Sketches. V

John Clare b.
*Felicia Dorothea Hemans
  b.*
Gilbert White d.
William Robertson d.
*'The British Critic'
  founded by W. Jones
  and Robert Nares.*
*Joseph Ritson's 'English
  Anthology'.*
*Herder, 'Humanitäts-
  briefe'.*
*Schiller, 'Über Anmut
  und Würde'.*

*President U.S.A.
  Washington (2nd
  term).*

Blake (1757): Songs of Experience.
  Songs of Innocence and Experience [n.d.].
  Europe (Prophetic Books). V
  Book of Urizen (Prophetic Books). V
Coleridge (1777): Monody on Chatterton [in
  Cambridge edition of Rowley Poems]. V
Cumberland (1732): The Jew. C
Darwin (1731): Zoonomia. P
Dwight, Timothy (1752): Greenfield Hill. V
Gifford (1756): Baviad. V
Gisborne, Thomas (1758): Walks in a Forest. V
Godwin (1756): Caleb Williams. P
Hayley (1745): Life of Milton [in Boydell's and
  Nicol's ed. of Milton: separately 1796].
Holcroft (1745): Hugh Trevor [concl. 1797]. P
Hurd (1720): Preface to Warburton's Works. P
Knight (1750): The Landscape. V
Mathias, James (1754?): Pursuits of Literature
  [concl. 1797]. V
Mickle, William (d. 1788): Collected Poems, in-
  cluding The Concubine [enlarged 1807].
Paine (1737): Age of Reason, pt. i [ii 1795, iii,
  incl. Essay on Dreams, 1811]. P
Paley (1743): Evidences of Christianity. P
Price, Uvedale (1747): Essay on the Picturesque. P
Radcliffe (1764): Mysteries of Udolpho. P
Southey (1774): Fall of Robespierre [with
  Coleridge]. T
  Trs. Bion and Moschus [with R. Lovell]. V
Taylor, William: Trs. Goethe's Iphigenie.
Wolcot (1738): Works [concl. 1796; later ed.
  1812].

John Gibson Lockhart b.
George Grote b.
William Whewell b.
Anna Jameson b.
Edward Gibbon d.
George Colman, senr., d.
William Cobbett's pamph-
  let ' On the Emigration
  of Dr. Priestley'.
Joseph Ritson's ' Scottish
  Songs' (anthology).
' The Morning Advertiser'
  (daily) started.
André Chénier d.
Fichte, 'Wissenschafts-
  lehre'.
Goethe, 'Reineke Fuchs'.

1795

Blake (1757): Book of Los (Prophetic Books). V
  Book of Ahania (Prophetic Books). V
  Song of Los. V
Chatterton (d. 1770): The Revenge: a Burletta.
  Poetical Works [in Anderson's British Poets:
  see 1803].
Coleridge (1772): Conciones ad Populum. P
Cumberland (1732): Henry. P
  Wheel of Fortune. D
D'Israeli (1766): Essay on the Literary Character. P
Edgeworth (1767): Letters for Literary Ladies. P
Gifford (1756): Mæviad. V
Holcroft (1745): Deserted Daughter. C
Landor (1775): Poems.
  Moral Epistle to Earl Stanhope. V
Macneill, Hector: Scotland's Scaith. V
More (1745): Cheap Repository Tracts. P
Paine (1737): First Principles of Government. P

John Keats b.
Thomas Carlyle b.
Thomas Arnold b.
Julius Hare b.
George Darley b.
James Boswell d.
Alexander Wilson's poem
  ' Watty and Meg'.
William Ireland's forgery,
  ' Miscellaneous Papers
  of Shakespeare', starts
  controversy.
Joseph Ritson's ed. of
  poems of Laurence
  Minot and collection of
  Robin Hood poems.
Lindley Murray's 'Eng-
  lish Grammar'.
Goethe, 'Wilhelm Meisters
  Lehrjahre' (concl.
  1796).

Taylor, William: Trs. Wieland's Dialogues of the Gods.

Wakefield, Priscilla (1751): Juvenile Anecdotes, founded on Facts [concl. 1798].

White (d. 1793): A Naturalist's Calendar. P

Williams, Helen Maria (1762): Paul and Virginia [trs. Bernardin de Saint Pierre]. P

Letters containing a Sketch of the Politics of France. P

1796

Bage (1728): Hermsprong. P

Barlow, Joel (1754): Hasty Pudding. V

Burges, James (1752): Birth and Triumph of Love. V

Burke (1729): Letter to a Noble Lord. P

Letters I and II on Regicide Peace [see 1797]. P

Burney, Charles (1726): Life of Metastasio. P

Burney, Frances (1752): Camilla. P

Coleridge (1772): The Watchman [ten nos.].

Poems on Various Subjects [cont. poems by Lamb omitted in 3rd ed.].

Vision of the Maid of Orleans [in Southey's Joan of Arc: re-named Destiny of Nations]. V

Ode on the Departing Year.

Four Sonnets [in Selected Sonnets of Bowles, Lamb, and others].

Colman, jnr. (1762): The Iron Chest. D

D'Israeli (1766): Miscellanies. P

Edgeworth (1767): Parent's Assistant, or Stories for Children, pt. i [complete, with Little Plays, 1800].

Gibbon (d. 1794): Miscellaneous Works, with memoir by himself, ed. Lord Sheffield [concl. 1814].

Holcroft (1745): Man of Ten Thousand. C

Inchbald (1753): Nature and Art. P

Lewis (1775): The Monk. P

Macneill, Hector (1746): Waes o' War. V

Moore, John (1729): Edward. P

Roscoe (1753): Life of Lorenzo de Medici. P

Scott (1771): The Chase, William and Helen [version of Bürger's Leonore]. V

Southey (1774): Joan of Arc. P

Strutt, Joseph (1749): Dresses and Habits of English People [concl. 1799]. P

Taylor, William: Trs. Select Fairy Tales from Wieland.

Trs. Bürger's Leonore. V

White, James (1775): Original Letters of Sir John Falstaff. P

Wollstonecraft (1759): Letters Written from Norway, Sweden, and Denmark. P

Schiller, 'Briefe über ästhetische Erziehung' (concl. 1796).

Hartley Coleridge b.

Robert Burns d.

James Macpherson d.

Thomas Reid d.

William Beckford starts construction of Fonthill Abbey.

'The Monthly Magazine' (concl. 1843).

William Ireland's 'Vortigern' performed, occasioning controversy.

George Ellis's ed. of Gregory Lewis Way's trs. of 'Fabliaux'.

Stephen Jones's 'Biographical Dictionary in Miniature'.

Goethe, 'Alexis und Dora'.

Goethe and Schiller, 'Xenien'.

Jean Paul (Richter), 'Quintus Fixlein'.

Bewick, Thomas (1753): History of British Birds. P
Burke (1729): Letter to Duke of Portland on
  Conduct of the Minority in Parliament. P
  Thoughts on French Affairs. P
  Letter III on a Regicide Peace [Letter IV in
  Works, 1812: see 1796]. P
  Letter on Affairs in Ireland. P
Gifford (editor), **Canning, Frere, Ellis, Pitt,** &c.:
  The Anti-Jacobin [20 Nov. 1797–9 July
  1798; collected edd. of poetry, 1799, 1801,
  1852 (ed. Edmonds), 1854 (ed. Gilray), and
  1890. Best-known pieces: Needy Knife-
  grinder, Progress of Man, Loves of the Tri-
  angles, The Rovers, and The New Morality].
Godwin (1756): The Enquirer. P
Inchbald (1753): Wives as they were. D
Lee, Harriet (1757): Canterbury Tales, vol. i [with
  Sophia Lee: concl. 1805]. P
  Clara Lennox. P
Lewis (1775): The Minister [from Schiller's
  Kabale und Liebe]. D
Morton (1764 ?): Cure for the Heart Ache. C
Pinkerton, John (1758): History of Scotland. P
Radcliffe (1764): The Italian. P
Reynolds (d. 1792): Works, ed. Malone [cont.
  complete series of Discourses, 1769–90].
Southey (1774): Poems.
  Letters written in Spain and Portugal. P
Tytler, Alexander Fraser: Essay on Principles of
  Translation. P
Wilberforce (1759): Practical Christianity. P

Alaric Alexander Watts b.
Samuel Lover b.
Sir Charles Lyell b.
Edmund Burke d.
Horace Walpole d.
Mary Wollstonecraft d.
Charles Macklin d.
William Mason d.
*Mary Wollstonecraft God-
  win (Shelley) b.*
*Friendship of Coleridge
  and Wordsworth (earli-
  est meeting perhaps at
  Bristol 1795).*
*John Bell's 'British
  Theatre'.*
*Cobbett's 'Porcupine Gaz-
  ette' (concl. 1799).*
Alfred de Vigny b.
*Goethe, 'Hermann und
  Dorothea'. Goethe and
  Schiller, 'Balladen'.*
Tieck, 'Volksmärchen'.
*Hölderlin, 'Hyperion'
  (1797–9).*
*Schlegel trs. of Shake-
  speare (1797–1801).*
*Joseph Warton's ed. of
  Pope.*
*Wackenroder, 'Herzens-
  ergiessungen'.*

*President U.S.A.
John Adams.*

1798

Baillie (1762): Plays on the Passions, vol. i.
Brown, C. B. (1771): Wieland. P
Coleridge (1772): Fears in Solitude. France, an
  Ode. Frost at Midnight [see below: Words-
  worth]. V
Colman, jnr. (1762): Blue Beard. D
Cowper (1731): Two Poems.
Coxe, William (1747): Memoirs of Sir Robert
  Walpole. P
Drake, Nathan: Literary Hours. P
Edgeworth (1767): Practical Education. P
Gilpin (1724): Picturesque remarks on Western
  parts of England and Isle of Wight.
Godwin (1756): Memoirs of Mary Wollstonecraft. P
  Ed. Posthumous Works of Mary Wollstone-
  craft.
Holcroft (1745): He's much to blame. C
Inchbald (1753): Lovers' Vows [from Kotzebue]. D
Lamb (1775): Blank Verse [with Charles Lloyd].
  Tale of Rosamond Gray. P

*Wordsworth and Coleridge
  visit Germany.*
*Stephen Jones's 'Pro-
  nouncing and Explana-
  tory Dictionary' (stereo-
  type ed. 1816).*
*Schiller, 'Wallensteins
  Lager'.*
*Goethe, 'Propyläen' (till
  1800). 'Das Athe-
  näum' (Manifesto of
  German Romanticism).*
Tieck, 'Franz Sternbald'.

Landor (1775): Gebir. V
Lewis (1775): Castle Spectre. D
Lloyd (1775): Edmund Oliver. P
Malthus (1766): Principle of Population as it
    affects the Future of Society [2nd ed. 1803,
    substantially a new book].
Morton (1764?): Secrets worth Knowing. C
    Speed the Plough. C
Roche, Regina (1764?): Children of the Abbey. P
Rogers (1763): Epistle to a Friend. V
Sheridan (1751): Collected Speeches [later edd.:
    1816, 1842; Speeches on Warren Hastings,
    ed. Bond, 1859–61].
Smith, Charlotte (1749): Minor Morals. P
Sotheby, William: Trs. Wieland's Oberon.
Vancouver, George: Voyage of Discovery. P
Wakefield, Priscilla (1751): Reflections on the
    present condition of the Female Sex. P
Walpole (d. 1797): Works, ed. Berry [cont. first
    instalment of letters to Conway, &c.].
Williams (1762): Tour in Switzerland. P
Wordsworth (1770) **and Coleridge** (1772): Lyrical
    Ballads [Ancient Mariner (see 1817), Tintern
    Abbey, Expostulation, &c.: see 1800]. V

1799

Bowles (1762): Battle of the Nile. V
Brown, C. B. (1771): Ormond. P
    Edgar Huntley. P
    Arthur Mervyn [Pt. 2 1800]. P
Campbell (1777): Pleasures of hope. V
Coleridge (1772) **and Southey** (1774): Devil's
    Thoughts [anon.: acknowledged ed. 1830].
Darwin (1731): Phytologia. P
Glover (d. 1785): Jason. T
Godwin (1756): St. Leon. P
Ireland, William: Vortigern and Rowena. D
    Henry II. D
Jones, Sir William (d. 1794): Works, ed. Lord
    Teignmouth [concl. 1804].
Lewis (1775): Tales of Terror [see 1801]. V
    East Indian [later called Rich and Poor]. C
More (1745): On Modern System of Female
    Education. P
Park, Mungo (1771): Travels in the Interior of
    Africa in 1795–7. P
Scott (1771): Goetz of Berlichingen [trs. Goethe]. T
    Apology for Tales of Terror. V.
Seward (1747): Sonnets.
Sheridan (1751): Pizarro [from Kotzebue]. T
Turner, Sharon (1768): History of England to
    the Norman Conquest [see 1839]. P

Thomas Hood b.
George Payne Rainsford
    James b.
George Finlay b.
Napoleon Buonaparte
    First Consul.
'Religious Tract Society'
    founded.
Hardenberg ('Novalis'),
    Hymnen an die Nacht'.
Schiller, 'Die Piccolo-
    mini'. 'Wallensteins
    Tod', 'Das Lied von
    der Glocke'.
Honoré de Balzac b.
Friedrich   Schlegel,
    'Lucinde'.

Bloomfield, Robert (1766): Farmer's Boy. V
Burns (d. 1796): Works, with Life, New Poems, and Correspondence, ed. Currie [Principal later edd.: Cunningham 1834, Hogg and Motherwell 1834–6, Pickering 1839, Chambers 1856–7 (revised Wallace 1896), Macmillan (ed. A. Smith 1865), Scott Douglas 1877–9, Henley and Henderson 1896].
Coleridge (1772): Poems [in Annual Anthology]. Trs. Schiller's Wallenstein. D
Dibdin, Charles: History of the English Stage. P
Edgeworth (1767): Castle Rackrent. P
Gifford (1756): Epistle to Peter Pindar. V
Malone, Edmond (1741): Ed. Dryden's Prose Works, with Life.
Moore (1779): Trs. Odes of Anacreon.
Scott (1771): Eve of St. John. V
Sotheby, William: Trs. Virgil's Georgics.
Wordsworth (1770) **and Coleridge** (1772): Lyrical Ballads [vol. i poems of 1798; vol. ii new poems and the preface, see also 1815]. V

Thomas Babington Macaulay b.
Edward Bouverie Pusey b.
Charles Jeremiah Wells b.
William Cowper d.
Joseph Warton d.
Mrs. Elizabeth Montagu d.

Jean Paul, 'Titan' (concl. 1803).
Mme de Staël, 'De la littérature considerée dans ses rapports avec les institutions sociales'.
Schiller, 'Maria Stuart'.

1801

Bowles (1762): Sorrows of Switzerland. V
Brown, C. B. (1771): Clara Howard. P
  Jane Talbot. P
Burges, Sir James: Richard the First. V
Burns (d. 1796): Poems ascribed to Robert Burns [incl. Holy Willie, The Jolly Beggars, &c.; ed. Stewart]. V
Cobbett (1762): Porcupine's Works [concl. 1802]. The Porcupine [daily Oct.–Nov.].
Cowper (d. 1800): Poems from the Fr. of Mme de la Motte Guyon, with original poems.
Dibdin, Thomas (1771): The Cabinet. Opera.
Edgeworth (1767): Moral Tales. P
  Belinda. P.   Early Lessons. P
Goldsmith (d. 1774): Works, with Life by Percy [Life by Prior, 1837, by J. Forster 1848, 1854: Works ed. J. W. M. Gibbs, 1884–6].
Graves (1715): Senilities, or Amusements in Prose and Verse.
Hamilton, Elizabeth (1758): Letters on Education. P
Hogg (1770): Scottish Pastorals, Poems, Songs.
Holcroft (1745): Deaf and Dumb. D
Huddesford, George (1749): Collected Poems [Salmagundi, originally pub. 1791, Topsy Turvy 1793, Bubble and Squeak 1799, Crambe Repetita 1799].

John Henry Newman b.
Robert Bage d.
H. J. Todd's Variorum ed. of Milton's Poetical Works (rev. 1808, 1826, 1834).
George Ellis, 'Specimens of Early English Poets' (2nd ed., with Historical Sketch of Progress of English Poetry; 1st ed. in 1790).
Fourth ed. of 'Encyclopaedia Britannica' (Millar editor).
Hardenberg ('Novalis') d.
Schiller, 'Jungfrau von Orleans'.
Chateaubriand, 'Atala'.
Lemercier, 'Pinto'.

President U.S.A. Jefferson.

Hunt (1784): Juvenilia. V
Jefferson (1843): Manual of Parliamentary
   Practice. P
Lewis (1775): Tales of Wonder [with contribu-
   tions by Scott, Southey, Leyden, and others:
   includes Tales of Terror 1779]. P and V
 Adelmorn, or the Outlaw. D
 Alphonso, King of Castile. D
Macneill, Hector (1746): Poetical Works [later
   edd.: 1806, 1812, 1856].
Moore (1779): Poems by Thomas Little.
Murphy (1727): Life of David Garrick. P
Opie (1769): Father and Daughter. P and V
Pye (1745): Alfred. V
Sotheby, William (1757): Julian and Agnes. D
Southey (1774): Thalaba. V
Strutt, Joseph (1749): Sports and Pastimes of the
   People of England. P
Wakefield, Priscilla (1751): The Juvenile Travel-
   lers. P
Williams (1762): History of Perourou [dramatized
   as Lady of Lyons by E. B. Lytton]. P
 Sketches of the State of Manners and Opinions
   in the French Republic. P

1802

Baillie (1762): Plays on the Passions, vol. ii.
Bloomfield (1766): Rural Tales. V
Clarke, Adam (1762 ?): Bibliographical Dictionary
   [concl. 1806].
Colman, jnr. (1762): Poor Gentleman. C
Dibdin, Thomas (1776): Introduction to the
   Knowledge of Rare and Valuable Classics. P
Edgeworth (1767): Essay on Irish Bulls (with
   R. L. Edgeworth).
Gifford (1756): Trs. of Juvenal (cont. Auto-
   biography P).
Holcroft (1745): A Tale of Mystery. D
Lamb (1775): John Woodvil, a tragedy.
Landor (1775): Poetry by author of Gebir.
Opie (1769): Poems.
Paley (1743): Natural Theology. P
Pye (1745): Verses on Several Subjects.
Ritson, Joseph (1752): Bibliographia Poetica. P
Scott (1771): Ed. Border Minstrelsy, vols. i, ii [iii
   1803]. V
Smith (1779): Trevanion. P
Spencer, William Robert (1769): Urania. C

Peace of Amiens.
Winthrop Mackworth
   Praed b.
Letitia Elizabeth Landon b.
Isaac Williams b.
Harriet Martineau b.
Erasmus Darwin d.
Wordsworth's marriage.
William Cobbett starts the
   'Weekly Political Regis-
   ter' (contd. to 1835).
'The Edinburgh Review'
   started by Sydney Smith,
   Jeffrey and Brougham
   (publisher Constable).
Leyden, ed. 'Scottish De-
   scriptive Poems.'
Étienne Dumont's 'Traité
   de la législation civil et
   pénale' based on Ben-
   tham's MSS.
Dumas b.
Victor Hugo b.
Chateaubriand, 'Génie du
   christianisme'.
Mme de Staël, 'Delphine'.
Hardenberg ('Novalis'),
   'Heinrich von Ofter-
   dingen'.

Boswell, Sir Alexander (1775): Songs chiefly in Scottish Dialect.

Bowles (1762): The Picture. V

Burney, James (1750): History of Discoveries in the South Sea [concl. 1817]. P

Chatterton (d. 1770): Collected Works, ed. R. Southey and J. Cottle [ed. Willcox 1842, Skeat 1875, Roberts 1906, Sidney Lee 1906–9: see 1777].

Cowper (d. 1800): Letters [in Life and Posthumous Writings, ed. Hayley. Later and fuller edd. of letters: ed. Hayley 1804, 1809, 1812, ed. J. Johnson 1824, ed. Southey 1834–7, ed. T. Wright 1904].

Darwin (d. 1802): Temple of Nature. V

Dibdin, Charles, senr. (1745): Professional Life of Mr. Dibdin [with 600 songs].

Godwin (1756): Life of Chaucer [including Memoirs of John of Gaunt]. P

Hayley (1745): Life of Cowper. P

Holcroft (1745): Hear both Sides. C

Lancaster, Joseph (1778): Improvements in Education. P

Le Noir, Elizabeth (1755?): Village Annals. P novel.

Leyden, John (1775): Scenes of Infancy. V

Montagu (d. 1762): Works, including Letters [see 1763], Poems [see 1747], and Essays, ed. J. Dallaway [2nd ed. with Letters to Mrs. Hewitt 1817; another ed. with Introductory Anecdotes, ed. Wharncliffe, 1837; another ed., by Moy Thomas, 1861].

Porter, Jane (1776): Thaddeus of Warsaw. P novel.

Reed, Isaac (1742): Ed. of Shakespeare [known as the 1st variorum ed.; revised as the 2nd variorum ed. in 1813].

Repton, Humphrey (1752): Theory and Practice of Landscape Gardening. P

Sayers, Frank (1763): Nugæ Poeticæ [chiefly versifications of Jack the Giant Killer and Guy of Warwick]. V

Southey (1774): Trs. of Amadis of Gaul.

Struthers, John (1776): Anticipation. V

Turner (1768): Vindication of Genuineness of Ancient Poems of Aneurin, Taliesin, &c. P

White (1785): Clifton Grove. V

Woodhouse, James (1735): Norbury Park, and Other Poems.

War with France renewed.

Richard Henry (or Hengist) Horne b.

Thomas Lovell Beddoes b.
George Borrow b.

Douglas Jerrold b.
Ralph Waldo Emerson b.
Richard Hurrell Froude b.
Edward George Bulwer (Lytton) b.
James Beattie d.
William Cobbett starts 'The Parliamentary Debates' which in 1812 passed on to Hansard.
William Stewart Rose's trs. of 'Amadis de Gaule'.
Sydney Gazette', first Australian newspaper.

Klopstock d.
Schiller, 'Braut von Messina'.
H. von Kleist, 'Die Familie Schroffenstein'.
Kotzebue, 'Deutscher Kleinstädter'.
Mérimée b.
Alfieri d.

Baillie (1762): Miscellaneous Plays [Rayner, Country Inn, Constantine Paleologus].

Blake (1757): Jerusalem. V
Milton, a Poem. V

Bowles (1762): Spirit of Discovery. V

Brown, Thomas (1778): Poems.
Observations on the Relation of Cause and Effect [enlarg. ed. 1806; 3rd ed. 1818]. P

Du Bois, Edward: Trs. Decameron with Remarks on Boccaccio. P

Edgeworth (1767): Popular Tales. P
Modern Griselda. P

Grahame, James (1765): The Sabbath [anon.]. V

Hamilton, Elizabeth (1758): Memoirs of Agrippina. P

Hayley (1745): Triumphs of Music. V

Holcroft (1745): Travels from Hamburg. P

Le Noir, Elizabeth (1755): Village Anecdotes. P

Lewis (1775): Bravo of Venice [from German: dramatized as 'Rugantino' 1805].

Opie (1769): Adeline Mowbray. P

Peacock (1785): Monks of St. Mark. V

Pitt, Earl of Chatham (d. 1778): Letters to his Nephew, Thomas Pitt, ed. Grenville.

Porter, Anna (1780): Lake of Killarney. P

Richardson (d. 1761): Correspondence, ed. with Life by Mrs. Barbauld.

Seward (1747): Memoir of Erasmus Darwin. P

Smith, Charlotte (1749): Conversations introducing Poetry. P

Spencer, William (1769): Year of Sorrow. V

Struthers, John (1776): Poor Man's Sabbath. V

Taylor, Anne and Jane: Original Poems for Infant Minds. V

Nathaniel Hawthorne b.
Sir Richard Owen b.
Benjamin Disraeli b.
William Gilbert b.
Charlotte Lennox d.
Richard Graves d.
John Wilkes d.
Joseph Priestley d.
Scott's ed. of 'The British Drama'.
Napoleon Buonaparte Emperor.
Sainte-Beuve b.
Sénancour, 'Obermann'.
Kant d.
Schiller, 'Wilhelm Tell'.
Goethe, 'Natürliche Tochter'.
Tieck, 'Kaiser Octavianus'.
George Sand b.

Adams, John (1735): Discourses on Davilla. P
Anderson, Robert (1770): Ballads in Cumbrian Dialect. V
Brydges, Egerton (1762): Censura Literaria (1805–9). P
Campbell (1777): Collected Poems [later edd.: 1810, 1824, 1828–33, 1837, ed. Hill 1851, Rogers 1871, Rossetti 1871, Robertson 1901].
Cary (1772): Trs. Inferno [see 1814]. V
Colman, jnr. (1762): John Bull [n.d.]. D
Who wants a Guinea? D
Foster, John (1770): Essays. P
Gifford (1756): Ed. of Massinger [another ed. 1813].
Godwin (1756): Fleetwood. P
Fables. P
Graves (d. 1804): The Triflers. P and V
Hayley (1745): Ballads on Anecdotes of Animals [illustr. Blake]. V
Hazlitt (1778): Principles of Human Action. P
Holcroft (1745): Lady of the Rock. D
Memoirs of Bryan Perdue. P
Inchbald (1753): To Marry or not to Marry. C
Johnson (d. 1784): Account of his own Life. P
Knight (1750): Principles of Taste. P
Lamb (1775): King and Queen of Hearts. V
Montgomery (1771): The Ocean. V
Morgan, Sydney, Lady (1783?): Novice of St. Dominick. P
Morton (1764?): School of Reform. C
Roscoe (1753): Life of Leo X. P
Sayers, Frank (1763): Miscellanies, Antiquarian and Historical. P
Scott (1771): Lay of the Last Minstrel. V
Southey (1774): Madoc. V
Tobin, John (d. 1804): The Honey Moon. C
Trimmer (1741): Comparative View of the Plan of Education promulgated by Mr. Joseph Lancaster. P
Walpole (d. 1797): Reminiscences (written 1788). P

Battles of Trafalgar and Austerlitz.
William Harrison Ainsworth b.
James Martineau b.
Frederick Denison Maurice b.
Robert Surtees b.
Arthur Murphy d.
William Paley d.
George Ellis's 'Specimens of Early English Romances in metre'.
William Taylor's trs. of 'Nathan the Wise'.
Correspondence of Lady Hertford and Lady Pomfret, 1738–1741.
Thomas Park's 'British Poets' (1805–15).
Chateaubriand, 'René'.
Schiller d.
Arnim and Brentano, 'Wunderhorn' (1805–8).

President U.S.A. Jefferson (2nd term).

Bloomfield (1766): Wild Flowers. V
Bowles (1762): Bowden Hall. V
　Ed. of Pope.
Byron (1788): Fugitive Pieces. V
Edgeworth (1767): Leonora. P
　Letters. P
Franklin (d. 1790): Complete Works in Philosophy, Politics & Morals. P
Hazlitt (1778): Free Thoughts on Public Affairs. P
Holcroft (1745): The Vindictive Man. C
　Tales in Verse.
Hutchinson, Lucy (1620): Life of Colonel [John] Hutchinson [written between 1664 and 1671; cont. autobiographical fragment; re-ed., with additions, Firth 1904].
Lancaster, Joseph (1778): Plan for educating Ten Thousand Poor Children. P
Landor (1775): Simonidea [incl. Gunlung and Helga]. V
Lingard (1771): Antiquities of Anglo-Saxon Church [see 1845]. P
Montgomery (1771): Wanderer of Switzerland. V
Moore (1779): Epistles, Odes, and Other Poems. V
Morgan, Sydney, Lady (1783 ?): Wild Irish Girl. P
Opie (1769): Simple Tales. P
Peacock (1785): Palmyra. V
Roscoe (1753): Butterfly's Ball and Grasshopper's Feast [in the Gentleman's Magazine: Sept. 1807]. V
Scott (1771): Ballads and Lyrical Pieces. V
　Ed. Diary of Sir Henry Slingsby [abbreviated: see 1836].
Struthers, John (1776): The Peasant's Death. V
Webster, Noah (1758): Compendious Dictionary of the English Language [his American Dictionary of the English Language 1st ed. 1828].

Elizabeth Barrett (Browning) b.
John Stuart Mill b.
Charles James Lever b.
Henry Kirke White d.
Charlotte Smith d.
Charles James Fox d.
William Pitt d.
Mrs. Inchbald's 'British Theatre' (contd. 1809).
William Cobbett's 'Parliamentary History of England' begins to appear.
'The Monthly Repository of Theology and General Literature' starts (ed. Aspland: contd. 1837).

Barlow, Joel (1754): The Columbiad. V

Barrett, Eaton Stannard (1786): All the Talents. V

Byron (1788): Hours of Idleness. V

   Poems on Various Occasions. V

Campbell (1777): Annals of Great Britain. P

Copleston, Edward (1776): Advice to a Young Reviewer. P

Coxe, William (1747): History of the House of Austria. P

Crabbe (1754): Poems [cont. Parish Register and Sir Eustace Percy among new poems].

Cumberland (1732): Memoirs written by Himself. P

Dorset, Catherine (1750?): The Peacock 'At Home'. V

   The Lion's Masquerade. V

Douce, Francis (1757): Illustrations of Shakespeare. P

Godwin (1756): Faulkener. D

Grahame, James (1765): Poems (collected).

Heber (1783): Palestine. V

Hogg (1770): The Mountain Bard. V

Hunt (1784): Critical Essays on the Performers of the London Theatres. P

   Classic Tales, with Critical Essays on the Authors. P

Irving, Washington (1783): Salmagundi [1807–8]. P

Lamb, Mary (1764) **and Charles** (1775): Tales from Shakespeare. P

Lewis (1775): Adelgitha. T

   Feudal Tyrants. P

Malthus (1766): Letter to Whitbred on Poor Laws. P

Maturin (1782): Fatal Revenge. P

Moore (1779): Irish Melodies [1807–35; music by Sir John Stevenson].

Morton (1764?): Town and Country. C

Porter, Anna (1780): Hungarian Brothers. P

Pye (1745): Comments on Commentators of Shakespeare. P

Ramsay, David (1749): Life of Washington. P

Smith, Charlotte (d. 1806): Beachy Head, with Other Poems.

Smith, 'Horace' (1779): Horatio. P

Smith, Sydney (1771): Letters on the Subject of Catholics by Peter Plymley [concl. 1808]. P

Sotheby, William (1757): Saul. V

Southey (1774): Letters from England by Don Espriella. P

   Trs. of Spanish Chronicle of Palmerin of England.

   Specimens of the later English Poets.

Tannahill, Robert (1774): Poems and Songs.

Richard Chenevix Trench b.

Henry Wadsworth Longfellow b.

John Greenleaf Whittier b.

Clara Reeve d.

John Pinkerton's 'Collection of Voyages and Travels' (concl. 1814).

Fichte, 'Reden an die deutsche Nation'.

Mme de Staël, 'Corinne'.

Turner, Elizabeth: The Daisy, or Cautionary Stories in Verse.
White (d. 1806): Remains, ed. with Life by Southey. V
Wordsworth (1770): Poems in Two Volumes [Ode to Duty, Intimations of Immortality, Miscellaneous Sonnets, &c.].

1808

Bryant, William Cullen (1794): The Embargo. V
Burns (d. 1796): Reliques, ed. R. Cromek.
Clarkson, Thomas (1760): History of the Abolition of the African Slave Trade. P
Colman, jnr. (1762): Heir at Law (acted 1797). D
Battle of Hexham. D
Surrender of Calais. D
Cowper (d. 1800): Trs. of Milton's Italian and Latin Poems. V
Dalton, John (1766): New System of Chemical Philosophy [concl. 1810]. P
Fox, Charles James (d. 1806): History of the Early Part of the Reign of James II. P
Hamilton, Elizabeth (1758): Cottagers of Glenburnie. P
Hemans (née Browne) (1793): Poems.
England and Spain. V
Hunt (1784): London Theatres [originally in The News]. P
Lamb, Mary (1764), and **Charles** (1775): Mrs. Leicester's School. P
Le Noir, Elizabeth (1755 ?): Clara de Montfier. P
Lewis (1775): Romantic Tales. P
Venoni, or the Novice of St. Mark. T
Mangin, Edward (1772): Essay on Light Reading. P
Maturin (1782): Wild Irish Boy. P
Moore (1779): Corruption, Intolerance. V
Opie (1769): Warrior's Return, and Other Poems.
Scott (1771): Marmion. V
Ed. of Dryden [re-ed. Saintsbury 1882].
Southey (1774): Trs. of Spanish Romance of the Cid. P
Tobin, John (d. 1804): School for Authors. C

Peninsular War begun.
John Home d.
Leigh Hunt starts 'The Examiner' (contd. to 1821).
Rudolf Ackermann's 'Microcosm of London' (concl. 1811; words by William Combe and W. H. Pyne).
Charles Lamb's 'Specimens of English dramatic Poets'.
Mrs. Inchbald's 'British Theatre'.
Thomas Park's ed. of Harleian Miscellany (concl. 1813).
Catalogue of Harleian MSS. by Nares, Ellis, and Horne (concl. 1812).
Stephen Jones's ed. of Thomas Davies's 'Life of Garrick', with additions (see 1780).
C. J. Ingersoll's 'Rights and Wrongs of the U.S.A.'
Gérard de Nerval b.
Goethe, 'Faust', pt. 1.
H. von Kleist, 'Penthesilea'.

Adams, John Quincy (1767): American Principles. P

Blake (1757): Descriptive Catalogue. P

Byron (1788): Imitations and Translations from Classics with Original Poems. V
  English Bards and Scotch Reviewers. V

Campbell (1777): Gertrude of Wyoming and Other Poems [2nd ed. 1810]. V

Carter, Elizabeth (d. 1806): Letters to Miss Catherine Talbot and Mrs. Vesey. P

Coleridge (1772): The Friend [cont. to 15 March 1810; reissued with supplementary matter 1812; new and greatly altered ed. 1818]. P

Combe (1741): The Schoolmaster's Tour [in *The Poetical Magazine*: see 1812]. V

Dibdin, Thomas (1776): Bibliomania [enlarg. edd. 1811, 1842]. P

Edgeworth (1767): Tales of Fashionable Life, First series [Eunice, The Dun, Manœuvring, Almeria: see 1812]. P

Freneau, Philip (1752): Poems written during the American Revolutionary War. V

Godwin (1756): Essay on Sepulchres. P

Hobhouse, John (1786): Travels through Albania during 1809–10. P

Hope, Thomas (1770 ?): Costumes of the Ancients. P

Irving, Washington (1783): Diedrich Knickerbocker's History of New York. P

Lamb, Charles (1775) **and Mary** (1764): Poetry for Children. V

Montagu (d. 1800): Letters, vols. i, ii [iii and iv in 1813].

Montgomery (1771): West Indies. V

Moore (1779): The Sceptic. V

More (1745): Cœlebs in Search of a Wife [anon.]. P

Morgan, Sydney, Lady (1783 ?): Woman, or Ida of Athens. P

Porter, Anna (1780): Don Sebastian. P

Wordsworth (1770): Concerning Relations of Great Britain, Spain, and Portugal as affected by the Convention of Cintra. P

William Ewart Gladstone b.
Edgar Allen Poe b.
Oliver Wendell Holmes b.
Alfred Tennyson b.
Alexander William Kinglake b.
Charles Darwin b.
Richard Monckton Milnes (Lord Houghton) b.
Edward Fitzgerald b.
Thomas Gordon Hake b.
Abraham Lincoln b.
Hannah Cowley d.
Anna Seward d.
Thomas Paine d.
Thomas Holcroft d.
'Quarterly Review' started with Gifford as editor.
William Cobbett's (later known as Howell's) 'Collection of State Trials' (concl. 1826).
Scott's ed. of Somers Tracts (concl. 1815; see 1748).
Mrs. Inchbald's 'The Modern Theatre' and 'Collection of Farces'.
Rudolf Ackermann's 'Repository of Arts, Literature', etc. (concl. 1828).
Chateaubriand, 'Martyrs'.
Goethe, 'Wahlverwandtschaften'.
August Schlegel, 'Über dramatische Kunst und Literatur' (concl. 1811).

President U.S.A.
Madison.

Aikin (1781): Epistles on Women. V
Baillie (1762): Family Legend. T
Barrett, Eaton Stannard (1786): Woman, and Other Poems. V
Brunton, Mary (1778): Self-Control. P
Brydges, Egerton (1762): British Bibliographer [concl. 1814]. P
Clarke, Edward (1769): Travels. P
Conder, Josiah, and others (1789): Associate Minstrels. V
Crabbe (1754): The Borough. V
Dibdin, Thomas (1776): Ed. of Joseph Ames's Typographical Antiquities [concl. 1819: see 1749, 1785].
Hawker, Peter (1786): Journal. P
Hogg (1770): Forest Minstrel. V
Lancaster, Joseph (1778): Instructions for forming a Society for the Education of the Labouring Classes. P
Macneill, Hector (1746): Pastoral or Lyric Music of Scotland. V
Mitford, Mary (1787): Miscellaneous Poems.
Peacock (1785): Genius of the Thames. V
Pocock, Isaac (1782): Hit or Miss. D
Porter, Jane (1776): The Scottish Chiefs. P
Rogers (1763): Voyage of Columbus [privately printed 1808]. V
Scott (1771): Lady of the Lake. V
    Ancient British Drama [anthology].
Seward (d. 1809): Poetical Works, ed. Scott.
Shelley (1792): Original Poetry by Victor and Cazire [with Elizabeth Shelley]. V
    Zastrozzi. P
    Posthumous fragments of Margaret Nicholson. V
Sotheby, William (1757): Constance de Castille. V
Southey (1774): Curse of Kehama. V
    History of Brazil [concl. 1819]. P
Stewart (1753): Philosophical Essays. P
Taylor, Jane and Ann: Hymns for Infant Minds. V
Taylor, William (1765): Tales of Yore [trs. from Fr. and Ger.] P
Wordsworth (1770): Topographical Description of the Country of the Lakes [in Joseph Wilkinson's Select Views in Cumberland: see 1820, '22]. P

Elizabeth Gaskell b.
Martin Tupper b.
Margaret Fuller b.
Coleridge lectures on Shakespeare.
Letters of Marquise du Deffand to Horace Walpole, ed. Berry.
Mrs. Barbauld's 'British Novelists'.
Alexander Chalmers's 'English Poets'.
Robert Cromek's 'Select Scottish Songs' and 'Nithsdale and Galloway Song'.
Leigh Hunt starts 'The Reflector' (only four numbers).
Mme de Staël, 'De l'Allemagne' (1810–13).
Goethe, 'Pandora'.
C. J. Ingersoll's 'Inchiquin'.
Blake's Canterbury Pilgrims (engraving) published.
Musset b.
H. von Kleist, 'Käthchen von Heilbronn', 'Erzählungen (–1811).

Austen (1775): Sense and Sensibility [anon.]. P
Barbauld (1743): Eighteen Hundred and Eleven.
     V

  Female Speaker [P and V anthology].
Bloomfield (1766): Banks of the Wye. V
D'Israeli (1766): Despotism. P
Hunt (1784): Feast of the Poets [in The Reflector:
     book form 1814]. V
Kerr, Robert: History and Collection of Voyages
     [concl. 1824]. P
Knowles (1784): Brian Boroihme. D
Lamb (1775): Prince Dorus. V
Mitford, John (1781): Agnes, the Indian Captive
     and Other Poems. V
Mitford, Mary (1787): Christina. V
Moore (1779): M.P., or The Blue Stocking. D
     comic opera.
More (1745): Practical Piety. P
Scott, Jonathan (1754): Trs. of the Arabian
     Nights. P
Scott (1771): Vision of Don Roderick. V
     Ed. of Secret History of the Court of James I.
     Ed. of Abel Boyer's trs. of Memoirs of Count
     Grammont [see 1713–14].
     Modern British Drama [anthology].
Seward (d. 1809): Correspondence, 1784–1807.
Shelley (1792): Necessity of Atheism. P
     St. Irvyne. P
     Poetical Essay on Existing State of Things. V
Spencer, William (1769): Poems.
Stewart (1753): Biographical Memoirs. P
Struthers, John (1776): Wintry Day. V
Tighe, Mrs. Mary (d. 1810): Psyche, or the Legend
     of Love [privately printed 1805]. V
Turner, Elizabeth: The Cowslip, or More Caution-
     ary Stories in Verse.
Warton, Joseph and John: Ed. Poems of Dryden
     [ed. Christie 1870; Sargeaunt 1910].

Prince of Wales Regent.
*William   Makepeace
     Thackeray b.*
William Bell Scott b.
Thomas Percy d.
Richard Cumberland d.
Charles Kean d.
*Shelley's expulsion from
     Oxford and marriage
     with Harriet Westbrook.*
*National Society for the
     Education of the Poor
     founded.*
*Étienne Dumont's 'Théorie
     des peines et des récom-
     penses' based on the
     MSS. of Jeremy Ben-
     tham (see 1825).*
*Edward Mangin's ed. of
     Richardson.*
*Chateaubriand,   'Itiné-
     raire'.*
Fouqué, 'Undine'.
Gautier b.
H. von Kleist d.
*Goethe, 'Dichtung und
     Wahrheit' (concl. 1831).*

Baillie (1762): Plays on the Passions, Third series.
Barton (1784): Metrical Effusions. V
Byron (1788): Childe Harold, cantos i and ii (with 20 other poems, including those during his travels and those addressed to Thyrza. Canto iii 1816, iv 1818, complete 1819]. V
Curse of Minerva. V
Cary (1772): Trs. Purgatorio and Paradiso. V
Combe (1741): Tour of Dr. Syntax in Search of the picturesque [first sep. ed.; originally as 'The Schoolmaster's Tour' in the Poetical Magazine, 1809 ff.: see 1820–1; illustrated by T. Rowlandson]. V
Crabbe (1754): Tales in Verse.
D'Israeli (1766): Calamities of Authors. P ·
Edgeworth (1767): Tales of Fashionable Life, 2nd series [Vivian, Absentee, Mme de Fleury, Emilie de Coulanges: see 1809]. P
Heber (1783): Poems and Translations. V
Hemans (1793): Domestic Affections, and Other Poems. V
Jones, Stephen (1763): Biographia Dramatica, 3rd ed. [see 1764, 1782]. P
Lancaster, Joseph (1778): Schools for all. P
Landor (1775): Count Julian, a Tragedy.
Maturin (1782): Milesian Chief. P
Mitford, Mary (1787): Blanch of Castile. V
Montgomery (1771): World before the Flood. V
Nichols, John, senr. (1745): Literary Anecdotes of the Eighteenth Century [concl. 1815]. P
Opie (1769): Temper, or Domestic Scenes. P
Peacock (1785): Philosophy of Melancholy. V
Shelley (1792): Address to Irish People. P
Proposals for Association of Philanthropists for Ireland. P
Declaration of Rights. P
Letter to Lord Ellenborough. P
The Devil's Walk. V
Smith, 'Horace' (1779): Rejected Addresses [with James Smith]. V
Southey (1774) **and Coleridge** (1772): Omniana. P
Tennant, William (1784): Anster Fair [anon.]. V
Wilson (1785): Isle of Palms and Other Poems. V

French retreat from Moscow.
Robert Browning b.
Charles Dickens b.
Edward Lear b.
Samuel Smiles b.
John Forster b.
Horne Tooke d.
Isaac Bickerstaffe d.?
Edmond Malone d.
Roxburghe Club [for reprinting rare English books] founded by Thomas Dibdin and others.
Rudolf Ackermann's 'Westminster Abbey'.
Chalmers's 'General Biographical Dictionary' (enlarg. from ed. of 1761, completed 1817).
Jacob and Wilhelm Grimm, 'Kinder- und Hausmärchen' (concl. 1815).
Hegel, 'Logik' (concl. 1816).
John and L. Hunt's libel in 'Examiner' on Prince Regent.

Aubrey, John (d. 1697): Lives [in Letters Written by Eminent Persons in 17th and 18th Centuries; ed. Clark 1898].
Austen (1775): Pride and Prejudice [anon.]. P
Byron (1788): Bride of Abydos. V
  Waltz [anon.]. V
  Giaour. V
Coleridge (1772): Remorse. D
Cowley (d. 1809): Collected Works.
Coxe, William (1747): Memoirs of Kings of Spain. P
Cunningham, Allan (1784): Songs chiefly in the Rural Dialect of Scotland. V
Hogg (1770): Queen's Wake. V
Lingard (1771): Collection of Tracts connected with the Civil and Religious Principles of the Catholics. P
Mitford (1787): Poems on the Female Character. V
Moore (1779): Intercepted Letters, or The Two-penny Post Bag. V
More (1745): Christian Morals. P
Northcote, James (1746): Memoirs of Reynolds. P
Opie (1769): Tales of Real Life. P
Owen, Robert (1771): New View of Society [concl. 1816]. P
Pocock, Isaac (1782): Miller and his Men. D
Reresby, Sir John (d. 1689): Travels and Memoirs [see 1734].
Scott (1771): Rokeby. V
  Bridal of Triermain. V
Shelley (1792): Queen Mab. V
  Vindication of Natural Diet. P
Smith, 'Horace' (1779): Horace in London [with James Smith] V
Southey (1774): Life of Nelson. P

Mark Pattison b.
William Aytoun b.
Sir Arthur Helps b.
H. J. Pye d.
Southey becomes poet-laureate.
Leigh Hunt in prison 1813-15.
Wagner b.
Wieland d.
Fouqué, 'Der Zauberring'.
E. T. A. Hoffmann, 'Peter Schlemihl'.

President U.S.A. Madison (2nd term).

1814

Aikin (1781): Lorimer, a Tale. P
Austen (1775): Mansfield Park [anon.]. P
Barrett, Eaton Stannard (1786): The Heroine. P
Brunton, Mary (1778): Discipline. P
Brydges, Egerton (1762): Restituta: or Titles, Extracts, and Characters of Old Books Revived [concl. 1816]. P
Burney, Frances (1752): The Wanderer. P
Byron (1788): The Corsair. V
  Ode to Napoleon. V
  Lara. V
Cary (1772): Trs. Dante complete [see 1805]. V
Coleridge (1772): Essays on the Fine Arts [in Felix Farley's Journal]. P

Abdication of Napoleon.
Charles Reade b.
Aubrey Thomas De Vere b.
Shelley's departure from England.
Colburn's 'New Monthly Magazine' and 'New British Theatre' (ed. John Galt).
'The British Critic' (new series) begun (became quarterly in 1826; ed. John Newman 1836-41, T. Mozley 1841-3).

D'Israeli (1766): Quarrels of Authors. P
Edgeworth (1767): Patronage. P
Hawker, Peter (1786): Instructions to Young
    Sportsmen. P
Horne, Thomas (1780): Introduction to Study of
    Bibliography. P
Hunt (1784): Feast of the Poets [originally in The
    Reflector 1811]. V
Morgan, Sydney, Lady (1783?): O'Donnel, a
    National Tale. P
Nicholson, William (1782?): Tales in Verse and
    Miscellaneous Poems.
Quillinan, Edward (1791): Dunluce Castle. V
Stanzas by Author of Dunluce Castle. V
Reynolds, John Hamilton (1794): Safie, an East-
    ern Tale. V
Eden of Imagination. V
Richmond, Legh (1772): Annals of the Poor
    [Dairyman's daughter, Young Cottager,
    Negro Servant: originally in Christian
    Guardian between 1809 and 1814]. P
Rogers (1763): Jacqueline [with Byron's Lara]. V
Scott (1771): Waverley [anon.]. P.
    Border Antiquities of England and Scotland
    [concl. 1817]. P
    Eyrbiggia Saga [in Weber's Northern Anti-
    quities].
    Essays on Chivalry and Romance [in Encyclo-
    paedia Britannica]. P
    Ed. of Swift.
Sheil, Richard Lalor (1791): Adelaide, or The
    Emigrants. D
Shelley (1792): Refutation of Deism. P
Sotheby, William (1757): Song of Triumph on the
    Peace. V
    Five Tragedies [Confession, Orestes (2nd ed.,
    1st in 1802), Ivan, Death of Darnley,
    Zamorin and Zama].
Southey (1774): Roderick. V
Odes to the Prince Regent and King of Prussia. V
Stewart (1753): Philosophy of the Human Mind,
    vol. ii [see 1792, 1827]. P
Struthers, John (1776): Poems, Moral and
    Religious.
Turner (1768): History of England from Norman
    Conquest to 1509 [concl. 1823].
Wolcot (1738): The Regent and the King. V
Royalty Fogbound. V
Wordsworth (1770): The Excursion, being a
    portion of The Recluse [cont. the Essay upon
    Epitaphs from The Friend of 22 Feb. 1810:
    The Recluse in 1888].

*Capell   Lofft's   (senr.)
    'Laura, or Anthology
    of Sonnets'.
Thomas Mathias's ed. of
    Gray.
Rudolf   Ackermann's
    'University of Oxford'.
Chateaubriand,   'Bona-
    parte et les Bourbons'.
Fichte d.
Chamisso, 'Peter Schle-
    mihl'.*

Boswell, Sir Alexander: Tyrant's Fall. V
Bowles (1762): Missionary of the Andes. V
Burnet (d. 1715): Memorial offered to the Princess Sophia. P
Byron (1788): Hebrew Melodies. V
  Collected Works [Murray].
Combe (1741): Life of Napoleon. V
  English Dance of Death. V
Cowper (d. 1800): Poems, ed. J. Johnson [later edd.: early poems with anecdotes by Lady Hesketh, ed. J. Croft, 1825, with new letters, ed. Southey, 1834–7, ed. Grimshawe 1835, ed. Bruce 1865 (Aldine), ed. Benham 1889 (Globe), ed. Milford 1905 (Oxford)].
Glen, William (1789): Poems, chiefly Lyrical.
Godwin (1756): Lives of Edward and John Philips. To which are added Collections for the Life of Milton by J. Aubrey, and Life of Milton by Edward Philips. P
Hogg (1770): Pilgrims of the Sun. V
Hubbard (d. 1815): General History of New England. P
Hunt (1784): Descent of Liberty, a Masque. V
Johnstone, Christian (1781): Clan Albin. P
Keightley, Thomas (1789): Outlines of History. P
Key, Francis Scott (1780): The Star-spangled Banner. V
Knowles (1784): Caius Gracchus. T
Malcolm, Sir John (1769): History of Persia. P
Malthus (1766): Inquiry into Rent. P
Milman (1791): Fazio. D
Moore (1779): National Airs [music by Sir J. Stevenson]. V
More (1745): Essay on Character and Writings of St. Paul. P
Porter, Jane (1776): Pastor's Fireside. P
Scott (1771): Guy Mannering. P
  Lord of the Isles. V
  Field of Waterloo. V
  Paul's Letters to his Kinsfolk. P
Stewart (1753): Dissertation on the Progress of Philosophy, pt. i [pt. ii 1821]. P
Tannahill, Robert (d. 1810): Collected Works [other edd.: 1817, 1822, Ramsay 1838, Semple 1873].
Trench, Melesina (1768): Campaspe, and Other Poems. V
West, Sir Edward (1782): Application of Capital to Land. P
Wordsworth (1770): White Doe of Rylstone [incl. Force of Prayer]. V
  Poems including Lyrical Ballads, Miscellaneous Pieces, and (revised) Preface. V

Battle of Waterloo (18 June).
Anthony Trollope b.
Richard William Church b.
George Boole b.
Arthur Penrhyn Stanley b.
Byron married.
Thomas Dibdin's anthology, 'London Theatre' (concl. 1818).
'Encyclopaedia Britannica', 5th ed.
'North American Review' started.
Charles Lloyd's trs. of tragedies of Alfieri.
'The Military Adventures of Johnny Newcome' (illustr. by T. Rowlandson and letterpress probably by David Roberts).
Rudolf Ackermann's 'University of Cambridge.
Benjamin Constant, 'Adolphe'.
F. Schlegel, 'Vorlesungen über die Geschichte der Alten und Neuen Literatur'

Austen (1775): Emma [anon.]. P
Bentham (1748): Defence of Usury. P
　Chrestomathia. P
Byron (1788): Siege of Corinth. V
　Parisina. V
　Prisoner of Chillon and Other Poems.
　Childe Harold, canto iii. V
　Monody on Death of Sheridan. V
　Poems on his Domestic Circumstances.
Coleridge (1772): Christabel, Kubla Khan, Pains
　of Sleep. V
　The Statesman's Manual, a Lay Sermon. P
Cowper (d. 1800): Memoirs of Early Life, written
　by Himself. P
D'Israeli (1766): Character of James I. P
Heber (1783): Christian Comforter. P
Hogg (1770): Poetic Mirror. V
　Madoc of the Moor. V
Holcroft (d. 1809): Memoirs [completed by
　Hazlitt]. P
Hunt (1784): Story of Rimini. V
Johnson (d. 1784): Diary of a Journey into N.
　Wales in 1774. P
Lamb, Lady Caroline (1785): Glenarvon [anon.:
　called the Fatal Passion, 1865]. P
Maturin (1782): Bertram. D
Moore (1779): Sacred Songs. V
　On the Death of Sheridan. V
Morgan, Sydney, Lady (1783): Florence M'Carthy. P
Opie (1769): Valentine's Eve. P
Peacock (1785): Headlong Hall. P
Quillinan, Edward (1771): Sacrifice of Isabel. V
Ramsay, David (1749): The History of the U.S.A. P
Reynolds, John Hamilton (1794): The Naiad and
　Other Poems.
Scott (1771): Antiquary. P
　Tales of my Landlord [Black Dwarf. Old
　Mortality]. P
Shelley (1792): Alastor and Other Poems [see
　1876]. V
Sheridan (d. 1816): Speeches.
Southey (1774): Carmen Nuptiale. V
　Poet's Pilgrimage to Waterloo. V
　Lay of the Laureate. V
Trench, Melesina (1768): Laura's Dream [anon.]. V
Wilson (1785): City of the Plague and Other
　Poems. V
Wordsworth (1770): Letter to a Friend of Burns
　[James Gray]. P
　Thanksgiving Ode [with other short pieces]. V

Charlotte Brontë b.
Philip James Bailey b.
Sir Theodore Martin b.
Richard Brinsley Sheridan d.
Suicide of Harriet Westbrook and Shelley's marriage with Mary Godwin.
Byron's final departure from England.
Coleridge settles at Highgate.
'Albyn's Anthology' (Scottish Songs), ed. A. Campbell.
Robert Surtees's 'History of Durham' (concl. 1840).
Leigh Hunt's essay on Shelley and Keats entitled 'Young Poets' in 'The Examiner', 1 Dec.
Étienne Dumont's 'Tactique des Assemblées legislatives et Traité de Sophismes politiques' from the MSS. of Bentham.
William Gifford's ed. of Ben Jonson.
John Mitford's ed. of Gray.
Goethe, 'Italienische Reise'.
Jacob & Wilhelm Grimm, 'Deutsche Sagen' (concl. 1818).
Hegel, 'Philosophie des Rechts'.

Bentham (1748): Table of the Springs of Action [prtd. 1815]. P

Brackenridge, Henry Mane (1786): South America. P

Burges, Sir James (1752): Dramas [collected].

Byron (1788): Manfred. D
Lament of Tasso. V

Carter, Elizabeth (d. 1806): Letters to Mrs. Montagu. P

Chesterfield (d. 1773): Letters to A. C. Stanhope on the education of his Godson [see 1890]. P

Cobbett (1762): English Grammar. P

Coleridge (1772): Sibylline Leaves [first publication of marginal glosses on Ancient Mariner]. V.
Blessed are ye that sow, a Lay Sermon. P
A Hebrew Dirge. V
Biographia Literaria. P
Zapolya. A Christmas Tale. D

Combe (1741): Dance of Life. V

Croly, George (1780): Paris in 1815. V

Dibdin, Thomas (1776): Bibliographical Decameron. P

Drake, Nathan (1766): Shakespeare and his Times. P

Edgeworth (1767): Harington, Ormond. P
Comic Dramas. P

Frere (1769): Monks and the Giants, cantos i, ii [iii and iv in 1818; collected ed. 1818; original title Prospectus and Specimen of an intended National Work]. V

Godwin (1756): Mandeville. P

Hazlitt (1778): Characters of Shakespeare's Plays. P
The Round Table [from The Examiner, 1815–17: with Leigh Hunt]. P

Hemans (1793): Modern Greece. V

Hogg (1770): Brownie of Bodsbeck. P
Dramatic Tales. P

Hogg, with Lockhart and Wilson: Translations from Ancient Chaldee MSS. [attack on The Edinburgh Review: in Blackwood's Magazine for October. In the same issue of Blackwood's Lockhart and Wilson attack Coleridge, Shelley, Leigh Hunt, and Keats in article 'The Cockney School of Poets'.]

Henry David Thoreau b.
George Henry Lewes b.
Tom Taylor b.
Branwell Brontë b.
Benjamin Jowett b.
Jane Austen d.
William Hone imprisoned.
William Jerdan starts 'The Literary Gazette'.
'The Scotsman' started.
'Blackwood's Magazine' started in April (ed. William Blackwood: first six numbers called 'Edinburgh Monthly Magazine'; in June number Charles Wolfe's 'Burial of Sir John Moore').
Richard Cumberland's anthology 'The British Drama'.
John Thomas Smith, 'Vagabondiana' (with Introduction by Francis Douce).
Arnim, 'Kronenwächter'.
Mme de Staël d.
Grillparzer, 'Die Ahnfrau'.

President U.S.A.
Monroe.

Keats (1795): Poems [Sleep and Poetry, I Stood Tiptoe, &c.]. V

Maturin (1782): Manuel. T
Fredolfo. T

Mill (1773): History of British India [ed. with continuation by Horace Hayman Wilson, 1858). P

Moore (1779): Lalla Rookh. V

Nichols, John (senior) (1745): Illustrations of the Literary History of the 18th Century [concl. 1822: continued by Nichols, jnr., 1828–58]. P

Owen, Robert (1771): Report to the Committee on the Poor Law. P

Peacock (1785): Melincourt. P

Porter, Anna (1780): Knight of St. John. P

Priestley (d. 1804): Works, with Memoirs and Correspondence, ed. Rutt [concl. 1832].

Ricardo (1772): Principles of Political Economy and Taxation. P

Scott (1771): Harold the Dauntless. V
Ballad of the Noble Moringer [in Edinburgh Annual Register]. V
Rob Roy. P

Sheil, Richard Lalor (1791): The Apostate. T

Shelley (1792): Proposal for putting Reform to the Vote [anon.]. P
Address to the People on the Death of Princess Charlotte. P
History of a Six Weeks' Tour [with Mrs. Shelley]. P
Laon and Cythna [see 1818]. V

Southey (1774): Wat Tyler [written 1794: a pirated and a genuine ed. in 1817]. D
Letter to W. Smith. P
Ed. of Malory.

Wolcot (1738): Epistle to Emperor of China. V

Aikin (1781): Memoirs of the Court of Queen Elizabeth. P

Austen (d. 1817): Northanger Abbey, Persuasion [with biography by Henry Austen]. P

Barton (1784): The Convict's Appeal. V
Poems by an Amateur. V

Bowdler, Thomas (1754): The Family Shakespeare.

Burges, Sir James: The Dragon Knight. V

Byron (1788): Childe Harold, canto iv. V
Beppo. V
Suppressed Poems [English Bards and Scotch Reviewers, Land of the Gaul, Windsor Poetics: published].

Coleridge (1772): Essay on Method [in Encyclopaedia Metropolitana: reprtd. 1845]. P

Coxe, William (1747): Memoirs of the Duke of Marlborough. P

Dwight, Timothy (d. 1817): Theology Explained. P

Egan (1772): Boxiana, vols. i, ii [iii 1821, iv 1824]. P

Evelyn (d. 1706): Diary 1641–1706, ed. Bray [later edd.: Upcott 1827, Wheatley 1879, Dobson 1906, de Beer 1955].

Ferrier, Susan (1782): Marriage. P

Hallam (1777): Europe during the Middle Ages. P

Hazlitt (1778): Lectures on the English Poets. P
Review of the English Stage. P

Hemans (1793): Translations from Camoens and Other Poets. V

Horne, Thomas (1780): Introduction to the Study of the Scriptures. P

Karl Marx b.
James Anthony Froude b.
Emily Brontë b.
John Mason Neale b.
Matthew Gregory Lewis d.
Isaac D'Israeli d.
Shelley's final departure from England. Attack on Keats (probably by Lockhart) in 'Blackwood's Magazine' for August.
Attack on Keats (probably by Gifford) in 'Quarterly Review' in September (in a number dated April: see 1819).
Grillparzer, 'Sappho'.

Hunt (1784): Foliage. V
· Literary Pocket Book [miscellany: concl. 1822].
Keats (1795): Endymion. V
Lamb (1775): Collected Works [later fuller col-
    lections: Talfourd 1838–40, Shepherd 1874,
    Fitzgerald 1875, Ainger 1899–1900, Lucas
    1903–5, Macdonald 1903, Hutchinson 1908].
Maturin (1782): Women, or Pour et Contre. P
Milman (1791): Samor. V
Mitford, John ('Alfred Burton') (1782): Adven-
    tures of Johnny Newcombe in the Navy
    [illustrated by T. Rowlandson]. V
  Poems of a British Sailor. V
Moore (1779): Fudge Family in Paris. V
Newman (1801): St. Bartholomew's Eve [with
    J. W. Bowden]. V
Opie (1769): New Tales. P
Peacock (1785): Nightmare Abbey. P
  Rhododaphne, or the Thessalian Spell. V
Pocock, Isaac (1782): Rob Roy Macgregor. D
Scott (1771): Tales of my Landlord, 2nd series
    [Heart of Midlothian]. P
Sheil, Richard Lalor (1791): Bellamira. T
Shelley, Mary (1797): Frankenstein. P
Shelley (1792): Revolt of Islam [originally printed
    as Laon and Cythna, 1817]. V
Sherwood, Mary (1775): Fairchild Family, pt. i
    (ii 1842, iii 1847). P
Sotheby, William (1757): Farewell to Italy, and
    Occasional Poems.
Struthers, John (1776): The Plough. V
Walpole (d. 1797): Letters to George Montagu. P
  Letters to William Cole. P

Balfour, Alexander (1767): Campbell. P

Bentham (1748): Radical Reform Bill. P

Brackenridge, Henry Marie (1786): Voyage to South America. P

Brunton, Mary (d. 1818): Literary Remains [incl. Emmeline] with Correspondence and Life, ed. A. Brunton.

Byron (1788): Mazeppa [with fragment of Vampire]. V

Don Juan, cantos i and ii. V

Crabbe (1754): Tales of the Hall. V

Field, Barron (1786): First Fruits of Australian Poetry. V

Hazlitt (1778): Lectures on English Comic Writers. P

Political Essays, with Sketches of Public Characters. P

Letter to William Gifford [in reply to G.'s attack on Keats: see 1818]. P

Hemans (1793): Tales and Historic Scenes. V

Meeting of Bruce and Wallace. V

Hone, William (1780): Political House that Jack built. P

Hope, Thomas (1770?): Anastasius. P

Hunt (1784): Hero and Leander, Bacchus and Ariadne. V

The Indicator [journal: concl. 1821].

Irving, Washington (1783): Sketch Book. P

Keats (1795): Ode to the Nightingale [in Annals of the Fine Arts, July]. V

Leyden, John (d. 1811): Poetical Remains, ed. with Memoir by James Morton.

Lingard (1771): History of England [concl. 1830]. P

Lloyd, Charles (1775): Nugae Canorae. V

Peterloo massacre.
Queen Victoria b.
Charles Kingsley b.
John Ruskin b.
James Russell Lowell b.
Arthur Hugh Clough b.
Mary Ann Evans ('George Eliot') b.
Herman Melville b.
Walt Whitman b.
John Wolcot ('Peter Pindar') d.
'Harp of Caledonia', ed. John Struthers.
William Whewell's 'Treatise on Mechanics'.
William Tennant's ed. of Allan Ramsay.
Thomas Campbell's 'Specimens of British Poets'.
James Hogg's 'Jacobite Relics of Scotland' (verse anthology, 2nd vol. 1821).
Kotzebue d.
Goethe, 'West-Oestliche divan'.
Schopenhauer, 'Wille und Vorstellung'.
Goethe, 'Westöstlicher Divan'.
Schopenhauer, 'Die Welt als Wille und Vorstellung'.
Chénier, 'Œuvres choisies'.

Lockhart (1794): Peter's Letters to his Kinsfolk.
   P
Macaulay (1800): Pompeii. V
Mitford (1787): Our Village [in The Lady's
   Magazine: in book form 1824–6–8–30–2].
Moncrieff, William (1794): Dandy Family. D
Montgomery (1771): Greenland. V
Moore (1779): Tom Crib's Memorial to Congress.
   V
More (1745): Moral Sketches of Prevailing
   Opinions of Manners. P
Procter (1787): Dramatic Scenes, and Other
   Poems. V
Reynolds, John Hamilton (1794): One, Two,
   Three, Four, Five. D
   Peter Bell [travesty of Wordsworth's poem]. V
Rogers (1763): Human Life. V
Ross, Sir John (1777): Voyage of Discovery for
   exploring Baffin's Bay and NW. Passage. P
Russell, Lord John (1798): Life of Lord William
   Russell. P
Scott (1771): Tales of my Landlord, 3rd series
   [Bride of Lammermoor. Legend of Mon-
   trose]. P
   Ivanhoe [bears date 1820]. P
   Description of Regalia of Scotland. P
Sheil, Richard Lalor (1791): Evadne. D
Shelley (1792): Rosalind and Helen, and Other
   Poems. V
   Cenci. T
Whately, Richard (1787): Historic Doubts rela-
   tive to Napoleon Buonaparte. P
Wordsworth (1770): Peter Bell [with four son-
   nets]. V
   The Waggoner [with sonnets]. V

Anderson, Robert (1770): Poetical Works.
Browning, E. B. (1806): Battle of Marathon. V

Barton (1784): Poems [2nd ed., with additions, 1821; 4th ed., with additions, 1825].
Belzoni, Giovanni (1778): Observations and Discoveries within Pyramids, Tombs, &c., in Egypt and Nubia. P
Brown, Thomas (d. 1820): Physiology of the Human Mind. P
 Collected Poems [cont. Paradise of Coquettes, pub. 1814, Wanderer in Norway, 1815, War-fiend, 1816, Bower of Spring, 1817, Agnes, 1818, Emily, 1819, and Other Poems].
Byron (1788): Marino Faliero. T
Clare (1793): Poems, Descriptive of Rural Life. V
Combe (1741): Second Tour of Dr. Syntax in Search of Consolation [see 1812, 1821]. V
Crabbe (1754): Collected Works [later collections: ed. his son, with letters, journals, and life, 1834, ed. Ward 1905, ed. Carlyle 1908]. V
Croly, George (1780): Angel of the World. V
 May Fair. V

Edgeworth, Richard Lovell (d. 1817): Memoirs [completed by Maria Edgeworth]. P
Foster, John (1770): On the Evils of Popular Ignorance. P
Galt (1779): Ayrshire Legatees. P
Godwin (1756): Of Population, in answer to Mr. Malthus. P
Hemans (1793): The Sceptic. V
Heraud, John (1799): Legend of St. Loy and Other Poems. V
 Tottenham, a Poem.
Hogg (1770): Winter Evening Tales. P
Hunt (1784): Trs. Tasso's Amyntas. V
Irving, Washington (1783): The Sketch Book of Geoffrey Crayon. P
Keats (1795): La Belle Dame sans Merci [in The Indicator]. V
 Lamia, Isabella, Eve of St. Agnes, Hyperion, and Other Poems. V
Knowles (1784): Virginius. D
Lamb (1775): Essays of Elia [in London Magazine, between Aug. 1820 and Dec. 1822 separately 1823: see 1833]. P

Landor (1775): Idyllia Heroica Decem [pub. at Pisa].

Luttrell, Henry (1765?): Advice to Julia [3rd ed. entitled Letters to Julia, 1822]. V

Lytton (1803): Ismael and Other Poems. V

Malthus (1766): Principles of Political Economy [2nd ed., revised, with memoir by Otter, 1836]. P

Maturin (1782): Melmoth the Wanderer. P

Milman (1791): Fall of Jerusalem. D

Moncrieff, William (1794): Lear of the Private Family. D

Moultrie, John (1799): My Brother's Grave. V
Godiva. V

Opie (1769): Tales of the Heart. P

Peacock (1785): Four Ages of Poetry [in Ollier's Literary Pocket Book: provoked Shelley's Defence of Poetry, written 1821, first pub. in Works 1840]. P

Procter (1787): Marcian Colonna, with Three Dramatic Scenes, and Other Poems.
A Sicilian Story and Other Poems.

Reynolds, John Hamilton (1794): The Fancy, or Poetical Remains of Peter Corcoran [cont. Fields of Tothill]. V

Scott (1771): The Monastery. P
The Abbot. P
Miscellaneous Poems, collected [other edd.: 1821–7–30, Lockhart 1833, Palgrave 1866, Rossetti 1870, Robertson 1904, Lang 1905].

Shelley (1792): Œdipus Tyrannus. V
Prometheus Unbound and Other Poems.

Southey (1774): Life of John Wesley. P

Spence (d. 1768): Anecdotes [both Singer's and Malone's edd.]. P

Walpole (d. 1797): First collected ed. of Correspondence [later and fuller collections: Wright 1840, Cunningham 1857–9, Toynbee 1903].

Wordsworth (1770): The River Duddon, a Series of Sonnets. Vaudracour and Julia, and other Poems. Topographical Description of the Country of the Lakes [see 1810, '22].

Baillie (1762): Metrical Legends. V
Beddoes (1803): The Improvisatore, with Other Poems.
Bryant, William Cullen (1794): Poems.
Byron (1788): Prophecy of Dante. V
   Sardanapalus, a Tragedy; The Two Foscari, a Tragedy; Cain, a Mystery.
   Don Juan, iii–v. V
   Letter on W. L. Bowles's Strictures on Pope.
Clare (1793): Village Minstrel, and Other Poems.
Cobbett (1762): Monthly Religious Tracts [afterwards called Twelve Sermons. Concl. 1822]. P
   American Gardener [altered as English Gardener, 1827]. P
   Cottage Economy. P
Combe (1741): Third Tour of Doctor Syntax in Search of a Wife [see 1812, 1820]. V
Cooper, James Fenimore (1789): The Spy. P
De Quincey (1785): Confessions of an Opium Eater [in London Magazine, Oct. and Nov.; separately 1822, enlarg. 1856].
Dibdin, Thomas (1776): Bibliographical Tour in France and Germany. P
Dwight, Timothy (1752): Travels in New England and New York. P
Egan (1772): Life in London [illustr. George and Robert Cruikshank: see 1828]. P
Galt (1779): Annals of the Parish. P
Gifford (1756): Trs. Satires of Persius. V
Hall, John Vine (1774): Sinner's Friend. P
Hazlitt (1778): Lectures on Elizabethan Drama. P
   Table Talk [concl. 1822].
Hunt (1784): The Months. P

Greek War of Liberation begins.
Henry Thomas Buckle b.
George John Whyte-Melville b.
John Keats d.
Hester Lynch (Thrale) Piozzi d.
John Scott, editor of 'London Magazine', killed in duel following controversy with Lockhart and others of 'Blackwood's'.
'Manchester Guardian' started.
Rudolf Ackermann's 'The World in Miniature' (illustr. T. Rowlandson and W. H. Pyne).
John Struthers's 'British Minstrel' (anthology).
William Moncrieff's 'Tom and Jerry', dramatic adaptation of Pierce Egan's 'Life in London' produced.
Goethe, 'Wilhelm Meisters Wanderjahre'.
Baudelaire b.
Flaubert b.
Napoleon d.
Grillparzer, 'Das Goldene Vliess'.
H. von Kleist, 'Prinz Friedrich von Homburg'.

President U.S.A.
  Monroe (2nd Term).

Landon (1802): Fate of Adelaide. **V**
Lloyd, Charles (1775): Desultory Thoughts in London, Titus Gisippus, and Other Poems. **V**
  Poetical Essays on the Character of Pope. **V**
Lockhart (1794): Valerius, a Roman Story. **P**
Macaulay (1800): Evening. **V**
Malone (d. 1812): Ed. Shakespeare, completed by James Boswell, jnr. [see 1790].
Mill (1773): Elements of Political Economy. **P**
Parry, William Edward (1790): Journal of a Voyage for Discovery of NW. Passage in 1795–7 [concl. 1824: see 1824, 1826]. **P**
Procter (1787): Mirandola, a Tragedy. **V**
Reynolds, John Hamilton (1794): Garden of Florence and Other Poems [incl. Romance of Youth and Sonnets]. **V**
Russell, Lord John (1798): Essay on English Constitution. **P**
Scott (1771): Kenilworth. **P**
  Biographies [in Ballantyne's Novelists]. **V**
  Account of George IV's Coronation. **V**
  Edition of Fielding's Novels. **V**
Shelley (1792): Epipsychidion. **V**
  Adonais. **V**
Smith, 'Horace' (1779): Amarynthus the Nympholept. **D**
Southey (1774): Carmen Triumphale. **V**
  Vision of Judgment [provoked Byron's Vision of Judgment 1823]. **V**
  Expedition of Orsua, and the Crimes of Aguirre. **P**
  Life of Cromwell [in Quarterly Review]. **P**
Waldegrave, James, Earl (d. 1763): Memoirs [1754–8]. **P**

Aikin (1781): Memoirs of the Court of James I. P
Barton (1784): Napoleon and Other Poems. V
Beddoes (1803): Bride's Tragedy. D
Bentham (1748): Influence of Natural Religion upon Temporal Happiness. P
Bloomfield (1766): May Day with the Muses. V
Bowles (1762): Grave of the Last Saxon. V
Byron (1788): Werner, a Tragedy.
The Vision of Judgment [in The Liberal: see 1821, Southey]. V
Croly, George (1780): Catiline. T
Cunningham, Allan (1784): Sir Marmaduke Maxwell. D
Traditional Tales of English and Scottish Peasantry.
Darley, George (1795): Errors of Ecstasie. V
De Vere, Sir Aubrey (1788): Julian the Apostate. V
Digby, Kenelm (1800): Broad Stone of Honour [enlarged 1826–7]. P
Galt (1779): Steamboat. P
The Provost. P.   Sir Andrew Wylie. P
Grattan, Henry (d. 1820): Speeches, ed. his son [ed. Madden 1845]. Miscellaneous Works.
Hemans (1793): Welsh Melodies. V
Hogg (1770): Three Perils of Man. P
Irving, Washington (1783): Bracebridge Hall. P
Lamb, Lady Caroline (1785): Graham Hamilton. P
Lloyd, Charles (1775): Duke d'Ormond. T
Beritola. V
Lockhart (1794): Adam Blair. P
Milman (1791): Martyr of Antioch. V
Belshazzar. V
Opie (1769): Madeline. P
Peacock (1785): Maid Marian. P
Rhodes, William Barnes (1772): Bombastes Furioso. D burlesque.
Rogers (1763): Italy, pt. i (ii 1828; complete 1830). V
Scott (1771): The Pirate. P
Fortunes of Nigel. P
Peveril of the Peak. P.   Halidon Hill. V
Shelley (1792): Hellas. V lyrical drama.
Walpole (d. 1797): Memoirs of the Last Ten Years of the Reign of George II. P
Wells (1799?): Stories after Nature. V
Wilson (1785): Lights and Shadows of Scottish Life. P
Wilson, Lockhart, Hogg, and Maginn: Noctes Ambrosianae [in Blackwood, 1822–35]. P
Wordsworth (1770): Ecclesiastical Sketches. V
Memorials of a Tour on the Continent. V
Description of the Scenery of the Lakes [see 1810, 1820, 1835]. P

Matthew Arnold b.
Sir Henry Maine b.
Thomas Hughes b.
David Masson b.
Sir Francis Galton b.
Percy Bysshe Shelley d.
Leigh Hunt starts 'The Liberal' (4 nos. 1822–3).
'Sunday Times' started.
Robert Nares's 'Glossary'.
Reginald Heber's ed. of Jeremy Taylor (rev. C. P. Eden 1847–52).
Francis Place's 'Illustrations and Proofs of the Principle of Population'.
Edmond de Goncourt b.
H. Heine, 'Gedichte'.

Baillie (1762): Poetic Miscellanies [cont. poems by Scott, Mrs. Hemans, Miss Fanshawe, &c.].

Berkeley (d. 1753): Three Dialogues between Hylas and Philonous. P

Bowles (1762): Ellen Gray. V

Bowles, Caroline (1786): Tales of the Factories. V

Byron (1788): Age of Bronze. V
Island. V
Don Juan, vi–xiv. V
Contributions to The Liberal [Vision of Judgment, Letter to the editor of my Grandmother's Review, Epigrams on Castlereagh, Heaven and Earth, The Blues, Morgante Maggiore]. V

Carlyle (1795): Life of Schiller [in London Magazine, 1823–4; separately 1825]. P

Cooper, James Fenimore (1789): The Pioneers. P
The Pilot. P

De Quincey (1785): Letters to a Young Man whose Education has been neglected [in London Magazine, Jan., Feb., Mar., and May]. P

De Vere, Sir Aubrey (1788): Duke of Mercia. D
Lamentation of Ireland and Other Poems. V

Elliott (1781): Love, a Poem. V

Franklin, Sir John (1786): Narrative of a Journey to Polar Sea in 1819–22 [see 1828]. P

Galt (1779): The Entail. P
Gathering of the West. P

Hazlitt (1778): Liber Amoris. P
Characteristics. P

Hogg (1770): Three Perils of Women. P

Hunt (1784): Literary Examiner [27 nos.].
Ultra-Crepidarius, a Satire on W. Gifford. V

Lamb, Lady Caroline (1785): Ada Reis, a Tale. P

Lamb (1775): Essays of Elia [collected: see 1820, 1833]. P

Lloyd, Charles (1775): Poems.

Lockhart (1794): Reginald Dalton. P
Ancient Spanish Ballads [trs.]. V

Lytton (1803): Delmour and Other Poems.

Mitford (1787): Julian. D

Moore (1779): Fables for the Holy Alliance. V
Loves of the Angels. V

Procter (1787): Flood of Thessaly, Girl of Provence and Other Poems.

Scott (1771): Quentin Durward. P

Shelley (d. 1822): Poetical Pieces. V

Shelley, Mary (1797): Valperga. P

Southey (1774): History of Peninsular War [concl. 1832].

Tennant, William (1784): Cardinal Bethune. T

Watts (1797): Poetical Sketches. V

Wilson (1785): Trials of Margaret Lyndsay. P

Edward Augustus Freeman b.
Charlotte Mary Yonge b.
Coventry Patmore b.
Friedrich Max Müller b.
Ann Radcliffe d.
Bannatyne Club founded, with Scott as president.
'*Encyclopaedia Britannica*', 6th ed.
Jeremy Bentham's '*Rationale of Judicial Evidence*' *in Dumont's* '*Traité des preuves judiciaires*' (*see 1827*).
Dumont's '*De l'organisation judiciaire et codification*' (*based on Bentham's MSS.*).
John Cumberland's '*British Theatre*' (*anthology*).
William Whewell's '*Treatise on Dynamics*'.
Joseph Bosworth's '*Anglo-Saxon Grammar*'.
William Stewart Rose's trs. of '*Orlando Inamorato*' (*concl. 1831*).
'*The Lancet*' (*weekly*).
Lamartine, '*Nouvelles Méditations*'.
Renan b.

Barton (1784): Poetic Vigils. V
Bentham (1748): Book of Fallacies. P
Byron (d. 1824): Don Juan, xv–xvi. V
  Deformed transformed. V
Campbell (1777): Theodoric and Other Poems.
Carlyle (1795): Trs. Goethe's Wilhelm Meister's
  Apprenticeship [see 1827]. P
Cobbett (1762): History of the Protestant Re-
  formation [concl. 1827]. P
De Quincey (1785): Dialogue of the Three Temp-
  lars [in London Magazine, Apr. and May]. P
Ferrier (1782): Inheritance. P
Godwin (1756): History of the Commonwealth of
  England [concl. 1828]. P
Gore, Catherine (1799): Theresa Marchmont. P
Hazlitt (1778): Sketches of the Principal Picture-
  galleries of England [enlarg. as Criticisms on
  Art, 1843–4].
Hogg (1770): Confessions of a Justified Sinner
  [later called ' Of a Fanatic ']. P
Irving, Washington (1783): Tales of a Traveller. P
Johnson, John (1777): Typographia, or the
  Printer's Instructor. P
Landon (1802): Improvisatrice. V
Landor (1775): Imaginary Conversations, i, ii
  [iii–iv 1828, v 1829]. P
Lockhart (1794): History of Matthew Wald. P
Maturin (1782): Albigenses. P
Medwin, Thomas (1788): Journal of Conversations
  with Lord Byron.
Mitford (1787): Our Village [concl. 1832]. P
Moncrieff, William (1794): Cataract of the
  Ganges. D
Moore (1779): Memoirs of Captain Rock. P
Morier, James (1780 ?): The Adventures of Hajji
  Baba of Ispahan. P
Parry, William Edward (1790): Journal of a
  Second Voyage for Discovery of NW.
  Passage in 1821–3 [see 1821, 1826].
Scott (1771): Redgauntlet. P
  St. Ronan's Well. P
  Ed. Richardson's Novels.
Shelley (d. 1822): Posthumous Poems, ed. Mary
  Shelley [incl. Julian and Maddalo, Witch of
  Atlas, Triumph of Life, Epistle to Maria Gis-
  borne].
Southey (1774): Book of the Church. P
Thompson, William (1785 ?): Enquiry into the
  Principles of the Distribution of Wealth. P
Wells (1799): Joseph and his Brethren [by
  ' H. L. Howard ': revised by Swinburne
  1876]. V

George MacDonald b.
Sydney Thompson Dobell b.
Francis Turner Palgrave b.
William Wilkie Collins b.
William Allingham b.
Lord Byron d.
' *Westminster   Review*'
  started (later amalga-
  mated with ' London
  Review').
' *The Literary Souvenir*'
  started   (ed.   Alaric
  Watts; concl. 1838).
' *Grimm's Tales*' *(concl.*
  1826; illustr. G. Cruik-
  shank).
William Roscoe's ed. of
  Pope.

Bentham (1748): Rationale of Reward [from the Fr. of Étienne Dumont: see 1811]. P

Brougham, Henry (1778): Practical Observations on Education. P

Byron (d. 1824): Correspondence, ed. R. C. Dallas. P

Coleridge (1772): Aids to Reflection. P

Coleridge, Sara (1802): Trs. Bayard's Memoirs. P

Conder, Josiah (1789): Modern Traveller. P

Croker, Thomas Crofton (1798): Fairy Legends and Traditions of South Ireland. P

Cunningham, Allan (1784): Songs of Scotland. V

De Quincey (1785): Walladmor. P

Egan (1772): Life of an Actor. P

Galt (1779): The Omen. P

Gamba, Count Peter: Lord Byron's Last Journey. P

Hazlitt (1778): Spirit of the Age. P

   Select Poets of Great Britain. V

Hemans (1793): Forest Sanctuary [2nd ed. 1829 cont. Casabianca]. V

   Lays of Many Lands. V

Hood (1799) **and Reynolds** (1794): Odes and Addresses to Great People. V

Knowles (1784): William Tell. D

Landon (1802): The Troubadour and Other Poems.

Lauder, Sir Thomas (1784): Lochindhu. P

Lytton (1803): Sculpture. V

Macaulay (1800): Essay on Milton (in Edin. Rev.). P

McCulloch, John Ramsay (1789): Principles of Political Economy. P

Mill, James (1773): Essays on Government [concl. 1828].

Milton (d. 1674): De Doctrina Christiana. P

Moore (1775): Life of Sheridan. P

   Evenings in Greece. V

Nicholson, John (1790): Airedale in Ancient Times. V

Opie (1769): Tales of the Pemberton Family.

Pepys (d. 1703): Diary, ed. Smith and Braybrook [later edd.: 1828–48–54; Bright (with new material) 1875–9; Wheatley 1893–9].

Scott (1771): The Betrothed, The Talisman. P

Smith, 'Horace' (1779): Gaieties and Gravities. P

Sotheby, William (1757): Poems.

Southey (1774): Tale of Paraguay. V

Wade, Thomas (1805): Tasso, and Other Poems.

Walpole (d. 1797): Letters to Earl of Hertford and Rev. Henry Zouch [in Works, vol. ix].

Ward, Robert Plumer (1765): Tremaine. P

Waterton, Charles (1782): Wanderings in South America. P

Wilson (1785): The Foresters. P

Wolfe, Charles (d. 1823): Remains.

Thomas Henry Huxley b

William Stubbs b.

Richard Doddridge Blackmore b.

Anna Barbauld d.

Samuel Parr d.

Charles Molloy Westmacott's 'The English Spy' (illustr. R. Cruikshank, T. Rowlandson and others).

John Poole's 'Paul Pry' acted.

Alexander Dyce's 'Specimens of British Poetesses' (anthology).

Richter d.

Grillparzer, 'König Ottokar'.

President U.S.A.
John   Quincy
Adams.

Baillie (1762): The Martyr. T

Barrett, E. B. (Browning) (1806): Essay on Mind, with Other Poems.

Barton (1784): Devotional Verse.

Bowdler, Thomas: Gibbon's Decline and Fall, with omissions of passages of irreligious or immoral tendency. P

Cooper, James Fenimore (1789): The Last of the Mohicans. P

Darley, George (1795): Labours of Idleness. P

De Quincey (1785): Trs. Lessing's Laocoon [in Blackwood's, Nov.]. P

Disraeli (1804): Vivian Grey, pt. i [ii. 1827]. P
Modern Dunciad [in Star Chamber]. V

Galt (1779): Last of the Lairds. P

Gleig (1796): The Subaltern. P

Grant Duff, James (1798): History of the Mahrattas. P

Hazlitt (1778): The Plain Speaker. P
Journey through France and Italy. P
Conversations of James Northcote [in Colburn's New Monthly Magazine; separately 1830; ed. Gosse 1894]. P

Hogg (1770): Queen Hynde. V

Hood (1799): Whims and Oddities, 1st series [see 1827]. P and V

Hook, Theodore (1788): Sayings and Doings [collective title for Passion and Principle, Cousin William, Gervase Skinner, Martha the Gipsy, and five other novels pub. between 1826 and 1829]. P

Jameson, Anna (1794): Diary of an Ennuyée. P

Lister, Thomas Henry (1800): Granby. P

Macnish, Robert (1802): Metempsychosis [in Blackwood's]. P

Milman (1791): Anne Boleyn. V

Mitford (1787): Foscari. T

Montgomery (1771): Pelican Island. V

Parry, William Edward (1790): Journal of a Third Voyage for Discovery of NW. Passage in 1824–5 [see 1821, 1824].

Patmore, Peter (1786): Rejected Articles. P

Porter, Jane and Anna: Tales round a Winter Hearth. P

Scott (1771): Woodstock. P

Shelley, Mary (1797): The Last Man. P

Smith, 'Horace' (1779): Brambletye House. P
Tor Hill. P

Southey (1774): Vindiciae Ecclesiae Anglicanae. P

Turner (1768): History of the Reign of Henry VIII. P

Whately, Richard (1787): Logic. P

Walter Bagehot b.
William Gifford d.
Reginald Heber d.
'*Encyclopaedia Metropolitana*'.
*William Hone's '*Everyday Book' (concl. 1827)*.
Samuel Singer's ed. of Shakespeare.
*Archibald Constable's '*Miscellany of original and selected publications' (concl. 1835)*.
*Burke's '*Peerage and Baronetage', 1st ed.*
*Eichendorff, '*Taugenichts'.*
*H. Heine, '*Reisebilder'.*

Barton (1784): Widow's Tale and Other Poems.
Bentham (1748): Rationale of Evidence, ed. J. S. Mill [see 1823]. P
Burke (d. 1797): Correspondence with Dr. French Laurence.
Carlyle (1795): German Romance [vol. i Musaeus and Fouqué; ii Tieck and Hoffman; iii Richter; iv Wilhelm Meister]. P
    Wotton Reinfried, Fragment of a Novel. P
Clare (1793): Shepherd's Calendar. V
Cooper, James Fenimore (1789): The Prairie. P
Crowe, William (1745): English Versification. P
Dana, Richard Henry (1787): The Buccaneer and Other Poems.
Darley, George (1795): Sylvia, or the May Queen. V
De Quincey (1785): Murder as one of the Fine Arts, pt. i [in Blackwood's]. P
Digby, Sir Kenelm (d. 1665): Private Memoirs. P
Egan (1772): Anecdotes of the Turf. P
Hallam (1777): Constitutional History. P
Hare, Julius and Augustus: Guesses at Truth. P
Heber (d. 1826): Hymns. V
Hood (1799): Plea of Midsummer Fairies. V
    Whims and Oddities, 2nd series. P and V
    National Tales.
Keble (1792): Christian Year. V
Landon (1802): Golden Violet. V
Luttrell, Henry (1765?): Crockford House. V
Lytton (1803): Falkland. P
    O'Neil, or the Rebel. V
Macnish, Robert (1802): Anatomy of Drunkenness. P
Mitford (1787): Dramatic Scenes, Sonnets, &c. V
Moore (1779): The Epicurean. P
Poe (1809): Tamerlane and Other Poems. V
Pollok, Robert (1798): The Course of Time. V
Scott (1771): Chronicles of the Canongate [Highland Widow, Two Drovers, Surgeon's Daughter]. P
    Life of Napoleon Buonaparte. P
    Miscellaneous Prose Works [later edd.: 1834–71, 1836].
    Ed. George Bannatyne Miscellany.
Smith, 'Horace' (1779): Reuben Apsley. P
Stewart (1753): Philosophy of the Human Mind, vol. iii [see 1792, 1814]. P
Taylor, Sir Henry (1800): Isaac Comnenus. D
Tennyson (1809): Poems by Two Brothers [with Charles Tennyson].
Ward, Robert Plumer (1765): De Vere, or the Man of Independence. P

University of London founded.
Edward Bradley ('Cuthbert Bede') b.
William Blake d.
Helen Maria Williams d.
Thomas Arnold becomes Head Master of Rugby.
'The Evening Standard' started.
William John Thoms's ed. of Early English Prose Romances (concl. 1828).
William Gifford's ed. of John Ford.
William Hone's 'Table Book' (concl. 1828).
Hugo, 'Préface de Cromwell'.
H. Heine, 'Buch der Lieder'.
Manzoni, 'I Promessi Sposi'.

Barton (1784): A New Year's Eve. V
Blanchard, S. L. (1804): Lyric Offerings. V
Bowles (1762): Days Departed. V
Bury, Lady Charlotte (1775): Flirtation. P
Carlyle (1795): Essay on Burns [in Edinburgh Review, Dec.].
Combe, George (1788): Constitution of Man. P
Cooper, James Fenimore (1789): The Red Rover. P
Disraeli (1804): Voyage of Captain Popanilla. P
D'Israeli (1766): Life and Reign of Charles I. P
Drake, Nathan (1766): Memorials of Shakespeare. P
Egan (1772): Finish to the Adventures of Tom, Jerry, and Logic [concl. of Life in London, 1821; illustr. R. Cruikshank]. P
Franklin, John (1786): a Second Expedition to the Polar Sea in 1825-7 [see 1823]. P
Hazlitt (1778): Life of Napoleon Buonaparte, vols. i–ii [iii–iv 1830; i–iv complete 1852]. P
Heber (d. 1826): Journey through India. P
Hemans (1793): Records of Women and Other Poems.
Hunt (1784): Lord Byron and his Contemporaries. P
  The Companion [28 nos.].
Landor, Robert Eyres (1781): Impious Feast. V
Landor (1775): Imaginary Conversations, iii–iv [see 1824]. P
Lockhart (1794): Life of Robert Burns. P
Lytton (1803): Pelham. P
Malcolm, Sir John: Sketches of Persia. P
Moir, David Macbeth (1798): Mansie Wauch. P
Montgomery, Robert (1807): Omnipresence of the Deity. V
Moore (1779): Odes upon Cash, Corn, Catholics. V
Morier (1780?): Hajji Baba in England. P
Napier (1785): History of the Peninsular War [concl. 1840]. P
Parr, Samuel (d. 1825): Collected Works.
Parry, William Edward (1790): Narrative of an Attempt to reach the N. Pole. P
Scott (1771): Tales of a Grandfather, 1st series [see 1829, 1830]. P
  Chronicles of Canongate, 2nd series [cont. Fair Maid of Perth]. P
  My Aunt Margaret's Mirror, The Tapestried Chamber, The Laird's Jock [in The Keepsake]. P
  Religious Discourses by a Layman. P
Smith, John Thomas (1766): Nollekens and his Times [ed. Edmund Gosse 1894]. P
Stewart (d. 1828): Philosophy of the Active and Moral Powers of Man. P
Tytler (1791): History of Scotland. P
Whately, Richard (1787): Rhetoric. P

Dante Gabriel Rossetti b.
George Meredith b.
Mrs. Margaret Oliphant b.
Dugald Stewart d.
'The Spectator' (weekly) started.
'The Athenaeum' (weekly) started.
Thomas Richardson's 'New Minor Drama' (anthology: concl. 1831).
Alaric Watts's 'Poetical Album and Register of Modern Fugitive Poetry', 1st series (2nd series 1829).
Julius Hare, Connop Thirlwell, and others, trs. Niebuhr's 'History of Rome' (concl. 1832).
Washington Irving, 'History of the Life and Voyages of Christopher Columbus'.
William Taylor, 'Historic Survey of German Poetry, with Translations' (concl. 1830).
Taine b.

Adams, John Quincy (1767): Correspondence. P
Arnold (1795): Sermons [later collections: Christian Life, 1841–2; Interpretation of Scriptures, 1845. Collected ed. 1878].
Carlyle (1795): Signs of the Times [in Edinburgh Review, June]. P
Croly, George (1780): Salathiel. P
Cunningham, Allan (1784): Lives of British Painters [concl. 1833]. P
Dibdin, Thomas: The Library Companion. P
Elliott (1781): Village Patriarch. V
Fanshawe, Lady Anne (d. 1680): Memoirs written by herself, with extracts from Correspondence of Sir Richard Fanshawe. P
Heber (d. 1826): Sermons preached in England. P
Hogg (1770): The Shepherd's Calendar. V
Hood (1799): Eugene Aram's Dream [in The Gem]. V
Epping Hunt. V
Irving, Washington (1783): Chronicle of the Conquest of Granada. P
Jefferson (d. 1826): Autobiography.
Jerrold (1803): Black-eyed Susan [acted]. D
Landon (1802): Venetian Bracelet. V
Landor (1775): Imaginary Conversations, v [see 1824]. P
Lytton (1803): The Disowned. P
Devereux. P
Marryat (1792): Frank Mildmay. P
Mill, James (1773): Analysis of the Human Mind. P
Milman (1791): History of the Jews. P
Peacock (1785): Misfortunes of Elphin. P
Poe (1809): Al Araaf, Tamerlane, and other Poems. V
Poole, John (1786 ?): Lodgings for Single Gentlemen [acted]. D
Scott, Michael (1789): Tom Cringle's Log [in Blackwood's, Sept. 1829–Aug. 1833; separately, 1836]. P
Scott (1771): Anne of Geierstein. P
History of Scotland [concl. 1830]. P
Tales of a Grandfather, 2nd series. P
Southey Caroline (1786): Chapters on Church Yards. V
Southey (1774): Sir Thomas More. P
All for Love, Pilgrim to Compostella. V
Taylor, Isaac (1787): Natural History of Enthusiasm. P
Tennyson (1809): Timbuctoo. V
Turner (1768): History of the Reigns of Edward VI, Mary, and Elizabeth. P
Wade, Thomas (1805): Woman's Love. D

Samuel Rawson Gardiner b.
Thomas William Robertson b.
Charles Knight's ' Library of Entertaining Knowledge'.
Murray's 'Family Library'.
Sir William Hamilton's article, 'The Philosophy of the Unconditioned', in 'Edinburgh Review', October.
Balzac, 'Comédie Humaine' (1829–48).
Goethe, 'Wilhelm Meisters Wanderjahre'.

President U.S.A. Jackson.

Alcott, Amos Bronson (1799): Infant Instruction. P

Bentham (1748): Rationale of Punishment. P
Constitutional Code for All Nations. P

Byron (d. 1824): Letters and Journals, with Life by Thomas Moore [see 1832].

Carleton, William (1794): Traits and Stories of the Irish Peasantry, 1st series [2nd 1833; new ed. with notes and illustrations 1843–4]. P

Channing, William Ellery (1780): Remarks on American Literature. P

Cobbett (1762): Rural Rides. P
Advice to Young Men. P

Coleridge (1772): On Constitution of Church and State. P

Forster, Thomas (ed.): Original Letters of Locke, Sidney, and Shaftesbury.

Frere (1769): Fables for Five Years Old.

Galt (1779): Lawrie Todd. P
Life of Byron. P

Godwin (1756): Cloudesley, a Tale. P

Gore, Catherine (1799): Manners of the Day. P

Hemans (1793): Songs of the Affections. V

Heraud, John Abraham: Descent into Hell. V

Herschel, Sir John (1792): Preliminary Discourse on the Study of Natural Philosophy. P

Hood (1799): Comic Annual [1830–9; 1842].

Hook, Theodore (1788): Maxwell. P

Hunt (1784): The Tatler [Sept. 1830–Feb. 1832].
Chat of the Week [13 nos.].

James, G. P. R. (1799): De l'orme. P

Jerrold (1803): Sally in our Alley [acted]. C

Keightley, Thomas (1789): History of the War of Greek Independence. P

Lamb (1775): Album Verses.

Lyell, Sir Charles (1797): Principles of Geology [concl. 1833]. P

Lytton (1803): Paul Clifford. P

Macaulay (1800): Essay on Robert Montgomery (in Edin. Rev.). P

Mackintosh (1765): History of England. P
Life of Sir Thomas More. P
Progress of Ethical Philosophy [in Encyclopaedia Britannica; separately, ed. Whewell, 1836]. P

Maginn, William (1793): Gallery of Illustrious Literary Characters [in Fraser's Magazine, 1830–8; separately 1873]. P

Marryat (1792): King's Own. P

Martineau (1802): Traditions of Palestine. P

Mitford (1787): Stories of American Life. P

Montgomery, Robert (1807): Satan. V
Puffiad. V

Accession of William IV.
Reform Bill, 1830–2.
Christina Rossetti b.
Alexander Smith b.
Henry Kingsley b.
Thomas Edward Brown b.
William Hazlitt d.
'*Fraser's Magazine*' (*1830–82; followed by Longman's Magazine*).
Lardner's '*Cabinet Cyclopaedia*'· (*concl. 1849*) *and* '*Cabinet Library*' (*concl. 1832*).
'*Encyclopaedia Britannica*', *7th ed.* (*concl. 1842*).
French '*Revolution of July*'.
Jules de Goncourt b.
Comte, '*Cours de philosophie positive*'.
Hugo, '*Hernani*'.

Moore (1779): Legendary Ballads. V
  Life of Byron [see Byron, above]. P
Scott (1771): Letters on Demonology and Witch-
    craft [in Murray's Family Library]. P
  House of Aspen [in The Keepsake].
  Doom of Devorgoil, Auchindrane. D
  Essays on Ballad Poetry. P
  Tales of a Grandfather, series III and IV
    [England and France].
Shelley, Mary (1797): Perkin Warbeck. P
Tennyson (1809): Poems, chiefly Lyrical.
Wade, Thomas (1805): Jew of Arragon. D
Webster, Daniel (1782): Speeches and Forensic
    Arguments. P

1831

Bell, Henry Glassford (1803): Summer and Winter
    Hours. V
Brewster, Sir David (1781): Treatise on Optics. P
Collier, John Payne (1789): History of English
    Dramatic Poetry and Annals of the Stage. P
Disraeli (1804): The Young Duke. P
Elliott (1781): Corn-Law Rhymes. V
Erskine, Thomas (1788): The Brazen Serpent. P
Ferrier (1782): Destiny. P
Galt (1779): Lives of the Players. P
Garrick (d. 1779): Private Correspondence, ed.
    with Memoir by Boaden [concl. 1832.
    Further unpub. correspondence, ed. G. P.
    Baker, 1907].
Godwin (1756): Thoughts on Man. P
Gore, Catherine (1799): School for Coquettes. C
    Mothers and Daughters. P
Grote (1794): Parliamentary Reform. P
Hogg (1770): Songs. V
Landon (1802): Romance and Reality. P
Lover, Samuel (1797): Legends and Stories of
    Ireland. P
Macaulay (1800): Essay on Boswell [in Edin.
    Rev.]. P
Moore (1779): Summer Fête. V
  Life of Lord Edward Fitzgerald. P
Peacock (1785): Crotchet Castle. P
Poe (1809): Poems. V
Porter, Jane (1776): Sir Edward Seaward's Narra-
    tive of his Shipwreck. P
Trelawny, Edward John (1792): Adventures of a
    Younger Son. P
Whitehead, Charles (1804): The Solitary. V
Whittier (1807): Legends of New England. V

*William Hale White
  ('Mark Rutherford') b.
Edward Robert Bulwer,
  Earl Lytton ('Owen
  Meredith') b.
Charles Stuart Calverley
  b.
Henry Mackenzie d.
William Roscoe d.
First meeting of the British
  Association.
John Cumberland's
  'Minor Theatre' (anth.).
Charles Knight's 'Results
  of Machinery' and
  'Capital and Labour'
  (reprtd. together as
  'Knowledge is Power',
  1855).
John Wilson Croker ed.
  Boswell's 'Life of John-
  son'.
Sotheby, trs. of Homer
  [concl. 1834].
Hegel d.
Stendhal, 'Le Rouge et le
  Noir'.
Grillparzer, 'Des Meeres
  und der Liebe Wellen'.*

Austin, John (1790): Province of Jurisprudence. P

Bell, Henry Glassford (1803): My Old Portfolio. V

Brackenridge, Henry Marie (1786): Letters to the Public. P

Bryant, William Cullen (1794): Poems.

Burney, Frances (1752): Memoirs of Dr. Burney. P

Byron (d. 1824): Works, with Letters, Journals, and Life by Thomas Moore [concl. 1835. New and rev. ed., E. H. Coleridge and Prothero, 1898–1904].

Darwin (1809): Narrative of the Surveying Voyages of H.M.S. Adventure and Beagle [concl. 1836; 2nd ed. 1845; 3rd ed. 1860].

De Quincey (1785): Klosterheim. P

Disraeli (1804): Contarini Fleming. P

Genest, John: Account of the English Stage. P

Hawker (1803): Records of the Western Shore. V

Hunt (1784): Poetical Works [2nd ed. 1844; ed. L. S. Adams 1857; Thornton Hunt 1860; Milford 1922].

  Sir Ralph Esher. P

  Christianism [privately prtd. Reissued as Religion of the Heart 1853]. P

Irving, Washington (1783): The Alhambra. P

James, G. P. R.: Henry Masterton. P

Jameson, Anna (1794): Characteristics of Women. P

Jerrold (1803): Rent Day. D

Knowles (1784): The Hunchback. D

Lytton (1803): Eugene Aram. P

Martineau (1802): Illustrations of Political Economy [concl. 1834]. P

Montgomery, Robert (1807): The Messiah. V

Procter (1787): English Songs. V

Scott (1771): Tales of My Landlord, 4th series [Count Robert of Paris. Castle Dangerous]. P

Shelley (d. 1822): Masque of Anarchy [with Preface by Leigh Hunt]. V

Stanhope, Fifth Earl (1805): History of the War of Succession in Spain. P

Tennyson (1809): Poems [Lady of Shalott, Miller's Daughter, Œnone, Palace of Art, Lotos-Eaters, Dream of Fair Women, &c.: bears date 1833].

Trollope, Frances (1780): Domestic Manners of the Americans. P

Warren, Samuel (1807): Passages from the Diary of a Late Physician [concl. 1838; originally in Blackwood's from 1830]. P

Charles Lutwidge Dodgson ('Lewis Carroll') b.

Sir Leslie Stephen b.

Theodore Watts-Dunton b.

Sir Edwin Arnold b.

Sir Walter Scott d.

Jeremy Bentham d.

George Crabbe d.

Sir James Mackintosh d.

'Chambers's Journal.'

'Tait's Edinburgh Magazine.'

Hugh James Rose founds 'The British Magazine' (concl. 1849).

Robert Chambers's 'Biographical Dictionary of Eminent Scotsmen' (concl. 1834).

Benjamin Thorpe's ed. of Cædmon with Eng. translation and notes.

Goethe d.

Goethe, 'Faust II'.

President U.S.A. Jackson (2nd Term).

Aikin, Lucy (1781): Memoirs of the Court of Charles I. P

Alison, Sir Archibald (1792): History of Europe, 1789–1815 [concl. 1842: see 1852]. P

Barrett, E. B Browning (1806): Prometheus Bound, trs. from Æschylus [cont. miscellaneous poems: see 1850]. V

Browning, R. (1812): Pauline. V

Carlyle (1795): Sartor Resartus [in Fraser's Magazine, Nov. 1833–Aug. 1834; separately Boston, 1835; London, 1838]. P

Coleridge, Hartley (1796): Poems [Leonard and Susan, Sonnets].
    Biographia Borealis [called Worthies of Yorkshire and Lancashire 1836]. P

Dana, Richard Henry (1787): Poems and Prose Writings.

Disraeli (1804): Wondrous Tale of Alroy, Rise of Iskander. P
    Ixion in Heaven [in Colburn's New Monthly]. P

Hayward, Abraham (1801): Trs. Goethe's Faust. P

Hemans (1793): Hymns on the Works of Nature. V

Knowles (1784): The Wife. D

Lamb (1775): Last Essays of Elia. P

Longfellow (1807): Outre-Mer. P

Lytton (1803): Godolphin. P
    England and the English. P

Macaulay (1800): Essay on Walpole [in Edin. Rev.]. P

Montgomery, Robert (1807): Woman, and Other Poems.

Moore (1779): Travels of an Irish Gentleman in Search of a Religion. P

Newman (1801): Arians of the Fourth Century. P

Newman, Pusey, John and Thomas Keble, R. H. Froude, Marriott, Palmer, Perceval: Tracts for the Times [90 nos. from 1833 to 1841]. P

Nyren, John: The Young Cricketer's Tutor. P

Shelley (d. 1822): Shelley Papers, with Memoir by Thomas Medwin.

Southey (1774): Lives of British Admirals [contd. by W. Bell 1840]. P
    Ed. Works of Cowper.

Walpole (d. 1797): Letters to Sir Horace Mann, 1741–60, ed. Dover [see 1843].

Hannah More d.
William Wilberforce d.
Arthur Henry Hallam d.
Richard Watson Dixon b.
The Oxford Movement commences with Keble's sermon, 'National Apostasy', on 14 July.
Charles Knight's 'Penny Cyclopaedia' (concl. 1844).

Ainsworth (1805): Rookwood. P

Bancroft, George (1800): History of the United States, vol. i [completed in 10 vols. in 1874].

Beckford (1759): Letters from Various Parts of Europe [incl. those of 1783 repub. with omissions, and adding new letters from Spain and Portugal]. P

Bentham (d. 1832): Deontology, ed. John Bowring. P

Blessington, Lady (1789): Conversations with Lord Byron. P

Brackenridge, Henry Marie (1786): Recollections. P

Brydges, Egerton (1762): Autobiography. P

Campbell (1777): Life of Mrs. Siddons. P

Crabbe (d. 1832): Poetical Works [cont. Letters, Journals, and Unpub. Poems, ed., with Life, by his son, see 1820; with more unpub. poems, ed. Ward, 1905].

Cunningham, Allan (1784): Ed. of Burns.

Disraeli (1804): Infernal Marriage [in Colburn's New Monthly]. P
Revolutionary Epic. V

Edgeworth (1767): Helen. P.   Orlandino. P

Elliott, Charlotte (1789): The Invalid's Hymn Book. V

Godwin (1756): Lives of Necromancers. P

Hallam, Arthur Henry (d. 1833): Essays and Remains.

Heraud, John (1799): Judgment of the Flood. V

Hogg (1770): Familiar Anecdotes of Sir Walter Scott. P

Hood (1799): Tylney Hall. P

Hunt (1784): Leigh Hunt's London Journal [concl. 1835].
The Indicator and The Companion [selections].

Landor (1775): Citation and Examination of William Shakespeare touching deer-stealing. Conference of Edmund Spenser with the Earl of Essex. P

Lytton (1803): Last Days of Pompeii. P

Marryat (1792): Peter Simple. P
Jacob Faithful. P

Martineau (1802): Illustrations of Taxation. P

More (d. 1833): Memoirs of Life and Correspondence, ed. Roberts.

Myers, Frederic (1811): Catholic Thoughts [privately printed. First pub. 1873]. P

Place, Francis (1771): Improvement of the Working People. P

Planché (1796): History of British Costumes. P

Pringle, Thomas (1789): African Sketches. P and V

William Morris b.
Lord Acton b.
Sir John Seeley b.
George Du Maurier b.
James Thomson b.
Henry James Byron b.
Charles Farrar Browne b.
Samuel Taylor Coleridge d.
Charles Lamb d.
Thomas Malthus d.
Augustus Hare d.
Surtees Society founded.
William Thomas Lowndes, 'Bibliographer's Manual'.
Lamennais, 'Paroles d'un Croyant'.
Wienbarg, 'Ästhetische Feldzüge'.

Scott, Michael (1789): Cruise of the Midge [in Blackwood s, Mar. 1834–June 1835; separately 1836].

Sigourney, Lydia Huntley (1791): Letters to Young Ladies.
Poems.

Somerville, Mary (1780): Connection of the Physical Sciences. P

Southey (1774): The Doctor [concl. 1847; vols. vi and vii, ed. J. W. Warter]. P

Taylor, Sir Henry (1800): Philip von Artevelde. D

Whitehead, Charles (1804): Autobiography of Jack Ketch. P
Lives and Exploits of English Highwaymen. P

Wilson, John Mackay (1804): Tales of the Borders [concl. 1840]. P

1835

Beckford (1759): Recollections of an Excursion to the Monasteries of Alcobaça and Batalha. P

Browning, R. (1812): Paracelsus. V

Callcott, Maria, Lady (1785): Little Arthur's History of England. P

Carleton, William (1794): Fardorougha, the Miser. P

Channing, William Ellery (1780): Slavery. P

Clare (1793): The Rural Muse. V

Cobbett (d. 1835): Legacy to Parsons. P
Legacy to Labourers. P

Coleridge (d. 1834): Specimens of Table Talk, ed. H. N. Coleridge [enlarg. ed. T. Ashe 1884].

Coleridge, Hartley (1796): Lives of Illustrious Worthies. P

Darley (1795): Nepenthe. V

Dickens (1812): Sketches by Boz, 1st series. P

Hunt (1784): Captain Sword and Captain Pen. V

Lytton (1803): Rienzi. P

Mitford (1787): Belford Regis. P

Moore (1779): The Fudges in England. V
History of Ireland [concl. 1846]. P

Procter (1787): Life of Edmund Kean. P

Shelley, Mary (1797): Lodore. P

Simms, William Gilmore (1806): The Yemassee. P
The Partisan. P

Thirlwall, Connop (1797): History of Greece [concl. 1844].

Wade, Thomas (1805): Mundi et Cordis Carmina. V

Wordsworth (1770): Yarrow Revisited, and Other Poems.
Lines after the Death of Charles Lamb [n.d.]. V
Guide through the Lakes [enlarg. from Description of Scenery of the Lakes, 1822]. P

Alfred Austin b.
Samuel Clemens ('Mark Twain') b.
Samuel Butler b.
Walter Skeat b.
James Hogg (Ettrick Shepherd) d.
William Cobbett d.
Felicia Dorothea Hemans d.
Chambers's 'Information for the People'.
Vigny, 'Chatterton'.
'New York Herald'.
Musset, 'Les Nuits' (1835–7).
Büchner, 'Dantons Tod'.

Bayly, Thomas Haynes (1797): Perfection, a Farce.
Bowles, Caroline (1786): The Birthday. V
Browning, R. (1812): Porphyria's Lover, Johannes Agricola [in Monthly Repository]. V
Channing, William Ellery (1780): Abolitionist. P
Coleridge (d. 1834): Literary Remains, ed. H. N. Coleridge [concl. 1838]. P and V
  Letters, Conversations, and Recollections, by T. Allsop. P
Croker (1780): Johnsoniana.
Dickens (1812): Sketches by Boz, 2nd series. P
  Pickwick Papers [monthly from April 1836 to Nov. 1837; collected 1837]. P
Emerson (1803): Nature. P
Forster, John (1812): Lives of the Statesmen of the Commonwealth, vol. i [complete 1840]. P
Gore, Catherine (1799): Mrs. Armytage. P
  Diary of a Désennuyée. P
Hazlitt (d. 1830): Literary Remains, with Memoir by his son [see 1839].
Holmes, Oliver Wendell (1809): Poems. V
Hook, Theodore (1788): Jack Brag. P
Landon (1802): Traits and Trials of Early Life. P
Landor (1775): Pericles and Aspasia. P and V
  Satire on Satirists and Admonition to Detractors [on Wordsworth]. P
Lane, Edward William (1801): Manners and Customs of Modern Egyptians. P
Lytton (1803): Duchesse de la Vallière. D
Mahony, Francis Sylvester (1804): Reliques of Father Prout [enlarg. 1860: see 1876].
Marryat (1792): Mr. Midshipman Easy. P
  Japhet in Search of a Father. P
Newman, Keble, Williams, R. H. Froude, Bowden, and Wilberforce: Lyra Apostolica [179 poems; 109 by Newman].
Slingsby, Sir Henry (d. 1658): Diary, ed. Daniel Parsons [first complete ed.: see Scott 1806].
Stanhope, Fifth Earl (1805): History of England from the Peace of Utrecht to the Peace of Versailles, 1713–83 [concl. 1853]. P
Talfourd, Sir Thomas Noon (1795): Ion, a Tragedy. D
Taylor, Sir Henry (1800): The Statesman. P
Temple (d. 1699): Memoirs of Life, Works, and Correspondence, ed. T. P. Courtenay [cont. extracts from Dorothy Osborne's letters now first pub.: see 1888].
Whitehead, Charles (1804): The Cavalier. D

Sir William Gilbert b.
Francis Bret Harte b.
Isabella Mary Mayson (Mrs. Beeton) b.
William Godwin d.
James Mill d.
George Colman jnr. d.
Richard Hurrell Froude d.
'*The Dublin Review.*'
Keble, ed. of Richard Hooker (rev. Church and Paget 1888).
Eckermann, 'Gespräche mit Goethe' (Eng. trans. Goebel, 1925).
Heine, 'Romantische Schule'.

Ainsworth (1805): Crichton. P
Apperley, Charles ('Nimrod') (1773): Memoirs of the Life of John Mytton. P
Browning, R. (1812): Strafford. T
Carlyle (1795): French Revolution. P
    Lectures on German Literature. P
Coleridge, Sara (1802): Phantasmion. P and V
Cooper, James Fenimore (1789): Gleanings in Europe. P
Dickens (1812): Mudfog Papers [in Bentley's Miscellany, 1837–9; collected 1880]. P
    Oliver Twist [in Bentley's Miscellany, 1837–8; collected 1838]. P
    The Strange Gentleman, a Comic Burletta.
    The Village Coquettes, a Comic Opera.
Disraeli (1804): Henrietta Temple. P
    Venetia. P
Hallam (1777): Literature of Europe during the 15th, 16th, and 17th Centuries [concl. 1839]. P
Hare (d. 1834): Alton Sermons.
Hawthorne (1804): Twice-Told Tales [2nd series 1842]. P
Horne (1803): Cosmo de Medici. T
    Death of Marlowe. T
Hunt (1784): Monthly Repository [9 nos.].
Knowles (1784): The Love-Chase. C
Lamb (d. 1833): Letters, ed. with Life by T. N. Talfourd [more letters in Final Memorials of Lamb, ed. Talfourd 1848, ed. by W. C. Hazlitt 1886, Purnell 1870, Harper 1907, Lucas 1935].
Landon (1802): Ethel Churchill. P   [and V
Landor (1775): Pentameron and Pentalogia. P
    High and Low Life in Italy [in Monthly Repository, Aug. 1837–Apr. 1838]. P and V
    Literary Hours, by Various Friends, ed. J. Ablett [cont. Six Imaginary Conversations and other contributions by L.].
Lockhart (1794): Life of Scott [concl. 1838]. P
Lover, Samuel (1797): Rory O'More. P
Lytton (1803): Ernest Maltravers [see 1838]. P
Macaulay (1800): Essay on Bacon [Edin. Rev.]. P
Mill, James (d. 1836): Principles of Toleration. P
Newman (1801): Parochial Sermons [concl. 1842].
Peacock (1785): Paper Money Lyrics. V
Ruskin (1819): Poetry of Architecture [in Loudon's Architectural Magazine]. P
Thackeray (1811): The Professor [in Bentley's Miscellany]. P
    Yellowplush Papers [Fraser's Mag. 1837–8]. P
Trollope, Frances (1780): Vicar of Wrexhill. P
Whewell (1794): The Inductive Sciences. P
Whittier (1807): Poems [2nd series 1865]. V

Accession of Queen Victoria.
Camden Society founded.
Henry Becque b.
Algernon Charles Swinburne b.
John Richard Green b.
William Dean Howells b.
Benjamin Webster, 'Acting National Drama' (anthology: concl. 1853).
Charles Knight's 'Pictorial History of England' (concl. 1844).
Bentley's 'Miscellany' (concl. 1868).
Joseph Cottle, Early Recollections of S. T. Coleridge.

President U.S.A.
Van Buren.

Arnold (1795): Early History of Rome [concl. 1843: see 1845].

Barrett, E. B (Browning) (1806): The Seraphim. V

Behtham (d. 1832): Collected Works, ed. J. Bowring [concl. 1843].

Bethune, Alexander (1804): Tales and Sketches of the Scottish Peasantry.

Bury, Lady Charlotte (1775): Diary Illustrative of the Times of George IV.

Carlyle (1795): Lectures on History of Literature. P Essay on Scott [in Westminster Review]. P

Cooper, James Fenimore (1789): Home as Found. P

Dibdin, Thomas (1776): Bibliographical Tour in the Northern Counties of England. P

Dickens (1812): Memoirs of Joseph Grimaldi. P Sketches of Young Gentlemen. P
Nicholas Nickleby [monthly from Apr. 1838 to Oct. 1839; collected 1839]. P

Froude, R. H. [d. 1836]: Remains, ed. Keble and Newman [pt. ii ed. Keble and Mozley 1839].

Guest, Lady Charlotte (1812): Mabinogion. P

Guest, Edwin (1800): History of English Rhythms [ed. Skeat 1882]. P

Hood (1799): Hood's Own, or Laughter from Year to Year [miscellany].

Jerrold (1803): Men of Character. P

Lane, Edward (1801): Trs. of Arabian Nights [from the Fr. of Galland; concl. 1840; ed. E. S. Poole 1859, S. Lane-Poole 1891]. P

Lyell, Sir Charles (1797): Elements of Geology. P

Lytton (1803): Alice, or the Mysteries [afterwards with Maltravers (see 1837) as Eleusinia]. P
Lady of Lyons. D. Richelieu. D

Macaulay (1800): Essay on Temple [in Edin. Rev.]. P

Milnes, Richard Monckton (1809): Poems of Many Years.

Newman (1801): Doctrine of Justification. P

Prescott (1796): Ferdinand and Isabella. P

Scott, William Bell (1811): Hades, or the Transit. V

Surtees (1805): Jorrocks's Jaunts and Jollities [orig. in New Sporting Mag. 1831–4]. P

Thackeray (1811): Some Passages in the Life of Major Gahagan [in New Monthly Magazine]. P

Trollope, Frances (1780): Widow Barnaby. P

Tupper (1810): Proverbial Philosophy, 1 series [II 1842, III 1867, I–IV complete 1876]. V

Williams (1802): The Cathedral. P
Thoughts in Past Years [enlarg. 1852]. V

Wordsworth (1770): Sonnets, with a few additional ones now first printed.

William Edward Lecky b.
Henry Sidgwick b.
James Bryce (Viscount Bryce) b.
John Morley (Viscount Morley) b.
Thomas Morton d.
Letitia Elizabeth Landon d.
English Historical Society founded.
Camden Society publications begin (First Series, 1838–72; New Series, 1871–97).
Joseph Bosworth, 'Anglo-Saxon Dictionary'.
Charles Knight, 'Pictorial Shakespeare' (concl. 1841).
Thomas Campbell, ed. of Shakespeare.
Milman, ed. Gibbon's 'Decline and Fall'.
Newman, Pusey, and Keble (editors); Church, Copeland, and others: Library of the Fathers of the Catholic Church (concl. 1885).

Ainsworth (1805): Jack Sheppard. P
Bailey (1816): Festus [11th or jubilee ed. considerably enlarged 1889]. V
Carlyle (1795): European Revolutions. P
Chartism. P
Critical and Miscellaneous Essays [collected].
Disraeli (1804): Tragedy of Count Alarcos. V
Domett, Alfred (1811): Venice. V
Faraday (1791): Experimental Researches in Electricity [concl. 1855]. P
Frere (1769): The Frogs [trs. Aristophanes: see 1840]. V
Grant, Sir Robert (d. 1838): Sacred Poems.
Hazlitt (d. 1830): Sketches and Essays, collected by his son [new ed. entitled Men and Manners; Sketches and Essays 1852]. P
Winterslow; Essays and Characters written there, collected by his son. P
Hemans (d. 1835): Collected Works.
Hood (1799): Up the Rhine. P
Hook, Theodore (1788): Births, Marriages, and Deaths. P
Landor (1775): Andrea of Hungary. Giovanna of Naples. D
Lever (1806): Harry Lorrequer. P
Longfellow (1807): Hyperion. P
Voices of the Night. V
Marryat (1792): Phantom Ship. P
Martineau (1802): Deerbrook. P
Milman (1791): Life of Gibbon. P
Poetical Works.
Moore (1779): Alciphron. V
Shelley (d. 1822): Poetical Works, ed. Mrs. Shelley [ed. Rossetti 1870–78–88; Forman 1876–82–92; Dowden 1890–96–1900; Hutchinson 1904–5–7].
Smith, Sydney (1771): Works [concl. 1840; incl. Letters of Peter Plymley 1807–8, Three Letters to Archdeacon Singleton 1837–8–9, The Ballot 1839, Edinburgh Review articles].
Sterling, John (1806): Poems.
Thackeray (1811): Catherine [in Fraser's Magazine 1839–40]. P
Stubbs's Calendar, or the Fatal Boots [in Cruikshank's Comic Annual]. P
Williams (1802): Hymns translated from the Parisian Breviary. V

Walter Pater b.
Louise De La Ramée ('Ouida') b.
William de Morgan b.
John Galt d.
Winthrop Mackworth Praed d.
'The New General Biographical Dictionary' (projected by Hugh James Rose) appears.
John Thomas Smith's 'Cries of London' (illustr. by himself and J. Bowyer Nichols).
First authentic ed. of Saint-Simon's Memoirs (many pirated edd. in 18th century).
Lowndes, 'The British Librarian' [concl. 1842].
Stendhal, 'Chartreuse de Parme'.

Ainsworth (1805): Tower of London. P

Barham, Richard (1788): Ingoldsby Legends, Series I [Series II and III 1847]. V

Browning, R. (1812): Sordello. V

Clive, Caroline (1801): IX Poems by V.

Coleridge (d. 1834): Confessions of an Enquiring Spirit, ed. H. N. Coleridge. P

Cooper, James Fenimore (1789): The Pathfinder. P

Dana, Richard Henry (1815): Two Years before the Mast. P

Darwin (1809): Voyage of H.M.S. Beagle. P

Dickens (1812): Sketches of Young Couples. P
Master Humphrey's Clock, Old Curiosity Shop, Barnaby Rudge [weekly from Apr. 1840 to Nov. 1841; collected 1840–1]. P

D'Israeli (1766): Amenities of Literature. P

Elliott, Charlotte (1789): Hours of Sorrow. V

Frere (1769): Trs. Acharnians, Knights, and Birds of Aristophanes [see 1839]. V

Hawker (1803): Ecclesia. V

Hunt (1784): The Seer [concl. 1841].
Legend of Florence. D
Prefaces to Moxon's edd. of Wycherley, Congreve, Vanbrugh, Farquhar, and Sheridan. P

Landor (1775): Fra Rupert. D

Lytton (1803): Money. D [P

Macaulay (1800): Essay on Clive [in Edin. Rev.].

Milman (1791): Christianity under the Empire. P

Pepys (d. 1703): Life, Journals, Correspondence, ed. John Smith.

Poe (1809): Tales of the Grotesque and Arabesque. P

Shelley (d. 1822): Essays, Letters from Abroad, Translations and Fragments, ed. Mrs. Shelley [new ed. 1852; Collected Prose, ed. Forman, 1880. Collected Letters, ed. Dobell 1908, Ingpen, 1912].

Strickland, Agnes and Elizabeth: Lives of the Queens of England [concl. 1848]. P

Thackeray (1811): Bedford Row Conspiracy [in New Monthly Magazine].
A Shabby Genteel Story [in Fraser's Magazine].
Paris Sketch Book. P
Essay on Genius of George Cruikshank. P
Barber Cox and the Cutting of his Comb. P
Character Sketches. P

Walpole (d. 1797): Collected Letters, ed. Wright [Letters to the Misses Berry now first pub.].

Whewell (1794): Philosophy of the Inductive Sciences. P

Wilberforce, Samuel (1808): Agathos. P

Williams and Copeland (editors); **Newman**, and others: Plain Sermons by authors of the Tracts for the Times [concl. 1848].

Marriage of Queen Victoria and Prince Albert.
John Addington Symonds b.
Austin Dobson b.
Thomas Hardy b.
Wilfrid Scawen Blunt b.
Frances Burney d.
Percy Society founded.
Parker Society founded.
First Eng. trs. of Ranke's 'History of the Popes during the 16th and 17th centuries'.
'The Dial' started (ended 1844).
Hartley Coleridge, edd. of Massinger and Ford.
Zola b.
Mérimée, 'Colomba'.
Sainte-Beuve, 'Port-Royal' (1840–59).
Hebbel, 'Judith'.
Grillparzer, 'Weh dem der lügt'.

Ainsworth (1805): Guy Fawkes. P
  Old Saint Paul's. P
Borrow (1803): The Zincali, or Account of the
  Gypsies of Spain. P
Boucicault (1820 ?): London Assurance. D
Browning, R. (1812): Pippa Passes [no. 1 of Bells
  and Pomegranates]. V
Carlyle (1795): Heroes, Hero-Worship, and the
  Heroic in History. P
Channing, William Ellery (1780): Works. P
Cooper, James Fenimore (1789): The Deerslayer. P
Crowe, Catherine (1800 ?): Adventures of Susan
  Hopley. P
Dickens (1812): Pic-Nic Papers, by various hands
  [cont. The Lamp-Lighter by Dickens].
Elphinstone, Mountstuart (1779): History of India
  [enlarg. ed., F. B. Cowell, 1866].
Emerson (1803): Essays: 1st series [2nd series
  1844].
Gore, Catherine (1799): Cecil. P
Heber (d. 1826): Poetical Works [collected].
Helps, Sir Arthur (1813): Essays written in the
  Intervals of Business. P
Hunt (1784) and others: Chaucer Modernized. V
Lever, Charles James (1806): Charles O'Malley. P
Lowell (1819): A Year's Life. V
Macaulay (1800): Essay on Warren Hastings [in
  Edin. Rev.]. P
Marryat (1792): Masterman Ready. P
Marston, John Westland (1819): Patrician's
  Daughter. D
Martineau (1802): The Playfellow, a Series of
  Tales. P
  The Hour and the Man. P
Miller, Hugh (1802): Old Red Sandstone. P
Thackeray (1811): History of Samuel Titmarsh
  and the Great Hoggarty Diamond [in
  Fraser's Magazine; separately 1849]. P
  Second Funeral of Napoleon, Chronicle of the
  Drum. P
  Comic Tales and Sketches [reprt. of earlier
  writings]. P
Trench (1807): Notes on the Parables. P
  Poems.
Ward, Robert Plumer (1765): De Clifford, or the
  Constant Man. P
Warren, Samuel (1807): Ten Thousand a Year
  [originally in Blackwood's from 1839]. P

William Black b.
William Henry Hudson b.
Sir Henry Morton Stanley
  (John Rowlands) b.
'*The Christian Remem-*
  brancer' *(concl. 1868).*
'*Punch*' *started.*
Shakespeare   Society,
  1841–53.
Last '*Tract of the Times*'
  (No. 90) by Newman.
A. Stifter, '*Hochwald*'.
'*New   York   Tribune*'
  *(from   1924   *'*N.Y.*
  Herald-Tribune').

President U.S.A.
Tyler.

Apperley, Charles ('Nimrod') (1773): Life of a Sportsman. P

Arnold (d. 1842): Study of Modern History. P

Browning (1812): King Victor and King Charles [no. 2 of Bells and Pomegranates]. V
Dramatic Lyrics [no. 3 of above]. V

Bryant, William Cullen (1794): The Fountain. V

Burney (d. 1840): Diary and Letters, 1778–1840, ed. Charlotte Barrett [concl. 1846: see 1889].

Campbell (1777): Pilgrim of Glencoe. V
Frederick the Great and his Times. P

Channing, William Ellery (d. 1842): The Duty of the Free States. P

Dickens (1812): American Notes for General Circulation. P

Drummond (d. 1649): Conversations with Ben Jonson in 1619, ed. from original MS. by David Laing [see 1711]. P

Hunt (1784): The Palfrey. V

Longfellow (1807): Ballads and Other Poems. V
Poems on Slavery. V

Lover (1797): Handy Andy. P

Lytton (1803): Zanoni. P
Eva, and Other Tales and Poems. V

Macaulay (1800): Lays of Ancient Rome [Ivry, first pub. in Quarterly Magazine in 1833, and Armada, first pub. in Friendship's Offering in 1833, added in 1848]. V

Manning, Henry Edward (1808): Sermons [collected; concl. 1850].

Marryat (1792): Percival Keene. P

Montgomery, Robert (1807): Luther, a Poem.

Taylor, Sir Henry (1800): Edwin the Fair. D

Tennyson (1809): Poems [among new pieces: Locksley Hall, Morte d'Arthur, Ulysses, Two Voices, Godiva, Sir Galahad, Vision of Sin, 'Break, break, break', &c.].

Thackeray (1811): Sultan Stork [in Ainsworth's Magazine]. P
Fitz-Boodle Papers [in Fraser's Magazine 1842–3]. P

Trench (1807): Poems from Eastern Sources, V
Genoveva, a Poem.

Tupper (1810): Proverbial Philosophy, 2nd series [see 1838]. V

Whitehead, Charles (1804): Richard Savage. P

Williams (1802): The Baptistry. V

Wilson (1785): Recreations of Christopher North. P

Wordsworth (1770): Poems chiefly of Early and Late Years, including The Borderers.

William James b.

Thomas Arnold d.

Allan Cunningham d.

'*Biographical Dictionary*', ed. George Long (*concl. 1844*).

'*Dictionary of Greek and Roman Antiquities*', ed. Sir William Smith.

William Thoms's ed. of Stow's 'Survey of London'.

'*Illustrated London News*' *started.*

John Payne Collier, ed. of Shakespeare (concl. 1844).

Copyright Act extends term of copyright to 42 years from publication or 7 years after the Author's death, whichever is the longer. See 1709, 1774, 1911.

Mallarmé b.

Stendhal d.

Droste-Hülshof, '*Die Judenbuche*'.

Ainsworth (1805): Windsor Castle. P
Bethune, Alexander (1804): The Scottish Peasant's Fireside.
Borrow (1803): Bible in Spain. P
Browning, R. (1812): Return of the Druses [no. 4 of Bells and Pomegranates]. D
　Blot on the Scutcheon [no. 5 of above]. D
Carlyle (1795): Past and Present. P
Church (1815): Life of St. Anselm [enlarg. 1870]. P
Dickens (1812): A Christmas Carol in Prose. P
　Martin Chuzzlewit [monthly from Jan. 1843 to July 1844; collected 1844]. P
Gore, Catherine (1799): The Banker's Wife. P
Hawker (1803): Reeds Shaken by the Wind. V
Hood (1799): Song of the Shirt [in Punch]. V
Horne (1803): Orion, an Epic Poem.
Hunt (1784): One Hundred Romances of Real Life. P
Jerrold (1803): Punch's Letters to his Son. P
Jones, Ebenezer (1820): Studies of Sensation and Event. V
Knowles (1784): The Secretary. D
Longfellow (1807): The Spanish Student. D
Lytton (1803): Last of the Barons. D
Macaulay (1800): Critical and Historical Essays. P
Martineau (1805): Endeavours after the Christian Life, 1st series [2nd 1847]. P
Mill, John Stuart (1806): System of Logic. P
Neale, John Mason (1818): Hymns for Children.
Prescott (1796): The Conquest of Mexico. P
Prichard, James Cowles (1786): Natural History of Man. P
Ruskin (1819): Modern Painters, vol. i [ii 1846, iii–iv 1856, v 1860]. P
Sidney, Henry, Earl of Romney (1641–1704): Diary of the Time of Charles II, ed. A. W. Blencowe.
Spencer (1820): Proper Sphere of Government. P
Surtees (1805): Handley Cross, or the Spa Hunt [expanded into Handley Cross, or Mr. Jorrocks's Jaunts 1854]. P
Thackeray (1811): Irish Sketchbook. P
　Men's Wives [in Fraser's Magazine]. P
　Bluebeard's Ghost [in Fraser's Magazine].
Walpole (d. 1797): Letters to Sir Horace Mann, 1760–85 [see 1833].

Henry James b.
Edward Dowden b.
Frederic William Henry Myers b.
Charles Montagu Doughty b.
Sir William Reynell Anson b.
Robert Southey d.
Wordsworth poet-laureate.
Condemnation and suspension of Pusey by Oxford University after his sermon, 'Holy Eucharist', preached on 14 May.
'The Economist' started by James Wilson.
Liddell and Scott's 'Greek-English Lexicon' (7th ed. 1883, 8th ed. 1897).
Charles Knight's 'Shakespeare's Biography'.
Anna Swanwick, trs. Selections from Dramas of Goethe and Schiller [see 1850].
Owen, 'Comparative Anatomy and Physiology of Invertebrate Animals' (concl. 1846); enlarg. 1855.

Barnes, William (1801): Poems of Rural Life in Dorset Dialect [a second collection 1859; third 1863; collected 1879].

Barrett, E. B. (Browning) (1806): Poems.

Browning, R. (1812): Colombe's Birthday [no. 6 of Bells and Pomegranates]. D

Bryant, William Cullen (1794): The White-Footed Deer. V

Burke (d. 1797): Correspondence 1744–97, ed. Fitzwilliam and Bourke.

De Quincey (1785): Logic of Political Economy. P

Dickens (1812): The Chimes, a Goblin Story. P

Disraeli (1804): Coningsby. P

Finlay, George (1799): Greece under the Romans [first pt. of History of Greece: see 1877]. P

Fuller, Margaret (1810): Summer on the Lakes. P

Haydon, Benjamin (1786): Lectures on Painting and Design [concl. 1846]. P

Hood (1799): Whimsicalities. P and V
Hood's Magazine and Comic Miscellany [concl. 1845].

Horne (1803): New Spirit of the Age. P

Hunt (1784): Collected Poems, 2nd ed., with Additions [see 1832].

James, G. P. R. (1799): Col. Novels [concl. 1849].

Jeffrey, Francis, Lord Jeffrey (1773): Contributions to Edinburgh Review [concl. 1853].

Jerrold (1803): Story of a Feather. P

Kinglake (1809): Eothen. P

Lever (1806): Tom Burke of Ours. P
Arthur O'Leary. P

Lowell (1819): Poems. V

Mill (1806): Essays on Some Unsettled Questions of Political Economy. P

Milnes (Lord Houghton) (1809): Palm Leaves. V

Newman (editor), Church, Dalgairns, Meyrick, Pattison, Faber, Froude, Coffin, Ornsby, Walker, Oakeley, Barrow: Lives of the English Saints.

Patmore (1823): Poems.

Sewell, Elizabeth (1815): Amy Herbert. P

Sleeman, Sir William (1788): Rambles and Recollections of an Indian Official. P

Stanley (1815): Life of Arnold. P

Thackeray (1811): Luck of Barry Lyndon [in Fraser's Magazine. Reprtd. in Miscellanies 1855, and as Memoirs of B. L. 1856]. P
History of the next French Revolution. P

Warburton, Bartholomew Elliot (1810): The Crescent and the Cross. P

Ward, William George (1812): Ideal of a Christian Church. P

Edward Carpenter b.
Andrew Lang b.
Robert Bridges b.
Gerard Manley Hopkins b.
William Beckford d.
Thomas Campbell d.
Henry Francis Cary d.
Keble's 'Prælectiones Academicæ'.
Caxton Society founded.
W. J. Thoms's ed. of 'Reynard the Fox' from Caxton.
'North British Review' (concl. 1871).
Robert Chambers's 'Cyclopaedia of English Literature'.
Sir William Smith's 'Dictionary of Greek and Roman Biography and Mythology' (concl. 1849).
Charles Knight's 'Weekly Volumes' and 'Old England'.
Robert Chambers, 'Vestiges of the Natural History of Creation'.
Anatole France b.
Verlaine b.
Dumas, 'Les Trois Mousquetaires'.
Hebbel, 'Maria Magdalene'.
Heine, 'Neue Gedichte'.
Droste-Hülshof, 'Gedichte'.

Arnold (d. 1842): History of the Later Roman Commonwealth [see 1838]. P

Miscellaneous Works, ed. Arthur Stanley.

Aytoun (1813) **and Martin** (1816): Bon Gaultier Ballads [in Tait's and Fraser's Magazines 1842–4; later collections 1849, 1855]. V

Browning, R. (1812): Dramatic Romances and Lyrics [no. 7 of Bells and Pomegranates]. V

Carlyle (1795): Ed. Letters and Speeches of Cromwell [ed. Lomas 1904]. P

Cooper, Thomas (1805): Purgatory of Suicides. V

Dickens (1812): Cricket on the Hearth. P

Disraeli (1804): Sybil. P

Ford, Richard (1796): Handbook for Travellers in Spain. P

Fuller, Margaret (1810): Woman in the 19th Century. P

Henslowe, Philip (d. 1616): Diary, 1592–1603, ed. J. P. Collier [Extracts in Malone's ed. of Shakespeare, 1790–1821. Ed. Greg, 1904–8].

Jerrold (1803): Time Works Wonders [acted]. D

Punch's Complete Letter-Writer. P

Lewes (1817): Biographical History of Philosophy [concl. 1846]. P

Lowell (1819): Conversations on some of the Old Poets. P

Lytton (1803): New Timon [completed 1847]. V

Martineau (1802): Dawn Island. P

Forest and Game Law Tales. P

Newman (1801): Essay on Development of Christian Doctrine. P

Poe (1809): Tales of Mystery and Imagination. P

The Raven. V

Smith, John Thomas (d. 1833): Book for a Rainy Day [ed. W. Whitten 1905]. P

Southey (d. 1843): Oliver Newman and other Poetical Remains, ed. Hill.

Thackeray (1811): Legend of the Rhine [in Cruikshank's Table-Book, June to Dec.]. P

Diary of Jeames de la Pluche [Punch 1845–6]. P

Walpole (d. 1797): Memoirs of the Reign of George III ed. Denis le Marchant [new ed. by G. F. R. Barker 1894]. P

Whewell (1794): Elements of Morality. P

Williams (1802): Sacred Verses.

George Saintsbury b.

Sidney Colvin b.

Thomas Hood d.

Sydney Smith d.

Richard Harris Barham d.

The Oxford Movement reaches a crisis with the condemnation by the University of William Ward's 'Ideal of a Christian Church' (pub. 1844) and the degradation of the author: Newman joins the Church of Rome on 9 October.

Meeting of Robert Browning and Elizabeth Barrett.

Mrs. Cowden Clarke, 'Concordance to Shakespeare's Plays'.

'Encyclopaedia Metropolitana.'

Joseph Hunter, 'New Illustrations of Shakespeare'.

Walter Farquhar Hook, 'Dictionary of Ecclesiastical Biography' (concl. 1852).

Lingard, 'History and Antiquities of Anglo-Saxon Church' (enlarg. from 'Antiquities of Anglo-Saxon Church', 1806).

Mérimée, 'Carmen'.

President U.S.A. Polk.

Blanchard, Laman (d. 1845): Sketches from Life. P

Brontë, Charlotte (1816), Emily (1818), and Anne (1820): Poems by Currer, Ellis, and Acton Bell.

Browning, R. (1812): Luria, A Soul's Tragedy [no. 8 of Bells and Pomegranates]. D
Bells and Pomegranates, 1841–6, reprtd.

Dickens (1812): Pictures from Italy [originally in Daily News, Jan. to Mar. 1846]. P
Battle of Life. P
Dombey and Son [monthly from Oct. 1846 to Apr. 1848; collected 1848]. P

Fuller, Margaret (1810): Literature and Art. P

'George Eliot' (1819): Trs. Strauss's Life of Jesus. P

Grote (1794): History of Greece, vols. i–ii [concluded 1856]. P

Hawker (1803): Echoes from Old Cornwall. V

Hawthorne (1804): Mosses from an Old Manse. P

Hume (d. 1776): Life and Correspondence, ed. Burton [Letters, ed. Greig 1932].

Hunt (1784): Wit and Humour selected from English Poets.
Stories from Italian Poets, with Lives of Writers. P

Jerrold (1803): Mrs. Caudle's Curtain Lectures [repub. from Punch]. P
Chronicles of Clovernook. P

Keble (1792): Lyra Innocentium. V

Landor, Robert Eyres (1781): Fawn of Sertorius. P

Lear (1812): Book of Nonsense. V

Longfellow (1807): The Belfry of Bruges. V

Lytton (1803): Lucretia, or Children of the Night. P

Marryat (1792): Privateer's Man. P

Martineau (1802): The Billow and the Rock. P

Melville (1819): Typee. P

Nairne (d. 1845): Lays from Strathearn. V

Owen (1804): British Fossil Mammals and Birds. P

Ruskin (1819): Modern Painters, vol. ii [see 1843]. P

Smith, H. (1779): Poetical Works [collected].

Thackeray (1811): Cornhill to Cairo. P
Snobs of England [in Punch 1846–7; separately, as Book of Snobs, 1848]. P
Mrs. Perkins's Ball [1847].

Trench (1807): Notes on the Miracles of Our Lord. P

Walpole (d. 1797): Memoirs of the Reign of King George II, ed. Lord Holland [see 1822].

Webster, Daniel (1782): Bunker Hill Speeches.

Whewell (1794): Lectures on Systematic Morality. P

Francis Herbert Bradley b.

John Hookham Frere d.

Marriage of Browning and Elizabeth Barrett.

Hakluyt Society founded.

Bohn's 'Standard Library'.

'The Guardian' started.

'The Daily News' started by Dickens.

John Thomas Smith, 'Antiquarian Rambles in the Streets of London'.

Lord Campbell, 'Lives of Lord Chancellors and Keepers of the Great Seal of England' (concl. 1847).

Barham (d. 1845): Ingoldsby Legends, 2nd and 3rd series [see 1840]. P and V

Boole, George (1815): Mathematical Analysis of Logic. P

Brontë, Anne (1820): Agnes Grey [by 'Acton Bell']. P

Brontë, Charlotte (1816): Jane Eyre [by 'Currer Bell']. P

Brontë, Emily (1818): Wuthering Heights [by 'Ellis Bell': pub. with Agnes Grey above]. P

Crowe, Catherine (1800 ?): Story of Lilly Dawson. P

Disraeli (1804): Tancred. P

Emerson (1803): Poems. V

Evelyn (d. 1706): Life of Mrs. Godolphin, ed. Bishop Wilberforce. P

Froude (1818): Shadows of the Clouds. P

Gaskell (1810): The Sexton's Hero, Christmas Storms & Sunshine [Howitt's Journal, 1847]. P

Helps, Sir Arthur (1813): Friends in Council, 1st series [concl. 1859]. P

Hunt (1784): Men, Women, & Books [selections]. P

Keble (1792): Sermons. P

Landor (1775): Hellenics, enlarged and completed [repub. with alterations 1859]. V

Lever (1806): The Knight of Gwynne. P

Lewes (1817): Ranthorpe. P

Longfellow (1807): Evangeline. V

Medwin, Thomas (1788): Life of Shelley. P

Melville (1819): Omoo. P

Morton, John Maddison (1811): Box and Cox [acted]. C

Prescott (1796): The Conquest of Peru. P

Surtees (1805): Hawbuck Grange. P

Taylor, Sir Henry (1800): Notes from Life. P Eve of the Conquest and Other Poems.

Tennyson (1809): The Princess [3rd ed. with Songs added 1850]. V

Thackeray (1811): Vanity Fair [serially Jan. 1847 to July 1848; collected 1848]. P Punch's Prize Novelists [3 Apr. to 9 Oct. 1847; later Novels by Eminent Hands]. P

Trollope (1815): Macdermots of Ballycloran. P

Whewell (editor), **Herschel, Hare, Lockhart, Hawtrey**: English Hexameter Translations.

Williams (1802): The Altar. V

Alice Thompson (Mrs. Meynell) b.

Sharon Turner d.

Layamon's 'Brut' ed. by Sir Frederick Madden.

Bohn's 'Antiquarian Library' and 'Scientific Library'.

Marx's Communist Manifesto.

Foundation of Communist League.

Adams, John Quincy (d. 1848): Poems of Religion and Society.

Ainsworth (1805): Lancashire Witches. P

Aytoun (1813): Lays of Scottish Cavaliers. V

Brontë, A. (1820): Tenant of Wildfell Hall. P

Clough (1819): Bothie of Toper-na-Fuosich [later Tober-na-Vuolich]. V

Coleridge (d. 1834): Hints towards a Comprehensive View of Life, ed. S. B. Watson. P

Crowe, Catherine (1800 ?): Night Side of Nature. P

Dickens (1812): The Haunted Man. P

Fairfax, Thomas, Lord Fairfax (d. 1671): Correspondence, ed. Johnson and Bell [concl. 1849].

Forster, John (1812): Life and Adventures of Oliver Goldsmith [enlarg. as Life and Times, &c., 1854]. P

Gaskell (1810): Mary Barton. P

Grant, James (1822): Adventures of an Aide-de-Camp. P

Hervey, John, Lord Hervey (d. 1743): Memoirs of the Reign of George II, ed. J. W. Croker.

Hunt (1784): Jar of Honey from Mount Hybla. V
The Town. P

Jameson, Anna (1794): Sacred and Legendary Art. P

Keats (d. 1821): Life, Letters, and Literary Remains, ed. Lord Houghton [rev. 1867].

Kingsley (1819): Saint's Tragedy. D

Landor (1775): Imaginary Conversation of King Carlo-Alberto and the Duchess of Belgioioso. P
Italics. V

Lowell (1819): The Biglow Papers [2nd series 1860]. V
A Fable for Critics. V.   Vision of Sir Launfal. V

Lytton (1803): Harold. P
King Arthur. V

Mill (1806): Principles of Political Economy. P

Newman (1801): Loss and Gain. P

Pusey (1800): Parochial Sermons, vol. i [ii 1853, iii 1869].

Rich, Mary, Countess of Warwick (d. 1678): Autobiography, ed. T. C. Croker.

Sterling, John (d. 1844): Essays and Tales. P

Thackeray (1811): A Little Dinner at Timmins's. P
History of Pendennis [serially Nov. 1848 to Dec. 1850; collected 1849–50]. P
Our Street. P

Trollope (1815): The Kellys and the O'Kellys. P

Walpole (d. 1797): Letters to Countess of Ossory. 1769–97, ed. R. Vernon Smith.

Bernard Bosanquet b.

Arthur James Balfour, Earl of Balfour b.

Richard Jefferies b.

George John Romanes b.

Branwell Brontë d.

Emily Brontë d.

Frederick Marryat d.

Isaac D'Israeli d.

Formation of the Pre-Raphaelite Brotherhood by Rossetti, Madox Brown, Woolner, Holman Hunt, and Millais, 1848–9.

Thomas Lacy, 'Acting Edition of Plays' (concl. 1873).

Bohn's 'Classical Library'.

Chambers's 'Instructive and Entertaining Library'.

Revolution in France.

J.-K. Huysmans b.

Chateaubriand d.

Chateaubriand, 'Mémoires d'Outre-Tombe'.

Hebbel, 'Herodes und Mariamne'.

Marx and Engels, 'Communist Manifesto'.

Arnold (1822): Strayed Reveller and Other Poems.

Barton (d. 1849): Selections from Poems and Letters, ed. Lucy Barton.

Brontë, C. (1816): Shirley. P

Campbell, Lord (1779): Lives of the Chief Justices of England [concl. 1857]. P

Clough (1819): Ambarvalia [with Thomas Burbidge]. V

Coleridge (d. 1834): Notes and Lectures on Shakespeare and some of the Old Dramatists, ed. Sara Coleridge [ed. from notes by J. P. Collier 1856; ed. T. Ashe 1885]. P

Curzon, Robert (1810): Visit to the Monasteries in the Levant. P

Dickens (1812): David Copperfield [monthly from May 1849 to Nov. 1850; collected 1850]. P

Emerson (1803): Miscellanies. P

Freeman (1823): Study of History. P

Froude (1818): Nemesis of Faith. P

Herschel, Sir John (1792): Outlines of Astronomy. P

Hunt (1784): Readings for Railways. P

Jerrold (1803): A Man made of Money. P

Macaulay (1806): History of England, vols. i–ii [iii–iv 1855; ed. Lady Trevelyan 1861]. P

Manning, Anne (1807): Mary Powell [with a sequel, Deborah's Diary, 1859]. P

Marston, John Westland (1819): Strathmore. D

Martineau (1802): History of England during the Thirty Years' Peace, 1815–1845. P

Household Education. P

Melville (1819): Mardi. P. Redburn. P

Owen (1804): History of British Fossil Reptiles [concl. 1884]. P

Parkman, Francis (1823): California and Oregon Trail. P

Ruskin (1819): Seven Lamps of Architecture. P

Southey (d. 1843): Commonplace Book, ed. J. W. Warter [concl. 1851]. P

Life and Correspondence, ed. C. C. Southey. P

Stephen, Sir James (1789): Essays in Ecclesiastical Biography. P

Thackeray (1811): Dr. Birch and his Young Friends. P

Thoreau (1817): A Week on the Concord. P

Wakefield, Edward Gibbon (1796): A View of the Art of Colonization. P

Wesley, Charles (d. 1788): Journal, 1736–56, with Selections from Correspondence, ed. Jackson.

Whitehead, Charles (1804): The Solitary and Other Poems [collected].

William Ernest Henley b.
Edmund Gosse b.
Horace Smith d.
Maria Edgeworth d.
Hartley Coleridge d.
Thomas Lovell Beddoes d.
Ebenezer Elliott d.
Anne Brontë d.
Bernard Barton d.
Edgar Allan Poe d.
'*Notes and Queries*' *founded by William John Thoms.*
'*Household Words*' (*weekly*) *started by Dickens.*
*Charles Knight, '*Studies of Shakespeare*'.*
*Sir Austen Layard, '*Nineveh and its Remains*'.*
William Smith, trs. Works of Fichte (*collected; separately 1845–9*).
*Gotthelf, '*Uli der Pächter*'.*

President U.S.A.
Taylor.

Alison, Sir Archibald (1792): Essays, Political, Historical and Miscellaneous.
Allingham, William (1824): Poems.
Beddoes (d. 1849): Death's Jest Book. V
Browning, E. B. (1806): Poems [cont. Sonnets from the Portuguese and entirely new version of Prometheus Bound: see 1833].
Browning, R. (1812): Christmas Eve and Easter Day. V
Bryant, William Cullen (1794): Letters of a Traveller. P
Carlyle (1795): Latter-Day Pamphlets. P
Church, Richard William (1815): Dante [in Christian Remembrancer: repub. 1878]. P
Coleridge (d. 1834): Essays on His Own Times, ed. Sara Coleridge.
Collins (1824): Antonina, or the Fall of Rome. P
Dobell (1824): The Roman, a Dramatic Poem.
Emerson (1803): Representative Men. P
Gaskell (1810): Moorland Cottage. P
Grant, James (1822): The Scottish Cavalier. P
Hawthorne (1804): The Scarlet Letter. P
Hunt (1784): Autobiography [enlarg. ed. Thornton Hunt 1860; ed. Ingpen 1903].
Leigh Hunt's Journal [1850–1].
Kingsley (1819): Alton Locke, Tailor and Poet. P
Landon (d. 1838): Collected Poems.
Longfellow (1807): Seaside and Fireside. V
Lytton (1803): The Caxtons. P
Marston, John Westland (1819): Philip of France. D
Marie de Méranie. D
Melville (1819): White Jacket. P
Merivale, Charles (1808): History of the Romans under the Empire [concl. 1864]. P
Neale, John Mason (1818): History of the Holy Eastern Church. P
Newman, F. W. (1807): Phases of Faith. P
Poe (d. 1849): Works. P and V
Rossetti (1828) and others: The Germ [four nos., Jan.–Apr. R.'s contributions: Hand and Soul, My Sister's Sleep, Blessed Damozel (original version), Carillon, Sonnets for Pictures, &c.].
Senior, William Nassau (1790): Political Economy. P
Smedley, Francis Edward: Frank Fairleigh. P
Spencer (1820): Social Statics. P
Tennyson (1809): In Memoriam. V
Thackeray (1811): The Kickleburys on the Rhine [2nd ed. with Preface, 1851]. P
Rebecca and Rowena. P
Watts (1797): Lyrics of the Heart. V
Wordsworth (d. 1850): The Prelude [1805 version, ed. E. de Sélincourt pub. 1926]. V

Robert Louis Stevenson b.
Frederic William Maitland b.
Lafcadio Hearn b.
Augustine Birrell b.
William Wordsworth d.
Francis, Lord Jeffrey d.
William Lisle Bowles d.
Tennyson poet-laureate.
Sir William Smith, 'New Classical Dictionary'.
Joseph Hunter, 'Milton: A Sheaf of Gleanings after his Biographers and Annotators'.
Sir Frederic Madden ed. Wiclif's 'Bible'.
'Harper's Magazine' started.
Guy de Maupassant b.
Honoré de Balzac d.
John Stuart Blackie, trs. of Æschylus.
Anna Swanwick, trs. Goethe's 'Egmont and Faust', pt. i (pt. ii in 1878: see 1843).
Keller, 'Der Grüne Heinrich (–1879).
Otto Ludwig, 'Der Erbförster'.
Stifter, 'Studien'.

President U.S.A. Fillmore.

Beddoes (d. 1849): Collected Poems, ed. Kelsall [ed. Gosse 1890, Colles 1907].

Borrow (1803): Lavengro. P

Browning, E. B. (1806): Casa Guidi Windows. V

Carlyle (1795): Life of John Sterling. P
Excursion (futile enough) to Paris. P

Coleridge, H. (d. 1849): Poems, ed. Derwent Coleridge [ed. Bailey-Kempling 1903].
Prose Remains, ed. Derwent Coleridge.

Dickens (1812): Child's History of England [in Household Words, Jan. 1851–Dec. 1853; collected 1852–4]. P

FitzGerald, Edward (1809): Euphranor, a Dialogue on Youth. P

Hawthorne (1804): House of the Seven Gables. P
The Snow Image. P

Helps, Sir Arthur (1813): Companions of my Solitude. P

Hunt (1784): Table-Talk [with Imaginary Conversations of Pope and Swift].

Jerrold (1803): Collected Works [concl. 1854].

Kingsley (1819): Yeast [in abridged form in Fraser's Magazine 1848]. P

Layard, Sir Austen (1817): Popular Account of Discoveries at Nineveh. P

Longfellow (1807): The Golden Legend. D

Lytton (1803): Not so bad as we seem. D

Manning, Anne (1807): Household of Sir Thomas More. P

Mansel, Henry Longueville (1820): Prolegomena Logica. P

Melville (1819): Moby Dick. P

Meredith (1828): Poems [incl. first version of Love in the Valley].

Napier, Sir William Francis (1785): History of Sir Charles Napier's Administration of Scinde. P

Parkman, Francis (1823): Conspiracy of Pontiac. P

Ruskin (1819): King of the Golden River. P
Pre-Raphaelitism. P
Stones of Venice, vol. i [ii–iii 1853]. P
Examples of the Architecture of Venice. P
Notes on the Construction of Sheepfolds. P

Trench (1807): Study of Words. P

Walpole (d. 1797): Letters to Mason, ed. Mitford.

Wordsworth (d. 1850): Memoirs, dictated by himself, ed. Christopher Wordsworth.

The Great Exhibition.

Coup d'état: Louis Napoleon Emperor.

Mary Augusta Arnold (Mrs. Humphry Ward) b.

Henry Arthur Jones b.

Sir Oliver Lodge b.

Andrew Cecil Bradley b.

Joanna Baillie d.

John Lingard d.

J. M. W. Turner d.

H. N. Hudson's ed. of Shakespeare (concl. 1856; repub. as Harvard ed. 1881).

J. Mitford's ed. of Milton's Works (prose and verse).

Robert Chambers's ed. of Burns.

'New York Times'.

Sainte-Beuve, 'Lundis' (1851–62).

Alison, Sir Archibald (1792): History of Europe, 1815–52 [concl. 1859: see 1833]. P
  Life of Marlborough. P

Arnold (1822): Empedocles on Etna, and other Poems [Tristram and Iseult, A Summer Night, Youth of Nature, Youth of Man, Isolation, &c.].

Browning, R. (1812): Essay on Shelley. P

Creasy, Sir Edward Shepherd (1812): Fifteen Decisive Battles of the World. P

Dickens (1812): Bleak House [monthly from Mar. 1852 to Sept. 1853; collected 1853]. P

Disraeli (1804): Life of Lord George Bentinck. P

Hamilton (1788): Philosophy and Literature. P

Hawthorne (1804): A Wonder Book for Boys and Girls. P

  The Blithedale Romance. P

Hayward, Abraham (1801): Art of Dining. P

Holland, Lord (d. 1840): Memoirs of the Whig Party. P

Kingsley (1819): Phaethon. P

Martineau (1802): Merdhen, the Manor and the Eyrie, and Old Landmarks and Old Laws. P

Melville (1819): Pierre. P

Miller, Hugh (1802): My Schools and Schoolmasters. P

Mitford (1787): Recollections of a Literary Life. P

Newman (1801): Scope and Nature of University Education [later ed. Idea of a University]. P

Reade, Charles (1814) and **Taylor, Tom**: Masks and Faces [acted]. D

Stowe, Harriet Beecher (1811): Uncle Tom's Cabin. P

Stirling-Maxwell, Sir William (1818): Cloister Life of the Emperor Charles V [enlarg. 1891]. P

Tennyson (1809): Ode on Death of Wellington. V

Thackeray (1811): History of Henry Esmond. P

George Moore b.
Lady Gregory b.
Thomas Moore d.
John Cassell's 'The Popular Educator' (concl. 1855).
John Payne Collier's 'Notes and Emendations to the Plays of Shakespeare' starts the controversy leading to his exposure.
Gautier, 'Émaux et Camées'.

1853

Arnold (1822): Poems [among new pieces: Sohrab and Rustum, Scholar Gipsy, Requiescat].

Blackmore (1825): Poems by Melanter. V

Brontë, C. (1816): Villette. P

Burton, John Hill (1809): History of Scotland [concl. 1870]. P

Coleridge (d. 1834): Notes on English Divines, ed. Derwent Coleridge.
  Notes, Theological, Political, and Miscellaneous, ed. Derwent Coleridge.

Crimean War 1853–6.
Sir Hall Caine b.
Amelia Opie d.
Charles Knight, 'English Cyclopaedia' (concl. 1861).
'Bohn's British Classics.'
'Cassell's Classical Library.'
'Encyclopaedia Britannica', 8th ed. (concl. 1860).

'**Cuthbert Bede**' (1827): Adventures of Mr. Verdant Green, pt. i [ii 1854, iii 1857]. P

De Quincey (1785): Collected Works [concl. 1860; enlarg. 1862–78; enlarg. ed. D. Masson 1889–90].

FitzGerald (1809): Trs. Six Dramas of Calderon [see 1865]. V

Fox (d. 1806): Memorials and Correspondence, ed. Earl Russell [concl. 1857].

Gaskell (1810): Ruth. P
  Cranford [originally in Household Words, 13 Dec. 1851–21 May 1853]. P

Hawthorne (1804): Tanglewood Tales. P

Haydon, Benjamin Robert (d. 1846): Autobiography and Journals, ed. Tom Taylor.

Kingsley (1819): Hypatia. P

Landor (1775): Last Fruit off an Old Tree. P and V

Lewes (1817): Comte's Philosophy of Sciences. P

Lytton (1803): My Novel. P

Manning, Anne (1807): Cherry and Violet. P

Martineau (1802): Philosophy of Comte, translated and condensed. P

Maurice (1805): Theological Essays. P

Moore (d. 1852): Memoirs, Journals, and Correspondence, ed. Earl Russell [concl. 1856].

Patmore (1823): Tamerton Church Tower. V

Reade (1814): Peg Woffington. P
  Christie Johnstone. P

Ruskin (1819): Architecture and Painting. P
  Stones of Venice, ii–iii [i 1851]. P

Smith, Alexander (1830): Life Drama. V

Surtees (1805): Mr. Sponge's Sporting Tour [3rd ed. Soapey Sponge's Sporting Tour 1893]. P

Thackeray (1811): English Humorists of the 18th Century. P
  The Newcomes [serially from Oct. 1853 to Aug. 1855; collected 1854–5]. P

Trench (1807): Lessons in Proverbs. P

Verney: Letters and Papers of the Verney Family to the end of the year 1639, ed. J. Bruce.

Wallace, Alfred Russel (1823): Travels on the Amazon and Rio Negro. P

Whewell, William (1794): Of the Plurality of Worlds [2nd ed. with Supplement, A Dialogue on the Plurality of Worlds 1854]. P

Whyte-Melville (1821): Captain Digby Grand. P

Yonge (1823): Heir of Redclyffe. P

J. O. Halliwell-Phillipps, ed. Shakespeare.
Johann Tieck d.
Francis William Newman, trs. Odes of Horace.
Gérard de Nerval; 'Les Chimères'.
Hebbel, 'Gyges und sein Ring'.

President U.S.A. Pierce.

Ainsworth (1805): Star Chamber. P
  Flitch of Bacon. P
Allingham (1824): Day and Night Songs. V
Aytoun (1813): Firmilian. V
Church (1815): Essays and Reviews. P
Cooke, John E. (1830): Youth of Jefferson. P
Dickens (1812): Hard Times [in Household Words
  and separately]. P
Dobell (1824): Balder. V
Ferrier, James Frederick (1808): Institutes of
  Metaphysic. P
Forster, John (1812): Life and Times of Oliver
  Goldsmith [see 1848]. P
Keats (d. 1821): Poetical Works, with Memoir, ed.
  Lord Houghton [new ed. 1861: see 1883].
Macaulay (1800): Speeches, corrected by himself.
Massey, Gerald (1828): Ballad of Babe Christabel. V
May, Sir Thomas (1815): Rules, Orders, and Forms
  of Procedure of the House of Commons.
Milman (1791): Latin Christianity [concl. '55]. P
Mitford (1787): Atherton, and Other Tales. P
Owen (1804): Geology and Inhabitants of the
  Ancient World. P
Patmore (1823): The Betrothal [pt. i of Angel in
  the House: see 1856–60–62]. V
Patmore, Peter George (1786): My Friends and
  Acquaintances. P
Rossetti, William Michael (ed.): Ruskin, Rossetti,
  and Pre-Raphaelitism [Papers: concl. 1861].
Scott, W. B. (1811): Poems. V
Shillaber, Benjamin (1814): Life and Sayings of
  Mrs. Partington. P
Smedley, Francis Edward (1818): Harry Cover-
  dale's Courtship. P
Stanley, Arthur Penrhyn (1815): Memorials of
  Canterbury. P
Stewart (d. 1828): Works, ed. Sir William Hamil-
  ton and John Veitch [concl. 1858].
Surtees (1805): Handley Cross, or Mr. Jorrocks's
  Hunt [illustr. Leech; originally monthly
  Mar. 1853 to Oct. 1854: see 1843]. P
Tennyson (1809): Charge of the Light Brigade [in
  The Examiner, 9 Dec.; separately 1855]. V
Thoreau (1817): Walden, or Life in the Woods. P
Whyte-Melville (1821): General Bounce. P
Williams, Isaac (1802): The Christian Seasons. V
Wiseman, Nicholas (1802): Fabiola. P
Yonge (1823): The Little Duke. P

*Caroline Cody (Marie
Corelli) b.*
Oscar Wilde b.
John Gibson Lockhart d.
*John Wilson ('Christo-
pher North') d.*
Susan Ferrier d.
James Montgomery d.
Working Men's College.
*George Eliot lives with
G. H. Lewes.*
*Sir William Smith's 'Dic-
tionary of Greek and
Roman Geography'
(concl. 1857).*
*Constable's 'Miscellany
of Foreign Literature'
(concl. 1855).*
*George Boole, 'Analysis of
the Laws of Thought on
which are founded the
Mathematical Theories
of Logic and Probabili-
ties'.*
*George Eliot, trs. Feuer-
bach's 'Essence of Chris-
tianity'.*
*Robert Bell, ed. of English
Poets (concl. 1857).*
Rimbaud b.
Lamennais d.

Arnold (1822): Poems, second series.
Bailey, Samuel (1791): Philosophy of the Human Mind. P
Bain, Alexander (1818): Senses and Intellect. P
Bancroft, George (1800): Literary and Historical Miscellanies. P
Blanchard, Laman (d. 1845): Corporation Characters. P
Browning, R. (1812): Men and Women. V
Burton, Sir Richard (1821): Pilgrimage to El-Medinah and Mecca [concl. 1856]. P
Clive, Caroline (1801): Paul Ferroll. P
Dickens (1812): Little Dorrit [monthly from Dec. 1855 to June 1857; collected 1857]. P •
Gaskell (1810): Lizzie Leigh, and Other Tales. P
North and South [originally in Household Words, Sept. 1854–Jan. 1855]. P
Hunt (1784): The Old Court Suburb. P
Stories in Verse.
Irving (1783): Life of George Washington [completed 1859]. P
Jowett (1817): Commentary to St. Paul's Epistles to the Thessalonians, Galatians, & Romans. P
Kingsley (1819): Westward Ho! P
Glaucus, or the Wonders of the Shore. P
Lewes (1817): Life of Goethe. P
Lewis, Sir George Cornewall (1806): Credibility of Early Roman History. P
Longfellow (1807): Hiawatha. V
Macaulay (1800): History of England, vols. iii–iv [see 1848, 1861]. P
Macdonald, George (1824): Within and Without. V
Maurice, Frederick Denison (1805): Plan of a Female College. P
Melville (1819): Israel Potter. P
Meredith (1828): Shaving of Shagpat. P
Motley, John Lothrop (1814): The Rise of the Dutch Republic. P
'Owen Meredith' (1831): Clytemnestra. V
Prescott (1796): Philip II [completed 1858]. P
Taylor, Tom (1817): Still Waters run Deep. D
Tennyson (1809): Maud and Other Poems.
Thackeray (1811): The Rose and the Ring. V
Miscellanies in Prose and Verse [collected].
Trench (1807): English Past and Present. P
Alma and Other Poems.
Trollope (1815): The Warden. P
Whitman, Walt (1819): Leaves of Grass. V
Wilson (d. 1854): Collected Works, ed. Ferrier.
Yonge (1823): The Lances of Lynwood. P

William Paton Ker b.
William Sharp ('Fiona Macleod') b.
Oliver Madox Brown b.
Arthur Pinero b.
Samuel Rogers d.
Charlotte Brontë d.
Julius Hare d.
Mary Mitford d.
Sir William Smith, 'Latin and English Dictionary'.
'Saturday Review' started.
'Daily Chronicle' started.
'Daily Telegraph' started.
Charles Knight, 'Knowledge is Power' (see 1831).
Thomas Keightley, 'Life, Opinions, and Writings of John Milton'.
William Chappell, ed. 'Popular Music of Olden Time' (concl. 1859; rev. Wooldridge, 1893).
Benjamin Thorpe, ed. of 'Beowulf', with Translation and Commentary.
Gérard de Nerval d.

Bradford, William (d. 1657): History of Plimouth Plantations. P

Carlyle (1795): Collected Works [later edd. 1869–71; 1871–4; 1885–7; Traill 1897–1901].

Curtis, George William (1824): Prue and I. P

Dobell (1824): England in Time of War. V

Emerson (1803): English Traits. P

Froude (1818): History of England, vols. i–ii [iii–iv 1858, v–vi 1860, vii–viii 1863, ix–x 1866, xi–xii 1870]. P

Kingsley (1819): The Heroes. P

Landor (1775): Antony and Octavius. P

Melville (1819): Piazza Tales. P

Mulock, Dinah Maria (1826): John Halifax, Gentleman. P

Newman (1801): Callista. P

Patmore (1823): The Espousals [pt. ii o Angel in the House: see 1854–60–62]. V

Reade (1814): It is Never too Late to Mend. P*

Rogers (d. 1855): Recollections, ed. Sharpe.

Rossetti (1828), Morris (1834), and others: Oxford and Cambridge Magazine [R. cont: Burden of Nineveh, Blessed Damozel, Staff and Scrip. M. cont: Winter Weather, Riding Together, Chapel in Lyoness, Pray but one prayer for me, prose tales and articles]. P and V

Ruskin (1819): Modern Painters, iii–iv [see 1843]. P

Schoolcraft, Henry Rowe (1793): The Myth of Hiawatha. P

Stanley (1815): Sinai and Palestine. P

Yonge (1823): Daisy Chain. P

George Bernard Shaw b.
William Archer b.
Sir William Hamilton d.
Hugh Miller d.
Charles Knight's ' Popular History of England' (concl. 1862).
John Stuart Blackie, 'Lays and Legends of Ancient Greece'.
Joseph Bosworth's ed. of King Alfred's Orosius.
G. W. Thornbury, 'Shakespeare's England'.
Freud b.
Heine d.
Flaubert, 'Madame Bovary'. ·
Hugo, 'Contemplations'.
Keller, 'Die Leute von Seldwyla'.
O. Ludwig, 'Zwischen Himmel und Erde'.

1857

Bacon (d. 1626): Works, ed. Ellis, Spedding, and Heath [concl. 1874].

Borrow (1803): Romany Rye. P

Boswell (d. 1795): Letters to Temple [Letters, ed. Tinker 1924].

Brontë, C. (d. 1855): The Professor. P

Browning, E. B. (1806): Aurora Leigh. V

Buckle (1821): History of Civilization in England, vol. i [ii 1861; together, 1866]. P

Gaskell (1810): Life of Charlotte Brontë. P

Hughes (1822): Tom Brown's Schooldays. P

Kingsley (1819): Two Years Ago. P

Lawrence, George Alfred: Guy Livingstone. P

Livingstone, David (1813): Missionary Travels in South Africa. P

Locker-Lampson (1821): London Lyrics. V

Luttrell, Narcissus (d. 1752): Brief Relation of State Affairs from 1678 to 1714. P

Macdonald (1824): Poems.

Indian Mutiny.
Joseph Conrad b.
George Gissing b.
John Davidson b.
Douglas Jerrold d.
Matthew Arnold Professor of Poetry at Oxford.
Rossetti visits Oxford and meets Burne-Jones, Morris, and Swinburne.
'Calendar of State Papers,' ed. Mary Everett Green and others, begun.
'The Standard' started.
'The Christian World' started.
Alexander Dyce, ed. of Shakespeare.
Musset d.
Baudelaire, 'Fleurs du Mal'.
Stifter, 'Der Nachsommer'.

Marston, John Westland (1819): A Life's Ransom. D
Melville (1819): The Confidence Man. P
Meredith (1828): Farina. P
Miller (d. 1856): Testimony of the Rocks. P
Newman (1801): Sermons on Various Occasions.
'Owen Meredith' (1831): The Wanderer. V
Ruskin (1819): Political Economy of Art. P
Smith, Alexander (1830): City Poems.
Smith, William Henry (1808): Thorndale. P
Spencer (1820): Essays, series I [II 1863, III 1874].
Story, Robert (1795): Poetical Works [collected].
Thackeray (1811): The Virginians [monthly from
    Nov. 1857 to Oct. 1859; collected 1858–9]. P
    Christmas Books [collected]. P
Trollope (1815): Barchester Towers. P
Walpole (d. 1797): Letters, ed. Cunningham
    [concl. 1859; ed. Toynbee, 1903–5].

*President U.S.A.
Buchanan.*

1858

Arnold (1822): Merope. D
Brown, John (1810): Horæ Subsecivæ, vol. i
    [ii 1861, iii 1882]. P
Carlyle (1795): Friedrich II (Frederick the Great),
    vols. i–ii [iii 1862, iv 1864, v–vi 1865]. P
Clough (1819): Amours de Voyage. V
Cory, William Johnson (1823): Ionica [2nd vol.
    1877; enlarg. edition 1891]. V
Farrar (1831): Eric, or Little by Little. P
Forster, John (1812): Essays [collected]. P
'George Eliot' (1819): Scenes of Clerical Life
    [in Blackwood's, 1857]. P
Gladstone (1809): Studies on Homer. P
Hare (d. 1855): Sermons.
Hogg, Thomas (1792): Life of Shelley. P
Holmes (1809): The Autocrat of the Breakfast-
    Table. P and V
Kingsley (1819): Andromeda, and Other Poems.
Landor (1775): Dry Sticks Fagoted. V
Leyden, John (d. 1811): Poems and Ballads.
Longfellow (1807): Courtship of Miles Standish. V
Lytton (1803): What will he do with it. P
Macdonald (1824): Phantastes. P
Marston, John Westland (1819): A Hard Struggle. D
Morris (1834): Defence of Guenevere. V
Peacock (1785): Memoirs of Shelley [in Fraser's
    Magazine 1858–60; collected in Works, 1875,
    vol. iii].
Procter, Adelaide (1825): Legends and Lyrics.
Sleeman, Sir William (d. 1856): A Journey
    through the Kingdom of Oudh. P
Trelawny, Edward John (1792): Recollections of
    Last Days of Shelley and Byron. P

*Sir William Watson b.
Robert Owen d.
William Aytoun, 'Ballads
    of Scotland' (anthology).
Dickens begins his public
    readings.
First volume of the 'Rolls
    Series' published.
Aytoun and Martin, trs.
    Poems and Ballads of
    Goethe.
'Atlantic   Monthly'
    started.*

Trollope (1815): Doctor Thorne. P
The Three Clerks. P.
Wiseman, Nicholas (1802): Recollections of the
Last Four Popes. P

1859

Arnold (1822): England and the Italian question. P
Bain, Alexander (1818): Emotions and Will. P
Boole (1815): Differential Equations [concl.
1865].
Boyd, A. K. H. (1825): Recreations of a Country
Parson. P
Brown, John (1810): Rab and his Friends. P
Darwin (1809): Origin of Species. P
Dickens (1812): Tale of Two Cities [in All the
Year Round, Apr.–Nov.; also separately]. P
FitzGerald (1809): Rubáiyát of Omar Khayyám
[2nd ed. much altered 1868; 3rd ed. 1872;
4th ed. 1879]. V
Gaskell (1810): Round the Sofa. P
'George Eliot' (1819): Adam Bede. P
The Lifted Veil [in Blackwood's]. P
Holmes (1809): The Professor at the Breakfast-
Table. P and V
Hughes (1822): Scouring of the White Horse. P
Kingsley, Henry (1830): Recollections of Geoffrey
Hamlyn. P
Lewes (1817): Physiology of Common Life. P
Mackay, Charles (1814): Collected Songs.
Masson (1822): Life of Milton [concl. 1880]. P
Meredith (1828): Ordeal of Richard Feverel. P
Mill (1806): On Liberty. P
Thoughts on Parliamentary Reform. P
Dissertations and Discussions, vols. i–ii [iii
1867, iv 1876]. P
Norton, Charles Eliot (1827): Notes of Travel. P
Ruskin (1819): The Two Paths. P
Elements of Perspective. P
Sewell, Mary (1797): Children of Summerbrook. V
Shaftesbury (d. 1683): Memoirs, Letters, and
Speeches, ed. W. D. Christie.
Shelley (d. 1822): Memorials, ed. Lady Shelley.
Smiles, Samuel (1812): Self-Help. P
Tennyson (1809): Idylls of the King [Enid,
Vivien, Elaine, Guinevere: see 1869, 1872]. V
Trench (1807): Select Glossary of English Words.
Trollope (1815): The Bertrams. P
Walpole (d. 1797): Journal of the Reign of George
III, 1771–83, ed. John Doran [new ed. by
A. F. Steuart 1910].

War of Italian Liberation.
Garibaldi in Sicily.
Kenneth Grahame b.
Francis Thompson b.
Arthur Conan Doyle b.
*Alfred Edward Housman
b.*
Sir Sidney Lee b.
Havelock Ellis b.
Thomas de Quincey d.
Leigh Hunt d.
Lord Macaulay d.
Henry Hallam d.
John Austin d.
*'Chambers's   Encyclo-
paedia' (concl. 1868).*
*Chambers's 'Domestic An-
nals of Scotland' (concl.
1861).*
*Dickens starts 'All the
Year Round' (weekly).*
*'Macmillan's Magazine'
started.*
'Sporting Life' started.
*Thomas Keightley, ed. of
Milton.*
*Hugo,   'Légende   des
siècles'.*

Boole (1815): Calculus of Finite Differences. P
Boucicault, Dion (1820?): Colleen Bawn. D
Bright, William (1824): History of the Church,
  A.D. 313–457. P
Browning, E. B. (1806): Poems before Congress.
  P
Campbell, John Francis: Popular Tales of the
  West Highlands [concl. 1862]. P
Collins (1824): Woman in White. P
Dickens (1812): Great Expectations [in All the
  Year Round, 1860–1; collected 1861]. P
  Uncommercial Traveller [enlarg. 1866]. P
  Hunted Down [in All the Year Round]. P
Doran, John: Their Majesties' Servants. P
Dundonald, Thomas Cochrane, 10th Earl of (d.
  1860): Autobiography of a Seaman. P
Emerson (1803): The Conduct of Life. P
Gaskell (1810): Right at Last, and Other Tales. P
'George Eliot' (1819): Mill on the Floss. P
Hawthorne (1804): The Marble Faun. P
Hook, Walter Farquhar (1798): Lives of the
  Archbishops of Canterbury [concl. 1876]. P
Howells, W. Dean (1837): Columbus. P
Hunt (d. 1859): Poetical Works, rev. by himself
  and ed. Thornton Hunt [ed. Milford 1922].
Macaulay (d. 1859): Miscellaneous Writings, ed.
  T. F. Ellis.
Motley (1814): The History of the United
  Netherlands, vol. i [vols. ii and iii in 1867].
'Owen Meredith' (1831): Lucile. V
Patmore (1823): Faithful for Ever [pt. iii. of
  Angel in the House: see 1854–6–62]. V
Peacock (1785): Gryll Grange [in Fraser's Maga-
  zine; separately 1861]. P
Pusey (1800): The Minor Prophets. P
Rogers (d. 1855): Table Talk, ed. Dyce.
Roscoe, William Caldwell (d. 1859): Poems and
  Essays, ed. R. H. Hutton.
Ruskin (1819): Modern Painters, vol. v [see 1843].
Swinburne (1837): The Queen Mother, Rosa-
  mond. D
Thackeray (1811): Lovel the Widower [in Corn-
  hill; separately 1861]. P
  The Four Georges [in Cornhill; sep. 1861].
Timrod, Henry (1829): Poems.
Trollope (1815): Castle Richmond. P
Tyndall, John (1820): Glaciers of the Alps. P
Whyte-Melville (1821): Holmby House. P
**Wilson (editor), Temple, Williams, Powell, Patti-
  son, Jowett, Goodwin**: Essays and Reviews. P
Yonge (1823): Pigeon Pie. P

Sir James Barrie b.
William Ralph Inge b.
Frederick Rolfe b.
Anna Jameson d.
*George Payne Rainsford
  James d.*
Sir William Napier d.
Ebenezer Jones d.
*'Cornhill   Magazine'
  (Thackeray editor up
  to 1862) started.*
*Thomas Corser, 'Collec-
  tanea   Anglo-Poetica'
  (concl. 1880).*
*Charles Bradlaugh starts
  the 'National Reformer'
  (concl. 1891).*
*Theodore Martin, trs. of
  Horace's Odes.*
*'London Review' (weekly;
  concl. 1869).*
*Wilberforce–Huxley de-
  bate at British Associa-
  tion meeting at Oxford.*
Schopenhauer d.

Arnold (1822): On Translating Homer: [see 1862]. P

Popular Education of France. P

Beeton, Mrs. (1836): Book of Household Management [originally pub. in parts 1859–60]. P

Buckle (1821): History of Civilization, vol. ii [see 1857]. P

Channing, William Henry (1810): The Civil War in America. P

Dixon (1833): Christ's Company. V

Du Chaillu, Paul (1835): Explorations in Equatorial Africa. P

'**George Eliot**' (1819): Silas Marner. P

Holmes (1809): Elsie Venner. P

Hughes (1822): Tom Brown at Oxford. P

Hunt (d. 1859): A Saunter through the West End. P

Kingsley, Henry (1830): Ravenshoe. P

Macaulay (d. 1859): History of England vol. v, ed. Lady Trevelyan [see 1848–55]. P

Maine (1822): Ancient Law. P

Max Müller (1823): Science of Language [concl. 1863]. P

May, Sir Thomas (1815): Constitutional History of England [concl. 1863]. P

Meredith (1828): Evan Harrington [originally in Once a Week 1860]. P

Mill (1806): Representative Government. P

Utilitarianism [in Fraser's Magazine; separately 1863]. P

Newman, F. W. (1805): Reply to Arnold's 'On Translating Homer'. P

Palgrave (1824): Golden Treasury [rev. and enlarg. 1896]. V

Piozzi (d. 1821): Autobiography, Letters, &c., ed. Hayward. P

Reade (1814): The Cloister and the Hearth [as A Good Fight in Once a Week 1859]. P

Rossetti (1828): Early Italian Poets [translations; revised as Dante and his Circle, 1874]. V

Sewell, Mary (1797): Stories in Verse.

Smith (1830): Edwin of Deira. V

Smith, William Henry (1808): Gravenhurst. P

Spencer (1820): Education. P

Stanhope, Fifth Earl of (1805): Life of William Pitt [concl. 1862].

Stanley (1815): History of the Eastern Church. P

Tennent, Sir James (1804): Natural History of Ceylon. P

Thackeray (1811): Adventures of Philip [in Cornhill 1861–2; separately 1862]. P

Trollope (1815): Framley Parsonage. P

Wood, Mrs. Henry (1814): East Lynne. P

Goldsworthy Lowes Dickinson b.
Mary Coleridge b.
Rabindranath Tagore b.
Maurice Hewlett b.
Walter Raleigh b.
Prince Albert d.
Elizabeth Barrett Browning d.
Arthur Hugh Clough d.
William Blades's 'Life and Typography of Caxton' (concl. 1863).
Benjamin Thorpe's ed. of 'Anglo-Saxon Chronicle'.
James Spedding's 'Life and Letters of Francis Bacon', 1861–74.
Outbreak of American Civil War (ended 1865).

President U.S.A. Lincoln.

Arnold (1822): On Translating Homer, Last Words [see 1861]. P

Austin, Alfred (1835): Human Tragedy. V

Borrow (1803): Wild Wales. P

Braddon, Mary (1837): Lady Audley's Secret. P

Browning, E. B. (d. 1861): Last Poems, ed. R. Browning.

Burton, John Hill (1809): The Book Hunter. P

Calverley (1831): Verses and Translations.

Carlyle (1795): Friedrich II, vol. iii [see 1858]. P

Clough (d. 1861): Collected Poems, with Memoir by F. T. Palgrave [ed. Milford, 1910].

Colenso, John William (1814): The Pentateuch Examined [concl. 1879]. P

Collins (1824): No Name. P

Cook, Edward Dutton (1829): Trials of the Tredgolds. P

Darwin (1809): On the Contrivances by which Orchids are fertilized. P

Faber, Frederick (1814): Hymns [complete ed.].

Farrar, Frederic William (1831): St. Winifred's. or the World of School. P

'George Eliot' (1819): Romola [in Cornhill, July 1862–Aug. 1863; separately 1863]. P

Howe, Julia Ward (1819): Battle Hymn of the Republic. V

Hunt (d. 1859): Correspondence, ed. T. Hunt.

Lytton (1803): A Strange Story. P

Meredith (1828): Modern Love. Poems of the English Roadside. V

Patmore (1823): Victories of Love [pt. 4 of Angel in the House: see 1854–6–60]. V

Rossetti, Christina (1830): Goblin Market and Other Poems.

Ruskin (1819): Unto this Last [in the *Cornhill*]. P

Sewell, Mary (1797): Patience Hart's Experiences in Service. P

Shelley (d. 1822): Relics of Shelley, ed. Richard Garnett.

Spencer (1820): A System of Synthetic Philosophy: First Principles. P

Stephen, Sir James Fitzjames (1829): Essays by a Barrister. P

Swinburne (1837): Dead Love [in Once a Week]. P

Taylor, Sir Henry (1800): St. Clement's Eve. D

Trollope (1815): Orley Farm. P

Wood, Mrs. Henry (1814): The Channings. P

Sir Henry Newbolt b.
Eden Phillpotts b.
Montagu Rhodes James b.
Henry Thomas Buckle d.
James Sheridan Knowles d.
Robert Chambers's 'Book of Days' (miscellany).
George Long's trs. of Marcus Aurelius.
John Payne Collier, ed. of Spenser.
Maurice Barrès b.
Maeterlinck b.
Hugo, 'Les Misérables'.
Hebbel, 'Die Nibelungen'.

Aldrich, Thomas Bailey (1836): Poems. V
Ashworth, John (1813): Strange Tales. P
Austin (d. 1859): Lectures on Jurisprudence. P
Bates (1825): The Naturalist on the Amazon. P
Blake (d. 1827): Life by Gilchrist and Selections from Works, ed. D. G. Rossetti.
Brown, John (1810): Marjorie Fleming. P
Browning, E. B. (d. 1861): The Greek Christian Poets and the English Christian Poets. P
Butler (1835): A First Year in Canterbury Settlement. P
Conington, John (1825): Trs. Odes of Horace. V
Cooke (1830): Life of Stonewall Jackson. P
Freeman (1823): History of Federal Government. P
Gardiner (1829): History of England from the Accession of James I [see 1883]. P
Gaskell (1810): A Dark Night's Work. P
　Sylvia's Lovers. P
　Crowley Castle [in All the Year Round]. P
Hawthorne (1804): Our Old Home. P
Huxley (1825): Man's Place in Nature. P
Ingelow, Jean (1820): Poems [a second series of Poems 1876, third series 1885].
Kinglake (1809): Invasion of the Crimea, vols. i–ii [iii–iv 1868, v 1875, vi 1880, vii–viii 1887]. P
Kingsley (1813): Water Babies. P
Landor (1775): Heroic Idylls. V
Le Fanu (1814): The House by the Churchyard. P
Lincoln (1809): Gettysburg Address. P
Longfellow (1807): Tales of a Wayside Inn. V
Lyell (1797): Antiquity of Man. P
Manning, Henry Edward (1803): Sermons on Several Subjects [concl. 1873].
Marston, John Westland (1819): Donna Diana. D
Maurice (1805): Claims of the Bible and of Science. P
Mill (1806): Utilitarianism [reprtd. from Fraser's Magazine 1861]. P
Oliphant, Mrs. (1828): Salem Chapel [series 1 of Chronicles of Carlingford]. P
　The Rector and the Doctor's Family [series 11 of above]. P
Reade (1814): Hard Cash. P
Reid (d. 1796): Works, ed. Hamilton and Mansel.
Smith, Alexander (1830): Dreamthorp. P
Speke, John Hanning (1827): Journal of Discovery of the Source of the Nile. P
Stanley (1815): History of Jewish Church. P
Thackeray (1811): Roundabout Papers [collected from Cornhill 1860–3].
Thoreau (d. 1862): Excursions. P
Whyte-Melville (1821): The Gladiators. P
Woolner, Thomas (1825): My Beautiful Lady. V

William Wymark Jacobs b.
Sir Arthur T. Quiller-Couch b.
William Makepeace Thackeray d.
Richard Whately d.
'The Church Times' (weekly).
Cambridge Shakespeare, ed. Clarke, Glover, and Wright (concl. 1866; new edd.: 1887, 1893).
Tyndall, 'Heat considered as a Mode of Motion' (later edd., each altered and enlarg., 1865–8–70–5–80).
Sir William Smith, 'Dictionary of the Bible'.
Edward Lane, 'Arabic-English Lexicon' (concl. 1892).
Hebbel d.
Alfred de Vigny d.
Taine, 'Histoire de la Littérature Anglaise' (concl. 1864; see 1872).
Renan, 'La Vie de Jésus'.
Saint-Beuve, 'Nouveaux Lundis' (1863–70).

Allingham (1824): Laurence Bloomfield in Ireland. V

The Ballad Book [Golden Treasury Series].

Arnold (1822): A French Eton. P

Babbage, Charles (1792): Passages from the Life of a Philosopher. P

Browning (1812): Dramatis Personae. V

Bryce (1838): Holy Roman Empire. P

Burton, John Hill (1809): Scot Abroad. P.

Cobbe, Frances Power (1822): Broken Lights. P

Carlyle (1795): Friedrich II, vol. iv [see 1858]. P

Cowper, Mary, Countess (d. 1724): Diary, 1714–20.

Dickens (1812): Our Mutual Friend [monthly May 1864 to Nov. 1865; collected 1865]. P

Dixon, Richard Watson (1833): Historical Odes. V

Forster (1812): Life of Sir John Eliot. P

Gaskell (1810): Cousin Phillis and Other Tales. P

'George Eliot' (1819): Brother Jacob [in Cornhill]. P

Hawker, R. S. (1803): Quest of the Sangraal. V

Huxley (1825): On the Classification of Animals. On the Vertebrate Skull. P

Le Fanu, Joseph Sheridan (1814): Uncle Silas. P

Long, George (1800): Decline of the Roman Republic [concl. 1874]. P

Lowell (1819): Fireside Travels. P

Meredith (1828): Emilia in England [called Sandra Belloni 1889]. P

Newman (1801): Apologia pro vita sua [repub. with passages dealing with Kingsley as History of my Religious Opinions 1865; original title readopted in later edd.].

Payn, James (1830): Lost Sir Massingberd. P

Praed (d. 1839): Poetical Works, ed. Derwent Coleridge [American edd. 1844, '57].

Robertson (1829): David Garrick [acted]. D

Spencer (1820): Principles of Biology, vol. i [ii 1867; enlarg. 1898–9]. P

Stanley, Edward, Earl of Derby (1799): Trs. of Iliad. V

Tennyson (1809): Idylls of the Hearth [later called Enoch Arden].

Thackeray (d. 1863): Denis Duval [in Cornhill; separately 1867]. P

Thoreau (d. 1862): Maine Woods. P
Cape Cod. P

Trollope (1815): The Small House at Allington. P
Can you forgive her? P

Westcott (1825): The Bible and the Church. P

Whateley (d. 1863): Miscellaneous Remains. P

Stephen Phillips b.
Leonard Trelawny Hobhouse b.
Israel Zangwill b.
Walter Savage Landor d.
Alaric Alexander Watts d.
John Clare d.
Robert Smith Surtees d.
George Boole d.
Adelaide Procter d.
Nathaniel Hawthorne d.
Controversy between Charles Kingsley and Newman starts with K.'s review of Froude's 'History of England' in 'Macmillan's Magazine' for January: K.'s pamphlet 'What then does Dr. Newman mean?' draws forth N.'s 'Apologia'.
'The Month' started.
Early English Text Society founded by F. J. Furnivall.
Henry Morley's 'English Writers' (vol. i before Chaucer, vol. ii up to Dunbar) 1864–7 (see 1887).
Vigny, 'Les Destinées'.

Alcott, Amos Bronson (1799): Ralph Waldo Emerson [2nd edition 1888]. P

Arnold (1822): Essays in Criticism, 1st series [see 1888]. P

Berry, Mary (d. 1852): Extracts from Journals and Correspondence.

Browne, Charles Farrar (1834): Artemus Ward: his Travels. P

Carlyle (1795): Friedrich II, vols. v–vi [see 1858]. P

Clough (d. 1861): Letters and Remains.

FitzGerald (1809): The Mighty Magician, Such Stuff as Dreams are made of [trs. from Calderon: see 1853]. V

Gaskell (d. 1865): The Grey Woman. P

Grote (1794): Plato and other Companions of Sokrates. P

Grote, John (1813): Exploratio Philosophica. P

Kingsley, Henry (1830): The Hillyars and Burtons. P

Lecky (1838): Rise and Influence of the Spirit of Rationalism in Europe. P

'Lewis Carroll' (1832): Alice in Wonderland. P

Lincoln (1809): Second Inaugural Address. P

Longfellow (1807): Trs. Divine Comedy. V

Lowell (1819): Commemoration Ode. V

Martin (1816): Trs. Faust, pt. i [ii. 1886]. V

Meredith (1828): Rhoda Fleming. P

Neale, John Mason (1818): Hymns. V

Newman (1801): Dream of Gerontius [in The Month; separately 1866]. V

Oliphant, Laurence (1829): Piccadilly [in Blackwood's; separately, 1870]. P

'Ouida' (1839): Strathmore. P

Owen (1804): Memoir on the Gorilla. P

Palgrave, William Gifford (1826): A Year's Journey through Central and Eastern Arabia. P

Parkman, Francis (1823): Pioneers of France. P

Pusey (1800): Eirenicon, pt. i [ii. 1869, iii 1870]. V

Ruskin (1819): Sesame and Lilies. P

Seeley (1834): Ecce Homo. P

Shaw, H. W. (1818): Josh Billings, his sayings. P

Smith, Goldwin (1823): England and America. P

Stirling, James Hutchinson (1820): Secret of Hegel. P

Swinburne (1837): Atalanta in Calydon. D
Chastelard. D

Trench, Richard (1807): Poems [collected].
Gustavus Adolphus. P

Trollope (1815): The Belton Estate. P

Whitman (1819): Drum-Taps. V
Sequel to Drum-Taps. V

Whittier (1807): Poems. V

Rudyard Kipling b.
William Butler Yeats b.
A. E. W. Mason b.
Laurence Housman b.
Isaac Williams d.
Elizabeth Gaskell d.
Mrs. Beeton d.
William Aytoun d.
Charles Cavendish Fulke Greville d.
'The Argosy' started.
'Fortnightly Review' ,,
'Pall Mall Gazette' ,,
'Sporting Times' ,,
'Nation' (American) ,,
Cassell's 'Illustrated History of England'.
John Payne Collier, 'Bibliographical and Critical Account of the Rarest Books in the English Language'.
Joseph Barber Lightfoot, 'Commentary on St. Paul's Epistle to the Galatians'.
Viscount Milton and W. B. Cheadle, 'The North-West Passage by Land'.
Assassination of Abraham Lincoln.
Goncourt brothers, 'Germinie Lacerteux'.
Stifter, 'Witiko' (concl. 1867).

President U.S.A. Johnson.

Baker, Sir Samuel (1821): The Albert Nyanza and Exploration of Nile Sources. P

Bell, Henry Glassford (1803): Romances. V

Blackmore (1825): Cradock Nowell. P

Carlyle (1795): On the Choice of Books. P

Collins (1824): Armadale. P

Conington, John (1825): Trs. Æneid. V

Dallas, Eneas Sweetland (1828): The Gay Science. P

Doyle, Sir Francis (1810): Return of the Guards. P

Gaskell (d. 1865): Wives and Daughters [completed by F. Greenwood: originally in Cornhill 1864–6]. P

'George Eliot' (1819): Felix Holt. P

Hinton, James (1822): Mystery of Pain. P

Howells, W. Dean (1837): Venetian Life. P

Kingsley (1813): Hereward the Wake. P

Lytton (1803): Lost Tales of Miletus. V

Macaulay (d. 1859): Collected Works, ed. Lady Trevelyan.

Mansel (1820): Philosophy of the Conditioned. P

Marston, John Westland (1819): Favourite of Fortune. D

Melville (1819): Battle Pieces. V

Neale (d. 1866): Sequences, Hymns, and other Ecclesiastical Verses.

'Ouida' (1839): Chandos. P

Owen (1804): Memoir on the Dodo. P
On the Anatomy of Vertebrates. P

Procter (1787): Charles Lamb [concl. 1868]. P

Reade (1814): Griffith Gaunt [originally in Argosy 1865]. P

Rogers, J. E. Thorold (1823): History of Agriculture and Prices in England, vols. i–ii [iii–iv 1882, v–vi 1887, vii 1902]. P

Rossetti, Christina (1830): Prince's Progress and Other Poems.

Ruskin (1819): Ethics of the Dust. P
Crown of Wild Olive. P

Swinburne (1837): Poems and Ballads, 1st series [see 1878, 1889].
Notes on Poems and Reviews. P

Thoreau (d. 1862): A Yankee in Canada. P

Webster, Augusta (1837): Dramatic Studies. V

Westcott (1825): Gospel of Resurrection. P

Whittier (1807): Snow-Bound. V

Yonge (1823): The Dove in the Eagle's Nest. P

Herbert George Wells b.
Gilbert Murray b.
Thomas Love Peacock d.
John Keble d.
William Whewell d.
John Mason Neale d.
Jane Welsh Carlyle d.
Richard Morris, ed. of Chaucer and 'Specimens of Early English' (concl. 1872).
'Contemporary Review' started.
'Aunt Judy's Magazine' started.
Sir William Rowan Hamilton, 'Elements of Quaternions'.
Romain Rolland b.

Arnold (1822): New Poems [Thyrsis, A Southern Night, Saint Brandan, &c.].
  On the Study of Celtic Literature. P
Bagehot (1826): English Constitution. P
Bailey (1816): The Universal Hymn. V
Browne, Charles Farrar (1834): Artemus Ward in London. P
Carlyle (1795): Shooting Niagara [in Macmillan's Magazine]. P
Dixon, William Hepworth (1821): New America. P
Emerson (1803): May Day and other pieces. V
Freeman (1823): History of Norman Conquest of England [concl. 1879]. P
Froude (1818): Short Studies on Great Subjects, series I [II 1871, III 1877, IV 1883]. P
Gordon (1833): Sea Spray and Smoke Drift. V
Harte (1836): The Lost Galleon. V
  Condensed Novels. P
Hazlitt (d. 1830): Memoirs, by W. C. Hazlitt.
Holmes (1809): The Guardian Angel. P
Howells (1837): Italian Journeys. P
Ingelow (1820): Story of Doom. V
Keble (d. 1866): Sermons. P
Lanier, Sidney (1842): Tiger Lilies. P
Liddon, Henry Parry (1829): Divinity of Our Lord and Saviour [Bampton Lecture, 1866].
Longfellow (1807): Flower-de-Luce. V
'Mark Twain' (1835): The Celebrated Jumping Frog. P
Marston, John Westland (1819): Hero of Romance. D
Max Müller (1823): Chips from a German Workshop [concl. 1875]. P
Meredith (1828): Vittoria. P
Morris (1834): Life and Death of Jason. V
Myers (1843): St. Paul. V
'Ouida' (1839): Under Two Flags. P
'Owen Meredith' (1831): Poetical Works.
Parkman, Francis (1827): The Jesuits in North America. P
Pater (1839): Essay on Winckelmann [in Westminster Review].
Robertson (1829): Caste [acted]. D
Ruskin (1819): Time and Tide. P
Seebohm, Frederic (1833): Oxford Reformers. P
Smith, Goldwin (1823): Three English Statesmen. P
Swinburne (1837): Song of Italy. V
  Appeal to England. V
Thackeray, Anne Isabella (1837): The Village on the Cliff. P
Thackeray (d. 1863): Collected Works [concl. 1869].

Arnold Bennett b.
Pearl Mary Craigie ('John Oliver Hobbes') b.
George William Russell ('Æ') b.
Lionel Johnson b.
John Galsworthy b.
Charles Edward Montague b.
Alexander Smith d.
Sir Archibald Alison d.
Michael Faraday d.
Alaric Watts's 'The Laurel and the Lyre' (anthology of fugitive verse).
Walter Skeat's ed. of 'Piers Plowman' (concl. 1884).
William Carew Hazlitt, 'Handbook to the Popular Poetical and Dramatic Literature of Great Britain'.
William Thomson, Lord Kelvin, and Peter Guthrie Tait, 'Natural Philosophy'.
Marx, 'Das Kapital', 1st vol. published (vols. II and III, ed. Engels, 1885–95).
Baudelaire d.

Trollope (1815): Last Chronicle of Barset [in parts
    1866]. P
The Claverings. P.   Nina Balatka. P
Tupper (1810): Proverbial Philosophy, series III
    [see 1838]. V
Tyndall (1820): Lectures on Sound. P
Whittier (1807): Maud Muller. V

1868

Ainsworth (1805): South Sea Bubble. P
Alcott, Amos Bronson (1799): Tablets. P
Alcott, Louisa (1832): Little Women. P
Arnold (1822): Schools and Universities on the
    Continent. P
Browne, Charles Farrar (1834): Artemus Ward:
    his book. P
Browning (1812): The Ring and the Book. V
Byron (1834): Uncle Dick's Darling [acted]. D
Church (1815): Oxford Sermons. P
Collins (1824): The Moonstone. P
Darwin (1809): Variation of Animals and Plants
    under Domestication. P
Digby, Sir Kenelm (d. 1665): Journal of the
    Scanderoon Voyage in 1628. P
Dilke, Charles Wentworth (1843): Greater Britain. P
'George Eliot' (1819): Spanish Gypsy. V
Helps (1813): Realmah. P
Lightfoot, Joseph Barber (1828): Commentary on
    St. Paul's Epistle to the Philippians. P
Longfellow (1807): New England Tragedies. V
Lowell (1819): Under the Willows. V
Mackay, Charles (1814): Poetical Works.
Martineau, J. (1805): Essays, Philosophical and
    Theological.
Maurice (1805): The Conscience. P
Milman (d. 1868): Ed. Annals of St. Paul's. P
Morris (1834): Earthly Paradise, vol. i [ii. 1869,
    iii 1870]. V
Newman (1801): Verses on various Occasions.
    Collected Works [concl. 1881].
Stanley (1815): Memorials of Westminster
    Abbey. P
Swinburne (1837): Siena. V
    William Blake. P
    Notes on the Royal Academy. P
Victoria, Queen (1819): Leaves from a Journal of
    our Life in the Highlands [ed. Sir A. Helps]. P

Gertrude Lowthian Bell b.
Henry Hart Milman d.
Lord Brougham d.
*The Ballad and Chaucer
    Societies founded by
    F. J. Furnivall.*
*The Royal Historical
    Society founded.*
*Edward Arber's series
    of 'English Reprints'
    (concl. 1870) starts with
    Milton's 'Areopagitica'.*
*F. J. Furnivall and J. W.
    Hales's ed. of the Percy
    Ballads MS.*
*F. J. Furnivall, ed. of
    'Canterbury Tales' (six-
    text ed.).*
*A. B. Grosart, 'Fuller
    Worthies Library' (39
    vols., concluded 1876;
    edd. of Sir John Davies,
    Fulke Greville, Henry
    Vaughan, Andrew Mar-
    vell, George Herbert,
    Richard Crashaw, John
    Donne, Robert South-
    well, Sir Philip Sidney,
    and others).*
*Alexander Bain, 'Mental
    and Moral Science'.*
*Philip Stanhope Worsley
    and John Conington,
    trs. Iliad (W.'s share,
    bks. i–xii, previously in
    1865).*

Paul Claudel b.

Alcott, Louisa (1832): Good Wives. P

Arnold (1822): Collected Poems [incl. Rugby Chapel, now first pub.].
Culture and Anarchy. P

Beecher, Henry Ward (1813): Sermons.

Blackmore (1825): Lorna Doone. P

Browne (1834): Artemus Ward's Panorama. P

Clough (d. 1861): Poems and Prose Remains, with Selection from Letters, ed. by his Wife.

Ewing, Juliana Horatia (1841): Mrs. Overtheway's Remembrances. P

Forster (1812): Life of Landor. P

Galton, Sir Francis (1822): Hereditary Genius. P

'George Eliot' (1819): Agatha, a Poem.

Gilbert (1836): Bab Ballads. V

Guiccioli, Teresa: Recollections of Lord Byron [Eng. trs.; original French 1868]. P

Hawker, R. S. (1803): Cornish Ballads. V

Keble (d. 1866): Sermons on Baptismal Service. Miscellany Poems, ed. Moberley.

Lecky (1838): History of European Morals. P

'Lewis Carroll' (1832): Phantasmagoria. P

Lightfoot (1828): Apostolic Fathers, pt. i.

'Mark Twain' (1835): Innocents Abroad. P

Maurice (1805): Lectures on Social Morality. P

Mill (1806): On the Subjection of Women. P

Morris (1834): Earthly Paradise, vol. ii [see 1868]. V Trs. Grettir's Saga. P

'Owen Meredith' (1831): Orval, or the Fool of Time. V

Reade (1814): Foul Play [with Dion Boucicault: dramatic version produced in 1868, and in 1877 as Scuttled Ship]. P

Robinson, Henry Crabb (d. 1867): Diary (selections), ed. T. Sadler.

Ruskin (1819): Queen of the Air. P

Stubbs, William, and Haddan, A. W.: Ed. Councils and Ecclesiastical Documents of Great Britain and Ireland. P

Tennyson (1809): Holy Grail and Other Poems [New Arthurian poems: Holy Grail, Coming of Arthur, Pelleas and Ettarre, Passing of Arthur; non-Arthurian: Lucretius, Higher Pantheism, Northern Farmer (new style), &c.: see 1859, 1872].

Thornton, William Thomas (1813): On Labour. P

Trollope (1815): Phineas Finn. P

Wallace (1823): The Malay Archipelago. P

Laurence Binyon b.

Gandhi b.

Harleian Society founded.
'Nature' started.
'The Academy' started.
'The Graphic' started.

Thomas Arnold (jnr.), ed. of the English Works of Wycliffe (concl. 1871).

William Chappell, ed. of Roxburghe Ballads, vols. i–iii (1869–79); see 1883).

E. A. Abbott, 'Shakesperian Grammar' (new ed. 1897).

André Gide b.

Sainte-Beuve d.

Lamartine d.

Flaubert, 'Éducation sentimentale'.

President U.S.A.
Grant.

Aldrich, Thomas Bailey (1836): The Story of a Bad Boy. P

Arnold (1822): St. Paul and Protestantism. P

Austen-Leigh, James (1798): Memoir of Jane Austen [2nd ed., '71].

Barker,Lady(1831):Station Life in New Zealand. P

Church (1815): Life of St. Anselm [enlarg. from ed. of 1843]. P

Collins (1824): Man and Wife. P

Cox, George William (1827): Mythology of Aryan Nations. P

Dickens (d. 1870): Mystery of Edwin Drood [unfinished; monthly Apr.–Sept.]. P

Disraeli (1804): Lothair. P

Emerson (1803): Society and Solitude. P

Ewing, Juliana Horatia (1841): The Brownies. P

Gordon (1833): Bush Ballads and Galloping Rhymes. V

Grote, John (d. 1866): Utilitarian Philosophy. P

Harte (1836): The Luck of Roaring Camp, and Other Sketches. P

Hunt (d. 1859): A Day by the Fire, and other papers hitherto uncollected. P

Huxley (1825): Lay Sermons, Addresses, and Reviews. P

Keble (d. 1866): Letters of Spiritual Counsel. P

Lowell (1819): The Cathedral. V
Among my Books. P

Miller, Joaquin (1839): Pacific Poems. V

Milman (d. 1868): Savonarola, Erasmus, and other Essays, ed. A. Milman. P

Newman (1801): Grammar of Assent. P

O'Shaughnessy, Arthur (1844): An Epic of Women. V

Reade (1814): Put Yourself in His Place [originally in Cornhill, 1869–70; dramatic version, Free Labour, performed 1870]. P

Rossetti (1828): Poems [collected: new and altered ed. 1881].

Ruskin (1819): Lectures on Art. P

Spencer (1820): Principles of Psychology [concl. 1872]. P

Stanhope, Fifth Earl (1805): History of England, comprising the Reign of Queen Anne until the Peace of Utrecht. P

Stubbs (1825): Ed. Select Charters and other Illustrations of English Constitutional History. P

Swinburne (1837): Ode on Proclamation of French Republic. V

Wallace (1823): Natural Selection. P

Whymper (1840): Scrambles amongst the Alps. P

Franco - Prussian War, 1870–1.

Education Act.

Thomas Sturge Moore b.

Hilaire Belloc b.

Charles Dickens d.

Benjamin Jowett Master of Balliol.

W. D. Christie, ed. Dryden's Poetical Works.

Historical MSS. Commission's Reports begin.

Brewer's 'Dictionary of Phrase and Fable'.

Dumas d.

Mérimée d.

Jules de Goncourt d.

Lenin b.

Alcott, Louisa (1832): Little Men. P
Arnold (1822): Friendship's Garland. P
Austen (d. 1817): Lady Susan, The Watsons [in 2nd ed. of Memoir (by J. E. Austen Leigh). First ed. of Memoir in 1870]. P
Beecher, Henry Ward (1813): Life of Jesus. P
Black, William (1841): A Daughter of Heth. P
Browning (1812): Balaustion's Adventure. V
  Prince Hohenstiel-Schwangau. V
Burroughs, John (1837): Wake-Robin. P
Cooke, John Esten (1830): Life of Robert E. Lee. P
Darwin (1809): Descent of Man. P
Erskine, Thomas (d. 1870): The Spiritual Order. P
Freeman (1823): Historical Essays, series I [II 1873, III 1879, IV 1892]. P
Froude (1818): Short Studies on Great Subjects, series II [see 1867]. P
'George Eliot' (1819): Middlemarch [in parts]. P
Gilbert (1836): Pygmalion and Galatea [acted]. D
Hardy (1840): Desperate Remedies. P
Hare (1834): Walks in Rome. P
Hay, John (1838): Pike County Ballads. V
  Castilian Days. P
Howells (1837): Their Wedding Journey. P
Hutton, Richard Holt (1826): Essays. P
Jowett (1817): Trs. Dialogues of Plato. P
Kingsley (1813): At Last. P
Lear (1812): Nonsense Songs and Stories. V
'Lewis Carroll' (1832): Through the Looking Glass. P
Lewis, Leopold David (1828): The Bells [acted]. D
Longfellow (1807): The Divine Tragedy. D
Lowell (1819): My Study Windows. P
Lytton (1803): The Coming Race. P
Macdonald (1824): At the Back of the North Wind. P
Maine (1822): Village Communities. P
Marston, Philip Bourke (1850): Songtide. V
Maurice (1805): Moral and Metaphysical Philosophy [collective ed., concl. 1872]. P
Maxwell, James Clerk (1831): Theory of Heat. P
Meredith (1828): Harry Richmond. P
Miller, Joaquin (1839): Songs of the Sierras. V
Morris, Sir Lewis (1833): Songs of Two Worlds, series I [II 1874, III 1875]. V
Reade (1814): A Terrible Temptation. P
Ruskin (1819): Fors Clavigera [concl. 1887]. P
Stephen (1832): Playground of Europe. P
Swinburne (1837): Songs before Sunrise. V
Whitman (1819): Democratic Vistas. V
  Passage to India. V

Abolition of religious tests at Oxford, Cambridge, and Durham.
John Millington Synge b.
William Henry Davies b.
Erskine Childers b.
George Grote d.
Thomas William Robertson d.
Robert Buchanan ('Thomas Maitland') attacks Rossetti in article, 'Fleshly School of Poetry', in 'Contemporary Review', Oct. R.'s reply, 'Stealthy School of Criticism', in 'Athenaeum', 16 Dec.
Walter Skeat, 'Specimens of English from 1394 to 1597'.
F. J. Furnivall, ed. of Chaucer's Minor Poems (concl. 1879).
Bayard Taylor trs.'Faust'.
Horace Howard Furness, 'Variorum Shakespeare' (publication begun).
W. Elwin and W. J. Courthope, ed. of Pope (concl. 1889).
Marcel Proust b.
Paul Valéry b.
Zola, 'Les Rougon-Macquart' (1871–93).

Alcott, Amos Bronson (1799): Concord Days. P
Bagehot (1826): Physics and Politics. P
Besant and Rice: Ready-Money-Mortiboy. P
Black (1841): Strange Adventures of a Phaeton. P
Blackmore (1825): Maid of Sker. P
Browning (1812): Fifine at the Fair. V
Butler (1835): Erewhon. P
Calverley (1831): Fly Leaves. V
Cooper, Thomas (1805): Life, written by himself. P
Darwin (1809): Expression of the Emotions in Man and Animals. P.
De Morgan, Augustus (d. 1871): Budget of Paradoxes. P
Domett, Alfred (1811): Ranolf and Amohia. V
Forster (1812): Life of Dickens, vol. i [ii 1873, iii 1874]. P
Freeman (1823): English Constitution. P
Froude (1818): The English in Ireland [concl. 1874]. P
Hardy (1840): Under the Greenwood Tree. P
Hare (1834): Memorials of a Quiet Life. P
Holmes (1809): The Poet at the Breakfast-Table. P and V
Ingelow (1820): Off the Skelligs. P
Lang (1844): Ballads and Lyrics of Old France. V
Lear (1812): More Nonsense Songs. V
Liddon, Henry (1829): Some Elements of Religion. P
Longfellow (1807): Three Books of Song. V
Macdonald (1824): The Princess and the Goblin. P
'Mark Twain' (1835): Roughing It. P
Morley (1838): Voltaire. P
Morris (1834): Love is Enough: a Morality [1873]. V
Pusey (1800): University Sermons [collected].
Reade, William Winwood (1838): Martyrdom of Man. P
Ruskin (1819): Munera Pulveris. P
　Aratra Pentelici: Six Lectures on Sculpture. P
　Michael Angelo and Tintoret. P
　Eagle's Nest. P
Stanley, H. M. (1841): Finding of Livingstone. P
Swinburne (1837): Under the Microscope [reply to Buchanan's attack in 1871]. P
Tennyson (1809): Gareth and Lynette. V
　Poems, first collected, with Epilogue to the Queen [concl. 1873; cont. Idylls of the King, complete and in sequence: see 1859, 1869].

Bertrand Russell, Earl Russell b.
Max Beerbohm b.
Charles James Lever d.
Frederick Denison Maurice d.
'The Light Green', ed. Arthur Clement Hilton (two nos. only).
Eng. trs. of Taine's 'History of English Literature' (see 1863).
Richard Morris, 'Historical Outlines of English Accidence'.
William Blades, 'Shakespeare and Typography'.
James Gairdner, ed. Paston Letters, 1440–1486 (concl. 1875, revised 1901, 1904). .
Gautier d.
Calendar of Clarendon State Papers, vol. i, ed. Ogle and Bliss [ii–iii ed. Macray 1869–76, vol. iv ed. Routledge 1932: see 1767].
Grillparzer d.
Keller, 'Sieben Legenden'.
Nietzsche, 'Die Geburt der Tragödie'.

Aldrich (1836): Marjorie Daw. P
Arnold (1822): Literature and Dogma. P
Bagehot (1826): Lombard Street. P
Barker, Lady (1831): Station Amusements in New Zealand. P
Bridges (1844): Poems. V
Brown, O. M. (1855): Gabriel Denver. P
Brown, T. E. (1830): Betsy Lee [in Macmillan's Magazine, Apr.: see 1881]. V
Browning (1812): Red Cotton Nightcap Country. V
Butler (1835): Fair Haven. P
Collins (1824): New Magdalen. P
Cooper, Thomas (1805): Paradise of Martyrs. V
Dobson (1840): Vignettes in Rhyme.
Ewing, Juliana Horatia (1841): A Flatiron for a Farthing. P
Freeman (1823): Essays, series II [see 1871]. P
Grote (d. 1871): Minor Works, ed. A. Bain.
Hardy (1840): Pair of Blue Eyes. P
Harte (1836): Mrs. Skaggs's Husbands. P
Howells (1837): Chance Acquaintance. P
Lytton (1803): Kenelm Chillingly. P
   The Parisians. P
'Mark Twain' (1835): The Gilded Age. P
Martineau, J. (1805): Hymns of Praise and Power.
Max Müller (1823): The Science of Religion. P
Maxwell, James Clark (1831): Treatise on Electricity and Magnetism. P
Mill (d. 1873): Autobiography. P
Morley (1838): Rousseau. P
Myers (d. 1851): Catholic Thoughts [see 1834]. P
Pater (1839): Studies in the Renaissance. P
Spencer (1820): Study of Sociology. P
   The English [first instalment of Descriptive Sociology. Eight instalments during S.'s lifetime 1873–81]. P
Stephen, Sir James Fitzjames (1829): Liberty, Equality, Fraternity. P
Stephen, Sir Leslie (1832): Essays on Freethinking and Plain Speaking. P
Stubbs (1825): Constitutional History of England
Taylor, Meadows (1808): Confessions of a Thug. P
Thackeray, Anne Isabella (1837): Old Kensington. P
Timrod, Henry (d. 1867): Collected Poems. V
Trollope (1815): The Eustace Diamonds. P
Tyndall (1820): Lectures on Light. P
Wills, William Gorman (1828): Charles the First. D
Yonge (1823): The Pillars of the House. P

Walter de la Mare b.
H. M. Tomlinson b.
John Stuart Mill d.
Edward John Bulwer-Lytton, Lord Lytton, d.
Samuel Wilberforce d.
The New Shakspere Society founded by F. J. Furnivall.
George Bannatyne MS. pub. by Hunterian Club (concl. 1902).
Henry Morley, 'First Sketch of English Literature'.
Anna Swanwick, trs. Aeschylus.
Charles Péguy b.
Rimbaud, 'Une Saison en Enfer'.

President U.S.A. Grant (2nd term).

Adams, John Quincy (d. 1848): Memoirs. P
Aldrich, Thomas Bailey (1836): Prudence Palfrey. P
Black, William (1841): A Princess of Thule. P
Blackie, John Stuart (1809): On Self-Culture. P
Cairnes, John Elliot (1823): Political Economy. P
Cox, George William (1827): History of Greece. P
Ewing, Juliana (1841): Lob-lie-by-the-Fire. P
Farrar (1831): Life of Christ. P
Fiske, John (1842): Cosmic Philosophy. P
Frere (d. 1846): Collected Works, ed. Bartle Frere.
'George Eliot' (1819): Legend of Jubal, &c. V
Green (1837): Short History of the English People. P
Greville (d. 1865): Greville Memoirs, series I, 1817–37 [II 1885, III 1887].
Hardy (1840): Far from the Madding Crowd. P
Jevons, William Stanley (1835): Principles of Science. P
Lewes (1817): Foundations of a Creed [Series I of Problems of Life and Mind: see 1877, 1879].
'Marcus Clarke' (1846): For the Term of His Natural Life. P
Mill (d. 1873): Three Essays on Religion. P
Morley (1838): On Compromise. P
Motley, John Lothrop (1814): The Life and Death of John of Barneveld. P
O'Shaughnessy (1844): Music and Moonlight. V
'Ouida' (1839): Two Little Wooden Shoes. P
'Owen Meredith' (1831): Fables in Song. V
Parkman, Francis (1827): The Old Régime in Canada. P
Pusey (1800): Lenten Sermons. P
Ruskin (1819): Val d'Arno. P
Sidgwick (1838): Methods of Ethics. P
Smiles, Samuel (1812): Lives of the Engineers [collected]. P
Stephen (1832): Hours in a Library, series I [II 1876; III 1879; collected and enlarg. 1907]. P
Stubbs (1825): Memorials of St. Dunstan. P
Swinburne (1837): Bothwell, a Tragedy. D
  Ed. of George Chapman.
Taylor (1817): Lady Clancarty [acted]. D
Taylor, Colonel Meadows (1808): Tara. P
Thomson (1834): City of Dreadful Night [in National Reformer, Mar.–May; separately, with other poems, 1880]. V
Trollope (1815): Phineas Redux. P
Wordsworth, Dorothy (d. 1855): Recollections of a Tour in Scotland (1803), ed. Shairp. P

Maurice Baring b.
Gilbert Keith Chesterton b
Winston Spencer Churchill b.
Gertrude Stein b.
Bryan Waller Procter ('Barry Cornwall') d.
Sydney Dobell d.
Agnes Strickland d.
Oliver Madox Brown d.
'Illustrated Sporting and Dramatic News' (weekly).
'The World' (weekly).
W. M. Rossetti, ed. of Blake.
Henry Sweet, 'History of English Sounds'.
Guizot d.

Arnold (1822): God and the Bible. P

Blades, William (1824): Some Early Type Specimen Books. P

Browning (1812): Aristophanes' Apology. V
The Inn Album. V

Burroughs, John (1837): Winter Sunshine. P

Byron (1834): Our Boys [acted]. D

Carlyle (1795): Early Kings of Norway. Essay on Portraits of John Knox. P

Dobell (d. 1874): Collected Poetical Works.

Dowden, Edward (1843): Shakespeare: his Mind and Art. P

Eddy, Mary Baker (1821): Science and Health [often revised and reprinted]. P

Emerson (1803): Letters and Social Aims. P

Harte (1836): Tales of the Argonauts. P

Howells, W. Dean (1837): A Foregone Conclusion. P

Keble (d. 1866): Sermons for the Christian Year [concl. 1880].

Lightfoot (1828): Commentary on St. Paul's Epistle to the Colossians.

Longfellow (1807): The Masque of Pandora. V

Marston, Philip Bourke (1850): All in All. V

Martin (1816) **and Aytoun** (1813): Life of the Prince Consort [concl. 1880]. P

Meynell, Alice (1847): Preludes. V

Morris (1834): Trs. Aeneid of Virgil [1876]. V
Trs. Three Northern Love-Stories from Icelandic [with E. Magnússon]. P

Norton, Charles Eliot (1827): William Blake. P

Palgrave (1824): Children's Treasury. V

Pattison (1813): Isaac Casaubon. P

Peacock (d. 1866): Works ed. Sir Henry Cole (ed. Brett-Smith 1924–35).

Ruskin (1819): Mornings in Florence [in six separate parts, 1875–7; collected 1889]. P
Proserpina [in ten parts, 1875–86]. P
Deucalion [concl. 1883]. P

Scott, W. B. (1811): Poems: Ballads, Studies from Nature, Sonnets, &c.

Swinburne (1837): Essays and Studies [collected]. P
Songs of Two Nations [reprint of Song of Italy 1867 and Ode on French Republic 1870]. V

Symonds (1840): Renaissance in Italy [concl. 1886]. P

Tennyson (1809): Queen Mary. D

Trollope (1815): The Way we live now. D

Ward, Adolphus William: History of English Dramatic Literature [new ed. 1899].

Whyte-Melville (1821): Katerfelto. P

Charles Kingsley d.
Sir Charles Lyell d.
Sir Arthur Helps d.
Connop Thirlwall d.
George Finlay d.
'*Encyclopaedia Britannica*', 9th ed. (concl. 1889).
The Gilbert-Sullivan opera series starts with '*Trial by Jury*' *at the Royalty.*
Swinburne's attack on Robert Buchanan, entitled '*The Devil's Due*', *in* '*The Examiner*', 28 Dec. (see 1871–2).
Charles Cowden Clarke, ed. of Shakespeare (called Cassell's Shakespeare, 1886).
Edward Arber, ed. of '*Stationers' Register*', 1554–1660 (concl. 1894).
Henry Morley, '*Library of English Literature*' (concl. 1881).
Sir William Smith, '*Dictionary of Christian Antiquities*' (concl. 1880).
J. W. Ebsworth, ed. of '*Westminster Drollery*' *and* '*Merry Drollery*'.
Max Müller's series of '*Sacred Books of the East*' *commences.*
Eng. trs. of Ranke's '*History of England, principally in the Seventeenth Century*'.
A. B. Grosart, '*Occasional Issues of Unique and very rare Books*'.

Bentham (d. 1832): Theory of Legislation [trs. Fr. of Dumont by R. Hildreth: see 1802]. P

Besant and Rice : The Golden Butterfly. P

Bradley, F. H. (1846): Ethical Studies. P

Bridges (1844): The Growth of Love. V

Brooke, Stopford (1832): English Literature. P

Brown (d. 1874): Literary Remains, ed. W. M. Rossetti and F. Hueffer.

Browning, R. (1812): Pacchiarotto. V

Dobell (d. 1874): Collected Prose Works.

Ewing, Juliana Horatia (1841): Jan of the Windmill. P

FitzGerald (1809): Trs. Aeschylus' Agamemnon. V

Forster (d. 1876): Life of Swift. P

'George Eliot' (1819): Daniel Deronda. P

Gilbert (1836): Original Plays [coll. ; concl. 1911]. P

Hardy (1840): Hand of Ethelberta. P

Harte (1836): Gabriel Conroy. P

Haydon, Benjamin Robert (d. 1846): Correspondence and Table Talk, ed. his son.

Houghton (1809): Collected Works.

James (1843): Roderick Hudson. P

Landor (d. 1864): Works, ed. Forster.

Lanier, Sidney (1842): Florida. P

'Lewis Carroll' (1832): Hunting of the Snark. V

Mahony, Francis Sylvester (d. 1866): Final Reliques of Father Prout [see 1836]. P

'Mark Twain' (1835): Tom Sawyer. P

Melville (1819): Clarel. V

Meredith (1828): Beauchamp's Career. P

Milnes (Lord Houghton) (1809): Collected Works.

Morris (1834): Two Sides of the River. V
Sigurd the Volsung, and Fall of the Niblungs [1877]. V

Shelley (d. 1822): Daemon of the World, pt. ii, ed. H. B. Forman [pt. i pub. with Alastor, 1816]. V

Spencer (1820): Principles of Sociology, vol. i [ii 1882, iii 1896]. P

Stephen (1832): English Thought in the Eighteenth Century. P
Hours in a Library, series II [see 1874]. P

Swinburne (1837): Erechtheus, a Tragedy. V
Note on the Muscovite Crusade. P

Tennyson (1809): Harold [1877]. D

Thackeray (d. 1863): Orphan of Pimlico. P

Trevelyan (1838): Life of Macaulay. P

Trollope (1815): The Prime Minister. P

Tupper (1810): Proverbial Philosophy, series I–IV complete [see 1838]. V

Wallace (1823): Geographical Distribution of Animals. P

Wordsworth (d. 1850): Prose Works, first collected ed. A. B. Grosart [ed. W. Knight 1896].

George Macaulay Trevelyan b.

Harriet Martineau d.

Henry Kingsley d.

John Forster d.

'Mind' started.

Thomas Arnold (jnr.), ed. of 'Beowulf', with trs.

Henry Sweet, 'Anglo-Saxon Reader'.

J. W. Ebsworth, ed. of 'Bagford Ballads' (concl. 1878).

A. B. Grosart, 'Chertsey Worthies Library' (concl. 1881; reprts. of Nicholas Breton, John Davies of Hereford, Joshua Sylvester, Francis Quarles, Joseph Beaumont, Henry More, Abraham Cowley).

William Carew Hazlitt, 'Bibliographical Collections and Notes' (concl. 1904).

George Sand d.

Mallarmé, 'L'Après-midi d'un faune'.

Acton (1834): History of Freedom in Antiquity, and History of Freedom in Christianity [Bridgnorth Addresses]. P

Alcott, Amos Bronson (1799): Table-Talk. P

Aldrich, Thomas Bailey (1836): The Queen of Sheba. P

Arnold (1822): Collected Poems (revised). V
Last Essays on Church and Religion. P

Bradley (1846): Mr. Sidgwick's Hedonism. P

Browning, E. B. (d. 1861): Letters to Richard Hengist Horne, ed. Mayer.

Browning, R. (1812): Trs. Agamemnon of Aeschylus. V

Burnett, Frances Hodgson (1849): That Lass o' Lowrie's. P

Butler (1835): Life and Habit. P

Coleridge (d. 1834): Letters to J. P. Estlin, ed. Bright [concl. 1884].

Dobson (1840): Proverbs in Porcelain. V

Domett, Alfred (1811): Flotsam and Jetsam. P

Finlay (d. 1875): History of Greece from its Conquest by the Romans to the Present Time [collected ed.; see 1844–51–6–61]. P

Froude (1818): Short Studies on Great Subjects, series III [see 1867]. P

Green (1837): Hist. of the English People [concl. 1880; distinct from Short Hist. '74]. P

James (1843): The American. P

Keble (d. 1866): Occasional Papers, ed. Pusey.

Lewes (1817): Physical Basis of Mind [series II of Problems of Life and Mind: see 1874, 1879]. P

Lanier (1842): Poems.

Mallock, William Hurrell: New Republic. P

Manning, Henry Edward (1808): Miscellanies [concl. 1878].

Martineau (d. 1876): Autobiography. P

Meredith (1828): Idea of Comedy [in New Quarterly Magazine; separately 1897]. P

Morris, Sir Lewis (1833): Epic of Hades. V

Patmore (1823): The Unknown Eros and Other Poems.

Procter (d. 1874): Autobiographical Fragment, ed. C[oventry] P[atmore].

Sewell, Anna (1820): Black Beauty. P

Swinburne (1837): Charlotte Brontë. P
A Year's Letters [see 1905]. P

Thomson, Sir Charles Wyville (1830): Voyage of the Challenger. P

Trollope (1815): The American Senator. P

Russo - Turkish War, 1877–8.
Walter Bagehot d.
'Truth' (weekly) started.
'Nineteenth Century' started.
Edward Arber, 'English Garner' (concl. 1896).
Sir William Smith, 'Dictionary of Christian Biography' (concl. 1887).
George Long, trs. of Epictetus.
F. J. Furnivall, ed. of Shakespeare.
Ibsen, 'Pillars of Society'.
Flaubert, 'Trois Contes'.
Zola, 'L'Assommoir'.

President U.S.A. Hayes.

Acton (1834): Democracy in Europe [in Quarterly Review, Jan.]. P

Besant and Rice: By Celia's Arbour. P
  Monks of Thelema. P

Black, William (1841): Macleod of Dare. P

Browning (1812): La Saisiaz, Two Poets of Croisic. V

Cowden Clarke, Charles and Mary: Recollections of Writers. P

Dixon, Richard Watson (1833): History of the Church of England 1529–1570 [concl. 1902]. P

Green, Anna Katharine (1847): The Leavenworth Case. P

Hardy (1840): Return of the Native. P

Hatton, Christopher, Viscount Hatton (d. 1706): Correspondence of the Hatton family, 1601–1704, ed. E. M. Thompson.

James (1843): Watch and Ward. P

Jefferies (1848): Gamekeeper at Home. P

Keats (d. 1821): Letters to Fanny Brawne, ed. H. B. Forman.

Lecky (1838): History of England in the Eighteenth Century [concl. 1890]. P

Longfellow (1807): Keramos. V

Martin (1816): Trs. Poems and Ballads of Heine. V

Max Müller (1823): Origin and Growth of Religion. P

Morley (1838): Diderot and the Encyclopaedists. P

Seeley (1834): Life and Times of Stein. P

Senior, William Nassau: Conversations with Thiers, Guizot, and other Persons during the Second Empire. P

Stanley (1841): Through the Dark Continent. P

Stephen (1832): Samuel Johnson [English Men of Letters Series]. P

Stevenson (1850): An Inland Voyage. P

Swinburne (1837): Poems and Ballads, series II [see 1866, 1889]. P

Trelawny (1792): Records of Shelley, Byron, and the Author [see 1858]. P

Trollope (1815): Is he Popenjoy? P

Wallace, Alfred Russel: Tropical Nature. P

Walpole, Sir Spencer: History of England from 1815 [concl. 1886. A Continuation, History of Twenty-five Years (1856–80), 1904–8].

Whistler (1834): Whistler *vs.* Ruskin. P
  Art *vs.* Art Critics. P

John Masefield b.
Wilfrid Gibson b.
Edward Thomas b.
George Henry Lewes d.
George John Whyte-Melville d.
'English Men of Letters' series started.
Edward Arber, 'English Scholars' Library' (concl. 1884).
Matthew Arnold's selection 'Six Chief Lives' from Johnson's 'Lives of the Poets'.
Grove's 'Dictionary of Music' (completed 1889).

Adams, Henry (1838): Life of Albert Gallatin. P

Anson (1843): Law of Contract. P

Arnold, Edwin (1832): Light of Asia. V

Arnold (1822): Mixed Essays. P

Bagehot (d. 1877): Literary Studies, ed. R. H. Hutton [1878]. P

Balfour (1848): A Defence of Philosophic Doubt. P

Barnes (1801): Poems of Rural Life in the Dorset Dialect [collected; separately 1844–63].

Bridges (1844): Poems. V

Browning (1812): Dramatic Idyls, series I. V

Burroughs (1837): Locusts and Wild Honey. P

Butler (1835): Evolution, Old and New. P

Cable (1844): Old Creole Days. P

Church (1815): Spenser. P

Clifford (d. 1879): Lectures and Essays, ed. Leslie Stephen and F. Pollock. P

Fiske, John (1842): Darwinism and other Essays. P

Freeman (1823): Essays, series III [see 1871]. P

'George Eliot' (1819): Theophrastus Such. P

Gladstone (1809): Gleanings from Past Years. P

Hodgkin, Thomas (1831): Italy and her Invaders [concl. 1899]. P

Howells (1837): A Lady of the Aroostook. P

Huxley (1825): David Hume. P

James (1843): Daisy Miller. P
  The Europeans. P
  Madonna of the Future. P
  Hawthorne. P

Lang (1844) **and Butcher**: Trs. Odyssey. P

Lewes (d. 1878): Study of Psychology [series III of Problems of Life and Mind: see 1874–7]. P

Meredith (1828): The Egoist. P

Morley (1838): Edmund Burke. P

Morris, Sir Lewis (1833): Gwen. V

Pattison (1813): Milton. P

Sewall, Samuel (d. 1730): Diary. P

Sidgwick (1838): Outlines of the History of Ethics. P

Spencer (1820): Principles of Ethics [concl. 1893]. P

Stephen (1832): Hours in a Library, series III. P

Stevenson (1850): Travels with a Donkey in the Cevennes. P

Taylor (d. 1876): Ralph Darnell. P

Tennyson (1809): The Lover's Tale [privately prtd. 1833; pirated 1875]. V

Trollope (1815): Thackeray. P

Edward Morgan Forster b.

Harold Monro b.

. *Charles Jeremiah Wells d.*

William Kingdon Clifford d.

'*The Cambridge Review.*'

'*Boys' Own Paper*' *started.*

Walter Skeat, '*Etymological Dictionary of the English Language*' (*concl. 1882*).

Mr. and Mrs. Cowden Clarke, '*Shakespeare Key*'.

Stalin b.

. *Ibsen,* '*A Doll's House*'.

Adams, Henry (1838): Democracy. P

Aldrich, Thomas Bailey (1836): The Stillwater Tragedy. P

Bagehot (d. 1877): Biographical Studies and Economic Studies, ed. R. H. Hutton.

Baring-Gould, Sabine (1834): Mehalah. P

Black, William (1841): White Wings. P
Sunrise. P

Blunt (1840): Love Sonnets of Proteus. V

Bridges (1844): Poems, Third Series. V

Browning (1812): Dramatic Idyls, series II [see 1879]. V

Cable, George Washington (1844): The Grandissimes. P

Dickens (d. 1870): Speeches, ed. R. H. Shepherd. Letters, ed. G. Hogarth and M. Dickens.

Disraeli (1804): Endymion. P

Gissing (1857): Workers in the Dawn. P

Groome, Francis Hindes (1851): In Gypsy Tents. P

Hardy (1840): Trumpet Major. P

Harris, Joel Chandler (1848): Uncle Remus: his Songs and Sayings.

Lang (1844): XXII Ballades in Blue China. V
Trs. Theocritus, Bion and Moschus. P

Lanier, Sidney (1842): The Science of English Verse. P

Longfellow (1807): Ultima Thule. V

Macdonald (1824): The Diary of an Old Soul. V

'Mark Twain' (1835): A Tramp Abroad. P

Meredith (1828): The Tragic Comedians [in Fortnightly Review and separately]. P

Morris, Sir Lewis (1833): Ode of Life. V

Norton, Charles Eliot (1827): Church-building in the Middle Ages. P

Oliphant (1828): A Beleaguered City. P

'Ouida' (1839): Moths. P

Ruskin (1819): Arrows of the Chace. P
Elements of English Prosody. P

Shorthouse, Joseph Henry (1834): John Inglesant. P

Stephen (1832): Alexander Pope. P

Swinburne (1837): Studies in Song. V
Songs of the Springtides. V
Heptalogia [parodies]. V
Study of Shakespeare. P

Tennyson (1809): Ballads and Other Poems.

Trevelyan (1838): The Early History of Charles James Fox. P

Trollope (1815): The Duke's Children. P

Turner, Charles Tennyson (d. 1879): Collected Sonnets.

Wallace, Lewis (1827): Ben Hur. P

Webster, Augusta (1837): Disguises. D

John Freeman b.
Giles Lytton Strachey b.
Alfred Noyes b.
Mary Ann Cross ('*George Eliot*') *d.*
Tom Taylor d.
'*The Stage*' (*weekly*).
T. Humphry Ward, '*English Poets*' (*anthology: with Preface by Matthew Arnold*).
A. B. Grosart, ed. of Spenser (*concl. 1888*).
Sir Richard Francis Burton, trs. *Lusiads of Camoens* (*Commentary and Life of C. 1881; trs. Lyrics 1884*).
'*The Bulletin*' (*Sydney*) *started.*
Apollinaire b.
Flaubert d.
Maupassant, '*Contes*' (*1880–90*).

Alcott, Amos Bronson (1799): New Connecticut. V
Besant and Rice: Chaplain of the Fleet. P
Bible: Revised Version of the New Testament.
Wescott and Hort, Greek New Testament.
Brown, T. E. (1830): Fo'c'sle Yarns [Betsy Lee
(see 1873) and three other poems].
Butler (1835): Alps and Sanctuaries of Piedmont
and the Canton Ticino. P
Carlyle (d. 1881): Reminiscences, ed. J.A. Froude.
Conway, Moncure (1832): Thomas Carlyle. P
Cox, George William (1827): Introduction to
Science of Comparative Mythology. P
Fitch, Sir Joshua: Lectures on Teaching. P
Halliwell-Phillipps, J. O. (1820): Outlines of Life
of Shakespeare (enlarg. edd. 1882-3-4-7). P
Hardy (1840): A Laodicean. P
Hill, George Birkbeck (1835): Colonel Gordon in
Central Africa. P
James (1843): Portrait of a Lady. P
Jefferies (1848): Wood Magic. P
Lang (1844): XXXII Ballades in Blue China [see
1880]. V
'Mark Rutherford' (1831): Autobiography of
Mark Rutherford. P
Matthews, Brander (1852): French Dramatists of
the 19th Century. P
Morley (1838): Life of Richard Cobden. P
O'Shaughnessy (d. 1881): Songs of a Worker, ed.
Deacon. V
'Rolf Boldrewood' (1826): Robbery Under Arms
[serialized *Sydney Mail*: see 1888].
Romanes, George John (1848): Animal Intelli-
gence. P
Rossetti, C. (1830): A Pageant, and Other Poems. P
Rossetti, D. G. (1828): Ballads and Sonnets [Rose
Mary, White Ship, King's Tragedy, Bride's
Prelude, &c.]. V
Southey (d. 1843): Correspondence with Caroline
Bowles, ed. Dowden. P
Stevenson (1850): Virginibus Puerisque. P
Swinburne (1837): Mary Stuart, a Tragedy. D
Trollope (1815): Dr. Wortle's School. P
Ayala's Angel. P
Wilde (1856): Poems.

*Pelham Grenville Wode-
house b.
Lascelles Abercrombie b.
Thomas Carlyle d.
Benjamin Disraeli, Earl
of Beaconsfield, d.
George Borrow d.
Arthur Penrhyn Stanley
d.
Arthur O'Shaughnessy d.
'The Evening News'
(daily).
Browning and Wiclif So-
cieties founded by F. J.
Furnivall.
F. J. Furnivall, ed. of
Chaucer's 'Troilus'.
Matthew Arnold, ed. of
Burke's Letters,
Speeches, and Tracts
on Irish Affairs.
A. B. Grosart, 'Huth
Library' (concl. 1886;
reprts. of Robert Greene,
Thomas Nashe, Gabriel
Harvey, Thomas Dek-
ker's Prose Tracts,
Samuel Daniel).
A. Beljame, 'Le public et
les hommes de lettres en
Angleterre au dix-
huitième siècle'.
R. Martin du Gard b.
G. Vigfússon d.
F. York Powell's 'Corpus
Poeticum Boreale'.
Ibsen, 'Ghosts'.
Jowett, trs. Thucydides.
Flaubert, 'Bouvard et
Pécuchet'.
Verlaine, 'Sagesse'.*

*President U.S.A.
Garfield (assassi-
nated), Arthur*

Alcott, Amos Bronson (1799): Sonnets and Canzonets. V

'Anstey, F.' (1856): Vice Versa. P

Arnold (1822): Irish Essays and Others. P

Bancroft, George (1800): Formation of the Constitution of the United States. P

Besant, Sir Walter (1836): All Sorts and Conditions of Men. P

Caine, Hall (1853): Recollections of D. G. Rossetti. P

Carlyle '(d. 1881): Reminiscences of my Irish Journey in 1849, ed. J. A. Froude. P
Last Words of Carlyle, ed. J. C. Aitken. P

Crawford, Francis Marion (1854): Mr. Isaacs. P

Creighton, Mandell (1843): History of the Papacy during the Reformation [concl. 1894]. P

Dickens (d. 1870): Plays and Poems, ed. R. H. Shepherd [suppressed; new ed. 1885].

Dutt, Toru (d. 1877): Ancient Ballads and Legends of Hindustan.

Fox, Caroline (d. 1871): Journals. P

Froude (1818): History of First Forty Years of Carlyle's Life [see 1884]. P

Green (1837): The Making of England. P

Hardy (1840): Two on a Tower. P

Howells (1837): A Modern Instance. P

Jefferies (1848): Bevis, the Story of a Boy. P

Jones (1851): The Silver King. D

Lang (1844): Helen of Troy. V

Longfellow (d. 1882): In the Harbour. V

Morris (1834): Hopes and Fears for Art. P

Mozley, Thomas (1806): Reminiscences, chiefly of Oriel and the Oxford Movement. P

'Ouida' (1839): In Maremma. P

Saintsbury (1845): A Short History of French Literature. P

Scott, W. B. (1811): A Poet's Harvest Home [enlarg. 1893]. V

Seeley (1834): Natural Religion. P

Sharp (1855): Human Inheritance, New Hope, Motherhood. V
Dante Gabriel Rossetti: a Record and a Study. P

Shaw (1856): Cashel Byron's Profession. P

Stephen (1832): Swift. P Science of Ethics. P

Stevenson (1850): Familiar Studies of Men and Books. P
Treasure Island. P
New Arabian Nights. P

Swinburne (1837): Tristram of Lyonesse, and Other Poems.

Whitman (1819): Specimen Days in America. P

Martin Armstrong b.
John Drinkwater b.
James Joyce b.
James Stephens b.
Virginia Woolf b.
William Harrison Ainsworth d.
Charles Darwin d.
Ralph Waldo Emerson d.
William Stanley Jevons d.
Henry Wadsworth Longfellow d.
Edward Bouverie Pusey d.
Dante Gabriel Rossetti d.
James Thomson d.
Anthony Trollope d.
Oxford Historical Society.
A. H. Bullen, 'Collection of Old English Plays' (concl. 1885; new series 1887–90).
W. Knight, ed. Wordsworth (Poetry: see 1896).
Jean Giraudoux b.
Franklin D. Roosevelt b.
Becque, 'Les Corbeaux'.
Fontane, 'L'Adultera'.
Keller, 'Das Sinngedicht'.

Aitken (1851): Tribes on my Frontier. P
Aldrich, Thomas Bailey (1836): Mercedes. V
Bradley (1846): Principles of Logic. P
Bridges (1844): Prometheus the Firegiver. V
Browning (1812): Jocoseria. V
Burnett, Frances Hodgson (1849): Through One Administration. P
Carlyle, Jane Welsh (d. 1866): Letters and Memorials, prepared by Thomas Carlyle and ed. J. A. Froude [New Letters and Memorials, 1903]. P
Carlyle (d. 1881): Correspondence with Emerson. P
Carpenter (1844): Towards Democracy. V
Crawford, F. Marion (1854): Dr. Claudius. P
Dixon (1833): Mano. V
Drummond, Henry (1851): Natural Law in the Spiritual World. P
Ewing, Juliana H. (1841): Jackanapes. P
Froude (1818): Short Studies, series IV [see'67]. P
Galton (1822): Inquiries into Human Faculty. P
Gardiner (1829): History of England from the Accession of James I [rev. ed.: see 1886, 1895]. P
Green, J. R. (d. 1883): Conquest of England. P
Green, T. H. (d. 1882): Prolegomena to Ethics. P
Harris (1848): Nights with Uncle Remus. P
Jefferies (1848): Story of my Heart. P
Lang (1844), Leaf, Myers: Trs. Iliad [see 1879]. P
Lanier, Sidney (1842): The English Novel. P
'Lewis Carroll' (1832): Rhyme? and Reason? V
Longfellow (1807): Michael Angelo. D
Lytton (d. 1873): Life, Letters, &c.
MacDonald (1824): The Princess and Curdie. P
'Mark Twain' (1835): Life on the Mississippi. P
Marston, Philip Bourke (1850): Wind Voices. V
Meredith (1828): Poems and Lyrics of the Joy of Earth. V
Myers (1843): Essays: Classical and Modern. P
Pusey (d. 1882): Parochial & Cathedral Sermons. P
Schreiner, Olive (1855): The Story of an African Farm. P
Seeley (1834): Expansion of England. P
Shaw (1856): An Unsocial Socialist. P
Sidgwick (1838): Political Economy. P
Stephen, Sir James Fitzjames (1829): History of the Criminal Law of England. P
Stevenson (1850): Silverado Squatters. P
Swinburne (1837): A Century of Roundels. V
Trollope (d. 1882): Autobiography. P
Victoria, Queen (1819): More Leaves from a Journal [see 1868]. P

Edward FitzGerald d.
John Richard Green d.
'The Oxford Magazine.'
J. W. Ebsworth, ed. of Roxburghe Ballads, vols. iv–ix (concl. 1899: see 1869).
Sir Richard Jebb, ed. of Sophocles with Eng. trs. (concl. 1896).
H. B. Forman, ed. Keats's Poetical Works (enlarged 1889, 1901–2, 1906).
Henry Morley, 'Universal Library' (concl. 1888).
Dobson, 'Fielding' (English Men of Letters Series).
English and Scottish Popular Ballads, ed. Child (5 vols., concl. 1898).
Rusden, 'History of Australia'; 'History of New Zealand'.
Mussolini b.
Karl Marx d.
Wagner d.
Nietzsche, 'Also sprach Zarathustra'.
Leopold von Ranke, 'Weltgeschichte' (concl. 1888).

Austen Jane (d. 1817): Letters [see 1932].
Bible: Revised Version of the Old Testament.
Birrell (1850): Obiter Dicta [vols. 1887, 1924] P
Browning (1812): Ferishtah's Fancies. V
Cable, George Washington (1844): Creoles of Louisiana. P
Crawford, F. Marion (1854): Roman Singer. P
Croker, John Wilson (d. 1857): Memoirs, Diaries and Correspondence, ed. L. J. Jennings.
De Vere, A. T. (1814): Poetical Works.
Dixon (1833): Odes and Eclogues. V
Emerson (d. 1882): Lectures and Biographical Sketches. P
Ewing, Juliana H. (1841): Daddy Darwin's Dovecote. P
Froude (1818): Carlyle's Life in London [see '82]. P
'George Eliot' (d. 1880): Essays, and Leaves from a Note Book, ed. C. L. Lewes. P
Gissing (1857): The Unclassed. P
Howells, W. Dean (1837): Rise of Silas Lapham. P
James (1843): Tales of Three Cities. P
Jefferies (1848): Life of the Fields. P
Lang (1844): Custom and Myth. P
Lanier, Sidney (d. 1881): Poems. V
'Mark Twain' (1835): The Adventures of Huckleberry Finn. P
Matthews, Brander (1852): Margery's Lovers. P
Moore, George (1852): A Mummer's Wife. P
Parkman, Francis (1827): Montcalm and Wolfe. P
Rogers, J. E. Thorold (1823): Six Centuries of Work and Wages. P
Ruskin (1819): Art of England. P
Pleasures of England. P
Sharp (1855): Earth's Voices. V
Spencer (1820): Man versus the State. P
Stevenson (1850) and Henley (1849): Beau Austin. D
Admiral Guinea. D
Swinburne (1837): A Midsummer Holiday. Poems.
Symonds (1840): Wine, Women, and Song: trs. Medieval Latin students' songs. V
Tennyson (1809): The Cup, and The Falcon. D
Becket. D
Thomson (d. 1882): Voice from the Nile and Other Poems, with Memoir by B. Dobell. V
Satires and Profanities. P
The New Lucian. P
Ward (1851): Miss Bretherton. P

James Elroy Flecker b.
Sean O'Casey b.
Hugh Walpole b.
Sir John Collings Squire b.
Charles Reade d.
Richard Henry (or 'Hengist') Horne d.
Henry James Byron d.
Charles Stuart Calverley d.
Mark Pattison d.
'Oxford English Dictionary' (ed. Sir James Murray) begins to appear (completed 1928).
John Earle, 'Anglo-Saxon Literature'.
Fabian Society founded.
Georges Duhamel b.
Huysmans, 'A Rebours'.

Austin, Alfred (1835): At the Gate of the Convent. V

Arnold (1822): Discourses in America. P

Beecher, Henry Ward (1813): Evolution and Religion. P

Birrell (1850): Life of Charlotte Brontë. P

Bridges (1844): Nero [Part II, 1894]. D
Eros and Psyche [rev. 1894]. V

Burton, Sir Richard Francis (1821): Trs. Arabian Nights [privately prtd.; concl. 1888; rev. 'for household reading' 1887-8]. P

Clifford, William Kingdon (d. 1879): Common Sense of the Exact Sciences, ed. K. Pearson.

Crawford, F. Marion (1854): Zoroaster. P

Disraeli (d. 1881): Home Letters, 1830-1 [new ed. by Ralph Disraeli 1887].

Dobson (1840): At the Sign of the Lyre. V

Ewing, Juliana H. (d. 1885): The Story of a Short Life. P

Fargus, Frederick ('Hugh Conway') (d. 1885): Called Back. P

Fiske, John (1842): American Political Ideas. P

George Eliot' (d. 1880): Life, as related in Letters and Journals, ed. J. W. Cross. P

Gordon, Charles George (d. 1885): Journals at Khartoum. P

Green, T. H. (d. 1882): Works, ed. Nettleship [later vols. 1886, 1888]. P

Greville (d. 1865): Memoirs, series II, 1837-52 [see 1874, 1887]. P

Haggard, Rider (1856): King Solomon's Mines. P

Holmes (1809): A Mortal Antipathy. P

Hudson (1841): The Purple Land. P

Lang (1844): Rhymes à la Mode. V

Lightfoot (1828): Apostolic Fathers, pt. ii [Ignatius and Polycarp].

'Mark Rutherford' (1831): Mark Rutherford's Deliverance. P

Martineau (1805): Types of Ethical Theory. P

'Owen Meredith' (1831): Glenaveril. V

Meredith (1828): Diana of the Crossways [originally in Fortnightly Review 1884-5]. P

Morris (1834): Pilgrims of Hope [in The Commonweal, 1885-6; separately 1886]. V

Pater (1839): Marius the Epicurean. P

Powell, Frederick York, and Tout, T. F.: History of England [concl. 1898]. P

Ruskin (1819): On the Old Road [collection of essays, pamphlets, &c., 1834-85].
Praeterita [concl. 1889]. P

Stannard, Henrietta ('John Strange Winter') (1856): Bootles' Baby. P

David Herbert Lawrence b.
Ezra Pound b.
Richard Monckton Milnes,
Lord Houghton, d.
Fall of Khartoum.
'Dictionary of National Biography', 1st vol. (ed. Leslie Stephen 1882-91, Sidney Lee 1891 ff.).
'The Commonweal' (contrib. by Morris, &c.) started.
Scottish History Society founded.
Henry Sweet's 'Oldest English Texts'.
François Mauriac b.
Jules Romains b.
Victor Hugo d.
Zola, 'Germinal'.

President U.S.A. Cleveland.

Stevenson (1850): Prince Otto. P
   Child's Garden of Verses. V
   More New Arabian Nights, The Dynamiter. P
   Macaire [with William Ernest Henley]. D
Swinburne (1837): Marino Faliero, a Tragedy. D
Tennyson (1809): Tiresias and Other Poems.
Ward (1851): Trs. Amiel's Journal Intime. P
Whistler (1834): The Ten o'clock Lecture. P

1886

Alcott, Louisa (1832): Jo's Boys. P
Anson, Sir William (1843): Law and Custom of
   the Constitution [concl. 1892]. P
Burnett, Frances Hodgson (1849): Little Lord
   Fauntleroy. P
Corelli (1854): A Romance of Two Worlds. P
Disraeli (d. 1881): Correspondence with his sister,
   1832–52, ed. Ralph Disraeli.
Dobson (1840): Steele. P
Dowden, Edward (1843): Life of Shelley. P
Froude (1818): Oceana. P
Gardiner (1829): History of the Great Civil War
   [concl. 1891: see 1883, 1895]. P
Gissing (1857): Isabel Clarendon. P
   Demos. P
Hardy (1840): Mayor of Casterbridge. P
James (1843): The Bostonians. P
   Princess Casamassima. P
Kipling (1865): Departmental Ditties. V
Lawless, Emily: Hurrish. P
Maine (1822): Popular Government. P
Rossetti (d. 1882): Collected Works, ed. W. M.
   Rossetti. V and P
Stevenson (1850): Dr. Jekyll and Mr. Hyde. P
   Kidnapped. P
   The Merry Men and Other Tales. P
Stubbs (1825): Lectures on Study of History. P
Swinburne (1837): A Study of Victor Hugo. P
   Miscellanies. P
Symons, Arthur (1865): Introduction to Brown-
   ing. P
Tennyson (1809): Locksley Hall, sixty years after.
   Promise of May, and Other Poems. V
Ward, James (1843): Psychology. P

Lennox Robinson b.
Ronald Firbank b.
Siegfried Sassoon b.
Richard Chevenix Trench
   d.
Sir Henry Taylor d.
Shelley Society.
'Scribner's Magazine'
   started.
'English Historical Re-
   view' (ed. Mandell
   Creighton).
'Cassell's National Lib-
   rary' (ed. Henry Mor-
   ley; concl. 1890).
Frederic Gard Fleay,
   'Chronicle History of
   Life and Work of
   Shakespeare'.
A. H. Bullen, 'Lyrics from
   the Song Books of the
   Elizabethan Age'.
Alain-Fournier b.
Nietzsche, 'Jenseits von
   Gut und Böse'.

Blackmore (1825): Springhaven. P
Brown, T. E. (1830): The Doctor and Other Poems.
Browning (1812): Parleyings with Certain People. V
Butler (1835): Luck or Cunning. P
Caine (1853): The Deemster. P
Carlyle (d. 1881): Early Letters, ed. Norton. P
  Correspondence with Goethe, ed. Norton. P

Crawford, F. Marion (1854): Marzio's Crucifix. P
  Saracinesca. P
Darwin (d. 1882): Life and Letters, with Auto-
  biography, ed. F. Darwin. P
Dixon (1833): Lyrical Poems. P
Doyle, Arthur Conan (1859): A Study in Scarlet. P
Freeman, Mary Eleanor Wilkins (1852): A
  Humble Romance and Other Stories. P
Gissing (1857): Thyrza. P
Greville (d. 1865): Memoirs, series III, 1852-60
  [see 1874, 1885]. P
Haggard, Rider (1856): She. P
  Allan Quartermain. P
Hardy (1840): The Woodlanders. P
Holmes (1809): One Hundred Days in Europe. P
Jefferies (d. 1887): Amaryllis at the Fair. P
Jessopp, Augustus (1823): Arcady, for better for
  worse. P
Lang (1844): Myth, Ritual, and Religion [rev.
  1899]. P
  Trs. Aucassin and Nicolette. P
Laughton, Sir John Knox (1830): Studies in Naval
  History. P
Lowell (1819): Democracy and other Addresses. P
'Mark Rutherford' (1831): Revolution in Tanner's
  Lane. P
Meredith (1828): Ballads and Poems of Tragic
  Life. V
Morison, James Cotter (1832): Service of Man. P
Morris (1834): Trs. Odyssey. V
Pater (1839): Imaginary Portraits. P
Saintsbury (1845): Elizabethan Literature. P
Stevenson (1850): Underwoods. V
  Memories and Portraits. P
Swinburne (1837): Locrine, a Tragedy. D
  The Question. V
  Selections from Poems, made by himself. V
Thackeray (d. 1863): Letters, 1847-55, ed. Brook-
  field [see 1945]. P
  Sultan Stork and other Stories and Sketches. P

Rupert Brooke b.
Edwin Muir b.
Edith Sitwell b.
Richard Jefferies d.
Selden Society founded.
George Birkbeck Hill, ed.
  of Boswell's 'Life of
  Johnson' (revised L. F.
  Powell, 1934-50).
Henry Morley, 'English
  Writers' (recast from ed.
  of 1864-7; concl. 1895).
Robert William Lowe,
  'Bibliographical Ac-
  count of English
  Theatrical Literature'.
G.E.C.'s Complete Peer-
  age (concl. 1898).
Goncourt brothers, 'Jour-
  nal', 1851-95 (concl.
  1896).
Zola, 'La Terre'.

Allingham (1824): Poetical Works [concl. 1893].

Archer (1856): Masks and Faces. P

Arnold (d. 1888): Essays in Criticism, series II [see 1865].

Barrie (1860): Auld Licht Idylls. P

Bellamy, Edward (1850): Looking Backward. P

Black (1841): Strange Adventures of a House-Boat. P

Bosanquet (1848): Logic. P

Bryce (1838): American Commonwealth. P

Butler (1835): Ex Voto. P

Dobson (1840): Goldsmith. P

Doughty (1843): Travels in Arabia Deserta. P

Garnett, Richard (1835): Twilight of the Gods and Other Tales. P

Gissing (1857): A Life's Morning. P

Hardy (1840): Wessex Tales. P

Henley (1849): A Book of Verses.
Deacon Brodie [with R. L. Stevenson; privately prtd. 1880]. D

Holmes (1809): Over the Teacups (completed 1890). P

Hume (d. 1776): Letters to Strahan. P

James (1843): The Reverberator. P
Partial Portraits. P

Kipling (1865): Soldiers Three. P
Plain Tales from the Hills. P

Lang (1844): Grass of Parnassus. V

Lowell (1819): Heartsease and Rue. V
Political Essays. P

Meredith (1828): A Reading of Earth. V

Moore (1852): Confessions of a Young Man. P

Morris (1834): Dream of John Ball. P
Signs of Change [Seven Lectures]. P

Osborne, Dorothy, Lady Temple (d. 1695): Letters, ed. E. A. Parry [complete: see 1836, ed. G. C. Moore Smith 1928].

Quiller-Couch (1863): Troy Town. P

Rogers, J. E. Thorold (1823): Economic Interpretation of History. P

'Rolf Boldrewood' (1826): Robbery Under Arms. P

Sharp (1855): Romantic Ballads and Poems of Phantasy. V

Stevenson (1850): Black Arrow. P
Wrong Box [with Lloyd Osbourne]. P
Deacon Brodie [with W. E. Henley]. D

Ward (1851): Robert Elsmere. P

Wilde (1856): Happy Prince and Other Tales. P

Wordsworth (d. 1850): The Recluse. V

Yeats (1865): Fairy and Folk Tales of the Irish Peasantry. P

Joyce Cary b.
Thomas Stearns Eliot b.
T. E. Lawrence b.
'Katherine Mansfield' b.
Eugene O'Neill b.
Matthew Arnold d.
Sir Henry Maine d.
Edward Lear d.
'The Star' started.
Accession of Kaiser Wilhelm II.
Georges Bernanos b.
Barrès, 'Le Culte du Moi'
(1888–91).

Adams, Henry (1838): History of the United States of America. P
Alexander, Samuel (1859): Moral Order and Progress. P
Bancroft, George (1800): Marten van Buren. P
Barrie (1860): A Window in Thrums. P
Booth, Charles (1840): Life and Labour of the People in London (9 vols. 1889–97). P
Bridges (1844): The Feast of Bacchus. D
Brown, T. E. (1830): Manx Witch and Other Poems. P
Browning, E. B. (d. 1861): Poetical Works, ed. R. Browning [concl. 1890; ed. Kenyon 1897].
Browning, R. (d. 1889): Asolando. V
Burney (d. 1840): Early Diary, 1768–78, with Letters, ed. A. R. Ellis [see 1842].
Caird, Edward (1835): Critical Philosophy of Immanuel Kant. P
Carpenter (1844): Civilisation, Its Cause and Cure. P
Coleridge (d. 1834): Critical Annotations, ed. from marginal notes in books, W. F. Taylor. P
Davidson (1857): Scaramouch in Naxos. D
An Unhistorical Pastoral. D
A Romantic Farce. D
Doyle (1859): The Sign of Four. P
Field, Eugene (1850): Western Verse. V
Profitable Tales. P
FitzGerald (d. 1883): Collected Works, with Letters and Literary Remains, ed. W. A. Wright [another éd. 1902].
Galton (1822): Natural Inheritance. P
Gissing (1857): The Nether World. P
Jerome, Jerome K. (1859): Idle Thoughts of an Idle Fellow. P
Three Men in a Boat. P
Kipling (1865): From Sea to Sea. P
Lear (d. 1888): Nonsense Drolleries. V
Levy, Amy (d. 1889): A London Plane Tree. V
Reuben Sachs. P
'Lewis Carroll' (1832): Sylvie and Bruno [concl. 1893]. P
Mandeville, Sir John: Travels [first Eng. version derived from the Egerton MS.; pub. by Roxburghe Club: see 1499, 1725]. P
'Mark Twain' (1835): A Connecticut Yankee in King Arthur's Court. P
Martin (1816): Song of the Bell, and other trs. from German Poets. V
Meredith (1828): Sandra Belloni [see 1864]. P
Morris (1834): House of the Wolfings. P and V
Pater (1839): Appreciations. P
Patmore (1823): Principle in Art, &c. P
Robertson (d. 1871): Principal Dramatic Works.

W. J. Turner b.
John Middleton Murry b.
Philip Guedalla b.
Robert Browning d.
Martin Tupper d.
Edward Bradley ('Cuthbert Bede') d.
Gerard Manley Hopkins d.
William Wilkie Collins d.
William Allingham d.
Parnell Commission.
British Record Society founded.
'The Granta.'
'The Scots Observer' started by Henley.
David Masson, ed. of De Quincey.
A. H. Bullen, ed. Works of Thomas Campion.
William Archer's trs. of 'A Doll's House' acted.
Tolstoy,'Kreutzer Sonata'.
Adolf Hitler b.
Fontane, 'Irrungen, Wirrungen'.
Hauptmann, 'Vor Sonnenaufgang'.

President U.S.A.
Harrison.

Shaw (1856): Fabian Essays in Socialism [with Webb, Clarke, Olivier, Besant, & Bland]. P
Stevenson (1850): Master of Ballantrae. P
Swinburne (1837): Poems and Ballads, series III.
  A Study of Ben Jonson. P
Tennyson (1809): Demeter and Other Poems.
Yeats (1865): The Wanderings of Oisin. V

1890

Barrie (1860): My Lady Nicotine. P
Booth, William (1829): In Darkest England. P
Bridges (1844): Shorter Poems [additional vol. 1893]. Palicio. D. Return of Ulysses. D Christian Captives. D. Achilles in Scyros. D
Caine (1853): Bondman. P
Chesterfield (d. 1773): Letters to his Godson, ed. Lord Carnarvon [see 1774, 1777]. P
Crawford, F. Marion (1854): Cigarette-maker's Romance. P
Dickinson, Emily (d. 1886): Poems [2nd series 1891, 3rd series 1896].
Dobson (1840): Horace Walpole. P
Frazer, James George (1854): The Golden Bough, [enlarged 3rd ed. 1907–8, concl. 1915]. P
Gilbert (1836): Original Comic Operas [Sorcerer, H.M.S. Pinafore, Pirates of Penzance, Iolanthe, Patience, Princess Ida. Mikado. Trial by Jury, Ruddigore, Yeomen of the Guard, Gondoliers]. D
  Foggerty's Fairy and Other Tales. P
  Songs of a Savoyard [from the Savoy operas]. V
Gissing (1857): The Emancipated. P
Grundy, Sidney (1848): A Pair of Spectacles. D
Hake (1809): The New Day. V
Hawker, Mary ('Lanoe Falconer'): Mdlle Ixe. P
Henley (1849): Views and Reviews: Literature. P
James, Henry (1843): The Tragic Muse. P
James, William (1842): Principles of Psychology. P
'Mark Rutherford' (1831): Miriam's Schooling. P
Martineau, J. (1805): Authority in Religion. P
Morris (1834): Roots of the Mountains. P
  News from Nowhere [in The Commonweal; sep. 1891]. P
North (d. 1734): Lives of the Norths [Francis, Dudley, and John] with Letters, and Roger North's Autobiography [see 1742, 1744]. P
'Rolf Boldrewood' (1826): The Miner's Right. P
Scott (d. 1832): Journal [see 1939].
Stanley, H. M. (1841): In Darkest Africa. P
Stevenson (1850): Ballads.
Watson (1858): Wordsworth's Grave. V
Whistler (1834): The Gentle Art of Making Enemies. P

John Henry Newman d.
Richard William Church d.
William Bell Scott d.
John Westland Marston d.
William Morris founds the Kelmscott Press.
'Daily Graphic'.
'Review of Reviews'.
Frederick Gard Fleay, 'Chronicle History of London Stage' (see 1891).
Marshall, 'Principles of Economics'.
William James, 'Principles of Psychology'.
Fall of Bismarck.
Ibsen, 'Hedda Gabler'.
Keller d.
Stefan George, 'Hymnen'.
Holz and Schlaf, 'Die Familie Selicke'.

Bierce, Ambrose (1842): Tales of Soldiers and Civilians. P

Bàrrie (1860): The Little Minister. P

Browning (d. 1889): Life and Letters, by Mrs. S. Orr.

Church (d. 1890): Oxford Movement. P

Davidson (1857): In a Music Hall and Other Poems.

Dobson (1840): William Hogarth. P

Doyle (1859): Adventures of Sherlock Holmes. P

Field, Eugene (1850): Echoes from the Sabine Farm. V

Freeman, Mary Eleanor Wilkins (1852): A New England Nun, and Other Stories. P

Garland, Hamlin (1860): Main-Travelled Roads. P

Gissing (1857): New Grub Street. P

Hardy (1840): Group of Noble Dames. P
Tess of the d'Urbervilles. P

Henley (1849): Lyra Heroica. V

Howells (1837): Criticism and Fiction. P

'John Oliver Hobbes' (1867): Some Emotions and a Moral. P

Jones (1851): Saints and Sinners. D

Keats (d. 1821): Letters to his Family and Friends, ed. Sidney Colvin [see 1931].

Kipling (1865): Life's Handicap. P
The Light that Failed. P

Meredith (1828): One of our Conquerors. P

Moore (1852): Impressions and Opinions. P

Morris (1834): Poems by the Way.
Story of the Glittering Plain. P
The Saga Library, ed. Morris and E. Magnússon [concl. 1895].

Pinero (1855): The Times. D
Lady Bountiful. D.   The Profligate. D

Schreiner (1855): Dreams. P

Shaw (1856): Quintessence of Ibsenism. P

Sidgwick (1838): Elements of Politics. P

Stephen, James Kenneth (1859): Quo Musa Tendis. V
Lapsus Calami. V

Wilde (1856): Lord Arthur Savile's Crime, and Other Stories. P
A House of Pomegranates. P
Picture of Dorian Gray [Preface separately in Fortnightly Review, Mar.]. P
Intentions [essays collected from reviews]. P

Alexander William Kinglake d.

Edward Robert Bulwer, Earl Lytton ('Owen Meredith') d.

James Russell Lowell d.

Herman Melville d.

F. G. Fleay, 'Biographical Chronicle of English Drama' (see 1890).

'Oxford Poets' ed. of Shakespeare (1st of the series).

'Life and Times of Anthony Wood,' ed. Andrew Clark (completed 1900).

The Chace Act makes it possible for foreigners to obtain copyright in the United States on condition of printing there.

Rimbaud d.

Huysmans, 'Là-bas'.

George, 'Pilgerfahrten'.

Hauptmann, 'Einsame Menschen'.

Wedekind, 'Frühlings Erwachen'.

Ivy Compton-Burnett b.
Edward Shanks b.
Victoria Sackville-West b.
Osbert Sitwell b.
Stella Benson b.
David Garnett b.
Lord Tennyson d.
Edward Augustus Freeman d.
Sir Richard Owen d.
London   Bibliographical Society founded.
G. Birkbeck Hill, ed. of Johnson's Letters.
E. Dowden, ed. of Wordsworth (poetry).
C. Plummer, ed. of 'Anglo-Saxon Chronicle'.
Henry Sweet, 'A New English Grammar'.
English trs. of 'Peer Gynt'.
Eng. trs. of Zola.
Renan d.
Maeterlinck, 'Pelléas et Mélisande'.
George, 'Algabal'; 'Blätter für die Kunst'.
Hauptmann, 'Die Weber'.
Hofmannsthal, 'Der Tod des Tizian'.
'Swanee Review' started.

Bierce, Ambrose (1842): Black Beetles in Amber. P

Birrell (1850): Res Judicatae. P

Bosanquet (1848): History of Aesthetic. P

Conway, Moncure (1832): Life of Thomas Paine. P

Dobson (1840): Eighteenth Century Vignettes [concl. 1896; other volumes of a similar character.] P

Du Maurier (1834): Peter Ibbetson [1891]. P

Field, Eugène (1850): With Trumpet and Drum. V

Freeman (d. 1892): Essays, IV series [see 1871]. P

Gissing (1857): Born in Exile. P
Denzil Quarrier. P

Harris (1848): Uncle Remus and his Friends. P

Henley (1849): Song of the Sword and Other Verses [incl. London Voluntaries which became the title of the 2nd ed., enlarg., 1893].
Views and Reviews: Art [see 1890]. P

Hudson (1841): A Naturalist in La Plata. P

James (1843): The Lesson of the Master. P

Kipling (1865): Barrack-Room Ballads. V
(with **W. Balestier**): The Naulahka. P

Max Müller (1823): Anthropological Religion. P

'Owen Meredith' (d. 1891): King Poppy [privately prtd. 1875]. V

Pinero (1855): Cabinet Minister. D
Hobby Horse. D

Ritchie, Mrs. Anne (1837): Records of Tennyson, Ruskin, and the Brownings. P

Romanes (1848): Darwin and after Darwin. P

Severn, Joseph (d. 1879): Life and Letters, ed. William Sharp.

Stevenson (1850): The Wrecker [with Lloyd Osbourne]. P.   Across the Plains. P

Swinburne (1837): The Sisters, a Tragedy. D

Tennyson (d. 1892): The Foresters. D
Death of Œnone, Akbar's Dream, and other poems.

Ward (1851): History of David Grieve. P

Watson (1858): Lachrymae Musarum. V

Whymper, Edward (1840): Travels amongst the Great Andes of the Equator. P

Williams, Isaac (d. 1865): Autobiography, ed. Sir George Prevost.

Yeats (1865): Countess Kathleen. V
Ed. Irish Fairy Tales.

Zangwill, Israel (1864): Children of the Ghetto. P

Benson, E. F. (1867): Dodo. P
Bierce, Ambrose (1842): Can Such Things be. P
Bradley (1846): Appearance and Reality. P
Bridges (1844): Milton's Prosody [originally two essays printed '87, '89; enlarged 1901]. P
   Humours of the Court. D
Brown, T. E. (1830): Old John. V
Carman, Bliss (1861): Low Tide on Grand Pré. V
Corelli (1854): Barabbas. P
Crackanthorpe, Hubert: Wreckage. P
Davidson (1857): Fleet Street Eclogues. V
De Tabley, John, Lord (1835): Poems, Dramatic and Lyrical [concl. 1895].
Doyle (1859): Memoirs of Sherlock Holmes. P
Emerson (d. 1882): Natural History of Intellect. P
Gissing (1857): The Odd Women. P
Grahame (1859): Pagan Papers. P
Grand, Sarah (1862): The Heavenly Twins. P
Hopkins (d. 1889): in Poets and Poetry of the Century, ed. Bridges.
Hort (d. 1892): The Way, the Truth, and the Life. P
Hudson (1841): Idle Days in Patagonia. P
Huxley (1825): Collected Essays [concl. 1894]. P
James (1843): The Private Life. P
Jones (1851): The Crusaders. D
Kipling (1865): Many Inventions. P
Liddon, Henry Parry (d. 1890): Life of Pusey.
Lowell (d. 1891): Letters. P
'Mark Rutherford' (1831): Catharine Furze. P
Matthews, Brander (1852): The Decision of the Court. D
Meynell (1847): Poems. V
Pater (1839): Plato and Platonism. P
Patmore (1823): Religio Poetæ. P
Pinero (1855): Dandy Dick. D
   Sweet Lavender. D
Smith, Goldwin (1823): The United States. P
Stevenson (1850): A Footnote to History. P
   Island Nights' Entertainments. P
   Catriona [sequel to Kidnapped 1886]. P
Thompson (1859): Poems [Hound of Heaven, Love in Dian's Lap, &c.].
Weyman (1855): A Gentleman of France. P
Wilde (1856): Lady Windermere's Fan. D
   Salomé [in original French in Paris: see '94]. D
Yeats (1865): Celtic Twilight. P
   Ed. Blake [with E. J. Ellis].

Robert Nichols b.
John Tyndall d.
Benjamin Jowett d.
John Addington Symonds d.
'*Westminster Gazette.*'
Bibliographical Society's 'Transactions', 1st vol.
Ibsen, 'The Master Builder' acted in England.
Taine d.
Guy de Maupassant d.
Hauptmann, 'Hannele'.
Hofmannsthal, 'Der Torr und der Tod'.

President U.S.A.
  Cleveland (2nd term).

Austin (1835): The Garden that I Love. P

Blackmore (1825): Perlycross. P

Blatchford, Robert (1851): Merrie England. P

Carman, Bliss (1861): Songs from Vagabondia [2nd series 1896].

Davidson (1857): Ballads and Songs.
Plays Collected [Bruce 1886, Smith 1888, An Unhistorical Pastoral 1889, A Romantic Farce 1889, Scaramouch in Naxos 1889].

Dickinson, Emily (d. 1886): Letters.

Du Maurier (1834): Trilby. P

Freeman, Mary Eleanor (1852): Pembroke. P

Froude (d. 1894): Life and Letters of Erasmus. P

Gissing (1857): In the Year of Jubilee. P

Grossmith, George (1847) and **Weedon** (1854): The Diary of a Nobody. P

Hake (1809): Poems, selected by Alice Meynell.

Hardy (1840): Life's Little Ironies. P

Hearn (1850): Glimpses of Unfamiliar Japan. P

'Hope, Anthony' (1863): The Prisoner of Zenda. P
The Dolly Dialogues. P

Jones (1851): Judah. D

Kipling (1865): Jungle Book. P

Lincoln (d. 1865): Complete Works. P

'Mark Twain' (1835): The Tragedy of Pudd'n Head Wilson and the Comedy. P

Meredith (1828): Lord Ormont and his Aminta. P

Moore (1852): Esther Waters. P

More, Paul Elmer (1864): The Great Refusal. P

Morris (1834): Wood beyond the World. P

Pater (d. 1894): The Child in the House. P

Pinero (1855): The Weaker Sex. D
The Schoolmistress. D

Raleigh (1861): The English Novel. P

Russell (Æ.; 1867): Homeward, Songs by the Way.

Steel, Flora Annie (1847): The Potter's Thumb. P

Stevenson (d. 1894): The Ebb-Tide [with Lloyd Osbourne]. P. Collected Works, ed. Colvin [concl. 1898; ed. Gosse 1905–7].

Swinburne (1837): Astrophel and Other Poems. Studies in Prose and Poetry. P

Thackeray (d. 1863): Loose Sketches, An Eastern Adventure [contributions to The Britannia 1841 and Punch's Pocket Book 1847].

Ward (1851): Marcella. P

Watson (1858): Odes and Other Poems.

Weyman (1855): Under the Red Robe. P

Wilde (1856): A Woman of no Importance. D
Salomé; Eng. trs. by Lord Alfred Douglas, and illustr. by Aubrey Beardsley [see 1893]. D
The Sphinx. V

Yeats (1865): Land of Heart's Desire. D

Aldous Huxley b.

Robert Louis Stevenson d.

James Anthony Froude d.

Walter Pater d.

Christina Rossetti d.

George John Romanes d.

Oliver Wendell Holmes d.

Walter Skeat ed. Complete Works of Chaucer.

Aubrey Beardsley and others, 'Yellow Book'.

John Bartlett, 'Concordance to Shakespeare's Plays and Poems'.

Israel Gollancz, 'Temple Shakespeare'.

Dreyfus Trial.

English translation of Maeterlinck.

Sidney and Beatrice Webb, 'History of Trade Unionism'.

Bateson, 'Study of Variation'.

M. Halbe, 'Jugend'.

Acton (1834): Lecture on Study of History.
Allen, Grant (1848): The Woman who did. P
Arnold (d. 1888): Letters, ed. G. W. E. Russell.
Balfour (1848): The Foundations of Belief. P
Barrie (1860): Sentimental Tommy. P
Bridges (1844): Essay on Keats. P
Carman, Bliss (1861): Behind the Arras. V
Coleridge (d. 1834): Letters, 1785–1834, ed. E. H. Coleridge. P

Anima Poetae, ed. E. H. Coleridge. P
Conrad (1857): Almayer's Folly. P
Corelli (1854): The Sorrows of Satan. P
Crackanthorpe, Hubert: Sentimental Studies. P
Crane (1871): The Red Badge of Courage. P
Froude (d. 1894): English Seamen in the Sixteenth Century. P
Gardiner (1829): History of Commonwealth and Protectorate [concl. 1901: see '83, '86]. P
Gissing (1857): Eve's Ransom. P
Paying Guest. P.   Sleeping Fires. P
Grahame (1859): The Golden Age. P
Hardy (1840): Jude the Obscure. P
Harris, Frank (1856): Elder Conklin. P
Hearn (1850): Out of the East. P
Holmes (d. 1894): Complete Poetical Works.
James (1843): The Reprobate. P   Terminations. P
Johnson (1867): Poems.
Kipling (1865): Second Jungle Book. P
Maitland (1850): History of English Law before Edward I [with Sir Frederick Pollock]. P
Mathews, Brander (1852): Books and Playbooks. P
His Father's Son. P
Meredith (1828): The Amazing Marriage. P
Moore (1852): Celibates. P
Morris (1834): Child Christopher and Goldilind the Fair. P   Trs. Beowulf. P
Pater (d. 1894): Greek Studies. P
Miscellaneous Studies. P
Paterson (1864): The Man from Snowy River.   V
Patmore (1823): Rod, Root, and Flower. P
Pinero (1855): The Notorious Mrs. Ebbsmith. D
The Second Mrs. Tanqueray. D
The Amazons. D
Rossetti (d. 1882): Family Letters, with Memoir by W. M. Rossetti.
Stevenson (d. 1894): Vailima Letters. P
Thompson, Francis (1859): Sister Songs.
Thomson, James (d. 1882): Poetical Works.
Ward (1851): Bessie Costrell. P
Wells (1866): Time Machine. P
Yeats (1865): Poems.

Robert Graves b.
Thomas Henry Huxley d.
Sir John Seeley d.
Thomas Gordon Hake d.
S. H. Butcher, ed. Aristotle's 'Poetics' with Trs.
W. J. Courthope, 'History of English Poetry' (concl. 1905).
W. R. Nicoll and T. J. Wise, 'Literary Anecdotes of the 19th Century'.
John Horace Round, 'Feudal England'.
Rashdall, 'The Universities of Europe in the Middle Ages' (revised, Powicke and Emden, 1936).
George, 'Das Buch der Hirten'.
Hauptmann, 'Florian Geyer'.
Wedekind, 'Erdgeist'.

Barrie (1860): Margaret Ogilvie. P
Beerbohm (1872): Works of Max Beerbohm. P
Belloc (1870): A Bad Child's Book of Beasts. V
Browning (d. 1889): Collected Works, ed. Birrell
    and Kenyon [Centenary ed. 1912 ff.].
Burroughs, John (1837): Whitman, a Study. P
Carpenter (1844): Love's Coming of Age. P
Coleridge, Mary (1861): Fancy's Following. V
Conrad (1857): An Outcast of the Islands. P
Corelli (1854): The Mighty Atom. P
Davidson (1857): Fleet Street Eclogues. V
Dickinson, G. L. (1861): The Greek View of Life. P
Dolling, Robert (1851): Ten Years in a Ports-
    mouth Slum. P
'Fiona Macleod' (1855): Green Fire. P
    From the Hills of Dreams. V
Froude (d. 1894): Council of Trent. P
Hearn (1850): Gleanings in Buddha Fields. P
Housman, A. E. (1859): A Shropshire Lad. V
Jacobs, W. W. (1863): Many Cargoes. P
James (1843): Embarrassments. P
    The Other House. P
Jones (1851): Michael and his Lost Angel. D
Kipling (1865): The Seven Seas. V
Lawson (1867): In the Days When the World
    Was Wide. V   While the Billy Boils. P
Lecky (1838): Democracy and Liberty. P
M'Taggart, John M'T. Ellis (1866): Studies in
    Hegelian Dialectic. P
'Mark Rutherford' (1831): Clara Hopgood. P
'Mark Twain' (1835): Personal Recollections of
    Joan of Arc. P
Meynell (1847): The Colour of Life. P
Morris (d. 1896): Well at the World's End. P
    Trs. Old French Romances. P
    Ed. Kelmscott Chaucer.
Pater (d. 1894): Gaston de Latour. P
Pinero (1855): Benefit of the Doubt. D
Romanes (d. 1894): Thoughts on Religion. P
Rossetti, C. (d. 1894): Poems, Unpublished or
    Uncollected, ed. W. M. Rossetti.
Stevenson (d. 1894): Weir of Hermiston. P
    Fables [in a new ed. of Jekyll and Hyde]. P
    Songs of Travel. V
Stout, G. F. (1860): Analytic Psychology. P
Swinburne (1837): Tale of Balen. V
Ward (1851): Sir George Tressady. P
Wells (1866): Island of Dr. Moreau. P
    Wheels of Chance. P
Wilson, Woodrow (1856): Mere Literature and
    Other Essays. P

Edmund Blunden b.
William Morris d.
Coventry Patmore d.
Thomas Hughes d.
George Du Maurier d.
*Alfred Austin poet-lau-
    reate.*
'Savoy' (8 numbers).
The 'Daily Mail' started.
*W. Knight, ed. of Words-
    worth (Prose and
    Poetry).*
*J. B. Bury, ed. Gibbon's
    'Decline and Fall', com-
    pleted 1900.*
'Temple Classics' started.
André Breton b.
Montherlant b.
Edmond de Goncourt d.
Verlaine d.
*Hauptmann, 'Die Ver-
    sunkene Glocke'.*
Schnitzler, 'Liebelei'.
*Legouis, 'La Jeunesse de
    William Wordsworth'.*

Beerbohm (1872): The Happy Hypocrite. P
Bellamy, Edward (1850): Equality. P
Browning, E. B. (d. 1861): Letters, ed. F. G. Kenyon.
Butler (1835): The Authoress of the Odyssey. P
Caine (1853): The Christian. P
Carman, Bliss (1861): Ballads of Lost Haven. V
Coleridge, Mary (1861): King with Two Faces. P
Conrad (1857): Nigger of the Narcissus. P
Cooper, E. H. (1867): Mr. Blake of Newmarket. P
Cory (d. 1892): Letters and Journals. P
Davidson (1857): New Ballads. V
Dowson (1867): Pierrot of the Minute. D
Du Maurier (d. 1896): The Martian. P
Ellis, Havelock (1859): Studies in Psychology of
  Sex, vol. i [5 more vols. concl. 1910].
Gissing (1857): The Whirlpool. P
Grant Duff, Sir Mountstuart Elphinstone (1829):
  Notes from a Diary [contd. 1898–1905].
Hardy (1840): The Well-Beloved. P
James, Henry (1843): What Maisie Knew. P
  The Spoils of Poynton. P
James, William (1842): The Will to Believe. P
'John Oliver Hobbes' (1867): School for Saints. P
Jones (1851): The Case of Rebellious Susan. D
Ker (1855): Epic and Romance. P
Kipling (1865): Captains Courageous. P
Maugham (1874): Liza of Lambeth. P
Meredith (1828): Essay on Comedy. P
Meynell (1847): Flower of the Mind [selections]. V
Morris (d. 1896): Water of the Wondrous Isles. P
Newbolt (1862): Admirals All. V
Raleigh (1861): Style. P
Robinson, Edwin Arlington (1869): The Children
  of the Night. V
Rossetti (d. 1882): Letters to William Allingham,
  ed. G. Birkbeck Hill.
Russell ('Æ.'; 1867): Earth Breath. V
Schreiner (1855): Trooper Peter Halket of Mash-
  onaland. P
Steel, Flora Annie (1847): On the Face of the
  Waters. P
Stevenson (d. 1894): St. Ives [completed by A. T.
  Quiller Couch]. P
Tennyson, Hallam: Alfred Tennyson: a Memoir. P
Thompson (1859): New Poems.
Tyrrell, George (1861): Nova et Vetera. P
Voynich, Mrs. E. L. (1864): The Gadfly. P
Ward, Wilfrid Philip (1856): Life and Times of
  Cardinal Wiseman. P
Watts-Dunton (1832): Coming of Love. V
Wells (1866): Invisible Man. P
  Plattner Story. P

Jean Ingelow d.
Thomas Edward Brown d.
Margaret Oliphant d.
*Francis Turner Palgrave
  d.*
'*Country Life*' (*weekly*).
*G. Birkbeck Hill, ed. of
  Johnsonian Miscella-
  nies.*
*Sidney and Beatrice Webb,
  'Industrial Demo-
  cracy'.*
*Gide, 'Nourritures ter-
  restres'.*
*Rostand, 'Cyrano de Ber-
  gerac'.*

*President U.S.A.
McKinley.*

Wordsworth, Dorothy (d. 1855): Journals, ed.
    W. Knight
Yeats (1865): Secret Rose. P. Tables of the Law.
    P.   Adoration of the Magi. P

1898

Bridges (1844): Poetical Works [completed in
    6 vols. 1905: enlarged ed. in 7 vols. 1912].
Carman, Bliss (1861): By the Aurelian Wall. V
Churchill, Winston (1871): The Celebrity. P
Conrad (1857): Tales of Unrest. P
Dunne, Finlay Peter (1867): Mr. Dooley in Peace
    and War. P
'Elizabeth': Elizabeth and her German Garden. P
Gissing (1857): Human Odds and Ends. P
    The Town Traveller. P. Charles Dickens. P
Grahame (1859): Dream Days. P
Hardy (1840): Wessex Poems.
Hewlett (1861): Forest Lovers. P
Hodgson, Shadworth Hollway (1832): Metaphysic
    of Experience. P
'Hope, Anthony' (1863): Rupert of Hentzau. P
Huxley (d. 1895): Scientific Memoirs, ed. Foster
    and Lankester [concl. 1903].
James (1843): In the Cage. P. The Two Magics. P
Jones (1851): The Rogue's Comedy. D
    The Tempter. D
Kipling (1865): The Day's Work. P
Lee, Sidney (1859): Life of Shakespeare. P
Maitland (1850): Roman Canon Law in the
    Church of England. P
    Township and Borough. P
Meynell (1847): The Spirit of Place. P
Morris (d. 1896): The Sundering Flood. P
Newbolt (1862): The Island Race. V
Phillips (1864): Poems.
Phillpotts, Eden (1862): The Children of the Mist. P
Saintsbury (1845): A Short History of English
    Literature. P
Shaw (1856): Plays Pleasant and Unpleasant
    [vol. i, Unpleasant: Widower's Houses, Phi-
    landerer, Mrs. Warren's Profession; vol. ii,
    Pleasant: Arms and the Man, Candida, Man
    of Destiny, You Never can Tell].
    The Perfect Wagnerite. P
Sidgwick (1838): Practical Ethics. P
Tyrrell, George (1861): Hard Sayings. P
Ward (1851): Helbeck of Bannisdale. P
Watson (1858): Collected Poems.
Watts-Dunton (1832): Aylwin. P
Wells (1866): War of the Worlds. P
Wilde (1856): Ballad of Reading Gaol. V

Ernest Hemingway b.
William Ewart Glad-
    stone d.
Charles Lutwidge Dodgson
    ('Lewis Carroll') d.
William Black d.
'Harmsworth's Magazine'.
Byron's Works and Letters,
    ed. Coleridge and Pro-
    thero (completed 1904).
Oxford Classical Texts
    begun.
Mallarmé d.
Fontane d.
George, 'Das Jahr der
    Seele'.
Bismarck, 'Gedanken und
    Erinnerungen'.

Bierce, Ambrose (1842): Fantastic Fables. P
Beerbohm (1872): More. P
Bosanquet (1848): Theory of the State. P
Browning, E. B. (d. 1861) and R. (d. 1889): Love-Letters, 1845–6, ed. F. G. Kenyon.
Churchill, Winston (1871): Richard Carvel. P
Churchill, Winston S. (1874): The River War. P
Davidson (1857): The Last Ballad. V
Dunne, Finlay Peter (1867): Mr. Dooley in the Hearts of his Countrymen. P
'Elizabeth': The Solitary Summer. P
'Fiona Macleod' (1855): Dominion of Dreams. V
Firth, Sir Charles (1857): The Protectorate. P
Gissing (1857): Crown of Life. P
Henley (1849): Hawthorn and Lavender. V
Hewlett (1861): Little Novels of Italy. P
Hornung (1866): The Amateur Cracksman [other Raffles books, 1901, '05, '09].
Inge (1860): Christian Mysticism. P
James, Henry (1843): The Awkward Age. P
James, William (1842): Talks on Psychology. P
Jones (1851): The Physician. D.
　　Triumph of the Philistines. D.
Kipling (1865): Stalky & Co. P
Lanier, Sidney (d. 1887): Letters.
Mackail, J. W. (1859): Life of William Morris. P
Nesbit (1858): The Treasure-Seekers. P
Norris, Frank (1870): McTeague. P
Norton, Charles Eliot (1827): Rudyard Kipling. P
Oliphant, Margaret (d. 1897): Autobiography. P
Phillpotts (1862): The Human Boy. P
Pinero (1855): Trelawny of the Wells. P
Quiller-Couch (1863): The Ship of Stars. P
Rossetti, William Michael (ed.): Ruskin, Rossetti and Pre-Raphaelitism [Papers 1854–62].
Somerville, Œ., and Ross, Martin: Some Experiences of an Irish R. M. [Further Experiences 1908]. P
Stephen (1832): Studies of a Biographer, series I [II 1902]. P
Stevenson (d. 1894): Letters, ed. S. Colvin.
Swinburne (1837): Rosamund, Queen of the Lombards. D
Tyrrell, George (1861): External Religion. P
Ward, James (1843): Naturalism and Agnosticism. P
Wells (1866): When the Sleeper Wakes. P
Whistler (1834): Baronet and Butterfly. P
Whiteing, Richard (1840): No. 5 John Street. P

Elizabeth Bowen b.
Noel Coward b.
Beginning of S. African War.
First Hague Conference.
Bridges, 'Yattendon Hymnal'.
G. C. Macaulay, ed. Works of Gower.
John Horace Round, 'The Commune of London'.
Armand Salacrou b.
Henry Becque d.
George, 'Der Teppich des Lebens'.
A. Holz, 'Revolution der modernen Lyrik'.
Thomas Mann, 'Der kleine Herr Friedemann'.

Wilde (1856): Ideal Husband. D
  Importance of being Earnest [acted 1895]. D
Yeats (1865): The Wind among the Reeds. V
  Poems.

1900

Brown, T. E. (d. 1897): Collected Poems.
Butler (1835): Trs. Odyssey. P
Conrad (1857): Lord Jim. P
Corelli (1854): Boy. P
Dreiser (1871): Sister Carrie. P
Dunne, Finlay Peter (1867): Mr. Dooley's Philo-
  sophy. P
'Fiona Macleod' (1855): Divine Adventure. P
  House of Usna [in National Review, 1 July]. D
  Immortal Hour [in Fortnightly Review, Nov.;
  separately 1908]. D
Firth, Sir Charles (1857): Oliver Cromwell. P
Harland, Henry (1861): Cardinal's Snuff Box. P
Henley (1849): For England's Sake. V
Housman, L. (1865): An Englishwoman's Love-
  letters [anonymous]. P
Hudson (1841): Nature in Downland. P
James (1843): The Soft Side. P
'John Oliver Hobbes' (1867): Robert Orange. P
Lang (1844): History of Scotland [concl. 1907]. P
Lawson (1867): On the Track, and Over the
  Sliprails. P
Lear (d. 1888): The Jumblies. V
Maitland (1850): Political Theories of the Middle
  Ages [trs. Otto Gierke, with Introduction]. P
'Mark Rutherford' (1831): Pages from a Journal.
  P
'Mark Twain' (1835): The Man That Corrupted
  Hadleyburg. P
Phillips (1866): Herod [acted]. D. Marpessa. V
Pinero (1855): Gay Lord Quex. D
Raleigh (1861): Milton. P
Rossetti, William Michael: Ed. Pre-Raphaelite
  Diaries and Letters [Papers 1835–54].
Saintsbury (1845): A History of Criticism [concl.
  1904]. P
Seton (1860): Wild Animals I Have Known. P
Shaw (1856): Three Plays for Puritans. D
Steel, Flora Annie (1847): Voices in the Night. P
Stephen (1832): English Utilitarians. P
Ward (1851): Eleanor. P
Wells (1866): Love and Mr. Lewisham. P
Yeats (1865): Shadowy Waters. D

Boxer Rising.
John Ruskin d.
Oscar Wilde d.
Henry Sidgwick d.
James Martineau d.
R. W. Dixon d.
Stephen Crane d.
Friedrich Max Müller d.
Richard Doddridge Black-
  more d.
Ernest Dowson d.
'The Daily Express'
  started.
British Museum Cata-
  logue (books to 1880).
'Oxford Book of English
  Verse', ed. Quiller-
  Couch (revised 1939).
Henry Sweet's 'History of
  Language'.
Tolstoy, first vols. of trs.
  by A. and L. Maude.
Nietzsche d.
Saint-Exupéry b.
Freud, 'Traumdeutung'.
Académie Goncourt
  founded.
Péguy, 'Cahiers' (1900–
  14).
Spitteler, 'Olympischer
  Frühling'.
Rilke, 'Geschichten vom
  lieben Gott'.

'Anthony Hope' (1863): Tristram of Blent. P
Belloc (1870): Robespierre. P
Butler (1835): Erewhon Revisited. P
Churchill, Winston (1871): The Crisis. P
Davidson (1857): Self's the Man. D
'George Bourn' (1863): The Bettesworth
    Book. P
Gissing (1857): By the Ionian Sea. P
Hardy (1840): Poems of the Past and Present. P
Hewlett (1861): New Canterbury Tales. P
Hudson (1841): Birds and Man. P
James (1843): The Sacred Fount. P
Jones (1851): The Liars. D
Kipling (1865): Kim. P
Lawson (1867): Joe Wilson and His Mates. P
M'Taggart (1866): Hegelian Cosmology. P
Meredith (1828): A Reading of Life. V
Meynell (1847): Later Poems.
Moore (1852): Sister Teresa. P
Nesbit (1858): The Wouldbegoods. P
Newbolt (1862): The Sailing of the Long Ships. V
Norris, Frank (1870): The Octopus. P
Pater (d. 1894): Essays from the Guardian. P
Wells (1866): First Men in the Moon. P
Yeats (1865): Poems. V

Queen Victoria d.
Sir Walter Besant d.
F. W. H. Myers d.
William Stubbs d.
Brooke Foss Westcott d.
Charlotte Mary Yonge d.
'World's Classics' begun.
Roy Campbell b.
André Malraux b.
Thomas Mann, 'Budden-
    brooks'.
President McKinley
    assassinated.

President U.S.A.
    Theodore Roose-
    velt.

1902

Barrie (1860): The Little White Bird. P
Belloc (1870): The Path to Rome. P
Bennett (1867): The Grand Babylon Hotel. P
Chesterton (1874): Robert Browning. P
Conrad (1857): Youth. P
Dobson (1840): Samuel Richardson. P
Doyle (1859): The Hound of the Baskervilles. P
FitzGerald (d. 1883): Letters and Literary Re-
    mains, ed. Aldis Wright.
Hudson (1841): El Ombú. P
Jacobs, W. W. (1863): The Lady of the Barge. P
James, Henry (1843): The Wings of the Dove. P
James, William (1842): The Varieties of Religious
    Experience. P
Kipling (1865): Just So Stories. P and V
Lee (1859): Life of Queen Victoria. P
Masefield (1878): Salt-Water Ballads. V
Mason (1865): The Four Feathers. P
Maugham (1874): Mrs. Craddock. P
Nesbit (1858): Five Children and It. P
Potter (1866): Peter Rabbit. P
'Ralph Connor' (1860): Glengarry School Days.
    P
Roberts (1860): The Kindred of the Wild. P

Lord Acton d.
P. J. Bailey d.
Samuel Butler d.
Lionel Johnson d.
Francis Bret Harte d.
G. Murray trs. of Euri-
    pides begun.
'Encyclopaedia Britan-
    nica,' 10th ed.
Zola d.
The British Academy
    founded.
'Cambridge Modern His-
    tory' (completed 1912).
Gide, 'L'Immoraliste'.

'Walter Ramal' (**W. de la Mare,** 1873): Songs of
  Childhood. V
Watson (1858): Ode on Coronation. V
Yeats (1865): Cathleen Ni Houlihan. D

1903

Adamson, Robert (d. 1902): Development of
  Modern Philosophy. P
Barrie (1860): Quality Street. D
  The Admirable Crichton. D
  Little Mary. D
Belloc (1870): Caliban's Guide to Letters. P
Butler (d. 1902): The Way of All Flesh. P
Chambers, E. K. (1866): The Mediaeval Stage. P
Childers (1870): The Riddle of the Sands. P
Conrad (1857): Typhoon. P
  [With **F. M. Hueffer**] Romance. P
Creevey (d. 1838): Creevey Papers. P
Dickinson, G. L. (1861): Letters from John China-
  man. P
Dobson (1840): Fanny Burney. P
Gissing (d. 1903): The Private Papers of Henry
  Ryecroft. P
Hudson (1841): Hampshire Days. P
James (1843): The Ambassadors. P
  The Better Sort. P
Kipling (1865): The Five Nations. V
London, Jack (1896): The Call of the Wild. P
Moore (1852): The Untilled Field. P
Moore, George Edward (1873): Principia Ethica. P
Morley (1838): Life of William Ewart Gladstone. P
Norris, Frank (1870): The Pit. P
O'Dowd (1866): Dawnward? V
Potter (1866): The Tailor of Gloucester. P
Raleigh (1861): Wordsworth. P
Russell (1872): Principles of Mathematics. P
Shaw (1856): Man and Superman. D
'Tom Collins' (1843): Such is Life. P
Traherne (d. 1674): Poetical Works, ed. Dobell. V
Tyrrell (1861): Lex Orandi. P
Ward (1851): Lady Rose's Daughter. P
Watson (1858): For England. V
Wells (1866): Mankind in the Making. P
Yeats (1865): Ideas of Good and Evil. P
  Where there is Nothing. D

Evelyn Waugh b.
Frederick William Farrar
  d.
George Gissing d.
William Ernest Henley d.
George Birkbeck Hill d.
William Edward Lecky d.
Herbert Spencer d.
James Macneill Whistler
  d.
Sir John Sandys,'History
  of Classical Scholar-
  ship,' vol. i (vols. ii–iii
  1908).
'Burlington • Magazine'
  started.
'Daily Mirror' started.
Mrs. Toynbee's ed. of
  Walpole's Letters (com-
  pleted 1905: supple-
  ments by P. Toynbee
  1918, '25).
Hofmannsthal, 'Elektra'.
Thomas Mann,'Tristan'.

Adams, Henry (1838): Mont-Saint-Michel and Chartres. P

Barrie (1860): Peter Pan [first pub. 1928]. D

Beerbohm (1872): The Poets' Corner. P

Belloc (1870): The Old Road. D

Bradley, A. C. (1851): Shakespearean Tragedy. P

Bridges (1844): Demeter, a Mask. V

Chesterton (1874): Napoleon of Notting Hill. P

Conrad (1857): Nostromo. P

Davidson (1857): Selected Poems.

De la Mare (1873): Henry Brocken. P

Ellis, Havelock (1859): Study of British Genius. P

Gissing (d. 1903): Veranilda. P

Hardy (1840): The Dynasts, Part I. D

Hewlett (1861): The Queen's Quair. P

Hudson (1841): Green Mansions. P

James, M. R. (1862): Ghost Stories of an Antiquary. P

Kipling (1865): Traffics and Discoveries.

London, Jack (1876): The Sea-Wolf. P

More, Paul Elmer (1864): Shelburne Essays [12 vols. 1904–28].

Munro ('Saki': 1870): Reginald. P

Nesbit (1858): The New Treasure-Seekers. P
The Phoenix and the Carpet. P

Newbolt (1862): Songs of the Sea. V

Porter, W. S. ('O. Henry', 1862): Cabbages and Kings. P

Rolfe (1860): Hadrian the Seventh. P

Sinclair, May (1879): The Divine Fire. P

Spencer (d. 1903): Autobiography. P

Sturgis, Howard (1855): Belchamber. P

Swinburne (1837): Channel Passage. V

Swinton, Sir Ernest (1868): The Defence of Duffer's Drift' [under the pseudonym of Backsight-Forethought]. P

Wells (1866): The Food of the Gods. P

Yeats (1865): The King's Threshold. D
The Hour-Glass. D

Sir Edwin Arnold d.
Lafcadio Hearn d.
Christina Rossetti d.
Samuel Smiles d.
Sir Leslie Stephen d.
Abbey Theatre, Dublin, founded.
Forrester, 'History of the Indian Mutiny'.
T. Hutchinson, ed. Shelley's Poetical Works.
Aldis Wright, ed. Ascham's English Works.
A. R. Waller, ed. Crashaw.
Chekhov d.
Rutherford, 'Radioactivity'.
Hesse,'Peter Camenzind'.
Rolland, 'Jean-Christophe' (1904–12).
Wedekind, 'Die Büchse der Pandora'.

1905

Barrie (1860): Alice Sit-by-the-Fire [pub. 1919]. D

Bentley, E. C. (1875): Biography for Beginners. V ('Clerihews').

Birrell (1850): In the Name of the Bodleian. P

Chesterton (1874): The Club of Queer Trades. P

Dickinson, G. L. (1861): A Modern Symposium. P

Dowson (d. 1900): Poems, with Memoir by A. Symons. V

George Macdonald d.
William Sharp d.
E. V. Lucas, 'Life of Charles Lamb'.
W. P. Courtney, 'Register of Bibliographies', 2 vols. (vol. iii 1912).
York Powell and Vigfusson, 'Origines Islandicae'.

Doyle (1859): The Return of Sherlock Holmes. P
Forster (1879): Where Angels Fear to Tread. P
Gissing (d. 1903): Will Warburton. P
Hudson (1841): A Little Boy Lost. P
James (1843): The Golden Bowl. P
Kipling (1865): They. P
Locke, W. J. (1863): The Morals of Marcus Ordeyne. P
Masefield (1878): Mainsail Haul. V
Moore (1852): The Lake. P
Orczy, Baroness : The Scarlet Pimpernel. P
Santayana (1863): The Life of Reason (5 vols. completed 1906). P
Shaw (1856): Major Barbara (pub. 1907). D
Slater (1876): Footpaths thro' the Veld. V
Swinburne (1837): Love's Cross-Currents [publ. as A Year's Letters (1877)]. P
Synge (1871): In the Shadow of the Glen. D
  Riders to the Sea. D.
  The Well of the Saints. D
Vachell, H. A. (1861): The Hill. P
Vinogradoff (1854): Growth of the Manor. P
Ward (1851): The Marriage of William Ashe. P
Wells (1866): A Modern Utopia. P. Kipps. P
Wharton, Edith (1862): The House of Mirth. P
Wilde (d. 1900): De Profundis [complete 'edn., 1949]. P

*George Saintsbury, **ed.** Minor Poets of Caroline Period (vol. 2 1906, vol. 3 1921).*
J. Sampson, ed. Blake.
A. R. Waller, ed. Samuel Butler.
A. R. Waller, ed. Cowley's 'English Writings'.
A. Ward, ed. Crabbe's Poems 1905–7.
A. R. Waller, ed. Prior's Poems.
Roger Fry, ed. Reynold's 'Discourses'.
British Museum Catalogue Supplement (books 1880–1900).
Jean-Paul Sartre b.

President U.S.A.
Theodore Roosevelt (2nd term).

1906

Barrie (1860): Peter Pan in Kensington Gardens. P
Belloc (1870): Hills and the Sea. P
  Esto Perpetua. P
Benson, A. C. (1862): From a College Window. P
Chesterton (1874): Charles Dickens. P
Churchill, Winston S. (1874): Lord Randolph Churchill. P
Conrad (1857): Mirror of the Sea. P
De la Mare (1873): Poems.
De Morgan (1839): Joseph Vance. P
Doughty (1843): Dawn in Britain. V
Fowler, H. W. (1858) **and F. G. :** The King's English [developed 1926 in H. W. F.'s Modern English Usage]. P
Galsworthy (1867): The Man of Property. P
Gregory, Lady (1852): Gods and Fighting Men. P
Hardy (1840): The Dynasts, Part II. D
Kipling (1865): Puck of Pook's Hill. P
Locke, W. J. (1863): The Beloved Vagabond. P
London, Jack (1876): White-Fang. P
Lucas, E. V. (1868): Listener's Lure. P

F. W. Maitland d.
'John Oliver Hobbes' d.
Richard Garnett d.
The English Hymnal.
'Everyman's Library' started.
Greg, 'Pastoral Poetry'.
Sidney and Beatrice Webb, 'English Local Government: The Parish and the County'.
Ibsen d.
P. S. Allen, ed. 'Letters of Erasmus' (completed 1947; last 3 vols. ed. Garrod and Mrs. Allen).
Rilke, 'Das Stundenbuch'.

M'Taggart (1868): Some Dogmas of Religion. P
Moore (1852): Memoirs of my Dead Life. P
Nesbit (1858): The Railway Children. P
Pinero (1855): His House in Order. D
Porter, W. S. ('O. Henry', 1862): The Four Million. P
Saintsbury (1845): History of English Prosody vol. i [vol. ii 1908, vol. iii 1910].
Sinclair, Upton (1878): The Jungle. P
Wallace, Edgar (1875): The Four Just Men. P

1907

Acton (d. 1902): Historical Essays and Studies. P History of Freedom and Other Essays. P
Bell (1868): The Desert and the Sown. P
Belloc (1870): Cautionary Tales for Children. V
Coleridge, Mary (d. 1907): Poems.
Colum, Padraic (1881): Wild Earth. V
Conrad (1857): The Secret Agent. P
Davidson (1857): The Triumph of Mammon. V
De Morgan (1839): Alice-for-Short. P
Fitzpatrick (1862): Jock of the Bushveldt. P
Flecker (1884): The Bridge of Fire. V
Forster (1879): The Longest Journey. P
Galsworthy (1867): The Country House. P
'George Bourn' (1863): Memoirs of a Surrey Labourer. P
Gibson, Wilfrid (1878): The Stonefolds. V
Gosse (1849): Father and Son. P
Hewlett (1861): The Stooping Lady. P
Hodgson, Ralph: The Last Blackbird. V
Housman, L. (1865), and Barker (1877): Prunella. D
James, William (1842): Pragmatism. P
Jerome, Jerome K. (1859): The Passing of the Third Floor Back and Other Stories. P
Joyce (1882): Chamber Music. V
Kipling (1865): The Brushwood Boy. P
Lucas, E. V. (1868): Character and Comedy. P
Maitland (d. 1906): Domesday Book and Beyond. P
Mason (1865): The Broken Road. P
Maugham (1874): Lady Frederick. D
Murray (1866): Rise of the Greek Epic. P
Porter, W. S. ('O. Henry', 1862): The Trimmed Lamp. P
Prior (d. 1721): Dialogues of the Dead, ed. A. R. Waller. P and V
Raleigh (1861): Shakespeare. P
Service (1874): Songs of a Sourdough. V
Shaw (1856): John Bull's Other Island. D

Wystan Hugh Auden b.
Christopher Fry b.
Louis Macneice b.
Mary Coleridge d.
Francis Thompson d.
'Cambridge History of Eng. Lit.' (completed 1916; index vol. 15, 1927).
'Nation' started.
William Archer trs. Ibsen, 1907–12.
J.-K. Huysmans d.
George, 'Der Siebente Ring'.
Rilke, 'Neue Gedichte'.

Synge (1871): Playboy of the Western World. D
   The Aran Islands. P
Trevelyan, G. M. (1876): Garibaldi's Defence of
   the Roman Republic. P
Tyrrell (1861): Lex Credendi. P
Victoria, Queen (d. 1901): Letters, 1837–61, ed.
   A. C. Benson and Viscount Esher. P
Wordsworth (d. 1850): Letters of the Words-
   worth Family, ed. William Knight.
Yeats (1865): Deirdre. D

1908

Abercrombie, Lascelles (1881): Interludes and
   Poems. V
Banfield (1852): The Confessions of a Beach-
   comber. P
Barrie (1860): What Every Woman Knows. D
Belloc (1870): Mr. Clutterbuck's Election. P
Bennett (1867): Buried Alive. P
   The Old Wives' Tale. P
Blackwood (1869): John Silence. P
Chesterton (1874): The Man Who was Thursday.
   P
Conrad (1857): A Set of Six. P
Davidson (1857): The Testament of John David-
   son. V
   Mammon and His Message. V
Davies (1871): The Autobiography of a Super-
   Tramp. P
De Morgan (1839): Somehow Good. P
Dickinson, G. L. (1861): Justice and Liberty. P
Doughty (1843): Adam Cast Forth. V
   Wanderings in Arabia [abridgement of Arabia
   Deserta]. P
Forster (1879): A Room with a View. P
Galsworthy (1867): A Commentary. P
'George Birmingham' (1865): Spanish Gold. P
Grahame (1859): The Wind in the Willows. P
Gunn (1870): We of the Never Never. P
Hardy (1840): The Dynasts, Part III. D
Henley (d. 1903): Complete Works, 7 vols.
'Henry . Handel Richardson' (1870): Maurice
   Guest. P
Lodge (1851): Man and the Universe. P
Lucas, E. V. (1868): Over Bemerton's. P
Maitland (d. 1906): Constitutional History of
   England. P
Masefield (1878): Captain Margaret. P
Montgomery (1874): Anne of Green Gables. P
Robinson (1886): The Clancy Name. D
Shaw (1856): Getting Married. D

Edward Caird d.
'Ouida' d.
G. Birkbeck Hill, ed.
   Johnson's 'Lives'.
Henry Sweet, 'The Sounds
   of English'.
Wallas, 'Human Nature
   in Politics'.
Sidney and Beatrice Webb,
   'English Local Govern-
   ment: The Manor and
   the Borough'.
'English Review' founded.
Anatole France, first Eng.
   trs.
Oxford translation of
   Aristotle (concl. 1952).

Swinburne (1837): The Age of Shakespeare. P
  The Duke of Gandia. D
Synge (1871): The Tinker's Wedding. D
Traherne (d. 1674): Centuries of Meditations. P
Wells (1866): The War in the Air. P
Yeats (1865): Collected Works, vols. i and ii.

1909

Barclay, Florence (1862): The Rosary. P
Barker (1877): Marrying of Ann Leete. D
  The Voysey Inheritance. D.   Waste. D
Beerbohm (1872): Yet Again. P
Binyon (1869): England and Other Poems.
Blackwood (1869): The Education of Uncle Paul.
  P
Bottomley, Gordon (1874): Riding to Lithend. D
Bradley, A. C. (1851): Oxford Lectures on Poetry.
  P
Browning (d. 1889): Letters to Alfred Domett. P
Buchan (1875): Prester John. P.
Carlyle, Thomas (d. 1881) **and Jane Welsh** (d.
  1869): Love Letters, ed. A. Carlyle. P
Davidson (d. 1909): Fleet Street. V
De Morgan (1839): It Never Can Happen Again.
  P
Emerson (d. 1882): Journals.
Galsworthy (1867): Plays, vol. i: The Silver Box,
  Joy, Strife. D
Gregory, Lady (1859): Seven Short Plays.
Hardy (1840): Time's Laughingstocks. V
Harris, Frank (1856): The Man Shakespeare. P
Hewlett (1861): Open Country. P
Hudson (1841): Afoot in England. P
Jacks, L. P. (1860): Mad Shepherds.
James, William (1842): The Meaning of Truth. P
Kipling (1865): Actions and Reactions. P
Lodge (1851): The Survival of Man. P
Lucas, E. V. (1868): One Day and Another. P
Masefield (1878): Multitude and Solitude. P
  The Tragedy of Nan and Other Plays. D
Meredith (d. 1909): Last Poems.
Pound, Ezra (1885): Personae and Exultations. V
Quiller-Couch (1863): True Tilda. P
Stein, Gertrude (1874): Three Lives. P
Swinton, Sir Ernest (1868): The Green Curve
  [under pseudonym of **Ole-Luk-Oie**].
Synge (d. 1909): Poems and Translations.
Thompson (d. 1907): Shelley. P
Trevelyan (1876): Garibaldi and the Thousand. P
Wells (1866): Ann Veronica. P
  Tono Bungay. P

Frances Marion Craw-
  ford d.   -
John Davidson d.
Sir Theodore Martin d.
George Meredith d.
John Millington Synge d.
Algernon Charles Swin-
  burne d.
J. C. Smith, ed. Spenser's
  'Faerie Queene'.
J. H. Round, 'Feudal
  England'.
P. Vivian ed. Campion's,
  Works.
United States Copyright
  Act fixes term of copy-
  right at 28 years, renew-
  able by the author or his
  executors or next of kin
  for a second 28 years.
  See 1911. In order to
  secure copyright, books
  written in English by
  foreign authors must still
  (see 1891) be printed in
  the United States.
A. L. Reade, 'Johnsonian
  Gleanings' (cont. to
  1946).
Evans, 'Scripta Minoa'.
Beveridge, 'Unemploy-
  ment' (revised 1930).
Masterman, 'The Con-
  dition of England'.
Gide, 'La Porte étroite'.
Maeterlinck, 'L'Oiseau
  bleu'.
'Nouvelle Revue Fran-
  çaise' founded.

President U.S.A.,
    Taft.

Acton (d. 1902): The French Revolution. P

Angell, Norman (1874): The Great Illusion. P

Arnold (d. 1888): Essays in Criticism, III.

Baring (1874): Diminutive Dramas. D
   Dead Letters. P

Belloc (1870): Verses.

Bennett (1867): Clayhanger. P

De la Mare (1873): The Return. P

Flecker (1884): Thirty-six Poems. V

Forster (1879): Howard's End. P

Galsworthy (1867): Justice. D

Gibson, Wilfrid (1878): Daily Bread. V

'Henry Handel Richardson' (1870): The Getting
   of Wisdom. P

Hewlett (1861): Rest Harrow. P

Hudson (1841): A Shepherd's Life. P

James (1843): The Finer Grain. P

Kipling (1865): Rewards and Fairies. P and V

'Mark Rutherford' (1831): More Pages from a
   Journal. P

Masefield (1878): Pompey the Great. D

Meredith (d. 1909): Celt and Saxon. P

Montague, C. E. (1867): A Hind let loose. P

Monypenny (1866): Life of Disraeli (completed
   1920 by G. E. Buckle).

Morris (d. 1896): Collected Works.

Munro (**'Saki'**; 1870): Reginald in Russia. P

Newbolt (1862): Songs of the Fleet. V

Raleigh (1861): Six Essays on Johnson. P

Robinson, Edwin Arlington (1869): The Town
   down the River. V

Russell (1872) **and Whitehead** (1861): Principia
   Mathematica, vol. i.

Sinclair, May (1879): The Creators. P

Synge (d. 1909): Deirdre of the Sorrows. D

Traherne (d. 1674): Poems of Felicity.

Wells (1866): The History of Mr. Polly. P

Yeats (1865): Poems: Second Series.

Young, Andrew (1885): Songs of Night. V

Edward VII d.

F. J. Furnivall d.

William James d.

*'Encyclopaedia Britan-
nica', 11th ed.*

*Chamberlain, 'Founda-
tions of the 19th Cen-
tury' (German ed.
1899).*

*Flexner, 'Medical Educa-
tion in U.S. and
Canada'.*

*J. H. Round, 'Peerage
and Pedigree'.*

*Spenser's 'Minor Poems',
ed. de Selincourt.*

*Sidney and Beatrice Webb,
'English Poor Law
Policy'.*

*J. H. Wicksteed, ed.
Blake's 'Vision of the
Book of Job'.*

Jean Anouilh b.

Tolstoy d.

*Rilke, 'Malte Laurids
Brigge'.*

Beerbohm (1872): Zuleika Dobson. P
Bell (1868): Amurath to Amurath. P
Bennett (1867): Hilda Lessways. P
   The Card. P
Blackwood (1869): The Centaur. P
Brooke (1887): Poems.
Chesterton(1874): The Ballad of the White Horse. V
   The Innocence of Father Brown. P
Conrad (1857): Under Western Eyes. P
Davies (1870): Songs of Joy. V
De Morgan (1839): A Likely Story. P
Dolben, Digby Mackworth (d. 1867): Poems, ed.
   with a Memoir by R. Bridges.
Douglas, Norman (1868): Siren Land. P
Ervine, St. John (1883): Mixed Marriage. D
Flecker (1884): Forty-two Poems.
Forster (1879): The Celestial Omnibus. P
Galsworthy (1867): The Patrician. P
Gosse (1849): Collected Poems.
Granville-Barker (1877): The Madras House. D
James, Henry (1843): The Outcry. P
James, M. R. (1862): More Ghost Stories of an
   Antiquary. P
Johnson (d. 1902): Post Liminium. P
Lawrence (1885): The White Peacock. P
Leacock, Stephen (1869): Nonsense Novels. P
Lucas, E. V. (1868): Old Lamps for New. P
Mansfield (1888): In a German Pension. P
Masefield (1878): The Everlasting Mercy. V
   Jim Davis. P.   Street of To-day. P
Maugham (1874): Loaves and Fishes. P
Montague (1867): Dramatic Values. P
Moore (1852): Hail and Farewell, vol. i. P
   The Apostle. P
Munro ('Saki': 1870): Chronicles of Clovis. P
Porter, W. S. ('O. Henry', d. 1910): The Gift of
   the Wise Men. P
   Collected Works. P
Pound, Ezra (1885): Canzoni. V
Shaw (1856): The Doctor's Dilemma, Fanny's
   First Play, The Showing-up of Blanco
   Posnet. D
Trevelyan (1876): Garibaldi and the Making of
   Italy. P
Wallace (1875): Sanders of the River. P
Walpole (1884): Mr. Perrin and Mr. Traill. P
Ward, James (1843): The Realm of Ends. P
Wells (1866): The New Machiavelli. P. The
   Country of the Blind. P
Wharton, Edith (1862): Ethan Frome. P

Sir Charles Dilke d.
Sir Francis Galton d.
Sir W. S. Gilbert d.
J. L. and Barbara Hammond, 'The Village Labourer'.
Legouis, 'Geoffrey Chaucer'.
Copyright Act extends term of copyright to 50 years from author's death (with certain limitations). See 1709, 1842, 1909.
Pollard, 'Records of the Bible'.
Fowler, H. W. and F. G., 'Concise Oxford Dictionary' (frequently revised).
'Cambridge Medieval History' (completed 1936).
Claudel, 'Cinq grandes odes'.
Hauptmann, 'Die Ratten'.
Hofmannsthal, 'Der Rosen-Kavalier'; 'Jedermann'.

Abercrombie (1881): Emblems of Love. V

Archer (1856): Play-Making. P

Beerbohm (1872): A Christmas Garland. P

Bennett (1867) **and Knoblock, E. :** Milestones. D

Bentley, E. C. (1875): Trent's Last Case. P

Bosanquet (1848): Individuality and Value. P

Butler (d. 1902): Note Books, ed. H. Festing Jones. P

Chesterton (1874): Manalive. P

Conrad (1857): Some Reminiscences. P.   'Twixt Land and Sea. P

De la Mare (1873): The Listeners and Other Poems. V

Galsworthy (1867): Plays, vol. ii: The Eldest Son, The Little Dream.

Houghton, W. S. (1881): Hindle Wakes. D

Lawrence (1885): The Trespasser. P

Leacock (1869): Sunshine Sketches of a Little Town. P

Lucas, E. V. (1868): London Lavender. P

Mackenzie, Compton (1883): Carnival. P

Masefield (1878): The Widow in the Bye Street. V

Meredith (d. 1909): Letters [2 vols.].

Moore (1852): Hail and Farewell, vol. ii. P

Munro ('Saki': 1870): The Unbearable Bassington. P

Newbolt (1862): Poems New and Old.

Pound, Ezra (1885): Ripostes. V

Saintsbury (1845): History of English Prose Rhythm. P

Shaw (1856): Pygmalion. D

Stephens, James (1882): The Charwoman's Daughter. P.   The Crock of Gold. P

Strachey (1880): Landmarks in French Literature. D

Tomlinson, H. M. (1873): The Sea and the Jungle. P

Walpole (1884): Prelude to Adventure. P

Wells (1866): Marriage. P

Williams, C. (1886): The Silver Stair. V

Yeats (1865): The Cutting of an Agate. P

Andrew Lang d.

William Walter Skeat d.

Henry Sweet d.

'Georgian Poetry, 1911–12'

'Daily Herald' started.

Tagore's 'Gitanjali', Eng. translation.

Elton, 'Survey of English Literature 1732–1880' (completed 1928).

'Oxford Book of Victorian Verse,' ed. Quiller-Couch.

Deloney's Works, ed. F. O. Mann.

Savile's Works, ed. Walter Raleigh.

Coleridge's Poetical Works, ed. E. H. Coleridge.

H. J. C. Grierson, ed. Donne's Poems.

Spurgeon, 'Mysticism in English Literature'.

A. Feuillerat, ed. Works of Sidney (completed 1926).

Dostoievsky, trs. by C. Garnett, 1912–31.

Chekhov, 'Cherry Orchard', first Eng. trs.

Barlach, 'Der tote Tag'.

Claudel, 'L'Annonce faite à Marie'.

A. France, 'Les Dieux ont soif'.

Austen-Leigh, W. and R. A.: Jane Austen, her Life and Letters. P
Barrie (1860): The Twelve-Pound Look. D
Bosanquet (1848): The Value and Destiny of the Individual. P
Bridges (1844): A Tract on the Present State of English Pronunciation [first printed 1910]. P
Chesterton (1874): Magic. D
Churchill, Winston (1871): The Inside of the Cup. P
Conrad (1857): Chance. P
De la Mare (1873): Peacock Pie. V
Flecker (1884): The Golden Journey to Samarkand. V
Frost, Robert (1875): A Boy's Will. V
Gregory, Lady (1859): New Comedies. D
Hickey (d. 1830): Memoirs, 1749–1809 [concl. 1925]. P
Hudson (1841): Adventures among Birds. P
Jacks, L. P. (1860): All Men are Ghosts. P
James (1843): A Small Boy and Others. P
Lawrence (1885): Love Poems.
  Sons and Lovers. P
Lindsay (1879): A Curate in Bohemia. P
Lucas, E. V. (1868): Loiterer's Harvest. P
Mackenzie, Compton (1883): Sinister Street, vol. i. P
Masefield (1878): Dauber. V
  The Daffodil Fields. V
Meynell (1847): Collected Poems.
Montague (1867): The Morning's War. P
Squire, J. C. (1884): Three Hills and Other Poems.
Stein, Gertrude (1874): Portrait of Mabel Dodge at Villa Caronio. P
Trevelyan (1876): Clio a Muse. P
Walpole (1884): Fortitude. P
Watson (1858): The Muse in Exile. V
Williams, William Carlos (1883): Transitional. V
Wilson, Woodrow (1856): The New Freedom. P

Alfred Austin d.
Edward Dowden d.
Frederick Rolfe d.
William Hale White d.
Robert Bridges poet-laureate.
The Society for Pure English founded by Robert Bridges: first tract published 1919.
'New Statesman' started.
Cole, 'The World of Labour'.
Murray, 'Four (later five) Stages of Greek Religion'.
Albert Camus b.
Alain-Fournier, 'Le Grand Meaulnes'.
Apollinaire, 'Alcools'.
Proust, 'A la recherche du temps perdu' (1913–28).
R. Becher, 'De Profundis'.
Th. Mann, 'Der Tod in Venedig'.
Rilke, 'Das Marienleben'.
F. Werfel, 'Wir sind'.

1914

Blunt (1840): Poetical Works.
Bradley (1846): Truth and Reality. P
Brennan (1870): Poems.
Chesterton (1874): The Flying Inn. P and V
  The Wisdom of Father Brown. P
De Morgan (1839): When Ghost meets Ghost. P
Dickinson, Emily (d. 1886): The Single Hound. V
Dickinson, G. L. (1861): Appearances. P
Ervine, St. John (1883): Jane Clegg. D
  Mrs. Martin's Man. P

Beginning of Great War (4 August).
Dylan Thomas b.
Sir William Anson d.
Theodore Watts-Dunton d.
Alain-Fournier d.
Charles Péguy d.
R. Becher, 'Verfall und Triumph'.
George, 'Der Stern des Bundes'.

Flecker (1884): The King of Alsander. P
Frost, Robert (1875): North of Boston. V
Galsworthy (1867): Plays, vol. iii: The Fugitive,
     The Pigeon, The Mob.
Hardy (1840): Satires of Circumstance. V
Holme, Constance (1880): The Lonely Plough. P
James (1843): Notes on Novelists. P
     Notes of a Son and Brother. P
Joyce (1882): Dubliners. P
Lawrence (1885): The Prussian Officer. P
     The Widowing of Mrs. Holroyd. D
Lowell, Amy (1874): Sword Blades and Poppy
     Seed. V
Macaulay, Rose (1881): The Two Blind Countries.
     V
Mackenzie (1883): Sinister Street, vol. ii. P
Masefield (1878): Philip the King. V
Meynell (1847): Collected Essays. P
Moore (1852): Hail and Farewell, vol. iii. P
Munro ('Saki': 1870): Beasts and Super-Beasts.
     P
Russell, Bertrand (1872): Our Knowledge of the
     External World. P
Shaw (1856): Misalliance, The Dark Lady of
     the Sonnets. D
Walpole (1884): The Wooden Horse. P
Yeats (1865): Responsibilities. P

Hasenclever, 'Der Sohn'.
G. Kaiser, 'Die Bürger
*   von Calais'.*

1915

Aldington (1892): Images. V
Balfour (1848): Theism and Humanism. P
Benson, Stella (1892): I Pose. P
Binyon (1869): The Winnowing Fan. V
Brooke (d. 1915): 1914 and Other Poems.
Buchan (1875): The Thirty-nine Steps. P
Chesterton (1874): Poems.
Conrad (1857): Victory. P.   Within the Tides:
     tales. P
Dennis (1876): The Songs of a Sentimental
     Bloke. V
Douglas (1868): Old Calabria. P
Dreiser (1871): The Genius. P
Ervine, St. John (1883): John Ferguson. D
Flecker (d. 1915): The Old Ships. V
Ford (1873): The Good Soldier. P
Keith, Sir Arthur (1866): Antiquity of Man. P
Lawrence (1885): The Rainbow. P
Leacock, Stephen (1869): Moonbeams from the
     Larger Lunacy. P
'Mark Rutherford' (d. 1913): Last Pages from a
     Journal. P

James Elroy Flecker d.
Mary Braddon d.
Rupert Brooke d.
Stephen Phillips d.
'Georgian Poetry, 1913–
*   15.'*
Herrick's Poetical Works,
*   ed. F. W. Moorman.*
Vaughan's   Works,   ed.
*   L. C. Martin.*

Masefield (1878): The Faithful. D
Masters, Edgar Lee (1869): The Spoon River
    Anthology. V
Maugham (1874): Of Human Bondage. P
Monro, Harold (1879): Trees. V
Moore (1852): Muslin. P
Pound, Ezra (1885): Cathay. V
Prichard (1884): The Pioneers. P
Read (1893): Songs of Chaos. P
Sitwell, Edith (1887): The Mother. V
Stein, Gertrude (1874): Tender Buttons. P
Wells (1866): Boon. P
Wodehouse (1881): Psmith, Journalist. P
Woolf, Virginia (1882): The Voyage Out. P
Yeats (1865): Reveries over Childhood and
    Youth. P

1916

Anderson, Sherwood (1876): Windy McPherson's
    Son. P
Barrie (1860): A Kiss for Cinderella. D
Bridges (1844): The Spirit of Man; an Antho-
    logy. P and V
Brooke (d. 1915): Letters from America. P
    Webster and the Elizabethan Drama. P
    Collected Poems.
Buchan (1875): Greenmantle. P
Davies (1871): Collected Poems.
Drinkwater (1882): Olton Pools. V
Flecker (d. 1915): Collected Poems.
Gibson, Wilfrid (1878): Battle. V
Graves, Robert (1895): Over the Brazier. V
Hankey, Donald (d. 1916): A Student in Arms. P
Hewlett (1861): The Song of the Plow. V
Joyce (1882): A Portrait of the Artist as a Young
    Man. P
Kaye-Smith (1887): Sussex Gorse. P
Lawrence (1885): Amores. V
    Twilight in Italy. P
Lodge (1851): Raymond, or Life and Death. P
Lowell, Amy (1874): Men, Women, and Ghosts. V
Masefield (1878): Sonnets and Poems.
Mew, Charlotte (1869): The Farmer's Bride. V
Moore (1852): The Brook Kerith. P
Pound (1885): Lustra. V
Powys, J. C. (1872) **and Ll.** (1884): Confessions
    of Two Brothers. P
Quiller-Couch (1863): The Art of Writing. P
Robinson, Edwin Arlington (1869): The Man
    against the Sky. V
Sandburg, Carl (1878): Chicago Poems. V

Henry James d.
Stopford Brooke d.
Hector Munro ('Saki') d.
'Wheels, an Anthology of
    Verse' (later volumes
    1917, 1918, 1919, 1920,
    1921).
Chekhov, trs. by C. Garnett
    1916–22.
Jung, 'Psychology of the
    Unconscious'.
'Shakespeare's England'
    (final ed., C. T. Onions).
Trotter, 'Instincts of the
    Herd in Peace and
    War' (with postscript
    1919).

Shaw (1856): Androcles and the Lion, Overruled.
D
Sitwell, E. (1887) **and O.** (1892): Twentieth Cen-
tury Harlequinade. V
Walpole (1884): The Dark Forest. P
Wells (1866): Mr. Britling sees it through. P

1917

Barrie (1860): Dear Brutus. D
The Old Lady shows her Medals. D
Binyon (1869): For the Fallen and Other Poems.
Bridges (1844): Ibant Obscuri. V
Cabell (1879): The Cream of the Jest. P
Colvin (1845): Life of John Keats. P
Conrad (1857): The Shadow Line—a Confession.
P
Dane, Clemence: Regiment of Women. P
Douglas, Norman (1868): South Wind. P
Drinkwater (1882): Poems, 1908–14.
Dunsany, Lord (1878): Plays of Gods and Men. D
Eliot, T. S. (1888): Prufrock. V
Garland, Hamlin (1860): A Son of the Middle
Border. P
Gibson, Wilfrid (1878): Livelihood. V
Gosse (1849): Life of Swinburne. P
Graves, Robert (1895): Fairies and Fusiliers. V
'Henry Handel Richardson' (1870): The For-
tunes of Richard Mahoney: Australia Felix
[vol. i of trilogy concl. 1929]. P
Hodgson, Ralph (1871): Poems. V
James (d. 1916): The Ivory Tower (unfinished). P.
The Middle Years. P.   The Sense of the Past
(unfinished). P
Kipling (1865): A Diversity of Creatures. P
The Years between. V
Lawrence (1885): Look! we have come through. V
Lowell, Amy (1874): Tendencies in Modern
American Poetry. P
'Mark Twain' (d. 1910): Letters.
Masefield (1878): Good Friday. D
Lollingdon Downs, and Other Poems.
Meynell (1847): A Father of Women. V
Monro, Harold (1879): Strange Meetings. V
More, Paul Elmer (1864): Platonism. P
Nichols, Robert (1893): Ardours and Endurances.
V
Pollard, A. W. (1859): Shakespeare's Fight with
the Pirates. P
Sackville-West, V. (1892): Poems of East and
West. V

Russian Revolution.
William de Morgan d.
Edward Thomas d.
'Georgian Poetry, 1916–
17.'
Lenin, 'Imperialism: The
State and Revolution'.
J. L. and B. Hammond,
'The Town Labourer'.
George, 'Der Krieg'.
Goering, 'Seeschlacht'.
Valéry, 'La Jeune Par-
que'.

President U.S.A.
Wilson   (2nd
term).

Sassoon (1886): The Old Huntsman. V
Squire (1884): The Lily of Malud. V
Thomas (d. 1917): Poems.
Walpole (1884): Maradick at Forty. P
Waugh, Alec (1898): The Loom of Youth. P
Wells (1866): God the Invisible King. P
     The Soul of a Bishop. P
Williams, C. (1886): Poems of Conformity.
Williams, William Carlos (1883): Al Que Quiere! V
Wodehouse (1881): Uneasy Money. P
Yeats (1865): The Wild Swans at Coole. V

1918

Bridges (1844): The Necessity of Poetry. P
     Britannia Victrix. V
Cather, Willa (1876): My Antonia. P
De la Mare (1873): Motley and Other Poems.
Drinkwater (1882): Abraham Lincoln. D
Fletcher, John Gould (1886): Japanese Prints.
Galsworthy (1869): Five Tales. P
Gibson, Wilfrid (1878): Whin. V
Hopkins (d. 1889): Poems, ed. Bridges [2nd ed. 1930].
Hudson (1841): Far Away and Long Ago. P
Huxley, Aldous (1894): The Defeat of Youth, and Other Poems. V
Inge (1860): The Philosophy of Plotinus. P
Joyce (1882): Exiles. D
Knox, Ronald (1888): A Spiritual Æneid. P
Lawrence (1885): New Poems.
Lewis, Wyndham (1884): Tarr. P
Lindsay (1879): The Magic Pudding. P
Lowell, Amy (1874): Can Grande's Castle. P
Newton, A. Edward (1864): The Amenities of Book-Collecting. P
Quiller-Couch (1863): Studies in Literature [2nd series 1922, 3rd series 1929]. P
Robinson, Lennox (1886): The Lost Leader. D
Sassoon (1886): Counter Attack. V
Sitwell, Edith (1887): Clown's Houses. V
Sitwell, Sacheverell (1897): People's Palace. P
Smith, Logan Pearsall (1865): Trivia. P
Squire (1884): Poems, 1st series.
Stein, Gertrude (1874): Mary, he giggled. P
Stopes, Marie Carmichael: Married Love and Wise Parenthood. P
Strachey (1880): Eminent Victorians. P
Swinburne (d. 1909): Letters, ed. Gosse and Wise.
Thomas (d. 1917): Last Poems.
Tomlinson, H. M. (1873): Old Junk. P

*End of Great War.
     (Armistice 11 Nov.)*   .
*Report of Machinery of
     Government Committee.*
*Murray, 'Euripides and
     His Age'.*
*Waley trs. 'A Hundred.
     and Seventy Chinese
     Poems'.*
Wilfred Owen d.
Apollinaire d.
Wedekind d.
G. Kaiser, 'Gas' (–1921).
*Th. Mann, 'Betrachtun-
     gen einesUnpolitischen'.*
*F. von Unruh, 'Ein
     Geschlecht'.*

Torr, Cecil (1857): Small Talk at Wreyland [2nd
    series 1921, 3rd series 1923]. P
Turner, W. J. (1889): The Dark Fire. V
Walpole (1884): The Green Mirror. P
Wells (1866): Joan and Peter. P
West (1892): The Return of the Soldier. P
Yeats (1865): Per amica silentia lunae. P

1919

Aldington (1892): Images of Desire. V
Anderson, Sherwood (1876): Winesburg, Ohio. P
Ashford, Daisy: The Young Visiters. P
Babbitt (1865): Rousseau and Romanticism. P
Barbellion (d. 1919): The Journal of a Dis-
    appointed Man. P.   Enjoying Life. P
Beerbohm (1872): Seven Men. P
Bennett (1867): Sacred and Profane Love. D
Benson, Stella (1892): Living Alone. P
Blunt (1840): My Diaries [2nd vol. 1920]. P
Buchan (1875): Mr. Standfast. P
Cabell (1879): Beyond Life. P.   Jurgen. P
Conrad (1857): The Arrow of Gold. P
De Morgan (d. 1917): The Old Madhouse. P
Dreiser (1871): Twelve Men. P
Firbank (1886): Valmouth. P
Galsworthy (1869): Saint's Progress. P
Hardy (1840): Collected Poems.
    Moments of Vision and Miscellaneous Verse.
Inge (1860): Outspoken Essays. P
James, M. R. (1862): A Thin Ghost and Others. P
Jones, Henry Festing (1851): Samuel Butler: a
    Memoir. P
Keynes, J. M. (1883): The Economic Conse-
    quences of the Peace. P
Masefield (1878): Reynard the Fox. V
Maugham (1874): The Moon and Sixpence. P
Mencken, H. L. (1880): Prejudices [further series
    1921-3-5-8]. P
Millin (1889): The Dark River. P
Milne (1882): First Plays. D
Moffatt, James (1870): The New Testament: a
    New Translation.
Moore (1852): Avowals. P
Murry (1889): Evolution of an Intellectual. P
O'Neill, Eugene (1888): The Moon of the Carib-
    bees and six other Plays. D
Pound. (1885): Quia Pauper Amavi. V
Read (1893): Naked Warriors. V
Sassoon (1886): War Poems.
Shaw (1856): Heartbreak House, Great Catherine,
    &c. D

*William Michael Rossetti
d.*
'*London Mercury*' started.
'*John o' London's Weekly*'
    started.
'*Georgian Poetry, 1918–
    19.*'
*C. K. Scott-Moncrieff,
    trs. 'Song of Roland'.*
*J. L. and B. Hammond,
    'The Skilled Labourer'.*
*Mencken, 'The American
    Language' (revised '21,
    '23,'36, supp. vols.,'45,
    '48).*
*Smith, 'Oxford History of
    India'.*
*Turgenev's novels trs. C.
    Garnett (17 vols. concl.
    '23).*
*Hofmannsthal, 'Die Frau
    ohne Schatten'.*

Sinclair, May (1879): Mary Olivier. P
Sitwell, Osbert (1892): Argonaut and Juggernaut. V

Squire (1884): The Birds, and Other Poems.
Walpole (1884): Jeremy. P.   The Secret City. P
Woolf (1882) : Night and Day. P
Yeats (1865): Two Plays for Dancers. D

1920

Alexander (1859): Space, Time and Deity. P
Barrie (1860): Mary Rose. D
Beerbohm (1872): And Even Now. P
Blunden (1896): The Waggoner. V
Bottomley (1874): King Lear's Wife. D
Bridges (1844): October and Other Poems. V
Chapman (1881): Portrait of a Scholar. P
Chesterton (1874): The Uses of Diversity. P
Clare (d. 1864): Poems [ed. Blunden and Porter].
Conrad (1857): The Rescue. P
De la Mare (1873): Poems, 1901–18.
Dickinson, G. L. (1861): The Magic Flute. P
Eliot (1888): The Sacred Wood. P
Fitzgerald, Scott (1896): This Side of Paradise. P
Flecker (d. 1915): Collected Prose.
Fry, Roger (1866): Vision and Design. P
Galsworthy (1869): In Chancery. P
   Awakening. P   The Skin Game. D
Gibson, Wilfrid (1878): Neighbours. V
Graves, Robert (1895): Country Sentiment. V
Guedalla (1889): Supers and Supermen. P
Hudson (1841): Dead Man's Plack. P
Huxley, Aldous (1894): Leda. V.   Limbo. P
James (d. 1916): Letters, ed. Lubbock. P
Kipling (1865): Letters of Travel. P
Lawrence (1885): Women in Love. P   The Lost
   Girl. P   Touch and Go. D
Lewis, Sinclair (1885): Main Street. P
Macaulay, Rose (1881): Potterism. P
Mander (1878): The Story of a New Zealand
   River. P
'Mansfield' (1888): Bliss, and Other stories. P
Masefield (1878): Enslaved, and Other Poems.
Nichols, Robert (1893): Aurelia. V
O'Neill, Eugene (1888): Beyond the Horizon. D
Owen, Wilfred (d. 1918): Poems, with an introduc-
   tion by Siegfried Sassoon [new ed., 1931].
Pound (1885): Umbra [Collected Early Poems].
Quiller-Couch (1863): The Art of Reading. P
Robinson, Lennox (1886): The White-headed
   Boy. D
Sandburg, Carl (1878): Smoke and Steel. V
Santayana (1863): Little Essays. P

A. H. Bullen d.
Mrs. Humphry Ward d.
*Albert Einstein, 'Relati-
   vity', authorized trans-
   lation.*
*Spengler, 'Decline of the
   West'.*
*Radio Broadcasting
   started in U.S.A.*
*G. Murray trs. of Aeschy-
   lus begun.*
F. von Unruh, 'Platz'.
*'English Madrigal Verse'
   ed. Fellowes.*

Shelley (d. 1822): Philosophical View of Reform. P

Sitwell, Edith (1887): The Wooden Pegasus. V

Thomas, Edward (d. 1917): Collected Poems.

Walpole (1884): The Captives. P

Wellesley (1889): Poems.

Wells (1866): Outline of History. P

Wharton, Edith (1862): The Age of Innocence. P

Williams, C. (1886): Divorce. V

Wodehouse (1881): The Coming of Bill. P

Wolfe, Humbert (1885): London Sonnets. V
  Shylock reasons with Mr. Chesterton. V

Yeats (1865): Michael Robartes and the Dancer. V

1921

Anderson, Sherwood (1876): The Triumph of the Egg. P

Archer (1856): The Green Goddess. P

Baring (1874): Poems 1914–19.

Barrie (1860): Shall we join the Ladies? D

Conrad (1857): Notes on Life and Letters. P

Coppard (1878): Adam and Eve and Pinch Me. P

Dane, Clemence: A Bill of Divorcement. D
  Will Shakespeare. D

De la Mare (1873): Memoirs of a Midget. P
  The Veil, and Other Poems. V

De Morgan (d. 1917): The Old Man's Youth. P

Drinkwater (1882): Mary Stuart. D
  Oliver Cromwell. D

Galsworthy (1869): To Let. P

Graves, Robert (1895): The Pier Glass. V

Holme, Constance (1880): The Trumpet in the Dust. P

Housman, L. (1865): Angels and Ministers. D

Hudson (1841): A Traveller in Little Things. P

Huxley, Aldous (1894): Crome Yellow. P

Kaye-Smith (1887): Joanna Godden. P

Lawrence (1885): Psychoanalysis and the Unconscious. P
  Sea and Sardinia. P   Tortoises. V

Lubbock, Percy (1879): The Craft of Fiction. P

M'Taggart (1866): The Nature of Existence. P

Maugham (1874): The Circle. D

Millin (1889): Middleclass. P

Moore (1852): Héloïse and Abélard. P

Myers (1881): The Orissers. P

O'Neill, Eugene (1888): The Emperor Jones. D

Richards (1893) **with Ogden and Wood**: Foundations of Aesthetics. P

Austin Dobson d.

J. C. Squire's 'Selections from Modern Poets' (2nd series 1925).

New Cambridge Shakespeare, ed. Quiller-Couch (to 1931) and Dover Wilson.

R. Becher, 'Um Gott'.

George, 'Drei Gesunge'.

G. Keynes, Bibliography of Wm. Blake.

Sampson, 'English for the English'.

Arthur Waley, 'The Nō Plays of Japan'.

Binyon, 'Court Painters of the Grand Mogul'.

President U.S.A. Harding.

Robinson, Edwin Arlington (1869): Collected Poems.
Russell, Bertrand (1872): The Analysis of Mind. P
Sackville-West (1892): Orchard and Vineyard. V
Shaw (1856): Back to Methuselah. D
Sitwell, Edith (1887): Troy Park. V˙
Smith, Logan Pearsall (1865): More Trivia. P
Strachey (1880): Queen Victoria. P
Tomlinson, H. M. (1873): London River. P
Walpole (1884): The Young Enchanted. P
Woolf (1882): Monday or Tuesday. P
Yeats (1865): Four Plays for Dancers. D

1922

Abercrombie (1881): Four Short Plays. D
Austen (d. 1817): Love and Freindship. P
Baring (1874): The Puppet Show of Memory. P
Beerbohm (1872): Rossetti and his Circle. P
Bennett (1867): Mr. Prohack. P
Benson, Stella (1892): The Poor Man. P
Blunden (1896): The Shepherd and Other Poems.
Byron (d. 1824): Letters ed. Murray. P
Chesterton (1874): The Ballad of St. Barbara. V
Colum, Padraic (1881): Dramatic Legends. V
Coppard (1878): Clorinda walks in Heaven. P
Cummings (1894): The Enormous Room. P
Davies (1870): Child Lovers, and Other Poems.
Drinkwater (1882): Preludes. V
Eliot (1888): The Waste Land. V
Fitzgerald, Scott (1896): Tales of the Jazz Age. P
　　The Beautiful and the Damned. P
Flecker (d. 1915): Hassan. D
Galsworthy (1867): The Forsyte Saga [in one vol.]. P　　Loyalties. D
Garnett (1892): Lady into Fox. P
Granville-Barker (1877): The Exemplary Theatre. P
Guedalla (1889): The Second Empire. P
Hardy (1840): Late Lyrics and Earlier. V
Housman, A. E. (1859): Last Poems. V
Housman, L. (1865): Little Plays of St. Francis.
Hudson (d. 1922): A Hind in Richmond Park. P
Huxley, Aldous (1894): Mortal Coils. P
Inge (1860): Outspoken Essays [2nd series]. P
Joyce (1882): Ulysses [Paris ed., Feb.; London, Oct.]. P
Lawrence (1885): Aaron's Rod. P.　Fantasia of the Unconscious. P.　　England, my England. P
Lewis, Sinclair (1885): Babbitt. P
'Mansfield' (1888): The Garden Party. P
Masefield (1878): Melloney Holtspur. D

Sir Walter Raleigh d.
Wilfrid Scawen Blunt d.
W. H. Hudson d.
Alice Meynell d.
Marcel Proust d.
'Georgian Poetry, 1920–22.'
'Encyclopaedia Britannica', 12th ed.
Incorporation of British Broadcasting Company, 15 Dec. (First programme, 14 Nov.; licence issued, 18 Jan., 1923; Royal Charter 1 Jan. 1927.)
Thomas J. Wise, Ashley Library Catalogue (concl. 1936).
'The Criterion.'
'Reader's Digest.'
Martin du Gard, 'Les Thibault' (1922–40).
Valéry, 'Charmes'.
Clive Bell, 'Since Cézanne'.
Carr-Saunders, 'Population Problems'.
Evans, 'Palace of Minos' (completed 1935).
Power, 'Medieval English Nunneries'.
C. K. Scott Moncrieff trs. of Proust, first part (the 8 parts in 12 vols. 11th vol. 1930, final vol. trs. Stephen Hudson, 1921).
Sidney and Beatrice Webb, 'Statutory Authorities'.

Maugham (1874): East of Suez. D
  The Land of Promise. D
  On a Chinese Screen. P
Millin (1889): Adam's Rest. P
Monro, Harold (1879): Real Property. V
Montague (1867): Disenchantment. P
Moore, George Edward (1873): Philosophical
  Studies. P
Murry (1889): Countries of the Mind. P
  The Problem of Style. P
O'Neill, Eugene (1888): Anna Christie. D
  The Hairy Ape. D
Priestley (1894): Brief Diversions. P
Raleigh (d. 1922): The War in the Air, vol. i. P
'Rebecca West' (1892): The Judge. P
Sitwell, Edith (1887): Façade. V
Sitwell, S. (1897): Hundred and One Harle-
  quins. V
Squire (1884): Poems [second series].
Strachey (1880): Books and Characters. P
Turner, W. J. (1889): The Man who ate the Popo-
  mack. D
Walpole (1884): The Cathedral. P
Williams, William Carlos (1883): Spring and All.
  V
Woolf (1882) : Jacob's Room. P
Yeats (1865): Later Poems.

1923

Abercrombie (1881): Phoenix. D
Aldington (1892): Exile and Other Poems.
Archer (1856): The Old Drama and the New. P
Baring (1874): A Triangle. P
Belloc (1870): On. P.   Sonnets and Verse. V
Bennett (1867): Riceyman Steps. P
Blunden (1896): To Nature. V
Chambers, E. K. (1866): The Elizabethan Stage.
  P
Churchill, Winston S. (1874): World Crisis [com-
  pleted '29; abridged '31]. P
Conrad (1857): The Rover. P
Davies (1870): Collected Poems (2nd series).
De la Mare (1873): The Riddle, & Other Stories. P
Drinkwater (1882): Collected Plays. D
  Collected Poems.   Robert E. Lee. D
Dunsany (1878): Plays of Near and Far. D
Firbank (1886): The Flower beneath the Foot. P
Forster (1879): Pharos and Pharillon. P
Frost, Robert (1875): New Hampshire. V
Guedalla (1889): Masters and Men. P
Hardy (1840): Tragedy of the Queen of Cornwall.
  D

Maurice Barrès d.
'Katherine Mansfield' d.
William Paton Ker d.
Maurice Hewlett d.
William Hurrell Mallock d.
Viscount Morley d.
'Proposals for the Revision
  of the Book of Common
  Prayer.'
'English Diaries', ed. A.
  Ponsonby.
Jane Austen's Novels,
  ed. R. W. Chapman.
Nonesuch Press started.
'Time' started.
J. L. and Barbara Ham-
  mond, 'Lord Shaftes-
  bury'.
Coulton, 'Five Centuries
  of Religion' (vol. iii,
  1936).
Cambridge Ancient His-
  tory (completed 1939).
Adolf Hitler, 'Mein
  Kampf' (completed
  1927, Eng. trs., 1933).

Housman, L. (1865): Followers of St. Francis. D
Hudson (d. 1922): Letters, ed. Garnett. P
Huxley, Aldous (1894): Antic Hay. P
  On the Margin. P
Huxley, Julian (1887): Essays of a Biologist. P
Ker (d. 1923): The Art of Poetry. P
Lawrence (1885): Birds, Beasts and Flowers. V
  Kangaroo. P.   Ladybird.   P.   Love
  Poems.   Studies in Classic American
  Literature. P
Lubbock, Percy (1879): Roman Pictures.
Macaulay, Rose (1881): Told by an Idiot. P
Madariaga (1886): The Genius of Spain. P
'Mansfield' (d. 1923): The Dove's Nest, and Other
  Stories. P.   Poems.
Masefield (1878): King Cole, and Other Poems. V
  A King's Daughter. D.   Collected Poems.
Maugham (1874): Our Betters. D
Meynell (d. 1922): Essays. P.   Last Poems.
Millin (1889): The Jordans. P
Montague (1867): Fiery Particles. P
Powys, T. F. (1875): Black Bryony. P
  The Left Leg. P
Pratt (1883): Newfoundland Verse.
Raleigh (d. 1922): Some Authors. P
  Laughter from a Cloud. P
Read (1893): Mutations of the Phoenix. V
Richards (1893) **with Ogden**: The Meaning of
  Meaning. P
Santayana (1863): Scepticism & Animal Faith. P
Stein, Gertrude (1874): Geography and Plays. P
Stevens, Wallace (1879): Harmonium. V
Walpole (1884): Jeremy and Hamlet. P
Wodehouse (1881): Leave it to Psmith. P

President U.S.A.
Coolidge.

1924

Anderson, Sherwood (1876): A Story Teller's
  Tale. P
Babbitt (1865): Democracy and Leadership. P
Baring (1874): 'C.' P
Bennett (1867): Elsie and the Child. P
Benson, Stella (1892): Pipers and a Dancer. P
Boswell (d. 1795): Letters, ed. C. B. Tinker.
Campbell (1901): The Flaming Terrapin. V
Clare (d. 1864): Madrigals and Chronicles, ed.
  E. Blunden. V
Conrad (d. 1924): Laughing Anne, and One Day
  More. D
Coward (1899): The Rat-trap. D.   The Vortex. D
Davies (1870): Secrets. V

William Archer d.
Francis Herbert Bradley
  d.
Joseph Conrad d.
Collingwood, 'Speculum
  Mentis'.
Hulme,   'Speculations'
  (ed. Read).
Anatole France d.
Kafka d.
Lenin d.
Woodrow Wilson d.
André Breton, 'Manifeste
  du Surréalisme'.
Thomas Mann, 'Zauber-
  berg'.

De la Mare (1873): Crossings. D
  Ding Dong Bell. V
Duggan (   ): Poems.
Dukes (1885): The Man with a Load of Mischief. D
Dunsany (1878): Five Plays. D
Eliot (1888): Homage to John Dryden. P
Ford (1873): Some Do Not. P
Forster (1879): A Passage to India. P
Galsworthy (1869): Old English. D
  The White Monkey. P
Garnett (1892): A Man in the Zoo. P
Gibson (1878): Kestrel Edge and Other Plays. D
Hemingway (1898): in our time. P
Housman, L. (1865): Trimblerigg. P
Huxley, Aldous (1894): The Little Mexican. P
Kennedy, Margaret (1896): The Constant Nymph.
  P
Lawrence (1885): The Boy in the Bush [with
  M. L. Skinner]. P
Macaulay, Rose (1881): Orphan Island. P
'Mansfield' (d. 1923): Something Childish, and
  Other Stories. P
Masefield (1878): Sard Harker. P
Melville (d. 1891): Billy Budd. P
Millin (1889): God's Stepchildren. P
Milne (1882): When We were Very Young. P
Montague (1867): The Right Place. P
Moore (1852): Conversations in Ebury Street. P
Mottram (1883): The Spanish Farm [trilogy
  completed '27]. P
O'Neill, Eugene (1888): All God's Chillun. D
  Desire Under the Elms. D
Robinson, Lennox (1886): The Round Table. D
  Crabbed Youth and Age. D
Selincourt, Hugh de (1878): The Cricket Match. P
Shaw (1856): St. Joan. D
Sitwell, Edith (1887): The Sleeping Beauty. V
Sitwell, Osbert (1892): Triple Fugue. P
Sitwell, Sacheverell (1897): Southern Baroque
  Art. P.   The Thirteenth Cæsar. V
Slater (1876): The Karroo and other poems.
Squire (1884): Grub Street Nights. P.
Tomlinson, H. M. (1873): Tidemarks. P
Walpole (1884): The Old Ladies. P
Webb, Mary (1881): Precious Bane. P
Wodehouse (1881): The Inimitable Jeeves. P
Wolfe, Humbert (1885): Kensington Gardens. V
Woodforde, James (d. 1803): Diary of a Country
  Parson, vol. i, ed. J. Beresford [1758–1802;
  concl. 1931]. P

Siegfried, 'L'Angleterre d'aujourd'hui'.

Aldington (1892): A Fool i' the Forest. V
Anderson, Sherwood (1876): Dark Laughter. P
Austen (d. 1817): Sanditon. P   Lady Susan. P
Baring (1874): Cat's Cradle. P   Collected
    Poems.
Belloc (1870): The Cruise of the Nona. P
    Mr. Petre. P
Benson, Stella (1892): The Little World. P
Blunden (1896): English Poems. Far East. V
    Masks of Time. V
Bottomley (1874): Poems of Thirty Years. V
Bridges (1844): New Verse written in 1921. V
    The Tapestry. V
Chesterton (1874): The Everlasting Man. P
Compton-Burnett: Pastors and Masters. P
Conrad (d.1924):Suspense. P Tales of Hearsay. P
Coppard (1878): Fishmonger's Fiddle. P
Coward (1899): Fallen Angels. D. Hay Fever. D
Cushing (1869): Life of Sir William Osler. P
Davies, W. H. (1871): A Poet's Alphabet. V
Day-Lewis, C. (1904): Beechen Vigil. V
De la Mare (1873): Broomsticks & Other Tales. P
Dreiser (1871): An American Tragedy. P
Drinkwater (1882): New Poems.
Eliot (1888): Poems, 1905–25.
Firbank (1886): Sorrow in Sunlight (new title
    Prancing Nigger, 1929). P
Fitzgerald, Scott (1896): The Great Gatsby. P
Flecker (d. 1915): Don Juan. D
Ford (1873): No more Parades. P
Galsworthy (1869): Caravan. P
Garnett (1892): The Sailor's Return. P
Gibson, Wilfrid (1878): I heard a Sailor. V
Graves (1895): Welchman's Hose. V
Hardy (1840): Human Shows, Far Fantasies. V
Hartley (1895): Simonetta Perkins. P
Heyward (1885): Porgy [dramatized '27; Gersh-
    win's opera, Porgy and Bess, 1935]. P
Huxley, Aldous (1894): Those Barren Leaves. P
    Along the Road. P
Lawrence, D. H. (1885): St. Mawr and the Prin-
    cess. P
Lewis, Sinclair (1885): Arrowsmith. P
'Lonsdale' (1881):.The Last of Mrs Cheney. D
    Spring Cleaning. D
Loos (1893) : Gentlemen Prefer Blondes. P
Lowell, Amy (1874): John Keats. P·   What's
    O'Clock? V
Masefield (1878): The Trial of Jesus. D
Maugham (1874): The Painted Veil. P
Millin (1889): Mary Glenn. P
Muir (1887): First Poems.
Murry (1889): Keats and Shakespeare. P

A. C. Benson d.
Sir Henry Rider Haggard
  d.
C. H. Wilkinson, ed.
  Poems of Lovelace.
Whitehead, 'Science and
  the Modern World'.
Smuts, 'Holism and
  Evolution'.
Cole, 'Short History of the
  British Working-class
  Movement' (completed
  1927, revised 1948).
Grierson, ed. Milton's
  Poems.
J. L. and Barbara Ham-
  mond, 'Rise of Modern
  Industry'.
G. L. Keynes, ed. Blake's
  Works.
Centenary Book of South
  African Verse, ed. F. C.
  Slater.
Curzon, 'British Govern-
  ment in India'.
Coulton, 'The Medieval
  Village'.
Arthur Waley, trs. 'The
  Tale of Genji' (6 vols.,
  concl. 1933).
C. H. Herford, Percy and
  Evelyn Simpson, ed.
  Ben Jonson (11 vols.,
  completed 1952).
Lee, 'King Edward VII'.
'Oxford Book of English
  Prose', ed. Quiller-
  Couch.
'New Yorker' started.

President U.S.A.
  Coolidge (2nd
  Term).

Myers (1881): The Clio. P
O'Casey (1884): Juno and the Paycock. D
O'Flaherty (1897): The Informer. P
Pound (1885): A Draft of XVI Cantos [and
  further Cantos, 1928, '30, '34, '37, '40, '48]. V
Powys, J. C. (1872) Ducdame. P
Powys, Ll. (1884): Black Laughter. P
Powys, T. F. (1875): Mr. Tasker's Gods. P
Priestley (1894): The English Comic Writers. P
Robinson, Edwin Arlington (1869): Dionysus in
  Doubt. V
Sackville-West, E. (1901): Piano Quintet. P
Smith, Pauline : The Little Karoo. P
Stein, Gertrude (1874): Making of Americans. P
Stephens, James (1882): A Poetry Recital.
Turner (1889): The Seven Days of the Sun. V
Walpole (1884): Portrait of a Man with Red Hair. P
Weils (1866): Christina Alberta's Father. P
Williams, C. (1886): Windows of Night. V
Wolfe, Humbert (1885): The Unknown Goddess. V
Woolf, Virginia (1882): The Common Reader. P
  [Second Series 1932] Mrs. Dalloway. P
Yeats (1865): A Vision. P

1926

Anderson, Sherwood (1876): Tar. P
Bennett (1867): Lord Raingo. P
Bromfield (1896): Early Autumn. P
Cabell, (1879): The Silver Stallion. P
Christie, Agatha (1891): The Murder of Roger
  Ackroyd. P
Conrad (d. 1924): Last Essays. P
Davies, W. H. (1871): The Birth of Song. V
  The Song of Love. V
De la Mare (1873): The Connoisseur. P
Drinkwater (1882): Persephone. V
Faulkner, W. (1897): Soldiers' Pay. P
Ferber (1887): Show Boat. P
Firbank (1886): Concerning the Eccentricities of
  Cardinal Pirelli. P
Fitzgerald, Scott (1896): All the Sad Young Men. P
Ford (1873): A Man could Stand Up. P
Fry, Roger (1866): Transformations. P
Galsworthy (1869): The Silver Spoon. P
Gibson (1878): Collected Poems.
  Sixty-three Poems.
Guedalla (1889): Palmerston. P
Hemingway (1898): The Sun also Rises. P
Howard, S. (1891): The Silver Chord. D
Hughes, L. (1902): The Weary Blues. V
Hughes (1900): Confessio Juvenis. V
Jeffers (1887): Roan Stallion, Tamar, and Other
  Poems.

Ronald Firbank d.
*Charles Montagu Doughty
  d.*
*Fowler, 'Modern English
  Usage'.*
*'Short Catalogue of Bible
  of 1640', Pollard.*
*'Oxford Book of 18th
  Century Verse', ed.
  Nichol Smith.*
*Short-Title Catalogue of
  English Books, 1475–
  1640 (Bibliographical
  Society, revised ed. in
  preparation).*
*Owst, 'Preaching in Medi-
  eval England'.*
*Book-of-the-Month Club
  founded (U.S.).*
*Inge, 'The Platonic Tradi-
  tion'.*
*Tawney, 'Religion and the
  Rise of Capitalism'.*
*'Encyclopaedia Britan-
  nica', 13th ed.*

Lawrence, D. H. (1885): The Plumed Serpent. P
Lawrence, T. E. (1888): Seven Pillars of Wisdom. P
'McDiarmid' (1892): Penny Wheep. V
  A Drunk Man Looks at a Thistle. V
McLaren (1887): My Crowded Solitude. P
Masefield (1878): Odtaa. P
Milne (1882): Winnie-the-Pooh. P
Muir (1887): Chorus of the Newly Dead. V
O'Casey (1884): The Plough and the Stars. D
O'Neill, Eugene (1888): The Great God Brown. D
Parker (1893): Enough Rope. V
Plomer (1903): Turbott Wolfe. P
Pound (1885): Personae [the collected poems].
Pratt (1883): Titans. V
Prichard (1884): Working Bullocks. P
Robinson (1886): The White Blackbird. D.
Sandburg, Carl (1878): Abraham Lincoln: The
  Prairie Years. P
Sassoon (1886): Satirical Poems.
Schreiner (d. 1920): From Man to Man. P
Scott, D. C. (1862): Collected Poems.
Sitwell, Edith (1887): Elegy on Dead Fashion. V
Sitwell, Osbert (1892): Before the Bombardment. P
Smith, Pauline (   ): The Beadle. P
Stribling (1881): Teeftallow. P
Turner (1889): Marigold. V
Van Vechten (1880): Nigger Heaven. P
Victoria, Queen (d. 1901): Letters, 1862–85 [com-
  pleted 1928]. P
Wallace (1875): The Ringer. D
Wells (1866): The World of William Clissold. P
Wilder (1897): The Cabala. P
Wolfe, Humbert (1885): Humoresque. V
  News of the Devil. V
Wordsworth (d. 1850): The Prelude [ed. de
  Selincourt, first ed. of 1805 text]. V

1927

Aiken, C. P. (1889): Blue Voyage. P
Austen, Jane (d. 1817): The Watsons. P
Behrman (1893): The Second Man. D
Bell, Gertrude (d. 1926): Letters. P
Binyon (1869): The Wonder of Night. V
Cather (1876): Death Comes for the Archbishop. P
Chesterton (1874): Collected Poems.
Cresswell (1896): Poems 1921–27.
Davies, W. H. (1871): A Poet's Calendar. V
De la Mare (1873): Stuff and Nonsense. V
De la Roche (1885): Jalna. P
Drinkwater (1882): Bird in Hand. D
Forster (1879): Aspects of the Novel. P
Fry, Roger (1866): Cézanne. P

*Mona Wilson, 'Life of
  Blake'.*
*Plowman, 'Introduction
  to the Study of Blake'.*
*Sidney and Beatrice Webb,
  'English Poor Law
  History'.*
*Beard, 'Rise of American
  Civilization'.*
*Haldane, 'Possible
  Worlds'.*
*Parrington, 'Main Currents
  in American Thought'
  (trilogy, concl. 1930).*
*Russell, 'Analysis of
  Matter'.*

Granville-Barker (1877): Prefaces to Shakespeare [cont. 1930, '37, '45, '48]. P

Mauriac, '*Thérèse Desqueroux*'.

Green, P. E. (1894): In Abraham's Bosom. D
Grove (1872): A Search for America. P
Hemingway (1898): Men without Women. P
Joyce (1882): Pomes Penyeach. V
Lawrence, D. H. (1885): Mornings in Mexico. P
Lehmann, Rosamund (1903): Dusty Answer. P
Lewis, Sinclair (1885): Elmer Gantry. P
'Lonsdale' (1881): On Approval. D
Lowell, Amy (d. 1925): Ballads for Sale. V
Lowes (1867): Road to Xanadu. P
Mackenzie, Compton (1883): Vestal Fire. P
'Mansfield' (d. 1923): Journal [enlarged ed., '54]. P
Marquis (1878): archy and mehitabel. V
Mason (1865): No Other Tiger. P
Maugham (1874): The Letter. D   The Constant Wife. D
Millin (1889): An Artist in the Family. P
Milne (1882): Now We are Six. P
Myers (1881): The Near and the Far. P
Nicolson (1886): Some People. P
O'Neill, Eugene (1888): Marco Millions. D
Pickthall (d. 1922): Complete Poems.
Plomer (1903): I Speak of Africa. P
Robinson, Henry Crabb (d. 1867): Correspondence, ed. Morley. P
Rölvaag (1876): Giants in the Earth [trilogy concl. 1931]. P
Sandburg, Carl (1878): The American Songbag. V
Santayana (1863): The Realm of Being [4 vols. concl. 1940]. P
Sinclair, Upton (1878): Oil! P
Sitwell, Edith (1887): Rustic Elegies. V
Sitwell, Osbert (1892): England Reclaimed. V
Sitwell, Sacheverell (1897): The Cyder Feast. V
Tomlinson (1873): Gallions Reach. P
Turner (1889): The Aesthetes. P
Waddell (1889): The Wandering Scholars. P
Walpole (1884): Jeremy at Crale. P
Wharton, Edith (1862): Twilight Sleep. P
Wilder (1897): Bridge of San Luis Rey. P
Williamson, Henry (1897): Tarka the Otter. P
Wolfe, Humbert (1885): Cursory Rhymes. V   Requiem. V   Veni Creator! V
Woolf, Virginia (1882): To the Lighthouse. P
Yeats (1865): October Blast. V

Abercrombie (1881): Twelve Idylls. V

Belloc (1870): A Conversation with an Angel. P

Benét, S. V. (1898): John Brown's Body. V

Blunden (1896): Japanese Garland. V   Retreat. V
 Winter Nights. V   Undertones of War. P

'Brent of Bin Bin': Up the Country. P

Callaghan, Morley (1903): Strange Fugitive. P

Campbell (1901): The Wayzgoose. V

Day-Lewis (1904): Country Comets. V

Eliot (1888): For Lancelot Andrewes. P

Ford (1873): Last Post. P

Forster (1879): The Eternal Moment. P

Galsworthy (1869): Swan Song. P

Gibson (1878): The Golden Room. V

Hardy (d. 1928): Winter Words. V

Huxley, Aldous (1894): Point Counter Point. P

Joyce (1882): Anna Livia Plurabelle (from Finnegans Wake). P

Lawrence (1885): Lady Chatterley's Lover. P
 The Woman Who Rode Away. P
 Collected Poems.

Lewis, Wyndham (1884): The Childermass [vol. i
 of The Human Age: vol. ii and iii, 1955]. P

McCrae (1876): Satyrs and Sunlight. V

Mackenzie, Compton (1883): Extraordinary
 Women. P

'Mansfield' (d. 1923): Letters [and 1951]. P

Masefield (1878): Midsummer Night. V

Maugham (1874): Ashenden. P

Milne (1882): The House at Pooh Corner. P

Monro (1879): The Earth for Sale. V

Nichols (1893): Epic Wind. V

O'Casey (1884): The Silver Tassie. D

O'Neill, Eugene (1888): Strange Interlude. D

Powys, T. F. (1875): Mr. Weston's Good Wine. P

Russell ('Æ.', 1867): Midsummer Eve. V

Sandburg, Carl (1878): Good Morning, America.
 V

Sassoon (1886): The Heart's Journey. V
 Memoirs of a Fox-hunting Man. P

Schreiner (d. 1920): Undine. P

Sitwell, Edith (1887): Five Poems.

Turner (1889): New Poems.

Waugh, E. (1903): Decline and Fall. P

Wolfe, Humbert (1885): The Silver Cat. V   This
 Blind Rose. V

Woolf, Virginia (1882): Orlando. P

Yeats (1865): The Tower. V

Clive Bell, 'Civilization'.

*'Oxford Book of Regency
 (later called Romantic)
 Verse', ed. Milford.*

*Shaw, 'Intelligent
 Woman's Guide to
 Socialism'.*

*Wicksteed, ed. Blake's
 'Songs of Innocence
 and Experience'.*

Edmund Gosse d.

Thomas Hardy d.

First talking pictures.

'Life and Letters'.

*Eddington, 'The Nature
 of the Physical World'.*

André Breton, 'Nadja'.

*Remarque, 'Im Westen
 nichts Neues'.*

*Brecht, 'Die Dreigro-
 schenoper'.*

Aiken (1889): Selected Poems.
Aldington (1892): Death of a Hero. P
Baring (1874): The Coat without Seam. P
Blunden (1896): Near and Far. V
Bowen, Elizabeth (1899): The Last September. P
Bridges (1844): The Testament of Beauty. V
Cecil (1902): The Stricken Deer. P
Compton Burnett : Brothers and Sisters. P
Davies, W. H. (1871): Ambition. V
Day-Lewis (1904): Transitional Poem.
Dickinson (d. 1886): Further Poems.
Eliot (1888): Dante. P
Faulkner, W. (1897): Sartoris. P   The Sound
    and the Fury. P
Glasgow (1874): They Stooped to Folly. P
Graves (1895): Goodbye to all That. P
Greene, Graham (1904): The Man Within. P
Hamilton (1904): Rope. D
Hemingway (1898): A Farewell to Arms. P
Henry Green (1905): Living. P
Hughes, Richard (1900): A High Wind in Jamaica.
    P
Lawrence D. H. (1885): Pansies. V
Lewis, Sinclair (1885): Dodsworth. P
Linklater (1899): Poet's Pub. P
'Lonsdale' (1881): Canaries Sometimes Sing. D
MacNeice (1907): Blind Fireworks. V
Masefield (1878): South and East. V
Masters (1869): The Fate of the Jury. V
Maugham (1874): The Sacred Flame. D
Morgan, Charles (1894): Portrait in a Mirror. P
Plomer (1903): Paper Houses. P
Powys, J. C. (1872): Wolf Solent. P
Prichard (1884): Coonardoo. P
Priestley (1894): The Good Companions. P
'Rebecca West' (1892): Harriet Hume. P
Reitz (1882): Commando; a Boer journal of the
    Boer War. P
Rice, E. (1892): Street Scene. D
Russell ('Æ.', 1867): Dark Weeping. V
Sherriff (1896): Journey's End. D
Sitwell, Edith (1887): Gold Coast Customs. V
Sitwell, Sacheverell (1897): The Gothick North
    [concl. 1930]. P
Stephens, J. (1882): The Outcast. V
Wharton, Edith (1862): Hudson River Bracketed.
    P
Wolfe, T. (1900): Look Homeward, Angel. P
Woolf, Virginia (1882): A Room of One's Own. P
Yeats (1865): The Winding Stair. V

First year of the Depression.
Henry Arthur Jones d.
Russell, 'Marriage and Morals'.
Kenneth Clark, 'The Gothic Revival'.
F. A. Pottle, 'Boswell's Literary Career'.
Waddell, 'Medieval Latin Lyrics'.
Claudel, 'Le Soulier de Satin'.

President U.S.A.
Hoover.

Abercrombie (1881): Collected Poems.
Auden (1907): Poems.
Bax (1886): Socrates. D
Belloc (1870): New Cautionary Tales. V
Bennett (1867): Imperial Palace. P
Blunden (1896): Poems 1914–30. A Summer's
   Fancy. V Leigh Hunt. P
Bottomley (1874): Festival Preludes. V
'Brent of Bin Bin' (1883): Ten Creeks Run. P
'Bridie' (1888): The Anatomist. D Tobias
   and the Angel. D
Campbell (1901): Adamastor. V
Churchill, Winston S. (1874): My Early Life. P
Connelly (1890): Green Pastures. D
Coward (1899): Private Lives. D
Crane, H. (1899): The Bridge. V
Cresswell (1896): The Poet's Progress. P
De la Mare (1873): On the Edge. P
Dickinson (d. 1886): Poems: Centenary Edition.
Dos Passos (1896): The 42nd Parallel. P
Eliot (1888): Ash Wednesday. V
Empson (1906): Seven Types of Ambiguity. P
Faulkner, W. (1897): As I Lay Dying. P
Gibson (1878): Hazards. V
Hammett (1894): Maltese Falcon. P
Huxley, Aldous (1894): Brief Candles. P
Lawrence, D. H. (1885): The Virgin and the
   Gipsy. P
Lewis, Wyndham (1884): The Apes of God. P
MacLeish (1892): New Found Land. V
Maugham (1874): The Breadwinner. D Cakes
   and Ale. P
'McDiarmid' (1892): To Circumjack Cenrastus. V
Palmer (1885): The Passage. P
Porter (1894): Flowering Judas. P
Priestley (1894): Angel Pavement. P
Russell ('Æ.', 1867): Enchantment. V
Sackville-West, V. (1892): The Edwardians. P
Sassoon (1886): Memoirs of an Infantry Officer.
   P In Sicily. V
Shaw (1856): The Apple Cart. D
Sitwell, Edith (1887): Collected Poems.
Stephens, James (1882): Theme and Variations. V
Tomlinson (1873): All Our Yesterdays. P
Turner (1889): Miss America. V
Victoria, Queen (d. 1901): Letters, 1886–1901
   [completed 1932].
Waugh, E. (1903): Vile Bodies. P
Walpole (1884): Herries Chronicle. [4 vol. novel,
   concl. 1933].
Williams, C. (1886): War in Heaven. P
Wolfe, Humbert (1885): The Uncelestial City. V
Yeats-Brown (1886): Bengal Lancer. P

E. K. Chambers,
  'William Shakespeare'.
J. L. and Barbara Ham-
  mond, 'The Age of the
  Chartists'.
Inge, 'Christian Ethics
  and Modern Problems'.
J. M. Keynes, 'Treatise
  on Money'.
Jeans, 'The Mysterious
  Universe'.
Trevelyan, 'England
  under Queen Anne'
  (completed 1934).
Rutherford, Chadwick,
  and Ellis, 'Radiations
  from Radioactive Sub-
  stances'.
British Museum Cata-
  logue (revised) begins:
  vols. 1–51 appear
  1930–54.
Television started in
  U.S.A.
D. H. Lawrence d.
Kafka, 'The Castle', trs.
  W. and E. Muir.
Arthur Conan Doyle d.
Robert Bridges d.

Aiken, C. P. (1889): Preludes for Memnon. V
Baring (1874): In the End is my Beginning. P
Bax (1886): The Venetian. D   The Immortal Lady. D
Benét, S. V. (1898): Ballads and Poems
Benson, Stella (1892): Tobit Transplanted. P
Binyon (1869): Collected Poems.
Blunden (1896): To Themis. V
'Brent of Bin Bin' (1883): Back to Bool Bool. P
Bridges (d. 1930): Shorter Poems [enlarged ed.].
Buck (1892): The Good Earth. P
Campbell (1901): The Georgiad. V
Cather (1876): Shadows on the Rock. P
Compton-Burnett : Men and Wives. P
Coward (1899). Cavalcade. D
Cresswell (1896): Poems 1924–31.
Cronin (1896): Hatter's Castle. P
Davies, W. H. (1871): In Winter. V
Davison (1893): Man-Shy. P
Day-Lewis (1904): From Feathers to Iron. V
'Delafield', (1890): Diary of a Provincial Lady. P

Drinkwater (1882): Christmas Poems.
Eliot (1888): Thoughts after Lambeth. P
Faulkner, W. (1897): Sanctuary. P
Garnett (1892): The Grasshoppers Come. P
Granville-Barker (1877): On Dramatic Method. P
Guedalla (1889): The Duke. P
Hurst (1889): Back Street. P
Huxley (1894): The World of Light. D   The Cicadas. V
Johnston (1901): The Moon in the Yellow River. D
Lawrence, D. H. (d. 1930): The Man who Died. P
Linklater (1899): Juan in America. P
Macaulay, Rose (1881): Going Abroad. P
Myers (1881): Prince Jarli. P
O'Neill, Eugene (1888): Mourning Becomes Electra. D
Powell (1905): Afternoon Men. P
Robinson (1886): The Far-off Hills. D
Russell ('Æ.', 1867): Vale. V
Sackville-West, V. (1892): All Passion Spent. P
Santayana (1863): The Genteel Tradition. P
Sassoon (1886): Poems by Pinchbeck Lyre [pseud.]
Sherwood, Robert (1896): Reunion in Vienna. D
Sitwell, Edith (1887): Epithalamium. In Spring. V
Sitwell, Osbert (1892): Collected Satires and Poems.
Smith, Dodie (   ): Autumn Crocus. D
Steffens (1866): Autobiography. P

Keynes, 'Essays in Persuasion'.
Greg, 'Dramatic Documents from Elizabethan Playhouses'.
Tawney, 'Equality' (revised 1952).
Milton, Columbia edition (completed 1940).
Statute of Westminster.
Arnold Bennett d.
Buxton Forman, ed. Keats's Letters.
Telford, ed. John Wesley's Letters.
Stokes and Waddell ed. Cole's 'Blecheley Diary'.

Strachey (1880): Portraits. P
Thurber (1894): The Owl in the Attic. P
Turner (1889): Pursuit of Psyche. V
Wallace (1875): On the Spot. D
White, Gilbert (d. 1793) Journals, ed. Johnson.
Williams, C. (1886): Many Dimensions. P
  The Place of the Lion. P
Wilson, E. (1895): Axel's Castle. P
Wolfe, Humbert (1885): Snow. V
Woolf, Virginia (1882): The Waves. P

1932

Abercrombie (1881): Poetry, its Music and Meaning. P
Anderson, Sherwood (1876): Beyond Desire. P
Auden (1907): The Orators. V
Austen, Jane (d. 1817): Letters, ed. R. W. Chapman [revised 1952].
Bax (1886): The Rose without a Thorn. D
Bennett (d. 1931): Journals (1896–1928), ed. Newman Flower [3 vols., concl. '33].
Binyon (1869): Koya San: Four Poems from Japan.
Blunden (1896): Halfway House. V
Bottomley (1874): Lyric Plays.
Bowen, Elizabeth (1899): To the North. P
Bridge, Ann (   ): Peking Picnic. P
'Bridie' (1888): Jonah and the Whale. D
Caldwell (1903): Tobacco Road. P
Campbell (1901): Pomegranates. V
Cary (1888): Aissa Saved. P
Coward (1899): Design for Living. D
Davies, W. H. (1871): Poems 1930–31.
De la Mare (1873): Old Rhymes and New. V
De Voto (1897): Mark Twain's America. P
Dos Passos (1896): 1919. P
Eliot (1888): Selected Essays. P   Sweeney Agonistes. V
Farrell (1904): Studs Lonigan [trilogy, '32, '34, '35]. P
Faulkner, W. (1897): Light in August. P
Gibbons, Stella (1902): Cold Comfort Farm. P
Gibson (1878): Highland Dawn. V   Islands. V
Glasgow (1874): The Sheltered Life. P
Hardy (d. 1928): Collected Poems.
Hemingway (1898): Death in the Afternoon. P
Huxley, Aldous (1894): Brave New World. P
  Texts and Pretexts.
Isherwood (1904): The Memorial. P
Lawrence, D. H. (d. 1930): Letters, ed. A. Huxley.

Morison, 'The English Newspaper'.
'Oxford Book of 16th Century Verse', ed. Chambers.
'Scrutiny' (till 1953).
Sidney and Beatrice Webb, 'Methods of Social Study'.
Berenson, 'Italian Painters of the Renaissance'.
Calverton, 'Liberation of American Literature'.
Cole, 'The Intelligent Man's Guide through World Chaos'.
Wells, 'Work, Wealth and Happiness of Mankind'.
Romain, 'Les Hommes de Bonne Volonté'.
Saint-Exupéry, 'Vol de Nuit'.
Dobrée ed. Chesterfield's Letters.

President U.S.A.

Franklin D.

Roosevelt.

Leavis (1895): New Bearings in English Poetry. P

Lehmann, Rosamond (1903): Invitation to the Waltz. P

Macaulay, Rose (1881): They were Defeated. P

'McDiarmid' (1892): First Hymn to Lenin. V
Scots Unbound. V

MacLeish (1892): Conquistador. V

Mann (1895): Flesh in Armour. P

Masefield (1878): A Tale of Troy. V

Massingham (1888): World Without End. P

Maugham (1874): For Services Rendered. D

Morgan (1894): The Fountain. P

Muir (1887): Six Poems.

Nicolson (1886): Public Faces. P

Nordhoff (1887) **and Hall** (1887): Mutiny on the Bounty. P

O'Faoláin (1900): Midsummer Night Madness. P

O'Flaherty (1897): The Puritan. P   Skerrett. P

Plomer (1903): The Fivefold Screen. P

Powell (1905): Venusberg. P

Priestley (1894): Dangerous Corner. D

Runyon (1884): Guys and Dolls [and other humorous collections]. P

Sassoon (1886): Prehistoric Burials. V

Shaw (1856): Too True to be Good. D
Adventures of a Black Girl in search of God. P

Simpson (1897): Boomerang. P

Thurber (1894): The Seal in the Bedroom. P

Waugh, E. (1903): Black Mischief. P

Wharton, Edith (1862): The Gods Arrive. P

Williams, C. (1886): The Greater Trumps. P

Wright, F. L. (1869): Autobiography [revised 1943]. P

Wylie, E. (d. 1928): Collected Poems.

Yeats (1865): Words for Music perhaps. V

1933

Aldington (1892): All Men are Enemies. P

Allen, H. (1889): Anthony Adverse. P

Auden (1907): The Dance of Death. V

Austen, Jane (d. 1817): Volume the First [Volume the Third, 1951]. P

Barker (1913): Thirty Preliminary Poems.

'Bridie' (1888): A Sleeping Clergyman. D

Caldwell (1903): God's Little Acre. P

Campbell (1901): Flowering Reeds. V

Cary (1888): American Visitor. P

Compton-Burnett : More Women than Men. P

Cozzens (1903): The Last Adam [Eng. title, A Cure of Flesh]. P

Crane, H. (d. 1932): Collected Poems.

Mario Praz, 'The Romantic Agony'.

E. de Selincourt, 'Dorothy Wordsworth, a Biography'.

Turberville, ed. 'Johnson's England'.

Hicks, 'The Great Tradition'.

Inge, 'God and the Astronomers'.

Wells, 'The Shape of Things to Come'.

John Galsworthy d.

George Moore d.

Cummings (1894): Eimi. P
Curnow (1911): Valley of Decision. V
Dark (1901): Prelude to Christopher. P
Davies, W. H. (1871): The Lovers' Song Book. V
Day-Lewis (1904): The Magnetic Mountain. V
De la Mare (1873): The Fleeting. V
Drinkwater (1882): Summer Harvest. V
Eliot (1888): The Use of Poetry and the Use of
    Criticism. P
Fleming, Peter (1907): Brazilian Adventure. P
Hemingway (1898): Winner Take Nothing. P
Hilton (1900): Lost Horizon. P
Howard, S. (1891): Alien Corn. D
Lawrence, D. H. (d. 1930): The Ship of Death. V
    The Lovely Lady. P   Last Poems.
Lewis, C. S. (1898): Pilgrim's Regress. P
MacLeish (1892): Frescoes for Mr. Rockefeller's
    City. V
Maugham (1874): Sheppey. D
Millin (1889): Rhodes. P   Three Men Die. P
Monro (d. 1932): Collected Poems.
Nathan, R. (1894): One More Spring. P
O'Casey (1884): Within the Gates. D
O'Faoláin (1900): A Nest of Simple Folk. P
O'Neill, Eugene (1888): Ah, Wilderness. D
Powys, J. C. (1872): A Glastonbury Romance. P
Priestley (1894): Laburnum Grove. D
Read (1893): The End of a War. V
Reitz (1882): Trekking on. P
Roberts, K. (1885): Rabble in Arms. P
Sackville-West, V. (1892): Collected Poems.
Sassoon (1886): The Road to Ruin. V
Shaw (1856): On the Rocks. D.   Village
    Wooing. D
Sitwell, Edith (1887): Five Variations on a Theme.
    V
Sitwell, Osbert (1892): Miracle on Sinai. P
Sitwell, Sacheverell (1897): Canons of Giant Art.
    P
Spender (1909): Poems.
Stein, Gertrude (1874): The Autobiography of
    Alice B. Toklas. P
Strachey (d. 1932): Characters and Commentaries.
    P
Thurber (1894): My Life and Hard Times. P
West, Nathanael (1902): Miss Lonelyhearts.. P
Yeats (1865): Collected Poems [2nd ed. 1950,
    variorum ed., '57].

*Duhamel, 'Chronique de
    Pasquier' (concl. 1945).
Malraux, 'La Condition
    Humaine'.*

Beckett (1906): More Pricks than Kicks. P
Berners (1883): First Childhood. P
Blunden (1896): Choice or Chance. V
Bottome, Phyllis (1884): Private Worlds. P
Bowen, Elizabeth (1899): The Cat Jumps. P
Bridge, Ann (   ): The Ginger-Griffin. P
Byng (d. 1813): Torrington Diaries [ed. C. B.
    Andrews, concl. 1938]. P
Cain (1892): The Postman always Rings Twice. P
Callaghan (1903): Such is my Beloved. P
Creevey (d. 1838): Creevey's Life and Times. P
Day-Lewis (1904): A Hope for Poetry. P
Eliot (1888):The Rock. D.   After Strange Gods. P
Firbank.(d. 1926): The Artificial Princess. P
Fitzgerald, Scott (1896): Tender is the Night. P
Fleming, Peter (1907): One's Company. P
Gibson (1878): Fuel. V
Graves (1895): I Claudius. P.   Claudius the God. P
Greene, Graham (1904): It's a Battlefield. P
    The Basement Room. P
Hellman (1905): The Children's Hour. D
Herbert, A. P. (1890): Holy Deadlock. P
James, Henry (d. 1916): The Art of the Novel
    [ed. Blackmur]. P
Lee (1891): Children of the Poor. P
Linklater (1899): Magnus Merriman. P
Lomax (1872): American Ballads and Folk Songs.
Mason (1905): No New Thing, Poems 1924–29.
Muir (1887): Variations on a Time Theme. V
Nichols (1893): Fisbo. V
O'Hara (1905): Appointment in Samarra. P
Penton (1904): Landtakers. P
Pitter (1897): A Mad Lady's Garland. V
Pound (1885): The A.B.C. of Reading. P
Priestley (1894): Eden End. D
Rolfe (d. 1913): The Desire and Pursuit of the
    Whole. P
Russell ('Æ.', 1867): The House of the Titans. V
Sackville-West, E. (1901):The Sun in Capricorn. P
Saroyan (1908): The Daring Young Man on the
    Flying Trapeze. P
Spender (1909): Vienna. V
Stark (1893): The Valleys of the Assassins. P
Symons (   ): The Quest for Corvo. P
Thomas (1914): 18 Poems.
Turner (1889): Jack and Jill. V
Van der Post (1907); In a Province. P
Waugh, E. (1903): Handful of Dust. P
Wells (1866): Experiment in Autobiography. P
Williams, William Carlos (1883): Collected Poems.
Woollcott (1887): While Rome Burns. P
Yeats (1865): The King of the Great Clock Tower.
    V   Collected Plays [new ed. '52].
Young, Stark (1881): So Red the Rose. P

Arthur Pinero d.
J. L. Hammond, 'Life of
    C. P. Scott'.
Russell, 'Freedom and
    Organization'.
Toynbee, 'A Study of His-
    tory' (completed 1954).
'New Temple Shake-
    speare', ed. M. R.
    Ridley.
'Oxford Book of 17th
    Century Verse', ed.
    Grierson and Bullough.
'Early Victorian Eng-
    land', ed. G. M. Young.
'Partisan Review' started.
Powell, revised ed. Hill's
    Boswell (completed '50).

Anderson, Maxwell (1888): Winterset. VD

Auden (1907) and **Isherwood** (1904): The Dog Beneath the Skin. D

Bagnold, Enid ( ): National Velvet. P

Barker (1913): Poems.

Bowen, Elizabeth (1899): The House in Paris. P

Callaghan (1903): They Shall Inherit the Earth. P

Compton-Burnett : A House and its Head. P

Connolly (1903): The Rock Pool. P

Cronin (1896): The Stars Look Down. P

Dark (1901): Return to Coolami. P

Davies, W. H. (1871): Love Poems.

Day-Lewis (1904): A Time to Dance. V

Dyment (1914): First Day. V

Eliot (1888): Murder in the Cathedral. D

Empson (1906): Some Versions of Pastoral. P

Forester (1899): The African Queen. P

Glasgow (1874): Vein of Iron. P

Greene, Graham (1904): England Made Me. P

Hamilton (1904): Twenty Thousand Streets under the Sky. P

Hemingway (1898): Green Hills of Africa. P

Hopkins (d. 1889): Letters [concl. '38].

Isherwood (1904): Mr. Norris Changes Trains. P Lions and Shadows. P

Kingsley, S. (1906): Dead End. D

Lane, Margaret (1907): Faith, Hope, No Charity. P

Lewis, Sinclair (1885): It Can't Happen Here. P

Macaulay, Rose (1881): Personal Pleasures. P

MacLeish (1892): Panic. D

MacNeice (1907): Poems.

Moore, Marianne (1887): Selected Poems.

Myers (1881): The Root and the Flower. P

Odets (1906): Waiting for Lefty. D   Awake and Sing. D   Till the Day I die. D

O'Hara (1905): Butterfield 8. P

Pratt (1883): The Titanic. V

'Rebecca West' (1892): The Harsh Voice. P

Santayana (1863): The Last Puritan. P .

Sassoon (1886): Vigils. V

Sherwood, Robert (1896): The Petrified Forest. D

Smith, Dodie ( ): Call It a Day. D

Stead (1902): Seven Poor Men of Sydney. P

Steinbeck (1902): Tortilla Flat. P

Stevens, Wallace (1879): Ideas of Order. V

Tennant (1912): Tiburon. P

Thurber (1894): The Middle Aged Man on the Flying Trapeze. P

Williams, William Carlos (1883): An Early Martyr. V

Thomas Edward Lawrence d.

E. de Selincourt, ed. Letters of William and Dorothy Wordsworth (concl. 1939).

C. H. Dodd, 'The Bible and the Greeks'.

Morison, ed. 'History of "The Times"' (concl. 1952).

Sidney and Beatrice Webb, 'Soviet Communism, A New Civilization?'

Fisher, 'History of Europe'.

Powicke, 'The Christian Life in the Middle Ages'.

Spurgeon, 'Shakespeare's Imagery'.

Eddington, 'New Pathways in Science'.

Wodehouse (1881): Blanding's Castle. P
Wolfe, Humbert (1885): The Fourth of August.
    V   Stings and Wings. V   X at Ober-
    ammergau. V
Wolfe, Thomas (1900): Of Time and the River. P
Yeats (1865): A Full Moon in March. D

1936

Auden (1907): Look, Stranger! V
Auden (1907) **and Isherwood** (1904): The Ascent
    of F.6. D
Barnes, Djuna (1892): Nightwood. D
Barrie (1860): The Boy David. D
Benchley (1889): My Ten Years in a Quandary. P
Campbell (1901): Mithraic Emblems. V
Cary (1888): The African Witch. P
Collin (1893): The White Savannahs. P
Coward (1899): To-Night at 8.30. D
Cresswell (1896): Lyttelton Harbour. V
Dickinson (d. 1886): Unpublished Poems.
Dos Passos (1896): The Big Money. P
Eliot (1888): Collected Poems 1909–35.   Essays
    Ancient and Modern. P
Faulkner, W. (1897): Absalom, Absalom! P
Fleming, Peter (1907): News from Tartary. P
Forster (1879): Abinger Harvest. P
'Franklin' (1883): All that Swagger. P
Holtby (d. 1935): South Riding. P
Housman (d. 1936): More Poems
Huxley, Aldous (1894): Eyeless in Gaza. P
Hyde (1906): Passport to Hell. P   Check to
    Your King. P
Kaufman (1889) **and Hart, M.** (1904): You Can't
    Take it With You. D
Lawrence, T. E. (d. 1935): The Mint [New York
    ed. London ed., 1955]. P
Lewis, C. S. (1898): Allegory of Love. P
Masefield (1878): A Letter from Pontus. V
Millin (1889): General Smuts. P
Mitchell, Margaret (1900): Gone with the Wind.
    P
Morgan (1894): Sparkenbroke. P
Myers (1881): Strange Glory. P
Nehru (1889): An Autobiography. P
'O'Connor' (1903): Bones of Contention. P
Penton (1904): Inheritors [Eng. title, 'Giant's
    Stride']. P
Pitter (1897): A Trophy of Arms. V
Powys, J. C. (1872): Maiden Castle. P
Rattigan (1911): French without Tears. D
'Rebecca West' (1892): The Thinking Reed. P

George V d.
Edward VIII abdicated.
Gilbert Keith Chesterton d.
Rudyard Kipling d.
'*Oxford Book of Modern
    Verse*', ed. Yeats.
'*Oxford History of Eng-
    land*', ed. Clark (14
    vols, 10 published 1936–
    52).
*Television Service B.B.C.
    began officially, 2 Nov.*
*Ayer, '*Language, Truth,
    and Logic*'.*
*Keynes, '*General Theory
    of Employment, Inter-
    est and Money*'.*
*Young, '*Victorian
    England*'.*
*Brooks, '*Makers and
    Finders*' (Hist. of the
    writer in America,
    1800–1915, 5 vols.,
    concl. '52).*
'*New Writing*' (till 1939).
*Bernanos, '*Journal d'un
    Curé de Campagne*'.*
*Montherlant, '*Les Jeunes
    Filles*' (concl. 1939).*

President U.S.A.
Franklin D.
Roosevelt (2nd
term).

Sandburg (1878): The People, Yes. V
Sassoon (1886): Sherston's Progress. P
Shaw (1856): The Millionairess. D
Sherwood, Robert (1896): Idiot's Delight. D·
Stark (1893): The Southern Gates of Arabia. P
Steinbeck (1902): In Dubious Battle. P
Stevens, Wallace (1879): Owl's Clover. V
Thomas, Dylan (1914): Twenty-Five Poems.
Turner (1889): Songs and Incantations.
Williams, J. G. (   ) **and May, H. J.** (   ):
    I am black; the story of Shabala. P
Williams, William Carlos (1883): Adam & Eve
    and the City. V

1937

Auden (1907): Letters from Iceland (with Louis
    MacNeice). P and V
Barker (1913): Calamiterror. V
Bemelmans (1898): My War with the U.S. P
Blunden (1896): An Elegy and Other Poems.
Bottome (1884): The Mortal Storm. P
'Bridie' (1888): Susannah and the Elders. D
Cloete (1897): Turning Wheels. P
Compton-Burnett : Daughters and Sons. P
Cronin (1896): The Citadel. P
Dark (1901): Sun Across the Sky. P
De la Mare (1873): This Year, Next Year. V
Duggan (   ): Poems.
Ervine (1883): Robert's Wife. D
Hemingway (1898): To Have and Have Not. P
Hopkins (d. 1889): Note-books and Papers [ed.
    House].
Jeffers (1887): Such Counsels You Gave to Me. V
Jones, David (1895): In Parenthesis. P
Kipling (d. 1936): Something of Myself. P
Lewis, Wyndham (1884): Blasting and Bombar-
    diering. P   The Revenge for Love. P
MacKenzie, Compton (1883): The Four Winds of
    Love [concl. '45]. P
MacLeish (1892): The Fall of the City. V
Marquand (1893): The Late George Apley. P
Maugham (1874): Theatre. P
Muir (1887): Journeys and Places. V
Odets (1906): Golden Boy. D
Paul (1891): The Life and Death of a Spanish
    Town. P
Priestley (1894): Time and the Conways. D
    I Have Been Here Before. D
Roberts, K. (1885): Northwest Passage. P
Sackville-West, V. (1892): Pepita. P

J. M. Barrie d.
'Oxford Book of Greek
    Verse in Translation',
    ed. Higham and Bowra.
W. S. Lewis and others,
    ed. Walpole's Corre-
    spondence.
Kafka, 'The Trial', trs.
    W. and E. Muir.
Giraudoux, 'Électre'.
Harold Williams ed.
    Swift's Poems (2nd.
    ed. 1958).

Sayers, Dorothy (1893): The Zeal of Thy House.
D
Scott (d. 1832): Letters [ed. Grierson].
Simpson (1897): Under Capricorn. P
Steinbeck (1902): Of Mice and Men. P
Stevens, Wallace (1879): The Man with the Blue
Guitar. V
Tate (1899): Selected Poems.
Thurber (1894): Let Your Mind Alone. P
Tolkien (1892): The Hobbit. P
Warner, R. (1905): The Wild Goose Chase. P
Williams, C. (1886): Descent into Hell. P
Yeats (1865): Nine One-act Plays.

1938

Auden (1907) **and Isherwood** (1904): On the
Frontier. D
Beckett (1906): Murphy. P
Bowen, Elizabeth (1899): The Death of the Heart.
P
Bromfield (1896): The Rains Came. P
Cary (1888): Castle Corner. P
Connolly (1903): Enemies of Promise. P
Cummings (1894): Collected Poems.
Dark (1901): Waterway. P
Day-Lewis (1904): Overtures to Death. V
De la Mare (1873): Memory. V
Fairburn (1904): Dominion. V
Finlayson (1904): Brown Man's Burden. P
FitzGerald, R. D. (1902): Moonlight Acre. V
Gibson (1878): Coming and Going. V
Greene, Graham (1904): Brighton Rock. P
Hemingway (1898): The Fifth Column and the
First Forty-Nine Stories. D and P
Herbert, Xavier (1901): Capricornia. P
Hughes (1900): In Hazard. P
Hutchinson (1907): Testament. P
Hyde (1906): Nor the Years Condemn. P
Kilvert (d. 1879): Diaries [ed. Plomer, completed
1940]. P
Lawrence, T. E. (d. 1935): Letters [ed. David
Garnett].
MacNeice (1907): The Earth Compels. V
Manning, Olivia (   ): The Wind Changes. P
Maugham (1874): The Summing Up. P
Morgan: (1894) The Flashing Stream. P
Nash, O. (1902): I'm a Stranger Here Myself. V
Odets (1906): Rocket to the Moon. D
O'Hara (1905): Hope of Heaven. P
Priestley (1894): When We are Married. D
Rawlings (1896): The Yearling. P

*J. L. Hammond, 'Glad-
stone and the Irish
Nation'.*
*Mumford,'The Culture of
Cities'.*
Sartre,'La Nausée'.
*Waley trs. 'The Analects
of Confucius'.*

Richardson, Dorothy (1873): Pilgrimage [instalments from 1915]. P
'Rumer Godden' (1907): Black Narcissus. P
Sackville-West, V. (1892): Solitude. V
Shaw (1856): Geneva. D
Sherwood, Robert (1896): Abe Lincoln in Illinois. D
Smith, Dodie (   ): Dear Octopus. D
Smith, Logan Pearsall (1865): Unforgotten Years. P
Spender (1909). Trial of a Judge. D
Van Doren, C. (1885): Benjamin Franklin. P
Warner, R. (1905): The Professor. P
Waugh, E. (1903): Scoop. P
Wilder (1897): Our Town. D
Williams, C. (1886): Taliessin through Logres. V
Wilson, E. (1895): The Triple Thinkers. P
Wodehouse (1881): The Code of the Woosters. P
Woolf, Virginia (1882): Three Guineas. P   The Years. P
Yeats (1865): New Poems.

1939

Barry, P. (1896): Philadelphia Story. D
Benét, S. V. (1898): The Devil and Daniel Webster. D
'Bethell' (1874): Collected Poems.
Brasch (1909): The Land and the People. V
Bridge, Ann (   ): Four-Part Setting. P
Campbell (1901): Flowering Rifle. V
Cary (1888): Mister Johnson. P
Cecil (1902): The Young Melbourne. P
Cloete (1897): Watch for the Dawn. P
Compton-Burnett : A Family and a Fortune. P
Cresswell (1896): Present Without Leave. P
Curnow (1911): Not in Narrow Seas. V
Davies, W. H. (1871): The Loneliest Mountain. V
Dickens, M. (1915): One Pair of Hands. P
Eliot (1888): The Family Reunion. D
    The Idea of a Christian Society. P
    Old Possum's Book of Practical Cats. V
Faulkner, W. (1897): The Wild Palms. P
Forester (1899): Captain Hornblower, R.N. [containing The Happy Return '37, A Ship of the Line '38, Flying Colours '38]. P
Frost, Robert (1875): Collected Poems.
Fry, Christopher (1907): The Boy with a Cart. D
Hamilton (1904): Gas Light. D   Money with Menaces. RD   To the Public Danger. RD
Hellman (1905): The Little Foxes. D
Housman (d. 1936): Collected Poems.

Beginning of 2nd World War (3 Sept.).
William Butler Yeats d.
Clark, 'Leonardo da Vinci'.
Garrod, ed. Keats.
Lascelles, 'Jane Austen and her Art'.
Kierkegaard, 'Fear and Trembling' (1843), trs.
Pope, Twickenham edition, general ed., Butt (continued).
'Horizon' (till 1950).
'Poetry London' (till 1945).
'Kenyon Review'.
Sigmund Freud d.
Gide, 'Journal' (2nd vol. 1950: 1889–1949).

Huxley, Aldous (1894): After Many a Summer. P
Isherwood (1904): Goodbye to Berlin. P
Joyce (1882): Finnegans Wake. P
Kaufman (1889) **and Hart** (1904): The Man who
    came to Dinner. D
MacNeice (1907): Autumn Journal. V
Madariaga (1886): Christopher Columbus. P
Marquand (1893): Wickford Point. P
Morley, C. (1890): Kitty Foyle. P
Mulgan (1911): Man Alone. P
Parker (1893): Here Lies. P
Powell (1905): What's Become of Waring? P
Priestley (1894): Johnson Over Jordan. D
Sandburg, Carl (1878): Abraham Lincoln: The
    War Years. P
Saroyan (1908): The Time of Your Life. D
Scott (d. 1832): Journal [ed. Tait, completed
    '46].
Shaw (1856): In Good King Charles's Golden
    Days. D
Shaw, I. (1914): The Gentle People. D.
Spender (1909): The Still Centre. V
Steinbeck (1902): The Grapes of Wrath. P
Thomas, Dylan (1914): The Map of Love. V and
    P
Thompson, Flora (1877): Lark Rise [Trilogy:
    Over to Candleford, '41; Candleford Green,
    '43]. P
Thurber (1894): The Last Flower. P
Van Doren, Mark (1894): Collected Poems.
Wolfe, T. (d. 1938): The Web and the Rock. P
Yeats (d. 1939). Last Poems and Two Plays.

1940

Abercrombie (1881): Lyrics and Unfinished
    Poems.
Auden (1907): Another Time. V
Barker (1913): Lament and Triumph. V
Benson, E. F. (1867): Final Edition. P
Bentley (1875): Those Days. P
Betjeman (1906): Old Lights for New Chancels. V
Blunden (1896): Poems 1930–40.
Cary (1888): Charley is my Darling. P
Chandler, Raymond (1888): Farewell My Lovely.
    P
Cloete (1897): Yesterday is Dead. P
Cummings (1894): 50 Poems.
Day-Lewis (1904): Poems in Wartime.
Duggan (   ): New Zealand Poems.
Ellis, Havelock (d. 1939): My Life. P

William Henry Davies d.
'*Cambridge Bibliography*
of British Literature',
ed. F. W. Bateson.
E. de Selincourt and H.
Darbishire, ed. '*Words-*
worth's Poetical Works'
(*concl. 1949*).
C. B. Tinker and H. F.
Lowry, ed. '*Arnold's*
Poems'.
'*Meanjin*' (*Australia*)
started.
Knowles, '*The Monastic*
Order in England'.
McCormick, '*Letters and*
Art in New Zealand'.

Faulkner (1897): The Hamlet. P
Graves (1895): Sergeant Lamb of the Ninth. P
Greene, Graham (1904): The Power and the Glory. P
Hemingway (1898): For Whom the Bell Tolls. P
Holcroft (1902): The Deepening Stream. P
Kipling (d. 1936): Rudyard Kipling's Verse: Definitive Edition.
Klein (1909): Hath Not a Jew. V
Lewis, C. S. (1898): The Problem of Pain. P
Macaulay, Rose (1881): And No Man's Wit. P
MacLeish (1892): The Irresponsibles. P
McCullers (1917): The Heart is a Lonely Hunter. P
Morgan (1894): The Voyage. P
Muir (1887): The Story and the Fable [included in autobiography '54]. P
Myers (1881): The Pool of Vishnu. P
O'Casey (1884): The Star Turns Red. D
Purple Dust. D
Pratt (1883): Brébeuf and His Brethren. V
Read (1893): Thirty-five Poems.
Sadleir (1888): Fanny by Gaslight. P
Sargeson (1903): A Man and His Wife. P
Sassoon (1886): Rhymed Ruminations. V
Sherwood, Robert (1896): There Shall be no Night. D
Sitwell, Edith (1887): Poems New and Old.
Snow (1905): Strangers and Brothers. P
Thomas, Dylan (1914): Portrait of the Artist as a Young Dog. P
Thurber (1894) **and Nugent**: The Male Animal. D
Wilson, E. (1895): To the Finland Station. P
Wolfe, Humbert (1885): Kensington Gardens in War-Time. V
Wolfe, T. (d. 1938): You Can't Go Home Again. P
Wright, R. (1909): Native Son. P

Radhakrishnan, 'Eastern Religions and Western Thought'.
Russell, 'Meaning and Truth'.
'Penguin New Writing' (till 1950).

President U.S.A. Franklin D. Roosevelt (3rd term).

1941

Auden (1907): New Year Letter. V.
Berners (1883): Count Omega. P   Far from the Madding War. P
Binyon (1869): The North Star. V
Blunden (1896): Thomas Hardy. P
Bottome (1884): London Pride. P
Carr (1871): Klee Wyck. P
Cary (1888): Herself Surprised. P   The House of Children. P
Churchill, Winston S. (1874): Into Battle. P
Cloete (1897): The Hill of Doves. P
Compton-Burnett: Parents and Children. P

U.S.S.R., Japan, and U.S.A. enter war.
James George Frazer d.
James Joyce d.
Virginia Woolf d.
Nichol Smith and McAdam, ed. 'Johnson's Poems'.
Nehru, 'Unity of India'.
'Cambridge Economic History of Europe', vol. i (vol. ii, 1952).
E. de Selincourt, ed. 'The Journals of Dorothy Wordsworth'.

Coward (1899): Blithe Spirit. D.
Curnow (1911): Island and Time. V
Dark (1901): The Timeless Land. P
Davies, W. H. (d. 1940): Common Joys. V
De la Mare (1873): Bells and Grass. V   The
    Picnic. P
Fast (1914): The Last Frontier. P
Fitzgerald, Scott (d. 1940): The Last Tycoon. P
Gibson (1878): The Alert. V
Glasgow (1874): In This our Life. P
Hamilton (1904): Hangover Square. P
MacNeice (1907): Plant and Phantom. V
Marquand (1893): H. M. Pulham Esq. P
Mason (1905): This Dark Will Lighten. V
Matthiessen (1902): American Renaissance. P
Millay (1892): Collected Sonnets.
Morgan (1894): The Empty Room. P
Raddall (1903): His Majesty's Yankees. P
Ransom (1888): The New Criticism. P
Rodgers (1909): Awake! and other poems.
Stephens, James (1882): Collected Poems.
Tennant (1912): The Battlers. P
Warner (1905): The Aerodrome. P
Watkins (1906): The Ballad of the Mari Lwyd. V
Wilson, E. (1895): The Wound and the Bow. P
Woolf, Virginia (d. 1941): Between the Acts. P

Kierkegaard, 'Training in Christianity' (1849), trs. 'The Sickness unto Death' (1848), trs.
Brecht, 'Mutter Courage'.

1942

Bates (1905): The Greatest People in the World
    (by Flying Officer 'X'). P
Berners (1883): The Romance of a Nose. P
Birney (1904): David and Other Poems. V
Buck (1892): Dragon Seed. P
Carroll (1900): Shadow and Substance. D
Cary (1888): To be a Pilgrim. P
Cozzens (1903): The Just and the Unjust. P
De la Mare (1873): Collected Poems.   Time
    Passes. V   The Old Lion. P
Dickens, M. (1915): One Pair of Feet. P
Faulkner, W. (1897): Go Down Moses. P
Gibson (1878): Challenge. V
Keyes (1922): The Iron Laurel. V
Lewis, Alun (1915): Raider's Dawn. V
Lewis, C. S. (1898): The Screwtape Letters. P
Masefield (1878): A Generation Risen. V   Land
    Workers. V
Mortimer (1895): Channel Packet. P
Nichols (1893): Such was my Singing. V
O'Casey (1884): Red Roses for Me. D
Paul (1891): The Last Time I Saw Paris [Eng.
    title, 'A Narrow Street']. P

Greg, 'The Editorial Problem in Shakespeare' (revised 1951).
Collingwood, 'The New Leviathan'.
Gandhi, 'To the Hindus and Muslims'.
Julian Huxley, 'Evolution'.
Anouilh, 'Antigone'.

Piozzi, Hester Lynch (Thrale, d. 1821): Thraliana, ed. Balderston. P
Pritchett (1900): In My Good Books. P
Rattigan (1911): Flare Path. D
'Rebecca West' (1892): Black Lamb and Grey Falcon. P
Sitwell, Edith (1887): Street Songs. V
Spender (1909): Ruins and Visions. V
Stevens, Wallace (1879): Parts of a World. V
Thurber (1894): My World—and Welcome to It. P
Waugh (1903): Work Suspended. P   Put out More Flags. P
Wilder (1897): The Skin of Our Teeth. D
Woolf, Virginia (d. 1941): The Death of the Moth. P

1943

Beerbohm (1872): Lytton Strachey. P
Bowra (1898): The Heritage of Symbolism. P
'Bridie' (1888): Mr. Bolfry. D
Cloete (1897): Congo Song. P
Coward (1899): This Happy Breed. D   Present Laughter. D
Davies, W. H. (d. 1940): Collected Poems.
Day-Lewis (1904): Word over All. V
Durrell (1912): A Private Country. V
Dyment (1914): Selected Poems.
Fairburn (1904): Selected Poems.
Gascoyne (1916): Poems 1937–42.
Gibson (1878): The Searchlights. V
Graves (1895): Wife to Mr. Milton. P
Holcroft (1902): The Waiting Hills. P
Keyes (d. 1943): The Cruel Solstice. V
Millay (1892): Collected Lyrics.
Muir (1887): The Narrow Place. V
Plomer (1903): Double Lives. P
Priestley (1894): They Came to a City. D
Raine (1908): Stone and Flower. V
Rattigan (1911): While the Sun Shines. D
Reitz (1882): No Outspan. P.
Sackville-West, V. (1892): The Eagle and the Dove. P
Sitwell, Osbert (1892): Selected Poems: Old and New.
Smith, Arthur (1902): News of the Phoenix. V
Smith, Betty (1904): A Tree Grows in Brooklyn. P
Thomas, Dylan (1914): New Poems.
Ustinov (1921): House of Regrets. D
Woolf, Virginia (d. 1941): A Haunted House. P

Sidney Arthur Keyes d.
S. Morison, 'English Prayer Books' (revised ed. 1949).
Brogan, 'The English People'.
Brown, 'On Canadian Poetry'.
Gandhi 'Conquest of Self'. '
Stenton, 'Anglo-Saxon England'.
Richards, 'Basic English and its Uses'.

Auden (1907): For the Time Being. V
Barker (1913): Eros in Dogma. V
Bates (1905): Fair Stood the Wind for France. P
Baxter (1926): Beyond the Palisade. V
Betjeman (1906): New Bats in Old Belfries. V
Binyon (d. 1943): The Burning of the Leaves. V
Blunden (1896): Shells by a Stream. V Cricket Country. P
Cary (1888): The Horse's Mouth. P
Chase (1907): Harvey. D
Comfort (1920): The Powerhouse. P
Compton-Burnett: Elders and Betters. P
Corbett (1875): Man-Eaters of Kumaon. P
De la Mare (1873): Collected Rhymes and Verses.
Dyment (1914): The Axe in the Wood. V
Eliot (1888): Four Quartets [comprising East Coker '40, Burnt Norton '41, The Dry Salvages '41, and Little Gidding '42]. V
Gibson (1878): The Outpost. V
Grove (1872): The Master of the Mill. P
Hartley (1895): The Shrimp and the Anemone. P
Hersey (1914): A Bell for Adano. P
Johnson, Pamela Hansford (1912): The Trojan Brothers. P
Joyce (d. 1941): Stephen Hero. P
Lane, Margaret (1907): Where Helen Lies. P
Lee (1914): The Sun my Monument. V
Lehmann, Rosamond (1903): The Ballad and the Source. P
Maclaren-Ross (1909): The Stuff to Give the Troops. P
MacNeice (1907): Springboard. V
Maugham (1874): The Razor's Edge. P
Morgan (1894): Reflections in a Mirror. P
'O'Connor' (1903): Crab-Apple Jelly. P
Pratt (1883): Collected Poems.
Read (1893): A World Within a War. V
Santayana (1863): Persons and Places [3 vols., concl. 1953]. P
Sitwell, Edith (1887): Green Song. V
Williams, C. (1886): The Region of the Summer Stars. V
Williams, T. (1912): The Glass Menagerie. D
Williams, William Carlos. (1883): The Wedge. V

Alun Lewis d.
'Beveridge Report' on Full Employment.
Kierkegaard, 'Either/Or' (1843), trs.
C. L. Stevenson, 'Ethics and Language'.
Shaw, 'Everybody's Political What's What'.
Trevelyan, 'English Social History'.
Brogan, 'The American Problem'.
Sartre, 'Huit-Clos'.
Jean Giraudoux d.
Romain Rolland d.
Saint-Exupéry d.

President U.S.A.
Franklin D.
Roosevelt (4th
term).

Birney (1904): Now Is Time. V
Bowen, Elizabeth (1899): The Demon Lover. P
Bowra (1898): From Virgil to Milton. P
Carroll (1900): Three Plays. The Old Foolishness. D
Cloete (1897): Against These Three. P
Connolly (1903): The Unquiet Grave. P
Davin (1913): Cliffs of Fall. P
De la Mare (1873): The Burning Glass. V
Dickinson (d. 1886): Bolts of Melody. V
Eliot (1888): What is a Classic? P
Fergusson (1911): Beyond the Chindwin. P
Fitzgerald, Scott (d. 1940): The Crack-up. P
'Henry Green' (1905): Loving. P
Hutchinson (1907): Interim. P
Isherwood (1904): Prater Violet. P
Keyes (d. 1943): Collected Poems.
Lewis, Alun (d. 1944): Ha! Ha! Among the Trumpets. V
MacLennan (1907): Two Solitudes. P
'Mansfield' (d. 1923): Collected Stories. P
Mitford, Nancy (1904): Pursuit of Love. P
Newby (1918): A Journey to the Interior. P.
'George Orwell' (1903): Animal Farm. P
Pitter (1897): The Bridge. V
Ransom (1888): Selected Poems.
Sitwell, Edith (1887): The Song of the Cold. V
Sitwell, O. (1892): Left Hand, Right Hand! [autobiography, 5 vols., completed 1950]. P
Stein, Gertrude (1874): Wars I Have Seen. P
Thurber (1894): The Thurber Carnival. P
Watkins (1906): The Lamp and the Veil. V
Waugh, E. (1903): Brideshead Revisited. P
Wells (1866): Mind at the End of its Tether. P
Williams, C. (1886): All Hallows Eve. P

End of Second World War (Europe, 9 May; Japan, 2 Sept.).
'*New Centenary Book of South African Verse*', *ed. Slater.*
Ronald Knox, trs. Vulgate N.T. (O.T. '49).
'*Oxford History of English Literature*', *ed. Wilson and Dobrée, begun.*
*Gordon N. Ray, ed. '*Thackeray's Letters*' (concl. 1946).*
*Donald H. Wing, '*Short-title Catalogue of Books 1641–1700*' (cont.).*
*Sartre, '*Les Chemins de la Liberté*' vol. i.*
United Nations Educational Scientific and Cultural Organization (U.N.E.S.C.O.).
United Nations Organization Charter (U.N.O.).
Hitler d.
Mussolini d.
Roosevelt d.
Paul Valéry d.

President U.S.A.
Truman

Allen (1911): Rogue Elephant. P
Beerbohm (1872): Mainly on the Air [enlarged, 1957]. P
Blunden (1896): Shelley. P
Campbell (1901): Talking Bronco. V
Cary (1888): The Moonlight. P
Cloete (1897): The Third Way. P
Coppard (1878): Selected Tales. P
De la Mare (1873): The Traveller. V
Dreiser (1871): The Bulwark. P
Durrell (1912): Cities, Plains and People. V
Fergusson (1911): The Wild Green Earth. P
Finch (1900): Poems.
Fry (1907): The Firstborn. D   A Phoenix Too Frequent. D
'George Orwell' (1903): Critical Essays. P
Hartley (1895): The Sixth Heaven. P
'Henry Green' (1905): Back. P
Hersey, John (1914): Hiroshima. P
Holcroft (1902): Encircling Seas. P
Jenkins, Elizabeth (   ): Young Enthusiasts. P
Linklater (1899): Private Angelo. P
Macaulay, Rose (1881): They Went to Portugal. P
McCullers (1917): The Member of the Wedding. P
MacNeice (1907): The Dark Tower. RD
Masefield (1878): Collected Poems.
Muir (1887): The Voyage. V
O'Neill, Eugene (1888): The Iceman Cometh. D
Priestley (1894): An Inspector Calls. D
Raine (1908): Living in Time. V
Rattigan (1911): The Winslow Boy. D
Read (1893): Collected Poems.
'Rumer Godden' (1907): The River. P
Sackville-West (1892): The Garden. V
Sargeson (1903): That Summer. P
Spender (1909): Poems of Dedication.
Stein (1874): Brewsie and Willie. P
Taylor, Elizabeth (1912): At Mrs. Lippincote's. P
Thomas, Dylan (1914): Deaths and Entrances. V
Turner (1889): Fossils of a Future Time? V
Warren (1905): All the King's Men. P
Waugh, Evelyn (1903): Scott-King's Modern Europe. P
Williams, William Carlos (1883): Paterson [4 vols., concl. '51]. V
Wilson, E. (1895): Memoirs of Hecate County. P
Wright, Judith (1915): The Moving Image. V

Herbert George Wells d.
'Landfall' (N.Z.) started.
Collingwood, 'The Idea of History'.
'Book of N.Z. Verse', ed. Curnow.
Lower,' Colony to Nation'.
Russell, 'History of Western Philosophy'.
Nehru, 'Discovery of India'.

Bates (1905): The Purple Plain. P
'Bridie' (1888): Dr. Angelus. D
Carroll (1900): Two Plays.
Compton-Burnett : Manservant and Maidservant. P
Davies, W. Robertson (1913): The Diary of Samuel Marchbanks. P
Davin (1913): For the Rest of Our Lives. P   The Gorse Blooms Pale. P
Day-Lewis (1904): The Poetic Image. P
Eliot (1888): Milton. P
Fiennes, Celia (d. 1741): Diaries. P
Frye (1912): Fearful Symmetry: a Study of William Blake. P
Gaskell (1913): The Big Game. P
Gibson (1878): Coldknuckles. V
Graves (1895): The White Goddess. P
Hartley (1895): Eustace and Hilda. P
James (d. 1916): Notebooks [ed. Matthiessen and Murdock.]
Johnson, Pamela Hansford (1912): An Avenue of Stone. P
Lee (1914): The Bloom of Candles. V
MacKenzie (1883): Whisky Galore. P
Maclaren-Ross (1909): Of Love and Hunger. P
Malory, Sir Thomas (d. 1471): Works [ed.Vinaver, from Winchester MS. discovered 1934].
Miller, Arthur (1915): All My Sons. P
Morgan (1894): The Judge's Story. P
Mulgan (d. 1945): Report on Experience. P
'O'Connor' (1903): The Common Chord. P
Oman (1897): Nelson. P
Priestley (1894): The Linden Tree. D
Sadleir (1888): Forlorn Sunset. P
Sassoon (1886): Collected Poems.
Sitwell, Edith (1887): The Shadow of Cain. V
Snow (1905): The Light and the Dark. P
Stevens, Wallace (1879): Transport to Summer. V
Taylor, Elizabeth (1912): Palladian. P
Williams, T. (1912): A Streetcar Named Desire. D
Woolf, Virginia (d. 1941): The Moment. P

Pakistan established.
Gandhi, 'To the Protagonists of Pakistan.'
Camus, 'La Peste'.
Malraux, 'Psychologie de l'Art' (concl. 1950).

Auden (1907): The Age of Anxiety. V
Ballantyne (1924): The Cunninghams.   P
Baron (1917): From the City, from the Plough. P
Baxter (1926): Blow, Wind of Fruitfulness. V
Betjeman (1906): Selected Poems.
Brasch (1909): Disputed Ground.   V
Churchill, **Winston S.** (1874): Second World War
Corbett (1875): The Man-eating Leopard of
    Rudrapayag.   P
Courage (1903): The Fifth Child. P
Cozzens (1903): Guard of Honour. P
Curnow (1911): The Axe. V
Dark (1901): Storm of Time. P
Day-Lewis (1904): Collected Poems 1929–36.
    Poems 1943–7.
Durrell (1912): On Seeming to Presume. V
Eliot (1888): Notes towards the Definition of
    Culture. P
Faulkner, **W.** (1897): Intruder in the Dust. P
Finlayson (1904): Tidal Creek.
Graves (1895): Collected Poems 1914–47.
Greene, **Graham** (1904): The Heart of the Matter.
James (d. 1916): The Art of Fiction . P
Klein (1909): The Rocking Chair and other
    Poems. V
Leavis (1895): The Great Tradition. P
Lewis, **Alun** (d. 1944): In the Green Tree. P
MacNeice (1907): Holes in the Sky. V
Mailer, **Norman** (1923): The Naked and the
    Dead. P
Manning, **Olivia** (   ): Growing Up. P
Paton (1903): Cry, the Beloved Country. P
Rattigan (1911): The Browning Version. D
Shaw (1856): Buoyant Billions. D
Shaw, **I.** (1914): The Young Lions. P
Sherriff (1896): Miss Mabel. D
Soutar (d. 1943): Collected Poems.
Stark (1893): Perseus in the Wind. P
Thompson, **Flora** (d. 1947): Still Glides the
    Stream. P
Warner, **Sylvia** (1893): The Corner that Held
    Them. P
Watkins (1906): The Lady with the Unicorn. V
Waugh, **Evelyn** (1903): The Loved One. P

Republic of Ireland Act.
'Hudson Review' started.
Macnab and Gulston, ed.
    'South African Poetry'.
Georges Bernanos d.
Montherlant, 'Le Maître
    de Santiago'.
Kinsey,'Sexual Behaviour
    in the Human Male'.

Bates (1905): The Jacaranda Tree. P
Blunden (1896): After the Bombing. V
Bowen, Elizabeth (1899): The Heat of the Day. P
Bowles (1911): The Sheltering Sky. P
Bowra (1898): The Creative Experiment. P
'Bridie' (1888): Daphne Laureola. D
Campbell (1901): Collected Poems [2nd vol., '57].
Cary (1888): A Fearful Joy. P
Cole (1916): It was So Late. P
Compton-Burnett : Two Worlds and their Ways. P

Davin (1913): Roads from Home. P
Dyment (1914): Poems 1935–48.
Faulkner, W. (1897): Knight's Gambit. P
Fry (1907): The Lady's Not for Burning. D
Thor, with Angels. D
'George Orwell' (1903): Nineteen Eighty-Four. P
Huxley, Aldous (1894): Ape and Essence. P
Isherwood (1904): The Condor and the Cows. P
Kippenberger (1897): Infantry Brigadier. P
Kitchin (1895): The Auction Sale. P
Linklater (1899): Love in Albania. D
Macaulay, Rose (1881): Fabled Shore. P
Maclean (1911): Eastern Approaches. P
MacNeice (1907): Collected Poems 1925–48.
Manning, Olivia (   ): Artist among the Missing. P
Marquand (1893): Point of No Return. P
Miller, Arthur (1915): Death of a Salesman. D
Mitford (1904): Love in a Cold Climate. P
Morgan (1894): The River Line. P
Muir (1887): The Labyrinth. V
O'Hara (1905): A Rage to Live. P
Pound (1885): Pisan Cantos. V
Raine (1908): The Pythoness. V
Rattigan (1911): Adventure Story. D
Sackville-West, E. (1901): Inclinations. P
Sargeson (1903): I saw in My Dream. P
Sitwell, Edith (1887): The Canticle of the Rose. V
Snow (1905): Time of Hope. P
Tate (1899): Poems 1922–47.
Taylor, Elizabeth (1912): A View of the Harbour. P
Trevelyan (1876): Autobiography. P
Trilling (1905): The Middle of the Journey. P
Wilson, Angus (1915): The Wrong Set. P
Wright, Judith (1915): Woman to Man. V

Farrand, ed. Franklin's '*Memoirs*' (*Parallel text ed.*).
Clark, '*Landscape into Art*'.
Ryle, '*The Concept of Mind*'.
People's Republic of China proclaimed.

President U.S.A. Truman (*2nd Term*).

Auden (1907): Collected Shorter Poems 1930–1944.

Barker (1913): The Dead Seagull. V
The True Confession of George Barker. V

Boswell, James (d. 1795): London Journal 1762–3 [ed. Pottle]. P

Bowen, Elizabeth (1899): Collected Impressions. P

Bowra (1898): The Romantic Imagination. P

Courage (1903): Desire Without Content. P

De la Mare (1873): Inward Companion. V

Durrell (1912): Sappho. V

Eliot (1888): The Cocktail Party. D

Fry (1907): Venus Observed. D

Garrod (1878): Genius Loci. P

Gascoyne (1916): A Vagrant and other poems.

Gibson (1878): Within Four Walls. D

Grant, Douglas (1921): The Fuel of the Fire. P

Hartley (1895): The Boat. P

Hemingway (1898): Across the River and into the Trees. P

Herbert, A. P. (1890): Independent Member. P

Kennedy, Margaret (1896): The Feast. P

Macaulay, Rose (1881): The World My Wilderness. P

Millin (1889): King of the Bastards. P

'O'Connor' (1903): Travellers' Samples. P

Rattigan (1911): Who is Sylvia? D

Sherriff (1896): Home at Seven. D

Sitwell, Edith (1887): Poor Men's Music. V

Warren, R. P. (1905): World Enough and Time. P

Waugh, E. (1903): Helena. P

Wilson, Angus (1915): Such Darling Dodos. P

Woodham-Smith (   ): Florence Nightingale. P

Woolf, Virginia (d. 1941): The Captain's Death Bed. P

Young, Andrew (1885): Collected Poems.

North Atlantic Treaty Organization (N.A.T.O.).

Republic of India proclaimed.

Eric Blair ('George Orwell') d.

George Bernard Shaw d.

Nehru, 'Before and After Independence'.

Trilling, 'The Liberal Imagination'.

INDEX

301

British Critic started 1793, new series 1814.
British Drama 1817.
British Librarian 1737.
British Magazine 1760–7.
British Magazine started 1832.
British Theatre 1776–8.
British Theatre 1823.
Briton 1762–3.
BROKE, ARTHUR, d. 1563. Romeus and Juliet 1562.
BROME, RICHARD, d. 1652? Northern Lass 1632, Antipodes '40, Sparagus Garden '40, Jovial Crew '52, Five New Plays '53, Queen's Exchange '57, Five New Plays '59.
BROMFIELD, LOUIS [U.S.], 1896–1956. Early Autumn 1926, The Rains Came '38.
BRONTË, ANNE, 1820–49. Poems 1846, Agnes Grey '47, Tenant of Wildfell Hall '48.
BRONTË, CHARLOTTE, 1816–55. Poems 1846, Jane Eyre '47, Shirley '49, Villette '53, The Professor '57, Life by Mrs. Gaskell '57.
BRONTË, EMILY, 1818–1848. Poems 1846, Wuthering Heights '47.
BROOKE, FRANCES, 1724–89. Lady Julia Mandeville 1763, Siege of Sinope '81, Rosina '83, Marian '88.
BROOKE, HENRY, 1703?–83. Universal Beauty 1735, Gustavus Vasa '39, (with Edward Moore) Fables for the Female Sex '44, Earl of Essex '61, Fool of Quality '66, Redemption '72, Juliet Grenville '74.
BROOKE, RUPERT, 1887–1915. Poems 1911, 1914 and other Poems '15, Letters from America '16, John Webster '16, Collected Poems '16.
BROOKE, STOPFORD, 1832–1916. English Literature 1876.
BROUGHAM, HENRY, LORD BROUGHAM, 1778–1868. Practical Observations on Education 1825.
BROWN, CHARLES BROCKDEN, 1771–1810. Wieland 1798, Ormond '99, Edgar Huntley '99, Arthur Mervyn '99, 1800, Clara Howard '01, Jane Talbot '01.
BROWN, JOHN, 1715–66. Barbarossa 1755, Athelstane '56, Estimate of Manners and Principles '57, Poetry and Music '63.
BROWN, JOHN, 1810–82. Horae Subsecivae 1858, '61, '82, Rab and his Friends '59, Marjorie Fleming '63.
BROWN, OLIVER MADOX, 1855–74. Gabriel Denver 1873, Literary Remains '76.

BROWN, THOMAS, 1663–1704. Miscellany Poems 1699, Amusements 1700, Letters from the Dead '02, Dialogues '04, Works '07, Remains '21.
BROWN, THOMAS, 1778–1820. Poems 1804, Cause and Effect '04, Physiology of Human Mind '20, Collected Poems '20.
BROWN, THOMAS EDWARD, 1830–97. Betsy Lee 1873, Fo'c'sle Yarns '81, The Doctor '87, Manx Witch '89, Old John '93, Collected Poems 1900.
BROWNE, CHARLES FARRAR ('ARTEMUS WARD'), 1834–67. Artemus Ward: his travels 1865, Artemus Ward in London '67, Artemus Ward: his book '68, Artemus Ward's Panorama '69.
BROWNE, ISAAC HAWKINS, 1705–60. A Pipe of Tobacco 1736, Poems '68.
BROWNE, SIR THOMAS, 1605–82. Religio Medici (unauthorized ed.) 1642, (authorized ed.) '43, Pseudodoxia Epidemica '46, Hydriotaphia '58, Garden of Cyrus '58, Miscellany Tracts '84, Works '86, Letter to a Friend '90, Posthumous Works 1712, Christian Morals '16, '56 (with Life by Johnson).
BROWNE, THOMAS ALEXANDER ('ROLF BOLDREWOOD') [Au.], 1826–1915. Robbery under Arms, 1888, Miner's Right '90.
BROWNE, WILLIAM, 1591–1643? Britannia's Pastorals Pt. I 1613, Pt. II 1616, Pt. III 1852, Shepherd's Pipe 1614.
BROWNING, ELIZABETH BARRETT, 1806–61. Battle of Marathon 1820, Essay on Mind '26, Prometheus Bound '33, The Seraphim '38, Poems '44, Sonnets from the Portuguese '50, Casa Guidi Windows '51, Aurora Leigh '57, Poems before Congress '60, Last Poems '62, Greek Christian Poets '63, Letters to Horne '77, Poetical Works '89, Letters '97, '99.
BROWNING, ROBERT, 1812–89. Pauline 1833, Paracelsus '35, Porphyria's Lover, Johannes Agricola '36, Strafford '37, Sordello '40, Pippa Passes '41, King Victor and King Charles '42, Dramatic Lyrics '42, Return of the Druses '43, Blot on the Scutcheon '43, Colombe's Birthday '44, Dramatic Romances and Lyrics '45, Luria '46, Bells and Pomegranates (complete) '46, Christmas Eve and Easter Day '50, Essay on Shelley '52, Men and Women '55, Dramatis Personae '64, The Ring and the Book '68, Balaustion's Adventure '71, Prince Hohenstiel-Schwangau '71, Fifine at the Fair '72,

CABELL, JAMES BRANCH [U.S.], 1879–
. The Cream of the Jest 1917,
Beyond Life '19, Jurgen '19, Silver
Stallion '26.

CABLE, GEORGE WASHINGTON [U.S.],
1844–1925. Old Creole Days 1879,
The Grandissimes '80, Creoles of
Louisiana '84.

Caesar and Pompey 1607.

CAIN, JAMES M. [U.S.], 1892– .
Postman Always Rings Twice 1934.

CAINE, SIR HALL, 1853–1931. Recollections of D. G. Rossetti 1882, Deemster '87, Bondman '90, Christian '97.

CAIRD, EDWARD, 1835–1908. Critical
Philosophy of Kant 1889.

CAIRNES, JOHN ELLIOT, 1823–75. Principles of Political Economy 1874.

CALDERWOOD, DAVID, 1575–1650. History of Church of Scotland 1678.

CALDWELL, ERSKINE PRESTON [U.S.],
1903– . Tobacco Road 1932,
God's Little Acre '33.

Calendar of State Papers 1857.

CALLAGHAN, MORLEY [C.], 1903– .
Strange Fugitive 1928, Such is my
Beloved '34, They shall inherit the
Earth '35.

CALLCOTT, MARIA, LADY, 1785–1842.
Little Arthur's History of England
1835.

CALVERLEY, CHARLES STUART, 1831–84.
Verses and Translations 1862, Fly
Leaves '72.

*Cambridge Bibliography of British
Literature* 1940.

Cambridge Review 1879.

CAMBRIDGE, RICHARD OWEN, 1717–
1802. Scribleriad 1751.

Cambridge Shakespeare 1863.

Camden Society publications begin 1838.

CAMDEN, WILLIAM, 1551–1623. Bri-
tannia 1586, Remains Concerning
Britain 1605, Britannia (final ed.) '07,
Annales '15, '27.

CAMPBELL, LORD, 1779–1861. Lives of
the Lord Chancellors 1846, Lives of
the Chief Justices '49.

CAMPBELL, GEORGE, 1719–96. Miracles
1762, Rhetoric '76.

CAMPBELL, IGNATIUS ROY DUNNACHIE
[S.A.], 1901–57. Flaming Terrapin
1924, Wayzgoose '28, Adamastor '30,
Georgiad '31, Pomegranates '32,
Flowering Reeds '33, Mithraic Emblems '36, Flowering Rifle '39, Talking Bronco '46, Collected Poems '49.

CAMPBELL, JOHN, 1708–75. Lives of
Admirals 1742, State of Europe '50,
Survey of England '74.

CAMPBELL, JOHN FRANCIS, 1822–85.

Popular Tales of the West Highlands 1860.

CAMPBELL, THOMAS, 1777–1844. Plea-
sures of Hope 1799, Poems 1805,
Annals of Great Britain '07, Gertrude
of Wyoming '09, Specimens of British
Poets '19, Theodoric '24, Life of Mrs.
Siddons '34, Pilgrim of Glencoe '42,
Frederick the Great '42.

CAMPION, THOMAS, 1567–1620. Art of
English Poesie 1602, Masque in
honour of Lord Hayes '07, Two Books
of Airs '10, Third and Fourth Books
of Airs '12, Songs Bewailing Death of
Prince Henry '13, Entertainment
given by Lord Knowles '13, Masque
at Marriage of Earl of Somerset '14,
Works ed. Bullen 1889, ed. Vivian
1909.

'*Candor*', see FRANCIS, SIR PHILIP.

CANNING, GEORGE, 1770–1827. The
Microcosm 1786, in The Anti-Jacobin
'97–'98.

CAPELL, EDWARD, 1713–81. Prolusions
1760, ed. Shakespeare '68, Notes on
Shakespeare '83.

CAREW, BAMPFYLDE-MOORE, 1690–
1758. Life and Adventures 1745.

CAREW, RICHARD, 1555–1620. Godfrey
of Bulloigne 1594, Survey of Cornwall 1602, Excellency of the English
Tongue '05.

CAREW, THOMAS, 1595?–1639? Coelum
Britannicum 1634, Poems '40.

CAREY, HENRY, d. 1743. Poems 1713,
'29, Chrononhotonthologos '34,
Honest Yorkshire-Man '36, Dragon
of Wantley '37, Nancy '39.

CARLELL, LODOWICK, fl. 1629–64.
Deserving Favourite 1629, Arviragus
and Philicia Pts. I, II, '39, Fool would
be a Favourite '57, Osmond, the
Great Turk '57.

CARLETON, CAPT. GEORGE. Memoirs
1728 (? by Defoe).

CARLETON, WILLIAM, 1794–1869. Traits
of Irish Peasantry 1830, '33, Fardorougha, the Miser '35.

CARLYLE, JANE WELSH, 1801–66.
Letters and Memorials 1883, Love
Letters 1909.

CARLYLE, THOMAS, 1795–1881. Life of
Schiller 1823, trs. Wilhelm Meister
'24, German Romance '27, Wotton
Reinfried '27, Essay on Burns '28,
Signs of the Times '29, Sartor Resar-
tus '33, French Revolution '37,
Lectures in German Literature '37,
Lectures on History of Literature '38,
Essay on Scott '38, Lectures on Euro-
pean Revolutions '39, Chartism '39,

DAY, THOMAS, 1748–89. Sandford and Merton 1783–9.

DAY LEWIS, CECIL, 1904– . Beechen Vigil 1925, Country Comets '28, Transitional Poem '29, From Feathers to Iron '31, Magnetic Mountain '33, Hope for Poetry '34, Time to Dance '35, Overture to Death '38, Poems in Wartime '40, Word over All '43, Poetic Image '47, Collected Poems 1929–36 '48, Poems 1943–7 '48.

DEFOE, DANIEL, 1661?–1731. Essay upon Projects 1697, Occasional Conformity of Dissenters '98, True-born Englishman 1701, Shortest Way with Dissenters '02, Hymn to the Pillory '03, The Review '04, The Consolidator '04, Apparition of Mrs. Veal '06, Jure Divino '06, History of the Union '09, Appeal to Honour and Justice '15, Robinson Crusoe '19, Further Adventures '19, Memoirs of a Cavalier '20, Captain Singleton '20, Duncan Campbell '20, Journal of Plague Year '22, Moll Flanders '22, Colonel Jacque '22, Peter the Great '22, Roxana '24, Tour through Great Britain '24, Complete English Tradesman '25, New Voyage round the World '25, Jonathan Wild '25, Apparitions '27, (?) Memoirs of Capt. Carleton '28.

DEKKER, THOMAS, 1570?–1632. Shoemaker's Holiday 1600, Old Fortunatus 1600, Satiro-mastix '02, Wonderful Year '03, Patient Grissel '03, Honest Whore '04, The Magnificent Entertainment given to King James '04, Seven Deadly Sins of London '06, News from Hell '06, The Double P.P. '06, Whore of Babylon '07, Sir Thomas Wyatt '07, Westward Ho '07, Northward Ho '07, Jests to Make you Merry '07, Knight's Conjuring '07, Bellman of London '08, Lanthorn and Candlelight '08, Dead Term '08, Gull's Hornbook '09, Raven's Almanack '09, Four Birds of Noah's Ark '09, Work for Armourers '09, Troia Nova Triumphans '12, If it be not good '12, Strange Horse Race '13, Dekker his Dreame '20, Rod for Runaways '25, Honest Whore Pt. II '30, Match me in London '31, Penny-Wise Pound-Foolish '31, Wonder of a Kingdom '36.

'DELAFIELD, E. M.', *see* DE LA PASTURE.

DE LA MARE, WALTER ('WALTER RAMAL') 1873–1956. Songs of Childhood 1902, Henry Brocken '04, Poems '06, The Return '10, The Listeners '12, Peacock Pie '13, Motley '18,

Poems 1901–18, '20, Memoirs of a Midget '21, The Veil '21, The Riddle '23, Crossings '24, Ding Dong Bell' 24, Broomsticks '25, Connoisseur '26, Stuff and Nonsense '27, On the Edge '30, Old Rhymes and New '32, Fleeting '33, This Year, Next Year '37, Memory '38, Bells and Grass '41, Picnic '41, Collected Poems '42, Time Passes '42, Old Lion '42, Collected Rhymes and Verses '44, Burning Glass '45, Traveller '46, Inward Companion '50.

DE LA PASTURE, EDMÉE ELIZABETH MONICA ('E. M. DELAFIELD'), 1890–1943. Diary of a Provincial Lady 1931.

DE LA RAMÉE, MARIE LOUISE ('OUIDA'), 1839–1908. Strathmore 1865, Chandos '66, Under Two Flags '67, Two Little Wooden Shoes '74, Moths '80, In Maremma '82.

DE LA ROCHE, MAZO [C.], 1885– . Jalna 1927.

DELONEY, THOMAS, 1543?–c. 1600. Thomas of Reading 1612, History of John Winchcomb '19, Gentle Craft '37, Works ed. F. O. Mann 1912.

DE MORGAN, AUGUSTUS, 1806–71. Budget of Paradoxes 1872.

DE MORGAN, WILLIAM, 1839–1917. Joseph Vance 1906, Alice-for-Short '07, Somehow Good '08, It never can happen again '09, A likely Story '11, When Ghost meets Ghost '14, Old Madhouse '19, Old Man's Youth '21.

DENHAM, SIR JOHN, 1615–69. The Sophy 1642, Cooper's Hill '42, Cato Major '48, Anatomy of Play '51, Destruction of Troy '56, Instructions to a Painter '67, Collected Poems '68.

DENNIS, CLARENCE JAMES [Au.], 1876–1938. Songs of a Sentimental Bloke 1915.

DENNIS, JOHN, 1657–1734. Impartial Critic 1693, Letters '96, Usefulness of the Stage '98, Rinaldo and Armida '99, Iphigenia 1700, Modern Poetry '01, Operas after Italian Manner '06, Appius and Virginia '09, Genius and Writings of Shakespeare '11, Upon Public Spirit '11, Remarks upon Cato '13, Stage Defended '26.

DENT, ARTHUR, d. 1607. Plain Man's Pathway to Heaven 1610.

DE QUINCEY, THOMAS, 1785–1859. Confessions of an English Opium-Eater 1821, Letters to a Young Man '23, Three Templars '24, Walladmor '25, trs. Laocoön '26, Murder as one of the Fine Arts '27, Klosterheim

1764, Letter concerning Libels (?) '64, 'Junius' (?) '72.

FRANCKLIN, THOMAS, 1721–84. Trs. Cicero De Natura Deorum 1741, trs. Sophocles '59, trs. Voltaire '61–'74, Earl of Warwick '66, Matilda '75, trs. Lucian '80.

FRANKLIN, BENJAMIN [U.S.], 1706–90. Poor Richard's Almanac 1732–57, Autobiography, Pt. II (in French) '91, English version 1817, '68, Complete Works 1806.

'FRANKLIN', *see* FRANKLIN, STELLA MARIA SARAH MILES.

FRANKLIN, SIR JOHN, 1786–1847. Narrative of a Journey to Polar Sea 1823, Narrative of Second Expedition '28.

FRANKLIN, STELLA MARIA SARAH MILES ('BRENT OF BIN BIN' and 'FRANKLIN') [Au.], 1883–1954. Up the Country 1928, Ten Creeks Run '30, Back to Bool Bool '31, All That Swagger '36.

Fraser's Magazine started 1830.

FRAUNCE, ABRAHAM, fl. 1587–1633. Lamentations of Amyntas 1587, Arcadian Rhetorick '88, Countess of Pembroke's Ivychurch '91, Countess of Pembroke's Emanuel '91.

FRAZER, SIR JAMES GEORGE, 1854–1941. The Golden Bough 1890.

FREEMAN, EDWARD AUGUSTUS, 1823–92. Study of History 1849, History of Federal Government '63, Norman Conquest '67–'79, Historical Essays '71, '73, '79, '92, English Constitution '72.

FREEMAN, MARY ELEANOR WILKINS [U.S.], 1852–1930. Humble Romance 1887, New England Nun '91, Pembroke '94.

FRENEAU, PHILIP, 1752–1832. Poems 1786, 1809.

FRERE, JOHN HOOKHAM, 1769–1846. The Microcosm 1786, in The Anti-Jacobin '97–'98, Monks and Giants 1817–18, Fables for Five Years Old '30, trs. The Frogs '39, Acharnians, Knights, Birds '40, Collected Works '74.

FROST, ROBERT [U.S.], 1875–   . A Boy's Will 1913, North of Boston '14, New Hampshire '23, Collected Poems '39.

FROUDE, JAMES ANTHONY, 1818–94. Shadows of the Clouds 1847, Nemesis of Faith 1849, History of England '56–'70, Short Studies on Great Subjects '67–'83, The English in Ireland '72, Life of Erasmus '94, English Seamen '95, Council of Trent '96.

FROUDE, RICHARD HURRELL, 1803–36. Tracts for the Times 1833, in Lyra Apostolica '36, Remains '38.

FRY, CHRISTOPHER, 1907–   . Boy with a Cart 1939, Firstborn '46, Phoenix Too Frequent '46, Lady's Not for Burning '49, Thor, with Angels '49, Venus Observed '50.

FRY, ROGER, 1866–1934. Vision and Design 1920, Transformations '26, Cézanne '27.

FRYE, H. NORTHROP [C.], 1912–   . Fearful Symmetry: Study of Blake 1947.

FULLER, (SARAH) MARGARET, 1810–50. Summer on the Lakes 1844, Woman in the 19th Century '45, Papers on Literature and Art '46.

FULLER, THOMAS, 1608–61. David's Heinous Sinne 1631, Holy War '39, Joseph's Party-Coloured Coat '40, Holy and Profane State '42, Good Thoughts in Bad Times '45, Andronicus '46, Wounded Conscience '47, Good Thoughts in Worse Times '47, Pisgah Sight of Palestine '50, Church History of Britain '55, History of Cambridge University '55, Waltham Abbey '55, Injured Innocence '59, Mixt Contemplations '60, Alarum to England and Wales '60, Worthies '62.

FULWELL, ULPIAN, fl. 1586. Like will to Like 1568.

FURNESS, HORACE HOWARD, 1833–1912. New Variorum Shakespeare 1871–   .

FURNIVALL, FREDERICK JAMES, 1825–1910. Ed. Percy Folio 1868, ed. Canterbury Tales '68, ed. Chaucer's Minor Works '71, ed. Shakespeare '77.

FURPHY, JOSEPH ('TOM COLLINS') [Au.], 1843–1912. Such is Life 1903.

Galesus (by T. C.), 1560.

GALSWORTHY, JOHN, 1867–1933. Man of Property 1906, Country House '07, A Commentary '08, The Silver Box, Joy, Strife '09, Justice '10, Patrician '11, Eldest Son, '12, Little Dream '12, Fugitive, Pigeon, Mob '14, Five Tales '18, Saint's Progress '19, In Chancery '20, Awakening '20, Skin Game '20, To Let '21, Loyalties '22, Forsyte Saga '22, Old English '24, White Monkey '24, Caravan '25, Silver Spoon '26, Swan Song '28.

GALT, JOHN, 1779–1839. Ayrshire Legatees 1820, Annals of the Parish '21, Steamboat '22, Provost '22, Sir Andrew Wylie '22, Entail '23, Gathering

GILBERT, SIR WILLIAM SCHWENCK, 1836–1911. Bab Ballads 1869, Pygmalion and Galatea '71, Trial by Jury '75, Original Plays '76–1911, Original Comic Operas '90, Foggerty's Fairy '90, Songs of a Savoyard '90.

GILBY, GODDARD. Trs. Cicero's Epistle to Quintus 1561.

GILDON, CHARLES, 1665–1724. Examen Miscellaneum 1701, New Miscellany of Poems '01, Comparison between two Stages '02, Life of Betterton '10, Complete Art of Poetry '18, Laws of Poetry '21.

GILPIN, WILLIAM, 1724–1804. Observations on the Wye 1782, Cumberland '86, Highlands of Scotland '89, New Forest '91, Picturesque Beauty '92, Western Parts of England '98.

GISBORNE, THOMAS, 1758–1846. Walks in a Forest 1794.

GISSING, GEORGE, 1857–1903. Workers in the Dawn 1880, The Unclassed '84, Isabel Clarendon '86, Demos '86, Thyrza '87, A Life's Morning '88, The Nether World '89, The Emancipated '90, New Grub Street '91, Born in Exile '92, Denzil Quarrier '92, The Odd Women '93, In the Year of Jubilee '94, Eve's Ransom '95, Paying Guest '95, Sleeping Fires '95, The Whirlpool '97, Human Odds and Ends '98, The Town Traveller '98, Charles Dickens '98, Crown of Life '99, By the Ionian Sea 1901, Henry Ryecroft '03, Veranilda '04, Will Warburton '05.

GLADSTONE, WILLIAM EWART, 1809–98. Studies on Homer 1858, Gleanings from Past Years '79.

GLANVILL, JOSEPH, 1636–80. Vanity of Dogmatising 1661, Lux Orientalis '62, Concerning Witchcraft (Saducismus Triumphatus) '66, Plus Ultra '68, Blow at Modern Sadducism '68, Essays '76.

GLAPTHORNE, HENRY. Argalus and Parthenia 1639, Albertus Wallenstein '39, Hollander '40, Ladies Privilege '40, Wit in a Constable '40.

GLASGOW, ELLEN [U.S.], 1874–1945. They Stooped to Folly 1929, Sheltered Life '32, Vein of Iron '35, In this our Life '41.

GLASSE, HANNAH, fl. 1747. Art of Cookery 1747.

GLEIG, GEORGE ROBERT, 1796–1888. The Subaltern 1826.

GLEN, WILLIAM, 1789–1826. Poems 1815.

GLOVER, RICHARD, 1712–85. Leonidas 1737, London '39, Hosier's Ghost '39,

Boadicea '53, Medea '61, Athenaid '87, Jason '99.

'GODDEN, RUMER', *see* HAYNES DIXON, MARGARET RUMER.

Godly Queen Hester 1561.

GODWIN, WILLIAM, 1756–1836. Political Justice 1793, Caleb Williams '94, Enquirer '97, Mary Wollstonecraft '98, St. Leon '99, Life of Chaucer 1803, Fleetwood '05, Fables '05, Faulkner '07, Essay on Sepulchres '09. Lives of E. and J. Philips '15, Mandeville '17, Of Population '20, Commonwealth of England '24, Cloudesley '30, Thoughts on Man '31, Lives of Necromancers '34.

Golden Litany 1531.

Golden Treasury 1861.

GOLDING, ARTHUR, 1536?–1605? Histories of Justin 1563, Ovid's Metamorphoses '65, Caesar's Exploits in Gallia '65, Abraham's Sacrifice '77.

GOLDSMITH, OLIVER, 1730?–74. Memoirs of a Protestant 1758, State of Polite Learning '59, The Bee '59, Citizen of the World '60, '62, Mystery Revealed '62, Life of Nash, '62, Art of Poetry, '62, Brookes's Natural History '63, Hist. of England in Letters '64, Traveller '64, Essays '65, Edwin '65, Vicar of Wakefield '66, Poems for Young Ladies '67, Beauties of Eng. Poesy '67, Good-natur'd Man '68, Roman History '69, Deserted Village '70, Life of Parnell '70, Life of Bolingbroke '70, Hist. of England (4 vols.) '71, Threnodia Augustalis '72, She Stoops to Conquer '73, Retaliation '74, Grecian History '74, Animated Nature '74, Haunch of Venison '76, Experimental Philosophy '76, Works, with Percy's Life 1801, Prior's Life '37, Forster's Life '48, '54, Works, ed. Gibbs '84–'86.

GOMERSALL, ROBERT, 1602–46. Lodovick Sforza 1628.

Good Housewife's Jewell 1596.

GOOGE, BARNABE, 1540–94. Zodiake of Life 1560, Eclogs, Epitaphs, and Sonnets '63, Popish Kingdom '70, Four Books of Husbandry '77.

GOOKIN, DANIEL, 1612–87. Hist. Collections of Indians 1792.

Gorboduc (acted) 1561, (pub.) '65.

GORDON, ADAM LINDSAY [Au.], 1833–70. Sea Spray and Smoke Drift 1867, Bush Ballads and Galloping Rhymes '70.

GORDON, CHARLES GEORGE, 1833–85. Journals 1885.

Bookes Messenger '92, Philomela '92, Quip for an Upstart Courtier '92, Groatsworth of Wit '92, Greene's Vision '92, Repentance of Greene '92, Orlando Furioso '94, Looking Glass for London '94, Friar Bacon and Friar Bungay '94, Scottish History of James IV '98, Alphonsus King of Arragon '99, Orpharion '99, Alcida 1617.

GREGORY, AUGUSTA, LADY, 1852–1932. Gods and Fighting Men 1906, Seven Short Plays '09, New Comedies '13.

GREVILLE, CHARLES CAVENDISH, 1794–1865. Memoirs 1874, '85, '87.

GREVILLE, SIR FULKE (LORD BROOKE), 1554–1628. Tragedy of Mustapha 1609, Certain Learned and Elegant Works '33, Life of Sidney '52, Remains '70.

GREVILLE, ROBERT, 1608–43. Nature of Truth 1640.

GREW, NEHEMIAH, 1641–1712. Anatomy of Plants 1682.

GREY, ZACHARY, 1688–1766. Ed. Hudibras 1744, Notes on Shakespeare '54.

GRIEVE, CHRISTOPHER MURRAY ('McDIARMID'), 1892– . Penny Wheep 1926, Drunk Man Looks at Thistle '26, To Circumjack Cenrastus '30, First Hymn to Lenin '32, Scots Unbound '32.

GRIFFIN, BARTHOLOMEW. Fidessa More Chaste than Kind 1596.

GRIFFITH, ELIZABETH, 1720?–93. Double Mistake 1766, School for Rakes '69, Lady Barton '71, Morality of Shakespeare '75, Lady Juliana Harley '76, trs. Barbier de Séville '76.

GRIMALD, NICHOLAS, 1519–62. Trs. Three Books of Duties of Cicero 1533.

GRIMESTONE, EDWARD. Admirable and Memorable Histories 1607, History of the Netherlands '08.

GROOME, FRANCIS HINDES, 1851–1902. In Gypsy Tents 1880.

GROSE, FRANCIS, 1731–91. Antiquities of England and Wales 1773, Dictionary of the vulgar tongue '85, Antiquities of Scotland '91.

GROSSMITH, GEORGE, 1847–1912, and WEEDON, 1854–1900. Diary of a Nobody 1894.

GROTE, GEORGE, 1794–1871. Parliamentary Reform 1831, History of Greece '46–'56, Plato and other companions of Sokrates '65, Minor Works '73.

GROTE, JOHN, 1813–66. Exploratio Philosophica 1865, Utilitarian Philosophy '70.

GROVE, FREDERICK PHILIP [C.], 1872–1948. Search for America 1927, Master of the Mill '44.

GROVE, SIR GEORGE, 1820–1900. Dictionary of Music 1878–89.

GROVE, MATTHEW. Pelops and Hippodamia 1587.

Grub Street Journal 1730–7.

GRUNDY, SIDNEY, 1848–1914. A Pair of Spectacles 1890.

Guardian 1713.

Guardian started 1846.

GUEDALLA, PHILIP, 1889–1944. Supers and Supermen 1920, Second Empire '22, Masters and Men '23, Palmerston '26, Duke '31.

GUEST, LADY CHARLOTTE, 1812–95. Trs. Mabinogion 1838.

GUEST, EDWIN, 1800–80. History of English Rhythms 1838.

GUICCIOLI, COUNTESS TERESA GAMBA, 1801–73. Recollections of Lord Byron 1869.

GUILPIN, EDWARD. Skialethia 1598.

GUNN, MRS. AENEAS [Au.], 1870– . We of the Never Never 1908.

GUTHRIE, THOMAS ANSTEY ('F. ANSTEY'), 1856–1933. Vice Versa 1882.

HABINGTON, WILLIAM, 1605–54. Castara 1634, Queen of Arragon '40, History of Edward IV '40, Observations upon Historie '41.

HACKET, JOHN, 1592–1670. Scrinia Reserata 1693.

HADDAN, ARTHUR WEST, 1816–73. (With Stubbs) Councils and Eccles. Documents 1869.

HAGGARD, SIR HENRY RIDER, 1856–1925. King Solomon's Mines 1885, She '87, Allan Quatermain '87.

HAKE, EDWARD, fl. 1579. Trs. Imitatio Christi 1567.

HAKE, THOMAS GORDON, 1809–95. The New Day 1890, Selected Poems '94.

HAKLUYT, RICHARD, 1552?–1616. Divers Voyages 1582, Voyages made into Florida '87, Principall Navigations, '89, '98.

HALES, JOHN, 1584–1656. Golden Remains 1659, Several Tracts '77, Sermons at Eton '77.

HALIFAX, MARQUIS OF, see SAVILE, GEORGE.

HALL, ARTHUR, fl. 1563–1604. Trs. Ten Books of Homer 1581.

HALL, JAMES N., see NORDHOFF, CHARLES BERNARD.

HALL, JOHN, 1627–56. Horae Vacivæ

All in Due Time '55, *see also* HOPKINS, GERARD MANLEY.
Household Words started 1849.
HOUSMAN, ALFRED EDWARD, 1859–1936. Shropshire Lad 1896, Last Poems 1922, More Poems '36, Collected Poems '39.
HOUSMAN, LAURENCE, 1865–1959. An Englishwoman's Love-Letters 1900, (with H. Granville-Barker) Prunella '07, Angels and Ministers '21, Little Plays of St. Francis '22, Followers of St. Francis '23, Trimblerigg '24.
How a man may choose a good wife 1602.
HOWARD, EDWARD, fl. 1669. Women's Conquest 1671, Six Days Adventure '71.
HOWARD, JAMES, fl. 1674. English Mounsieur 1674.
HOWARD, SIR ROBERT, 1626–98. Poems 1660, Surprisal '65, Committee '65, Vestal Virgin '65, Indian Queen '65, Great Favourite '68.
HOWARD, SIDNEY [U.S.], 1891–1939. Silver Chord 1926, Alien Corn '33.
HOWE, JULIA WARD [U.S.], 1819–1910. Battle Hymn of the Republic 1862.
HOWELL, JAMES, 1594?–1666. Dodona's Grove 1640, Instructions for Foreign Travel '42, Epistolae Ho-elianae I '45, II '47, III '50, IV '55, Country of Scotland '49, Londinapolis '57.
HOWELL, THOMAS. Fable of Narcissus 1560, Arbor of Amitie '68, New Sonnets and Pretty Pamphlets '68, Howell his Devises '81.
HOWELLS, WILLIAM DEAN [U.S.], 1837–1920. Columbus 1860, Venetian Life '66, Italian Journeys '67, Their Silver Wedding Journey '71, Chance Acquaintance '73, Foregone Conclusion '75, Lady of the Aroostook '79, Modern Instance '82, Rise of Silas Lapham '84, Criticism and Fiction '91.
HUBBARD, WILLIAM, c. 1621–1704. Troubles with the Indians 1677, General History of New England 1815.
HUDDESFORD, GEORGE, 1749–1809. Collected Poems 1801.
HUDSON, WILLIAM HENRY, 1841–1922. The Purple Land 1885, Naturalist in La Plata '92, Idle Days in Patagonia '93, Nature in Downland 1900, Birds and Man '01, El Ombú '02, Hampshire Days '03, Green Mansions '04, A Little Boy Lost '05, Afoot in England '09, A Shepherd's Life '10, Adventures among Birds '13, Far Away

and Long Ago '18, Dead Man's Plack '20, A Traveller in Little Things '21, A Hind in Richmond Park '22, Letters '23.
HUGHES, JOHN, 1677–1720. Hist. of England 1706, Calypso '12, Siege of Damascus '20, Poems and Essays '35.
HUGHES, LANGSTON [U.S.], 1902– . Weary Blues 1926.
HUGHES, RICHARD, 1900– . Confessio Juvenis 1926, High Wind in Jamaica '29, In Hazard '38.
HUGHES, THOMAS, fl. 1587. Misfortunes of Arthur 1587.
HUGHES, THOMAS, 1822–96. Tom Brown's Schooldays 1857, Scouring of the White Horse '59, Tom Brown at Oxford '61.
HULL, THOMAS, 1728–1808. Sir William Harrington 1771, Henry II '74.
HUME, DAVID, 1711–76. Treatise of Human Nature 1739, Essays Moral and Political '41, Essays concerning Human Understanding '48, Enquiry concerning Principles of Morals '51, Political Discourses '52, History of England '54–'62, Four Dissertations '57, Suicide and Immortality '77, Own Life '77, Dialogues concerning Natural Religion '79, Life and Correspondence ed. Burton 1846, Letters to Strahan '88, Letters ed. Greig 1932.
Hundred Merry Tales 1526.
HUNNIS, WILLIAM, d. 1597. Certain Psalms 1550.
HUNT, JAMES HENRY LEIGH, 1784–1859. Juvenilia 1801, Critical Essays '07, Examiner started '08, London Theatres '08, Reflector '10, Feast of the Poets '11, '14, Descent of Liberty '15, Story of Rimini '16, Foliage '18, Literary Pocket Book '18, Hero and Leander; Bacchus and Ariadne '19, Indicator '19, trs. Tasso's Amyntas '20, The Months '21, Liberal '22, Literary Examiner '23, Ultra-Crepidarius '23, Lord Byron and his Contemporaries '28, Companion '28, Tatler '30, Chat of the Week '30, Poetical Works '32, Sir Ralph Esher '32, Christianism '32, London Journal '34, Indicator and Companion '34, Captain Sword and Captain Pen '35, Monthly Repository '37, Seer '40, Legend of Florence '40, Prefaces to Moxon's eds. of dramatists '40, Chaucer Modernized '41, The Palfrey '42, Hundred Romances of Real Life '43, Collected Poems '44, Wit and Humour '46, Stories from Italian Poets '46, Jar of Honey '48, The Town '48, Readings for Railways

'49, Autobiography '50, Leigh Hunt's Journal '50–'51, Table-Talk '51, Old Court Suburb '55, Stories in Verse '55, Poetical Works '60, Saunter through the West End '61, Correspondence '62, A Day by the Fire '70.

HURD, RICHARD, 1720–1808. Moral and Political Dialogues 1759, '62, Chivalry and Romance '62, Prophecies '72, Preface to Warburton '94.

HURST, FANNIE [U.S.], 1889– . Back Street 1931.

HUTCHESON, FRANCIS, 1694–1746. Ideas of Beauty and Virtue 1725, Passions and Affections '28, Moral Philosophy '55.

HUTCHINSON, LUCY, b. 1620. Life of Colonel Hutchinson 1806.

HUTCHINSON, RAY CORYTON, 1907– . Testament 1938, Interim '45.

HUTTON, HENRY. Folly's Anatomy 1619.

HUTTON, RICHARD HOLT, 1826–97. Essays 1871.

HUXLEY, ALDOUS, 1894– . Defeat of Youth 1918, Leda '20, Limbo '20, Crome Yellow '21, Mortal Coils '22, Antic Hay '23, On the Margin '23, Little Mexican '24, Those Barren Leaves '25, Along the Road '25, Point Counter Point '28, Brief Candles '30, Cicadas '31, World of Light '31, Brave New World '32, Texts and Pretexts '32, Eyeless in Gaza '36, After Many a Summer '39, Ape and Essence '49.

HUXLEY, JULIAN, 1887– . Essays of a Biologist 1923, Evolution '42.

HUXLEY, THOMAS HENRY, 1825–95. Man's Place in Nature 1863, Classification of Animals '64, Lay Sermons '70, David Hume '79, Collected Essays '93–'94, Scientific Memoirs '98–1903.

Hyckescorner 1510.

HYDE, ROBIN [N.Z.], 1906–39. Passport to Hell 1936, Check to Your King '36, Nor the Years Condemn '38.

HYLTON, WALTER, d. 1396. Scala Perfectionis 1494, Devout Book '94.

Hypneromachia 1592.

Ieronimo 1605.

Illustrated London News started 1842.

Illustrated Sporting and Dramatic News started 1874.

Impatient Poverty 1560.

INCHBALD, MRS. ELIZABETH, 1753–1821. Appearance is against them 1785, I'll tell you what '86, Such things are '88, Child of Nature '88, Simple Story

'91, Everyone has his Fault '93, Nature and Art '96, Wives as they were '97, Lovers' Vows '98, To Marry or not to Marry 1805, British Theatre '06.

INGE, WILLIAM RALPH, 1860–1954. Christian Mysticism 1899, Philosophy of Plotinus 1918, Outspoken Essays '19, '22, Platonic Tradition '26, Christian Ethics and Modern Problems '30, God and the Astronomers '33.

INGELEND, THOMAS. Disobedient Child 1547, '70.

INGELOW, JEAN, 1820–97. Poems 1863, '76, '85, Story of Doom '67, Off the Skelligs '72.

INGERSOLL, CHARLES JARED [U.S.], 1782–1862. Rights and Wrongs of U.S.A. 1808, Inchiquin '10.

Institution of a Gentleman 1555.

Intelligencer 1663.

Intelligencer 1728–9.

IRELAND, WILLIAM, 1777–1835. Miscellaneous Papers of Shakespeare 1795, Vortigern '96, '99, Henry II '99.

IRVING, WASHINGTON [U.S.], 1783–1859. Salmagundi 1807–8, Knickerbocker's History of New York '09, Sketch Book '19–'20, Bracebridge Hall '22, Tales of a Traveller '24, Life of Columbus '28, Conquest of Granada '29, Alhambra '32, Life of Washington '55–'59.

ISHERWOOD, CHRISTOPHER WILLIAM BRADSHAW, 1904– . Memorial 1932, Mr. Norris Changes Trains '35, Lions and Shadows '35, Goodbye to Berlin '39, Prater Violet '45. Condor and Cows '49, *see also* AUDEN, WYSTAN HUGH.

Jack Drum's Entertainment 1601.

Jack Straw 1593.

Jack Upland 1540.

Jacke Jugeler (acted) *c.* 1553, (pub.) *c.* 1562.

JACKS, LAWRENCE PEARSALL, 1860–1955. Mad Shepherds 1909, All Men are Ghosts '13.

Jacob and Esau 1568.

JACOB, GILES, 1686–1744. Poetical Register 1719.

Jacobite's Journal started 1747.

JACOBS, WILLIAM WYMARK, 1863–1943. Many Cargoes 1896, Lady of the Barge 1902.

JAGO, RICHARD, 1715–81. Edge Hill 1767, Collected Poems '84.

JAMES I of Scotland, 1394–1437. The Kingis Quair 1783.

Forman '83, ed. Garrod 1939, Letters ed. Colvin 1891, ed. Forman 1931.

KEBLE, JOHN, 1792–1866. Christian Year 1827, National Apostasy '33, ed. Hooker '36, Prælectiones Academicæ '44, Lyra Innocentium '46, Sermons '47, '67, Village Sermons '69, Miscellany Poems '69, Letters of Spiritual Counsel '70, Sermons for the Christian Year '75–'80, Occasional Papers '77.

KEIGHTLEY, THOMAS, 1789–1872. Outlines of History 1815, War of Greek Independence '30.

KEITH, SIR ARTHUR, 1866–1955. Antiquity of Man 1915.

KELLY, HUGH, 1739–77. Memories of a Magdalen 1767, False Delicacy '68, A Word to the Wise '70, School for Wives '74.

KELVIN, LORD, *see* THOMSON, WILLIAM.

KEMP, WILLIAM. Kemp's Nine Days Wonder 1600.

KENDALL, TIMOTHY. Flowers of Epigrams 1577.

KENNEDY, MARGARET, 1896–   . Constant Nymph 1924, Feast '50.

KENNET, WHITE, 1660–1728. Hist. of England 1706.

KER, WILLIAM PATON, 1855–1923. Epic and Romance 1897, Art of Poetry 1923.

KERR, ROBERT. History of Voyages 1811–24.

KEY, FRANCIS SCOTT, 1780–1843. The Star-Spangled Banner 1815.

KEYES, SIDNEY ARTHUR, 1922–43. Iron Laurel 1942, Cruel Solstice '43, Collected Poems '45.

KEYNES, JOHN MAYNARD, 1883–1946. Economic Consequences of the Peace 1919.

KILLIGREW, ANNE, 1660–85. Poems 1686.

KILLIGREW, HENRY, 1613–1700. Conspiracy 1638.

KILLIGREW, THOMAS, 1612–83. The Prisoners 1641, Claracilla '41, Comedies and Tragedies '64.

KILLIGREW, SIR WILLIAM, 1606?–95. Three Plays 1664, Four Plays (adding 1 new one) '66.

Killing no Murder 1657.

KILVERT, FRANCIS, 1840–79. Diaries ed. Plomer 1938.

KING, HENRY, 1592–1669. Poems 1657, '64.

King Leir 1605.

KING, WILLIAM, 1650–1729. De Origine Mali 1702.

KING, WILLIAM, 1663–1712. Journey to London in 1698, 1699, Dialogues of the Dead '99, Miscellanies 1705, Art of Cookery '08, Art of Love '09, Heathen Gods and Heroes '10.

KING, WILLIAM, 1685–1763. The Toast 1732.

KINGLAKE, ALEXANDER, 1809–91. Eothen 1844, Invasion of the Crimea '63, '68, '75, '80, '87.

King's Primer 1545.

KINGSLEY, CHARLES, 1819–75. Saint's Tragedy 1848, Alton Locke '50, Yeast '51, Phaethon '52, Hypatia '53, Westward Ho! '55, Glaucus '55, The Heroes '56, Two Years Ago '57, Andromeda '58, Water Babies '63, Hereward the Wake '66, At Last '71.

KINGSLEY, HENRY [Au.], 1830–76. Geoffrey Hamlyn 1859, Ravenshoe '61, The Hillyars and the Burtons '65.

KINGSLEY, SIDNEY [U.S.], 1906–   . Dead End 1935.

KIPLING, RUDYARD, 1865–1936. Departmental Ditties 1886, Plain Tales from the Hills '88, Soldiers Three '88, From Sea to Sea '89, Life's Handicap '91, Light that Failed '91, Barrack-Room Ballads '92, Naulahka '92, Many Inventions '93, Jungle Book '94, Second Jungle Book '95, Seven Seas '96, Captains Courageous '97, Day's Work '98, Stalky & Co. '99, Kim 1901, Just So Stories '02, Five Nations '03, Traffics and Discoveries '04, They '05, Puck of Pook's Hill '06, Brushwood Boy '07, Actions and Reactions '09, Rewards and Fairies '10, Diversity of Creatures '17, Years Between '17, Letters of Travel '20, Something of Myself '37, Verse '40.

KIPPENBERGER, SIR HOWARD KARL [N.Z.], 1897–1957. Infantry Brigadier 1949.

KITCHIN, CLIFFORD HENRY BENN, 1895–   . Auction Sale, 1949.

KLEIN, ABRAHAM [C.], 1909–   . Hath not a Jew 1940, Rocking Chair and other Poems '48.

Knacke to Know a Knave 1594.

Knacke to Know an Honest Man 1596.

KNIGHT, CHARLES, 1791–1873. Library of Entertaining Knowledge 1829, Penny Cyclopaedia '33–'44, Pictorial History of England '37–'44, Pictorial Shakespeare '38, Shakespeare's Biography '43, Weekly Volumes '44, Old England '44, Studies of Shakespeare '49, English Cyclopaedia '53, Knowledge is Power '55, Popular History of England '56.

MAY, THOMAS, 1595–1650. The Heir 1622, trs. Pharsalia '27, Tragedy of Antigone '31, Mirror of Minds '31, Henry II '33, Edward III '35, Cleopatra '39, Julia Agrippina '39, History of Long Parliament '47, Old Couple '58.

MAY, SIR THOMAS ERSKINE, 1815–86. Procedure of House of Commons 1854, Constitutional History of England '61.

Maying 1508.

MAYNE, JASPER, 1604–72. City Match 1639, Amorous War '59.

MEDWALL, HENRY, fl. 1486. Nature 1486 (printed 1525), Fulgens *c.* 1519.

MEDWIN, THOMAS, 1788–1869. Conversations with Lord Byron 1824, ed. Shelley Papers '33, Life of Shelley '47.

MELBANCKE, BRIAN, fl. 1583. Philotimus 1583.

MELVILLE, HERMAN, 1819–91. Typee 1846, Omoo '47, Redburn '49, Mardi '49, White-Jacket '50, Moby Dick '51, Pierre '52, Israel Potter '55, Piazza Tales '56, Confidence Man '57, Battle Pieces '66, Clarel '76, Billy Budd 1924.

MENCKEN, HENRY LOUIS [U.S.], 1880–1956. Prejudices 1919–28.

Mercurius Aulicus 1643–5.

Mercurius Britannicus 1643–6.

Mercurius Civicus 1643–6.

Mercurius Melancholicus 1647–9.

Mercurius Politicus 1650–60.

Mercurius Politicus 1716–20.

MEREDITH, GEORGE, 1828–1909. Poems 1851, Shaving of Shagpat '55, Farina '57, Ordeal of Richard Feverel '59, Evan Harrington '61, Modern Love '62, Poems of English Roadside '62, Emilia in England '64, Rhoda Fleming '65, Vittoria '67, Adventures of Harry Richmond '71, Beauchamp's Career '76, Idea of Comedy '77, Egoist '79, Tragic Comedians '80, Poems and Lyrics '83, Diana of the Crossways '85, Ballads and Poems of Tragic Life '87, A Reading of Earth '88, Sandra Belloni '89, One of our Conquerors '91, Lord Ormont and his Aminta '94, Amazing Marriage '95, Essay on Comedy '97, Reading of Life 1901, Last Poems '09, Celt and Saxon '10, Letters '12.

'MEREDITH, OWEN', *see* LYTTON, EDWARD ROBERT BULWER.

MERES, FRANCIS, 1565–1647. Palladis Tamia 1598.

MERIVALE, CHARLES, 1808–93. Romans under the Empire 1850–64.

MERRY, ROBERT, 1755–98. Laurel of Liberty 1790, Lorenzo '91.

Merry Devil of Edmonton 1608.

Merry Drollery 1661.

MEW, CHARLOTTE, 1869–1928. Farmer's Bride 1916.

MEYNELL, ALICE, 1847–1922. Preludes 1875, Poems '93, Colour of Life '96, Flower of the Mind '97, Later Poems 1901, Collected Poems '13, Collected Essays '14, Father of Women '17, Essays '23, Last Poems '23.

MICKLE, WILLIAM JULIUS, 1735–88. Concubine 1767 (Sir Martin '78), Voltaire in the Shades '70, trs. Lusiad '76, Collected Poems '94.

Micro-cynicon 1599.

MIDDLETON, CONYERS, 1683–1750. Life of Cicero 1741, Free Inquiry '49.

MIDDLETON, THOMAS, 1580?–1627. Wisdom of Solomon 1596, Blurt Master-Constable 1602, Father Hubbard's Tales '04, Blacke Booke '04, Michaelmas Term '07, Phoenix '07, Family of Love '08, A Mad World, my Masters '08, A Trick to Catch the Old One '08, Your Five Gallants '08, Roaring Girl '11, Faire Quarrell '17, Inner Temple Masque '19, Triumphs of Love and Antiquity '19, World Tost at Tennis '20, Sun in Aries '21, Entertainments composed for the City '21, Game at Chess '25, Chaste Maid in Cheapside '30, The Widow '52, Spanish Gipsie '53, Changeling '53, No Wit, no Help like a Woman's '57, Women beware Women '57, More Dissemblers besides Women '57, Mayor of Quinborough '61, Anything for a Quiet Life '62, The Witch 1778.

MILL, JAMES, 1773–1836. British India 1817, Elements of Political Economy '21, Essays on Government &c. '25, Analysis of the Human Mind '29, Principles of Toleration '37.

MILL, JOHN STUART, 1806–73. System of Logic 1843, Unsettled Questions of Political Economy '44, Principles of Political Economy '48, On Liberty '59, Thoughts on Parliamentary Reform '59, Dissertations and Discussions '59, '67, '76, Representative Government '61, Utilitarianism '61, '63, Subjection of Women '69, Autobiography '73, Three Essays on Religion '74.

MILLAY, EDNA ST. VINCENT [U.S.], 1892–1950. Collected Sonnets 1941, Collected Lyrics '43.

MILLER, ARTHUR [U.S.], 1915– .
All My Sons 1947, Death of a Salesman '49.

MILLER, HINER ('JOAQUIN MILLER')
[U.S.], 1839–1913. Pacific Poems
1870, Songs of the Sierras '71.

MILLER, HUGH, 1802–56. Old Red
Sandstone 1841, My Schools and
Schoolmasters '52, Testimony of the
Rocks '57.

'MILLER, JOAQUIN', *see* MILLER, HINER.

MILLIN, SARAH GERTRUDE [S.A.], 1889–
. Dark River 1919, Middleclass
'21, Adam's Rest '22, Jordans '23,
God's Stepchildren '24, Mary Glenn
'25, Artist in the Family '27, Rhodes
'33, Three Men Die '33, General
Smuts '36, King of the Bastards '50.

MILMAN, HENRY HART, 1791–1868.
Fazio 1815, Samor '18, Fall of Jerusa-
lem '20, Martyr of Antioch '22, Bel-
shazzar '22, Anne Boleyn '26, History
of the Jews '29, ed. Gibbon '38, Life
of Gibbon '39, Poetical Works '39,
Christianity under the Empire '40,
History of Latin Christianity '54–'55,
Annals of St. Paul's '68, Savonarola,
Erasmus &c. '70.

MILNE, ALAN ALEXANDER, 1882–1956.
First Plays 1919, When We were
Very Young '24, Winnie-the-Pooh
'26, Now We are Six '27, House at
Pooh Corner '28.

MILNES, RICHARD MONCKTON (LORD
HOUGHTON), 1809–85. Poems of Many
Years 1838, Palm Leaves '44, ed.
Keats's Life and Letters '48, Collected
Works '76.

MILTON, JOHN, 1608–74. Comus 1637,
Lycidas '38, Of Reformation touching
Church Discipline '40, Reason of
Church Government '42, Apology
for Smectymnuus '42, Doctrine and
Discipline of Divorce '43, Of Educa-
tion '44, trs. Bucer on Divorce '44,
Areopagitica '44, Tetrachordon '45,
Colasterion '45, Poems '45, Tenure of
Kings and Magistrates '49, Eikono-
klastes '49, Of Civil Power '59, Like-
liest Means '59, Ready and Easy
Way '60, Present Means '60, Paradise
Lost '67 (2nd ed. '74, ed. Bentley
1732), History of Britain '70, Para-
dise Regained and Samson Agonistes
'71, Poems upon various Occasions
'73, Epistolae Familiares '74, Muscovia '82, Letters of State '94, Poetical
Works '95, Prose Works '98, ed.
Birch 1738, Letters and Papers of
State '43, Poetical Works, ed. Newton
'49, De Doctrina Christiana 1825,

Poems, ed. Grierson 1925, Columbia
Edition '31.

Mind started 1876.

Minor Theatre 1831.

Mirror for Magistrates 1559, '78, 1610.

MITCHELL, MARGARET [U.S.], 1900–49.
Gone with the Wind 1936.

MITFORD, JOHN, 1781–1859. Agnes and
other poems 1811, ed. Milton '51.

MITFORD, JOHN, 1782–1831. Adventures of Johnny Newcombe 1818,
Poems of a British Sailor '18.

MITFORD, MARY RUSSELL, 1787–1855.
Miscellaneous Poems 1810, Christina
'11, Blanch of Castile '12, Poems on
Female Character '13, Our Village '19,
'24, Julian '23, Foscari '26, Dramatic
Scenes '27, Stories of American Life
'30, Belford Regis '35, Recollections
of a Literary Life '52, Atherton '54.

MITFORD, NANCY, 1904– . Pursuit
of Love 1945, Love in a Cold Climate
'49.

MITFORD, WILLIAM, 1744–1827. History
of Greece 1784–1810.

MOFFATT, JAMES, 1870– . New
Testament 1919.

MOIR, DAVID MACBETH, 1798–1851.
Mansie Wauch 1828.

MONBODDO, JAMES BURNETT, LORD,
1714–99. Origin of Language 1773,
Ancient Metaphysics '79.

MONCRIEFF, WILLIAM, 1794–1857.
Dandy Family 1819, Lear of the
Private Family '20, Cataract of the
Ganges '24.

Monitor started 1755.

MONRO, HAROLD, 1879–1932. Trees
1915, Strange Meetings '17, Real
Property '22, Earth for Sale '28,
Collected Poems '33.

MONTAGU, MRS. ELIZABETH (ROBINSON),
1720–1800. Essay on Shakespeare
1769, Letters 1809–13.

MONTAGU, LADY MARY WORTLEY,
1689–1762. Court Poems 1716, Town
Eclogues '47, Letters '63–'67, Poems
'68, Works 1803.

MONTAGUE, CHARLES EDWARD, 1867–
1928. A Hind let loose 1910,
Dramatic Values '11, Morning's War
'13, Disenchantment '22, Fiery Particles '23, Right Place '24.

MONTGOMERIE, ALEXANDER, 1556?–
1610? Cherry and Slae 1597, Mind's
Melodie 1605.

MONTGOMERY, JAMES, 1771–1854. The
Ocean 1805, Wanderer of Switzerland '06, West Indies '09, World
before the Flood '12, Greenland '19,
Pelican Island '26.

MONTGOMERY, LUCY MAUD [C.], 1874–
1942. Anne of Green Gables 1908.
MONTGOMERY, ROBERT, 1807–55.
Omnipresence of the Deity 1828,
Satan '30, Puffiad '30, Messiah '32,
Woman '33, Luther '42.
Month started 1864.
Monthly Magazine 1796–1843.
Monthly Review started 1749.
MONYPENNY, WILLIAM FLAVELLE, 1866–
1912. Life of Disraeli (completed by
Buckle) 1910–20.
MOORE, EDWARD, 1712–57. Fables for
the Female Sex 1744, Gamester '53,
Poems '56.
MOORE, GEORGE, 1852–1933. Mum-
mer's Wife 1884, Confessions of a
Young Man '88, Impressions and
Opinions '91, Esther Waters '94,
Celibates '95, Sister Teresa 1901,
Untilled Field '03, The Lake '05,
My Dead Life '06, Apostle '11, Hail
and Farewell '11–'14, Muslin '15,
Brook Kerith '16, Avowals '19, He-
loise and Abelard '21, Conversations
in Ebury Street '24.
MOORE, GEORGE EDWARD, 1873–1958.
Principia Ethica 1903, Philosophical
Studies '22.
MOORE, JOHN, 1729–1802. Zeluco 1786,
Edward '96.
MOORE, MARIANNE CRAIG [U.S.], 1887–
. Selected Poems 1935.
MOORE, THOMAS, 1779–1852. Trs.
Anacreon 1800, Poems by Thomas
Little 1801, Epistles, Odes &c., '06,
Irish Melodies '07, Corruption, In-
tolerance '08, Sceptic '09, M.P.
'11, Intercepted Letters '13, Sacred
Airs '15, Sacred Songs '16, Death
of Sheridan '16, Lalla Rookh '17,
Fudge Family in Paris '18, Tom
Crib's Memorial '19, Fables for Holy
Alliance '23, Rhymes on Road '23,
Loves of the Angels '23, Captain
Rock '24, Life of Sheridan '25, Even-
ings in Greece '25, Epicurean '27,
Odes upon Cash, Corn, &c. '28,
Legendary Ballads '30, Life of Byron
'30, Summer Fête '31, Life of Fitz-
gerald '31, Travels of Irish Gentle-
man '33, Fudges in England '35,
History of Ireland '35, Alciphron '39,
Journals and Correspondence '53.
MORE, HANNAH, 1745–1833. Search
after Happiness 1773, Inflexible Cap-
tive '74, Sir Eldred '76, Percy '77,
Essays for Young Ladies '78, Fatal
Falsehood '79, Sacred Drama '82,
Slavery '88, Manners of the Great
'88, Religion of the Fashionable

World '90, Village Politics '93,
Repository Tracts '95, Female Educa-
tion '99, Cœlebs in Search of a Wife
1809, Practical Piety '11, Christian
Morals '13, Essay on St. Paul '15,
Moral Sketches '19, Life and Corre-
spondence '34.
MORE, HENRY, 1614–87. Psychodia
Platonica 1642, Philosophical Poems
'47, Antidote against Atheism '53,
Conjectura Cabbalistica '53, Enthusi-
asmus Triumphatus '56, Immortality
of the Soul '59, Grand Mystery of
Godliness '60, Mystery of Iniquity
'64, Enchiridion Ethicum '67, Divine
Dialogues '68.
MORE, PAUL ELMER, 1864–1937. The
Great Refusal 1894, Shelburne Essays
1904–28, Platonism '17.
MORE, SIR THOMAS, 1478–1535. Life
of Pico della Mirandola 1510, Merry
Jest '16, Utopia '16, Supplication of
Souls '29, Dialogue of Diverse Matters
'29, Confutation of Tyndale's Answer
'32, Apology '33, History of Richard
III '43, Utopia, English trans. '51,
Dialogue of Comfort '53, Works
written in English '57.
More, Sir Thomas 1598 (printed 1844).
MORGAN, CHARLES, 1894–1958. Por-
trait in Mirror 1929, Fountain '32,
Sparkenbroke '36, Flashing Stream
'38, Voyage '40, Empty Room '41,
Reflections in Mirror '44, Judge's
Story '47, River Line '49.
MORGAN, SYDNEY, Lady Morgan,
1783?–1859. Novice of St. Dominick
1805, Wild Irish Girl '06, Ida of
Athens '09, O'Donnel '14, Florence
M'Carthy '16.
MORGANN, MAURICE, 1726–1802. Char-
acter of Falstaff 1777.
MORIER, JAMES, 1780?–1849. Hajji
Baba of Ispahan 1824, Hajji Baba
in England '28.
MORISON, JAMES COTTER, 1832–88.
Service of Man 1887.
MORLEY, CHRISTOPHER [U.S.], 1890–
1957. Kitty Foyle 1939.
MORLEY, HENRY, 1822–94. English
Writers 1864–7, First Sketch of
English Literature '73.
MORLEY, JOHN, 1st VISCOUNT, 1838–
1923. Voltaire 1872, Rousseau '73,
On Compromise '74, Diderot '78,
Edmund Burke '79, Life of Cobden
'81, Life of Gladstone 1903.
MORLEY, THOMAS, 1557–1604? Can-
zonets 1593, Madrigals '94, Book of
Ballets '95, Triumphs of Oriana 1601.
Morning Advertiser started 1794.

Good Morning, America '28, The People, Yes '36, Abraham Lincoln: War Years '39.

SANDFORD, JAMES, fl. 1567. Trs. Epictetus 1567, trs. Cornelius Agrippa '69.

SANDYS, GEORGE, 1578–1644. Relation of a Journey 1615, trs. Ovid's Metamorphoses '26, Paraphrase upon Psalms '36, Christ's Passion '40, Paraphrase upon Song of Solomon '41.

SANDYS, SIR JOHN, 1844–1922. History of Classical Scholarship 1903–8.

SANTAYANA, GEORGE [U.S.], 1863–1952. Life of Reason 1905, Little Essays '20, Scepticism '23, Realm of Being '27, Genteel Tradition '31, Last Puritan '35, Persons and Places '44.

SARGESON, FRANK [N.Z.], 1903– . Man and his Wife 1940, That Summer '46, I Saw in my Dream '49.

SAROYAN, WILLIAM [U.S.], 1908– . Daring Young Man on Flying Trapeze 1934, Time of Your Life '39.

SASSOON, SIEGFRIED, 1886– . Old Huntsman 1917, Counter-Attack '18, War Poems '19, Satirical Poems '26, Heart's Journey '28, Memoirs of a Fox-hunting Man '28, Memoirs of an Infantry Officer '30, In Sicily '30, Poems by Pinchbeck Lyre '31, Prehistoric Burials '32, Road to Ruin '33, Vigils '35, Sherston's Progress '36, Rhymed Ruminations '40, Collected Poems '47.

Saturday Review started 1855.

SAVAGE, RICHARD, d. 1743. Sir Thomas Overbury 1724, Nature in Perfection '28, Bastard '28, Wanderer '29, Progress of a Divine '35, Works '75.

SAVILE, GEORGE, Marquis of Halifax, 1633–1695. Letter to a Dissenter 1686, Character of a Trimmer '88, Lady's New Year Gift '88, Anatomy of an Equivalent '88, Miscellanies 1700, Character of Charles II '50, Works, ed. Walter Raleigh 1912.

SAVILE, SIR HENRY, 1549–1622. Trs. Histories of Tacitus 1591.

Savoy 1896.

SAYERS, DOROTHY LEIGH, 1893–1957. Zeal of Thy House 1937.

SAYERS, FRANK, 1763–1817. Dramatic Sketches 1790, Disquisitions '93, Nugæ Poeticæ 1803, Miscellanies '05.

School of Slovenrie 1605.

SCHOOLCRAFT, HENRY ROWE [U.S.], 1793–1864. Myth of Hiawatha 1856.

Schoolhouse of Women 1540.

SCHREINER, OLIVE (EMILIE ALBERTINA)

[S.A.], 1855–1920. Story of an African Farm 1883, Dreams '91, Trooper Peter Halket '97, From Man to Man 1926, Undine '28.

SCOGGIN, JOHN, fl. 1480. Scoggin his Jests 1613.

SCOT, REGINALD, 1538 ?–99. Perfit Platform of a hop garden 1574, Discoverie of Witchcraft '84.

SCOT, THOMAS. Philomythie 1610, Part II 1625.

Scots Magazine started 1739.

Scots Museum 1787–1803.

Scots New Testament 1520.

Scots Observer started 1889.

Scots Psalter 1564.

Scotsman started 1817.

SCOTT, DUNCAN CAMPBELL [C.], 1862–1947. Collected Poems 1926.

SCOTT, JOHN, 1730–83. Poetical Works 1782.

SCOTT, JONATHAN, 1754–1829. Trs. Arabian Nights 1811.

SCOTT, MICHAEL 1789–1835. Tom Cringle's Log 1829, Cruise of the Midge '34.

SCOTT, SIR WALTER, 1771–1832. The Chase; William and Helen 1796, Goetz of Berlichingen '99, Apology for Tales of Terror '99, Eve of St. John 1800, ed. Border Minstrelsy 1802–3, Lay of Last Minstrel '05, Ballads and Lyrical Pieces '06, Ed. Slingsby's Diary '06, Marmion '08, ed. Dryden '08, Lady of the Lake '10, Ancient British Drama '10, Don Roderick '11, ed. Secret History of Court of James I '11, ed. Memoirs of Count Grammont '11, Modern British Drama '11, Rokeby '13, Bridal of Triermain '13, Waverley '14, Border Antiquities '14, Eyrbiggia Saga '14, Essays on Chivalry and Romance '14, ed. Swift '14, Guy Mannering '15, Lord of the Isles '15, Field of Waterloo '15, Paul's Letters to his Kinsfolk '15, Antiquary '16, Black Dwarf '16, Old Mortality '16, Harold the Dauntless '17, Ballad of Noble Moringer '17, Rob Roy '17, Heart of Midlothian '18, Bride of Lammermoor '19, Legend of Montrose '19, Ivanhoe '19 ('20), Regalia of Scotland '19, Monastery '20, Abbot '20, Miscellaneous Poems '20, Kenilworth '21, Biographies in Ballantyne's Novelists '21, Account of George IV's Coronation '21, ed. Fielding '21, Pirate '22, Fortunes of Nigel '22, Peveril of the Peak '22, Halidon Hill '22, Quentin Durward '23, Redgauntlet '24, St.

Ronan's Well '24, ed. Richardson '24, The Betrothed '25, The Talisman '25, Woodstock '26, Highland Widow, Surgeon's Daughter, Two Drovers '27, Life of Napoleon '27, Miscellaneous Prose Works '27, ed. Bannatyne Miscellany '27, Tales of a Grandfather, 1st Series '28, 2nd Series '29, Fair Maid of Perth '28, Three Tales in the Keepsake '28, Religious Discourses '28, Anne of Geierstein '29, History of Scotland '29, Letters on Demonology '30, House of Aspen '30, Doom of Devorgoil '30, Essays on Ballad Poetry '30, Tales of a Grandfather, 3rd and 4th Series '30, Count Robert '32, Castle Dangerous '32, Journal '90, Letters, ed. Grierson 1937, Journal, ed. Tait '39.

SCOTT, WILLIAM BELL, 1811–90. Hades, or the Transit 1838, Poems '54, Poems '75, Poet's Harvest Home '82.

Scribner's Magazine started 1886.

SEDLEY, SIR CHARLES, 1639?–1701. Mulberry Garden 1668, Antony and Cleopatra '77, Bellamira '87, Poetical Works and Speeches 1702.

SEEBOHM, FREDERIC, 1833–1912. Oxford Reformers 1867.

SEELEY, SIR JOHN ROBERT, 1834–95. Ecce Homo 1865, Life and Times of Stein '78, Natural Religion '82, Expansion of England '83.

SELDEN, JOHN, 1584–1654. England's Epinomis 1610, Duello '10, Titles of Honour '14, De Diis Syris '17, History of Tithes '18, De Successionibus '31, Mare Clausum '35, De Jure Naturali '40, Power of Parliament '40, Privileges of Baronage '42, Uxor Ebraica '46, Table Talk '89.

Selimus, Tragical Raigne of, 1594.

SELINCOURT, HUGH DE, 1878– . Cricket Match 1924.

SENIOR, NASSAU WILLIAM, 1790–1864. Political Economy 1850, Conversations with Thiers, Guizot, &c., '78.

SERVICE, ROBERT W. [C.], 1874– . Songs of a Sourdough 1907.

SETON, ERNEST THOMPSON [C.], 1860–1946. Wild Animals I Have Known 1900.

SETTLE, ELKANAH, 1648–1724. Cambyses 1671, Empress of Morocco '73, Love and Revenge '75, Conquest of China '76, Ibrahim '77, Pastor Fido '77, Female Prelate '80, Fatal Love '80, Absalom Senior '82, Heir of Morocco '82, Distress'd Innocence '91, Fairy Queen '92, Ambitious Slave '94, Virgin Prophetess 1701.

SEVERN, JOSEPH, 1793–1879. Life and Letters 1892.

SEWALL, SAMUEL, 1652–1730. Diary 1879.

SEWARD, ANNA, 1747–1809. Sonnets 1799, Memoir of Erasmus Darwin 1804, Poetical Works '10, Correspondence '11.

SEWELL, ANNA, 1820–78. Black Beauty 1877.

SEWELL, ELIZABETH MISSING, 1815–1906. Amy Herbert 1844.

SEWELL, MARY, 1797–1884. Children of Summerbrook 1859, Stories in Verse '61, Patience Hart's Experiences '62.

SHADWELL, THOMAS, 1642?–92. Sullen Lovers 1668, Royal Shepherdess '69, Humorists '71, Miser '72, Epsom Wells '73, Tempest (opera) '74, Psyche '75, Libertine '76, Virtuoso '76, adapted Timon of Athens '78, True Widow '79, Woman Captain '80, Lancashire Witches '82, ?Medal of John Bayes '82, Squire of Alsatia '88, Bury Fair '89, Amorous Bigotte '90, Scowrers '91, Volunteers '93.

SHAFTESBURY, FIRST EARL OF, 1621–'83. Memoirs, Letters and Speeches 1859.

SHAFTESBURY, THIRD EARL OF, 1671–1713. Paradoxes of State 1702, Concerning Enthusiasm '08, Characteristics '11, Letters to a Student '16, Letters to Molesworth '21.

SHAKESPEARE, WILLIAM, 1564–1616. Venus and Adonis 1593, Lucrece '94, Titus Andronicus '94, King Richard II '97, Romeo and Juliet, Q. I '97 (Q. II '99), Richard III '97, Henry IV, Part I '98, Love's Labour's Lost '98, Julius Caesar (acted) c. '99, Henry IV, Pt. II 1600, Henry V 1600, Merchant of Venice 1600, Midsummer Night's Dream 1600, Much Ado about Nothing 1600, As You Like It (acted) c. 1600, Twelfth Night (acted) c. '01, Merry Wives of Windsor '02, Hamlet, Q. I '03, (Q. II '04), Troilus and Cressida (acted) c. '03, (printed) '09, Measure for Measure (acted) c. '04, Othello (acted) '04, (printed) '22, Macbeth (acted) c. '05, Timon of Athens '07, King Lear '08, Coriolanus '08, Sonnets '09, Pericles '09, Tempest '10, Cymbeline '10, Winters Tale '10, Henry VIII (acted) '13, Spurious Quartos '19, First Folio '23, Second Folio '32, Third Folio '63, Fourth Folio '85, ed. Rowe 1709, Pope '25, Theobald '34, Hanmer '43, Warburton